Social Media—New Masses

Edited by
Inge Baxmann, Timon Beyes and Claus Pias

diaphanes

1st edition
ISBN 978-3-03734-642-6
© diaphanes, Zurich-Berlin 2016
All rights reserved.

Layout: 2edit, Zurich-Berlin
Printed in Germany

www.diaphanes.com

Social Media—New Masses

Table of Contents

An Introduction in Ten Theses

The notion of "digital cultures" is presently associated with the description of a fundamental and historical transition. Its scope cannot simply be reduced to the convergence of various individual media or to the general digitalization of all areas of life. What is at stake is rather a new quality of recomposing the cultural and socio-technological configurations of modernity. Today, life is embedded in the omnipresence of active and intelligent artefacts, which partly interact without the involvement of human actors. As to the latter, our integration into digital networks, our increasing attachment to mobile media – and thus the state of being permanently connected to objects that communicate continuously and in real-time – constitute a transformation of the affective set-up of the present and create a multifarious and, to some degree, unconscious context of intensities, sensations, and stimulations. This situation is difficult to ignore, yet hard to describe and analyze.[1]

In these circumstances, the "old" question of the connection between mass phenomena and media technologies regains its relevance and urgency. In searching for answers to this question, the field of media studies plays a prominent role. After all, media studies' very existence is due to the various media upheavals of the twentieth century; in response to such upheavals, it has repeatedly proven its ability to adapt and reinvent itself.[2] Of course, the specific modes of inquiry and insights of media studies have been challenged and refined all along by those of other disciplines. In fields such as sociology, computer science, history, political science, and philosophy, scholars have likewise been concerned with recent developments and have come to accept, especially in the last few decades, what could be called a medial epistemology. Based on papers that were delivered at the Second Symposium for Media Studies, which took place in February of 2012 under the aegis of the German Research Foundation, the present volume adopts an "undisciplined" approach and presents exchanges between media studies and the fields named above in order to map out the new area of research that is concerned with "digital masses".

---

[1] Ulrik Ekman (ed.), *Throughout: Art and Culture Emerging with Ubiquitous Computing* (Cambridge, Mass.: MIT Press, 2013).

[2] Claus Pias (ed.), *Was waren Medien?* (Zurich: diaphanes, 2011).

Contained here are analyses of the difference between "old" and "new" masses, the various media-technological conditions that have engendered these differences, and the political consequences of current mass phenomena. The book is thus divided into three sections – "Which Masses?", "Which Media?", "Which Publics?" – each of which is furnished with its own brief introduction. The three sections are complemented with two invited commentaries on the overall endeavor, which conclude the book. The hypothesis that there is a fundamental difference between old and new masses represents a point of departure that is common to each of the texts gathered here. It is approached from different disciplinary perspectives, both historically and with explicit reference to current developments, both by way of established theories and (in some cases) through novel concepts and ideas. Interweaving the central research topics of this collection and indicating further issues to be explored, the remainder of this introduction is structured in ten theses concerning the implications and consequences of thinking about the nexus of social media and new masses.

1. *The present-day transitions provide an opportunity to reevaluate the cultural-historical approaches to understanding and describing mass phenomena.* Since the advent of modernity, various discourses on, and practices of, social control, communication, interaction, and community formation have arisen in response to the (positive or negative) phantasms and utopias concerned with masses or crowds. The motive of the inability of traditional concepts to describe masses and mass media; the well-established diagnosis of dispersed public spheres, which is fueled by the ubiquity of "social media"; the nearly unpredictable dynamics and effects of digital technologies; and the appearance of new notions of mass phenomena, such as swarms, flash mobs, and multitudes have all combined to create a field of research for reexamining the emergence, functions, and effects of now digitally mediated masses. The parameters of control and communication, of interaction and community formation may indeed have shifted, but such a shift allows new light to be shed on the traditional conceptualizations of (previous or "old") masses. If large crowds were once frequently imagined in terms of unconsciousness, unaddressability, or irrationality – and thus in some measure as the "dark side" of the enlightened and enlightening bourgeois public sphere – then the emergence of new masses calls for such interpretive paradigms to be revised and historicized.

2. *Today's digital mechanisms of connectivity and addressability require that we introduce and formulate a difference between the phenomena and descriptive forms of old masses and those of the new.* New masses not only afford a historicizing distance to traditional conceptualizations of mass phenomena; conversely, this critical engagement also enables us to recognize the specifically different nature of new masses with respect to the discourses and practices of current media technologies – and indicates our theoretical limitations. For it is the case that mass phenomena and the theories that conceptualize them are equally affected by the media technologies that happen to be dominant at the time. The challenge, then, is to think and explore the co-emergence and mutual conditioning of these two

poles. The "mediatic regime change," which Mark B. N. Hansen has proclaimed for the present day,[3] is therefore both a matter of media technology and a matter of the theories that are constructed around it. This includes the efforts to problematize traditional or established concepts of knowledge, for media upheavals invariably entail the restructuring of knowledge cultures.

3. *The difference between old and new masses is of an eminently technological nature. To think about digital masses is to examine the reciprocal reconfigurations of media technology and mass effects.* For the past twenty or so years, against the background of internet-supported and digital media cultures, there is a conspicuous trend to disassociate the concept of the masses from so-called mass media. Given the current media-technnological changes, critical engagement with the mass media, which since the middle of the nineteenth century had been shaping both the relevant issues and the memory of society, has begun to wane or at least fade into the background. As Wolfgang Hagen shows in his chapter, the internet, if measured according to classical criteria, is *not* a mass medium, even if it does organize both masses and, as a sort of new social memory, the immense masses of data that are produced in a globalized world. When investigating mass formation in the present era of social media, it is thus crucial to ask how it is that technological media are able to condition particular crowds and forms of sociality, at least to the extent that such media are regarded as being constitutive of these forms. A common thread throughout this book is thus the attempt to comprehend and describe the mediatization of masses in terms of the reciprocal relation between media-technological operations and social processes – that is, in terms of the mutual relationship between connectivity and collectivity.

4. *The research on new masses entails a heterogeneous search for appropriate terms and concepts, and much of this work relies on classic figures of thought.* This is especially true of the work of the sociologist Gabriel Tarde, which has enjoyed something of a renaissance in cultural studies and the social sciences. The prominence of his work is as clear to see in the Anglophone discourse about current mass phenomena as it is in the chapters of this book. Aside from their explanatory power, Tarde's writings on crowds, the public, and the mechanisms of imitation and contagion owe their current influence to their "rehabilitation" by such thinkers as Gilles Deleuze and Bruno Latour. They provide, moreover, an approach to a form of theorizing that is not based on an Enlightenment notion of the subject, a figure that is conspicuous by its absence in this book, too. On the one hand, it is worth asking whether the search for terms and concepts with which to describe the relationship between social media and new masses might benefit from a look back at other "classical" ideas. Walter Benjamin's concept of the mimetic faculty, for instance, could perhaps broaden Tarde's notion of imitation to yield a clearer understanding of *poiesis*, that is, the productive moment of creation. On the other hand, it would be valuable to discuss

---

[3]   Mark B. N. Hansen, "New Media," in *Critical Terms for Media Studies*, ed. W. J. T. Mitchell and
      Mark B. N. Hansen (Chicago: University of Chicago Press, 2010), 172–85, at 180.

the extent to which the application of Tarde's concepts is adequate enough to elucidate the media-*technological* conditions of current mass phenomena.

5. *Whereas the classical crowd theories of the late nineteenth and early twentieth century tend to describe the emergence of masses as a "dark" narrative of loss, more recent approaches exhibit an ambivalent relation to the political potential of digital masses. It is in this ambivalence that the contours of an affirmative critical understanding can be detected.* The focus is thus not, or only cursorily, on critiquing the function of social media for the politics of masses in the institutional sense. The issue is not, for instance, that of the mass-media coverage of representative politics or the use of the media by political actors. Nor does it suffice to simply diagnose the incorporation of media apparatuses and their mass effects into the mechanisms of political control. Rather, the current changes in the texture of mass phenomena and media apparatuses also seem to reopen the question of the political. "The political" here refers to making manifest the contingency of the social by way of gaps in, and ruptures of, the networks of institutionalized apparatuses and practices. This includes the awareness and acknowledgement of current forms of control and surveillance, which in the digital age increasingly take an algorithmic or protocological form and work through the modulation of affects and atmospheres. Beyond the mere diagnosis and revelation of digital mechanisms of domination, however, there is still some promise, as the articles in this volume demonstrate, in the possibility of forming new publics and in the political potential of digitally dispersed "crowd intelligence." Certain forms of digital masses, at least, cannot be thought without an ethical momentum concerned with ideals such as the invention of new forms of cooperation and community formation, and any critique of new masses will have to take this moment into consideration.

6. *The ambivalence of reflecting on the digital formation of crowds is based on the tension between the revitalization of the phantasm of controlling the (now digital) masses and the reproduction of the imaginary of a technologically conditioned, emancipatory public sphere.* On the one hand, the "phantasm of supervision," as discussed by Irina Kaldrack and Theo Röhle in this volume, is based on the conviction that the emergence of digital masses can be simulated and controlled (and profited from) by means of new identification technologies and evaluation procedures. New masses are thereby singled out as "data masses" whose correlations and analyses yields a self-referential circuit of interconnected masses. On the other hand, the idea of intelligent swarms revives the notion of a present experience of community, which resonates with the possibility of the masses' collective self-control. It is hardly a coincidence that the "techno-barbar" was regarded as a positive utopia by the modern avant-garde. The Futurists saw in the use of technology by modern masses a cultural-revolutionary strategy against the elitist and traditionalist culture of literacy and the book. The avant-garde discourse of barbarity recognized, in the direct and "unsullied" access of the masses to new technologies and materials, a chance to create a technologically determined and modern mass culture. Is it possible that today's utopian ideas about net democracy etc. are simply an extension

and actualization of this discourse under new conditions? In this regard, it is interesting that even such a performative and resolutely materialist understanding of the emergence of new and temporary publics (and their political effects) clings to the "old" idea of the principal possibility of emancipatory mass organization.

7. *The reconfigurations of cooperation, collectivity, and organization confront research on new masses with the notion of the social or sociality.* The term of sociality denotes the forms in which actors (and actants) relate to one another, connect to one another, and set themselves apart from one another. In this light, the popular term "social media" is quite fitting for describing the relevant "massified" areas of everyday digital life. Sociality and technology form a complex assemblage that requires analytical approaches in the interstices between cultural studies, media studies, and the social sciences. Technologically *and* socially networked collective structures have thus turned the network into a dominant mechanism or *dispositif* of sociality (think only of communication platforms such as Facebook, which define themselves as social networks). During the early years of network culture, however, the concept of "community" was also revitalized to address forms of sociality potentially neglected by the network *dispositif*. Our renegotiations of sociality thus also have to address the recent discussions concerned with phenomena such as "sharing", "peer structures" and, of course, the problematic of the "common," which has become a pressing issue for digital cultures. As several of the chapters in this volume suggest (indicating a rich spectrum of future research activities), it is perhaps impossible to understand and analyze new masses without taking into account their *social* media, their socio-technological conditions and effects.

8. *The explorative search for suitable terms and concepts with which to address digital masses is accompanied by methodological uncertainty regarding the appropriate ways to approach the current socio-technological configurations.* Under the present conditions, for instance, media studies seems to have exhausted its potential to conduct a sort of empirical social research that has to assume a random choice among evenly distributed viewers, listeners or readers in order to make "representative" statements about one phenomenon or another. The study of mass media, which had more or less been a branch of market research concerned with "linear" electronic media, has been replaced by the algorithmic analysis of "big data," social networks, search engines, and online commerce. This, in turn, raises the fundamental question regarding the methods that have been employed and should be employed to analyze the historically interconnected and fluid relationship between media and masses. The articles collected here reveal that the issues involved with the emergence, functions, and effects of new masses cannot be divorced from the process of problematizing and revising our methodologies. It has also become clear, moreover, that we are still at the early stages of this labor of revision. In the following chapters, there is a gesturing towards the problematic of new methods more than any detailed reflection or refinement. We certainly hope that we see the early stages of a newly found openness and experimental stance towards methodological issues. An openness of this sort was once a

distinguishing feature of media studies; it allowed generations of media theorists to build bridges between theoretical approaches that had traditionally been divided – e.g., hermeneutics and the history of technology, quantitative analysis and content analysis – and here it has allowed us to stage a productive exchange between a number of relevant disciplines.

9. *Under the media-ecological conditions of the digital, critical engagements with new masses cannot be severed from the "intrinsic logic of materiality" and thus cannot be isolated from the mediatization of the human sensorium and capacity for feeling.* Regarding the search for appropriate concepts, terms and methods, we are approaching difficult questions that go well beyond the topics treated in the present book. Today's mass phenomena are embedded in an affectively charged "mediosphere" that exerts control in a to some extent atmospheric and preconscious manner. Digital media are thus increasingly affecting and mediatizing the human sensorium itself. For this reason, phenomena such as the "technological unconscious," affective or atmospheric media – and thus issues concerning the organization of sensation and perception – have become important objects of investigation. These conditions not only problematize, in a fundamental way, the traditional methodological instruments that have been used to study media and masses; they also make it difficult to deal with concepts such as the public, the social, or the political insofar as the latter are related to a traditional understanding of the subject and the masses. In what ways, for instance, do we have to alter our understanding of public spheres, given that the latter are now influenced by a "technological capacity for feeling"[4] and that the technological unconscious – "a pre-personal substrate of guaranteed correlations, assured encounters, and therefore unconsidered anticipations"[5] – is constantly influencing thought, emotions, and behavior? In her commentary, Marie-Luise Angerer addresses such issues and speculates about the necessity of "mediamorphism," which would allow us to apprehend the interaction between technological and human actors (and the hybrid fusion of the two).

10. *The "anti-hermeneutic" approach to social media and new masses refers us to fundamental research questions about digital cultures' styles of perception, body techniques, and forms of knowledge.* Indicative of this is a broader understanding of body techniques that in turn come to shape styles of perception, styles of thought, and forms of knowledge, the investigation of which will prove to be among the most challenging objects of media-theoretical inquiry. If it is the case that changes in media technologies bring about changes in the styles of perception, communication, and interaction, then these changes are habitualized through embodied techniques of knowledge. It is probably not a coin-

---

[4]   Mark B. N. Hansen, "Medien des 21. Jahrhunderts, technische Empfinden und unsere originäre Umweltbedingung," in *Die technologische Bedingung: Beiträge zur Beschreibung der technischen Welt*, ed. Erich Hörl (Berlin: Suhrkamp, 2011), 365–409, at 367.

[5]   Nigel Thrift, "Movement-Space: The Changing Domain of Thinking Resulting from the Development of New Forms of Awareness," *Economy and Society* 33 (2004), 582–604, at 585.

cidence that the topic of "implicit knowledge" – of bodily and sensual knowledge – has been receiving more attention in recent years. This sort of knowledge, which pushes the boundaries of what can be apprehended and described, is corporeal and experiential. As a non-verbal "knowledge of doing", it can neither be objectively verified nor rationally substantiated. With reference to Marcel Mauss's idea of a cultural-comparative archive of body techniques, and with an eye on the current phase of media-technological transformation, it is possible to speculate about a mass reconfiguration of incorporated techniques of knowledge that re-code bodily perception and embodied habit (from running to sexuality, from the body techniques of work to the techniques of falling asleep).[6]

Inge Baxmann, Timon Beyes, and Claus Pias

Acknowledgements

Our gratitude extends first and foremost to the authors who kindly contributed to this volume. Warm thanks are also due to the other participants in the Symposium for Media Studies, to the members of the program committee, and to the collegial representatives of the German Research Foundation and the Society for Media Studies, notably Oliver Lerone Schultz, Stefan Ullrich, Deborah Weber-Wulff, Wolfgang Coy, Ute Holl, Geert Lovink, Stefan Rieger, Hartmut Winkler, Ulrike Bergermann, Malte Hagener, Hermann Kappelhoff, and Claudia Althaus. The Symposium was generously supported by the Leuphana University Lüneburg.

---

[6] See Marcel Mauss, "Techniques of the Body," in *Techniques, Technologies, and Civilization*, ed. Nathan Schlanger (New York: Durkheim Press, 2006), 77–95.

I. Which Crowds?

The concept of crowds and the concept of media (and more so the combination of both) are united by one factor in particular: their relative indeterminacy is inversely proportional to their distribution. From this initial position attempts to historicize crowds receive their motivation, and the essays collected here deal with these problems from different perspectives.

Such problems include, on the one hand, the question of crowds which is at the core of a crisis that is afflicting traditional models of the subject, the public, and the political.

Other questions concern the relationship between crowds and community and the processes used to control crowds – whether to influence them psychologically or simply to gather statistics on them. On the other hand, questions regarding the relationship between the construction of crowds and the construction of media technologies, their perspectives, and their discourses of reference arise. In this regard, I propose two general theses that bind together the chapters in this section:

1. *Since the advent of modernity, discourses about crowds reflect a fundamental crisis of descriptive cultures and control mechanisms within society.*

Since the late nineteenth and early twentieth centuries, crowds have been employed as a paradigm for processes of defining and forming the social. Anxieties of social contingency find their expression in describing crowds. Negative and positive phantasms and utopias of crowds have ignited modern discourses and practices of social control, communication, interaction, and community building. Constructions of crowds have thus been formed over a wide range of discourses, including sociology, psychology, anthropology, ethnology, and media studies.

The self description of modernity as the "age of crowds" implied a discursive turn in the collective cultural identity of the time. Whereas previously, History served as the main discourse for legitimizing modern society, now the interest shifted towards those sciences such as psychology and ethnology that were concerned with the unconscious and with the continuity of "archaic" features in modern man. These ideas were later taken up by sociology

Crowds problematize the traditional, Enlightenment-based model of the public sphere, according to which identifiable and rational subjects publically engage in non-hierarchical discussions in order to reach a consensus. This is because crowds – according to crowd theorists such as Le Bon, Tarde, Freud, and Canetti – are anonymous, unaddressable, and lack defining features. The specific processes of perception, communication, and interaction characterizing a crowd do not follow traditional notions of the subject and the social.

2. *Crowds can be distinguished by the styles in which they are imagined, and these styles are determined by the media technology dominant at a given time.*

Perception, the imaginary, and practices of crowds are determined through specific historical configurations which rely on the media technologies of the time. Therefore the contributions in this section are primarily concerned with the historical break that distinguishes "traditional crowds" of the late nineteenth and early twentieth centuries from the "digitalized crowds" of today. To what extent do traditional crowds differ from digital crowds regarding the construction and enactment of subjectivity and community? Which specific forms of perception, communication, and interaction can be said to be dominant in each case? And what kind of cultural historiography of mass media should result? It is important in this regard to reconstruct the historically specific configurations that determine the respective discourses, images, and practices of crowds.

In the discourses of the late nineteenth and early twentieth centuries, the types of behaviour of traditional crowds were described in analogy to the model of electricity. Thus the intrinsic logic of crowds, as Christian Borch demonstrates, is always already a mediated one. The crowd is always a unity already constructed – not only via its "leaders" or objects such as flags, but also through the mutual linkages established by its interaction.

Crowds, following the general assumption of modern crowd discourses, can only be controlled by means of their own impulses and energies. The intrinsic logic of crowds was believed to be determined by emotions and physicality. Crowds are charged with affect, and their mutual connectivity is based on motion. Coordination takes place pre-consciously by way of rhythmically induced synchronization, and in this manner the crowd – or so the theory goes – is able to generate its own coherence. According to Le Bon and Tarde, it is only possible to exert control over crowds with the help of collective myths and models of leadership. Crowds require a leader who transcends them and can thus unite them in the pursuit of a collective goal.

The visibility of crowds, as Christiane Heibach stresses in her contribution, is closely linked to media. It is photography, film, or the radio that first enabled crowds to experience themselves and to be experienced. These mass media were the precondition for a type of community defined by shared somatic states experienced in ecstatic mass presence.

Therefore, an understanding of traditional crowds must reconstruct the relationship between media technologies and respective changes taking place in the public sphere.

The mass media technologies of modernity were fundamental to the reconfiguration of collective styles of perception, communication, and interaction as described by anthropologists of traditional crowds (Tarde, Le Bon, Canetti). Here, crowds were the counter-model to the idea of the public sphere derived from the concept of the subject or individual inherited from the Enlightenment. Such an elitist cultural critique of crowds, as Heibach points out, has been perpetuated by the likes of Neil Postman and Peter Sloterdijk. Both rely on the concept of solitary and elite individuality as a sort of safeguard against the ecstatic collectivity of a somatic and spatio-temporally present community. Thus, the continuity of the traditional dichotomy between crowds and the public is maintained for the television crowd. The latter crowd is not physically present, but rather an isolated, unthreatening, and mediocre crowd of viewers, incapable of engaging in any sort of politically oriented collective activity.

The current dissolution of conceptual dichotomies such as individual/crowd, society/community, and public/private in actual debates on the relation of crowds and media, has given rise to a new sort of anthropology emerging in the context of digital crowds. This anthropology, which focuses on cultures of feeling, body techniques, and atmospheres, has brought forth new models of the subject and the collective. Have we moved away from the "stupid crowds" of modernity toward the "intelligent swarms" of the digital age? If so, this would represent a transition from a negative to a positive anthropology of crowds.

Traditional crowd theories described (from an elitist perspective) the formation of crowds as a narrative of loss, especially in regard to the relationship between the individual and the crowd and the disappearance of an enlightened public. Recent theories of crowds, at least since the discussion of the multitude initiated by Negri and Hardt, have instead emphasized the notion of crowd intelligence and the ethics of cooperation that such intelligence entails. In short, the many are more intelligent than the individual. It is thus no coincidence that behavioral biology has been invoked as a crucial reference point. Whether comparisons are made to schools of fish, flocks of birds, or to the organizational structure of termite colonies, the largely pre-conscious ability to synchronize in order to solve common problems has been revealed to be a decisive feature of human social behavior as well. Has swarm intelligence become the present-day phantasm of crowds? If so, how should we re-conceptualize the relationship between the individual and the community? Are digital crowds an "individualized multitude"?

This new anthropology has been exemplified by the work of Pierre Lévy, according to whom digital crowds or "molecular collectives" of network media, which possess the capacity for rationality and criticism, generate new public spheres. To digital crowds he also attributes -contrary to traditional crowds- an enlightened political competence.

Since modernity, crowds have been a symbol for social contingency and for limits of the regulation of society. At the same time, crowds have become an object of scientific study. Technologies used to identify crowds – and the phantasm of being able to govern them – have long been associated with processes of calculation, identification, and control. As Roland Meyer demonstrates, the modern belief in the possibility of controlling social contingency was fostered above all by the discourses and practices of biometrics. They were used to identify and filter repetitive patterns out of large quantities of data and to derive certain probabilities from this information. By such means, crowds could once again be analyzed and addressed in terms of their individual members, for it was primarily the disorderly and thus haphazard movements of crowds that rendered them socially unpredictable and unidentifiable.

Such anxiety about the mobility of crowds can be traced back to the French Revolution. An early precursor to biometrics, the first passport was issued in 1795 in response to the very fear that crowds, ever in motion, could not be identified unambiguously. In the eighteenth century, efforts were thus made to revive physiognomy, which reduced outward appearances to typical and recognizable patterns. An individual's features could thus be recorded in a document that had to be brought along whenever he or she ventured to travel.

The digital crowds, too, are "unaddressable". Fears concerning contingency on the one hand and new phantasms of controlling emergent and non-scalable processes on the other define the manner in which digital crowds are treated. Social complexity and obscurity is performed through practices. Whereas, in the early twentieth century, stable identity and addressability did not exist, already in the age of the Social Graph games with identity ("relational self" versus "individual sense of self") and processual ways of being (*prozessuale Seinsweisen*) emerge. Digital crowds operate within the framework of a complex interaction between community and individuality, an interaction engendered by the media-technological conditions of the internet.

Digital crowds and their forms of community building can be understood as a mutual reconfiguration of the media and crowds, as Irina Kaldrack and Theo Röhle demonstrate in the case of Facebook's Open Graph protocol. New forms of control became possible through the connection between technical infrastructure and online user practices.

By formalization, enactment, and user activity on Facebook, the Open Graph protocol has developed a logic of organization and communication. Its ability to scale from smaller to larger social groups (and back) has created new forms of control, sensitive to the intrinsic dynamics and self-organization of the groups themselves. By "sharing" content, users generate a form of co-presence. The technical processes of Open Graph systematically produce empty spaces that constantly need to be "filled in." As a result, a sort of phantasmatic excess of community has emerged as a technologically determined effect of inclusion.

On the one hand, a "phantasm of supervision" is fed by the belief that emergent processes and thus the self-organization of users can be accomplished by scaling – by stratifying the analytical processes of internet activity within the scope of new technologies designed to identify crowds. At the user level, on the other hand, what emerges is the phantasm of "sharing" as a present community experience that simultaneously implies the possibility that the crowds will collectively control themselves.

In any case, we can conclude that the egalitarian dream of interconnectivity as a new form of community has failed to come true on account of the emergent processes on the internet. These can best be compared to unpredictable flows whose undercurrents, sudden changes of direction, and unsteady formations always imply the potential engagement of different or conflicting interests. Groups of religious fundamentalists and efforts to control the network (currently epitomized by the NSA) are also, of course, elements of our network culture.

What do such findings mean for the cultural historiography of the mass media? One implication is that the media technologies of anonymization also have to be historicized:

Anonymous is a strategy of communitization. In unstable counter-publics and the ability to employ anonymous identities online, the imaginary of processes of digital assembly has recognized an opportunity for new democratic cultures of participation. WikiLeaks is an example of the ambivalent nature of this movement. The practice of disclosing confidential documents is related to an Enlightenment discourse that ultimately perpetuates the model of a bourgeois public sphere, the ideal of which can now – at last! – be realized by means of digital media technologies.

Accordingly, one possible way of historicizing the crowds and their media would be to produce a historical genealogy to trace the systematic connection between empty spaces and phantasmatic excess. Such is the impulse behind Florian Sprenger's call for a historiography of media that conceptualizes them in terms of difference, postponements, and synchronization. A genealogy of media theories and concepts, according to Sprenger, should be written as a history of their communities, which are based on techniques and technologies of connecting people and addressing them. This implies a critique of theoretical models that are teleological, such as McLuhan's utopian idea of immediate connections and unlimited communication, which envisions a new society in terms of media effects and connectivity. McLuhan's cultural historiography of media as a history of community formation is based on his idea of the "global village," which is the foundational myth of this community and its phantasm of simultaneity and immediacy. Sprenger argues that this model is perpetuated today when the globalized crowds are conceptualized in terms of accelerated immediacy.

By acknowledging the confrontation between the "traditional" and the "digital" crowds, a cultural historiography of crowds and their media also makes it possible to historicize the styles in which crowds have been imagined. It indicates discontinuities but also continuities and thus problematizes any critique of crowds that is based on dichotomies such as subject/crowd or private/public and that has usually been framed from the perspective of the social elite. That said, it has also become clear that a new form of critique requires a new set of concepts. Among these are a concept of subject and an understanding of community that takes into account the role of affect, body techniques, atmospheres, and mimetic behavior as conceptual fields between soma and psyche. This is a desideratum of both crowds and media research, because one of the objectives of the cultural historiography of mass media should be to reveal the systematic connections that exist between body techniques, cultures of feeling, and media-technological changes.

To this end it would be helpful to adopt the concept of "body techniques," as formulated by Marcel Mauss in the 1930s,[1] and to enhance it with a media-theoretical and media-historical perspective. Changes in perception, communication, and behaviour brought about by new media technologies manifest themselves in altered body techniques. This is essentially a knowledge of practices developed while engaging with new media technologies. The communicative and behavioral styles of crowds belong to an entire arsenal of

---

[1]   Marcel Mauss, "Techniques of the Body," in *Techniques, Technologies, and Civilization*, ed. Nathan Schlanger (New York: Durkheim Press, 2006), 77–95.

body techniques which, as a sort of "implicit knowledge," form the foundation of every cultural community.

Experiences of sensation, emotion, and perception are stored in motions, gestures, and rhythms. This knowledge, which is based on oral and gestural traditions, is materialized in artefacts, technologies, and non-verbal forms of expression. Knowledge of this sort has never been integrated into Western historiography and has thus remained marginal to European cultural understanding.

New media technologies alter our way of life by demanding recourse to submerged forms of knowledge, by engaging in new forms of knowledge, and by restructuring traditional forms of knowledge. New media technologies are historically specific cultural techniques that draw on and ultimately remodel bodily and sensual knowledge. Such a cultural historiography of crowds not only allows for a new view of modernity; it also enables a better understanding of new forms of knowledge and cultures of feeling as found in digital cultures. This includes last but not least the question of the ethics of cooperation within the communitization of crowds. For, increasingly, the web has become a place, where communication about transcendent goals of society takes place. Following Emile Durkheim these new forms of social self-description can be regarded as expressions of the sacred.

Inge Baxmann

CHRISTIAN BORCH

Crowd Mediation
On Media and Collective Dynamics

In his essay *Die Verachtung der Massen* of 2000, Peter Sloterdijk argues that we have entered a new age of mass mediation. Today, we are part of the masses not through our participation in street demonstrations, strikes, or the like. Rather, so Sloterdijk suggests, we are part of the mass when we sit on the couch and watch TV shows. The screen has replaced the street. The program principle has taken the place of the Führer principle.[1] While it can hardly be denied that the mass media, and more recently new social media, have had an impact on how crowd and mass phenomena are being materialized, experienced and orchestrated, an emphasis on epochal ruptures easily overshadows the fact that, from the very outset, the academic discussions of the role and nature of crowds, which emerged with the advent of crowd psychology in the late nineteenth century, revolved around a concept of crowds as inherently mediated entities. To be sure, the kinds of mediation attributed to crowd phenomena took different shapes, depending on the theoretical outlook. But there was a widespread agreement that some form of mediation was at play in the formation of crowds.

The present chapter aims to sketch how elements of this crowd mediation were articulated. How, in other words, was the relation between crowds and media observed and problematized in the field of crowd theory in the late nineteenth century, and how was this relation conceived by the heirs of this theoretical tradition? In the first part, I discuss how crowd mediation can be addressed and discussed on the basis of classical crowd theory. Specifically, I assert that the work of Gustave Le Bon and Gabriel Tarde points to a double, or even triple, crowd mediation process revolving around the mediation taking place in the crowd as such, and the mediation of the crowd through the leader (and vice versa). The second part discusses the role of mass media, focusing on how these might manipulate the masses through propaganda. Finally, I discuss how a rationalist-individualist conception of crowds emerged in sociology in the 1960s (still hegemonic in those specialized branches of sociology that continue to take an interest in crowd phenomena), and how

---

[1]   Peter Sloterdijk, *Die Verachtung der Massen. Versuch über Kulturkämpfe in der modernen Gesellschaft* (Frankfurt am Main: Suhrkamp, 2000).

this notion of crowds has produced an ignorance with regard to the idea that the crowd itself might be seen as a mediating entity.

Double mediation

While reflections on crowds can be dated back to the Ancient Greeks, it was only in the late nineteenth century that a distinctive science of crowds emerged under the label of crowd psychology – which, in spite of its name, was just as much a sociological as a psychological endeavor. The central contributions to this new field emanated from France, but important work was soon supplied also by German, Italian and US scholars. When looking only at the French debates, it is clear that they were based on a number of historical developments which, singularly and/or together, triggered a growing interest in crowd dynamics. These developments included especially France's revolutionary path, from 1789 to the 1871 Commune, but also the rise of socialism, industrialization, and urbanization.[2] What these and similar historical developments revealed was, according to many observers, the entry onto the stage of history of a new actor, namely the crowds.

Two of the key scholars occupied with understanding the nature of this new historical subject were Gustave Le Bon and Gabriel Tarde. Le Bon would become the more famous voice of the two, not least due to his 1895 essay *The Crowd: A Study of the Popular Mind*, in which he claimed that the society of his time was just about to enter the 'ERA OF CROWDS'.[3] This era was one painted in uniformly dark colors. Thus, claimed Le Bon, the crowds constituted in every possible way the complete contrast to modern civilized society: they were allegedly possessed by a barbarian nature, which meant that their rise to societal power signified several steps down the evolutionary ladder. The portrayal of crowds offered by Tarde was not altogether different from this. Tarde's entry into the crowd discussions in the early 1890s came from a criminological angle. He was concerned with the allegedly criminal nature of crowds, and not least with the apparent ability of crowds to seduce their members into all sorts of unruly, if not outright illegal, behavior that they would never have committed, had they not been part of a crowd.[4] In some of his later writings, Tarde approached the notion of crowds from a different point of view, as discussed below.

When accounting for the organizing principles of these seemingly disorderly crowds that appeared to take hold of still more domains of social life in the late nineteenth century, Le Bon, Tarde and others made reference to the notions of contagion and suggestion. 'In a crowd', wrote Le Bon, 'every sentiment and act is contagious, and contagious to such a

---

[2]   For extensive accounts, see Christian Borch, *The Politics of Crowds: An Alternative History of Sociology* (Cambridge: Cambridge University Press, 2012), Jaap Van Ginneken, *Crowds, Psychology, and Politics, 1871–1899* (Cambridge: Cambridge University Press, 1992).

[3]   Gustave Le Bon, *The Crowd: A Study of the Popular Mind* (New York: Dover, 2002), capitals in the original.

[4]   See Gabriel Tarde, "Les crimes des foules", *Archives de l'Anthropologie Criminelle* 7 (1892), 353–86; "Foules et sectes au point de vue criminal", *Revue des Deux Mondes* 332 (1893), 349–87.

degree that an individual readily sacrifices his personal interest to the collective interest'.[5] Tarde's description of the same phenomenon from the early 1890s was even more lucid and is worth quoting at length:

> A *mob* is a strange phenomenon. It is a gathering of heterogeneous elements, unknown to one another; but as soon as a spark of passion, having flashed out from one of these elements, electrifies this confused mass, there takes place a sort of sudden organization, a spontaneous generation. This incoherence becomes cohesion, this noise becomes a voice, and these thousands of men crowded together soon form but a single animal, a wild beast without a name, which marches to its goal with an irresistible finality. The majority of these men had assembled out of pure curiosity, but the fever of some of them soon reached the minds of all, and in all of them there arose a delirium. The very man who had come running to oppose the murder of an innocent person is one of the first to be seized with the homicidal contagion, and moreover, it does not occur to him to be astonished at this.[6]

It might be argued that the reference to contagion might work on a descriptive level, but that is does not have much relevance as an explanatory category. Consequently, Le Bon and Tarde put greater explanatory emphasis on the notion of hypnotic suggestion. In Le Bon's words:

> We know to-day that by various processes an individual may be brought into such a condition that, having entirely lost his conscious personality, he obeys all the suggestions of the operator who has deprived him of it, and commits acts in utter contradiction with his character and habits. ... All feelings and thoughts are bent in the direction determined by the hypnotiser.[7]

While some (small) measure of fascination of crowd hypnosis might be at play here, Le Bon was above all terrified by the crowd's ability to turn rational, civilized individuals into mere automatons.[8] This de-individualizing power attributed to the crowd was one of the main threats it posed and at the same time a key reason why the rise of crowds was so difficult to fight, according to Le Bon, *and* the starting point from which a new mode of political management might be instituted which took the age of the crowd seriously. Indeed, argued Le Bon, a profound knowledge of crowd dynamics, including the alleged suggestibility of crowds, could be utilized productively to create a new contemporaneous kind of government. This had two dimensions. The first was tied to recognizing the fact that, for Le Bon but also for Tarde, every crowd is constituted by a leader. 'A crowd is a servile flock that is incapable of ever doing without a master', stated Le Bon.[9] Similarly, Tarde argued that '[e]very mob, like every family, has a head and obeys him [*sic*] scrupulously'.[10]

---

[5]   Le Bon, *The Crowd: A Study of the Popular Mind*, 7.

[6]   Gabriel Tarde, *Penal Philosophy* (Montclair. N.J.: Patterson Smith, 1968), 323, italics in the original.

[7]   Le Bon, *The Crowd: A Study of the Popular Mind*, 7.

[8]   Ibid., 8.

[9]   Ibid., 72.

[10] Tarde, *Penal Philosophy*, 325.

Ignoring here the gendering that characterized the entire late-nineteenth-century crowd discourse, the key point was that without a leader there would be no crowd. The second dimension touched on the techniques available to the leader to exercise his or her hypnotic power over the crowd. Here Le Bon argued that in order to control the crowd, the leader should make simple statements (the blunter, the better) and simply repeat them over and over again. Soon these statements would spread contagiously through the crowd and the leader would be able to direct it in whatever direction he or she fancied.[11]

It makes sense, after this brief account of central ideas from classical crowd psychology, to return to the question of mediation. So how does mediation play out in and relate to crowd dynamics? Two central observations can be established on the basis of the above account. First, the leader produces a mediation without which there would be no crowd. It is precisely through the operations of the leader, especially the hypnotic-suggestive impulses emanating from him or her, that contagious dynamics are triggered and the crowd acquires a direction. So, in that view, crowd behavior is always leader-mediated behavior.

It might be noted here that the leader need not be a physical person. For example, Le Bon suggested that objects such as flags may work as non-human hypnotizers, i.e. as a functional equivalent to the leader as a person.[12] Furthermore, while very popular and widely accepted, leader-mediation has also been contested in debates on crowds. Most notably, perhaps, Elias Canetti offered a devastating critique of the idea of the constitutive leader in his *Crowds and Power*.[13] Drawing on his own personal experience with a crowd event in Vienna in 1927, Canetti argued that crowds need not rely on the guidance of some leader.

Second, although the leader is ascribed a constitutive role for the crowd, Le Bon and Tarde at the same time emphasized the *Eigenlogik* of crowds. The leader may propel events, but the internal dynamics of crowds have their own specific nature. This is precisely what Le Bon and Tarde sought to capture through reference to crowd contagion: once the crowd is set in motion, its action unfolds in a complex response to its own laws and the leader's words (in Le Bon's view, therefore, the clever political leader of the era of crowds is one who understands these internal dynamics and how they may be directed and guided externally). For the discussion of crowd mediation, the key point to stress here is that the crowd itself performs a mediation, namely of its members and their mutual ties. It does so by transforming the members of the crowd to precisely that: momentarily de-individualized entities that are subjected to what Le Bon referred to as '*the law of the mental unity of crowds*';[14] and, in a related move, by ensuring, to repeat Tarde's observations, that 'incoherence becomes cohesion', that 'noise becomes a voice'.[15] It is in other

---

11   See Le Bon, *The Crowd: A Study of the Popular Mind*, 77–80.

12   For a discussion of this, see Christian Borch, "Crowds and economic life: bringing an old figure back in", *Economy and Society* 36(4) (2007), 549–73; *The Politics of Crowds*, 301–2.

13   Elias Canetti, *Crowds and Power* (New York: Farrar, Straus and Giroux, 1984).

14   Le Bon, *The Crowd: A Study of the Popular Mind*, 2, italics in the original.

15   Tarde, *Penal Philosophy*, 323. A similar kind of transition, *but without an explanation of its mediating force (e.g. crowd dynamics)*, is identified by Giorgio Agamben in his analysis of how the *polis*,

words the crowd itself that enacts (mediates) this transition and creates cohesion, however temporary this cohesion might be.

I have discussed two main kinds of crowd mediation as they appear in early crowd psychology. What is worth noting at this point is a third kind of mediation which relates to how the leader and crowd are connected, but which goes in another direction than the one suggested in the work of Le Bon and Tarde. Thus, whereas these two French scholars tended to see the leader as the point from which at least one part of the crowd mediation was enacted, subsequently social scientists questioned this kind of unidirectional analysis. I already mentioned Canetti's critique of the emphasis on the leader. More important in the present context is Theodor Geiger's idea, put forward in his study of 1926, *Die Masse und ihre Aktion*, that:

> The typical leader of a crowd is not a 'demagogue', he [*sic*] does not consciously and coldly lead the crowd in a certain direction, but is rather himself affected the most by the ecstasy of the crowd experience, is himself the most unconcious person.[16]

Geiger's observation may be interpreted as a third form of crowd mediation along-side the two others discussed above. But it can also be seen as related to the second of the above-mentioned forms. Thus, Geiger in effect argued that it is the internal crowd dynamics, the mediation into crowd cohesion (and the related forms of ecstasy), which conditions [*konditioniert*], in a Luhmannian sense,[17] how the leader may exercise his or her government over the crowd. That is, the crowd itself mediates its leader.

Crowds and mass media

So far I deliberately refrained from discussing how crowds relate to media in the sense of mass media. There are two main reasons for this. First, I have tried to make clear that in early crowd psychology mediation is above all a question of internal crowd mediation and crowd–leader mediation. This is an important point since, secondly, the acknowledgment of internal crowd dynamics would disappear from view in the kind of collective behavior research that gained prominence in US sociology in the 1960s and 1970s, and which is still dominant in much contemporary crowd sociology (see the next section).

While I have argued that early crowd psychology is not per se mass media psychol-ogy, it is also clear that links between crowds and mass media were soon established.[18]

---

in Aristotle's view, performs a move from voice to language; see Giorgio Agamben, *Homo Sacer: Sovereign Power and Bare Life* (Stanford: Stanford University Press, 1998), 7–8.

[16] Theodor Geiger, *Die Masse und ihre Aktion. Ein Beitrag zur Soziologie der Revolutionen* (Stuttgart: Enke, 1987), 149.

[17] Niklas Luhmann, *Social Systems*, trans. John Bednarz, Jr., with Dirk Baecker (Stanford, California: Stanford University Press, 1995), 23.

[18] See for an interesting analysis Stefan Andriopoulos, *Possessed: Hypnotic Crimes, Corporate Fiction, and the Invention of Cinema*, trans. Peter Jansen and Stefan Andriopoulos (Chicago and London:

Here Tarde played a significant role.[19] Thus, in contrast to some of his writings from the early 1890s, Tarde's *L'opinion et la foule* from 1901 made an explicit attempt to relate crowds to what he referred to as *publics*, and more precisely to distinguish the two from one another.[20] The key point of the discussion of publics was to argue that new mass media had changed the social landscape, rendering the crowd somewhat less important than previously suggested within the field of crowd psychology.

Tarde pointed to several differences between crowds and publics. For example, he argued that, while crowds are based on physical proximity, the imitations of publics can work at great distance. According to Tarde, this 'contagion without contact' suggested a far more advanced social and mental evolution than represented by the crowd.[21] The 'simultaneous conviction or passion', which the members of a public share with one another, was made possible in modern society by the invention of printing and, as a more recent development, by newspapers and other means of 'instantaneous transmission of thought from any distance'.[22] While Tarde's age was one of newspapers, later mass media such as broadcasting would only make that point increasingly relevant. A further contrast between crowds and publics was that, while the former embodied spontaneous anarchy, publics were depicted as civilized entities that, if not rational by themselves, at least had the potential to accommodate rational deliberation. In the same vein, Tarde said, 'publics are less extremist than crowds, less despotic and dogmatic too'.[23]

Another way of putting all this was that '[t]he crowd is the social group of the past; after the family it is the oldest of all social groups'.[24] By contrast, since the public is not tied to physical co-presence, it can be 'extended indefinitely, and since its particular life becomes more intense as it extends', Tarde observed, 'one cannot deny that it is the social group of the future'.[25] This insistence on the modern predominance of publics made Tarde correct Le Bon's famous assertion: 'I therefore cannot agree with that vigorous writer,

---

University of Chicago Press, 2008).

[19] The following is based on Borch, *The Politics of Crowds*, 59–64.

[20] Gabriel Tarde, *L'opinion et la foule* (Paris: Les Presses universitaires de France, 1989).

[21] Ibid., 34.

[22] Ibid., 32, 37. Tarde's notion of the public has some affinity with the 'public sphere' that Habermas would later analyze in *The Structural Transformation of the Public Sphere*. Habermas mentions Tarde's *L'opinion et la foule* once in his book. According to Habermas, 'Tarde was the first to analyze [public opinion] in depth as "mass opinion"... It is considered [by Tarde] a product of a communication process among masses that is neither bound by the principle of public discussion nor concerned with political domination', see Jürgen Habermas, *The Structural Transformation of the Public Sphere: An Inquiry into a Category of Bourgeois Society*, trans. Thomas Burger (Cambridge: Polity Press, 1989). As Schmitz remarks, this quote demonstrates that Habermas completely misses the crucial point of Tarde's book, that crowd and public should not be conflated but distinguished from one another; see H. W. Schmitz, "Der Begriff der 'conversation' bei Gabriel Tarde", *Kodikas/ Code* 10(3/4) (1987), 287–99, here, 296.

[23] Ibid., 52.

[24] Ibid., 37.

[25] Ibid., 38.

Dr. Le Bon, that our age is the "era of crowds". It is the era of the public or of publics, and that is a very different thing'.[26]

Tarde's interest in publics was sparked not least by the Dreyfus Affair, which culminated in 1898–9, and which demonstrated that perhaps the greatest dangers to society were no longer to be found in the rage of crowds. Much more severe threats could result from the intervention of the press and its ability to manipulate public opinion. As Tarde remarked in *L'opinion et la foule* (with implicit reference to the Dreyfus Affair), 'I know of areas in France where the fact that no one has ever seen a single Jew does not prevent anti-semitism from flowering, because people there read anti-semitic papers'.[27] At the same time, such manipulation could only be successfully countered by the press itself, which in the Dreyfus Affair was made manifest by Zola's famous accusation in 1898. As Jaap van Ginneken notes in his discussion of the Affair's implications for Tarde (himself a Dreyfusard), the events suggested that '[t]he battle of crowds had turned into a battle of publics'.[28]

In spite of such dangers Tarde believed that the transition from crowd to public opened up positive paths. After all, as compared to the crowd, the public signified an evolutionary step forward, and it was therefore to be avoided that publics dissolved and regressed into crowds.[29] And while publics as such were no bulwark against disorder, the existence of a multiplicity of publics might well prevent one-sided media manipulation from occurring.

One final remark is warranted about Tarde's notion of publics. It was mentioned in the discussion above of early crowd psychology's concept of crowd mediation that the crowd–leader relation could be seen to constitute a dual mediation. Tarde's analysis of publics suggested that something similar applies to the relation between journalists and their publics: by producing the news that the public reads, the journalist affects the public; at the same time, however, the journalist will 'seek to please' his or her audience, whereby the public exerts an influence over the journalist.[30]

Tarde's discussion of crowds and publics is an early example of how mass media especially in the form of newspapers gave rise to reflections on how a new media reality seemingly rendered crowd formations less historically important – or, perhaps better, suggested that crowds, deliberately orchestrated or not, could be mediated through this new mass media landscape. This idea would attract still more attention in tandem with the increasing predominance of electronic mass media in the early twentieth century. For example, mass media such as broadcasting and movies would be closely scrutinized by a number of American sociologists.[31] One of the central figures here was Herbert Blumer who attributed several positive features to mass media, including an ability to gather people

---

<ol>
<li value="26">Ibid., 38.</li>
<li value="27">Ibid., 41.</li>
<li value="28">Van Ginneken, Crowds, Psychology and Politics, 217.</li>
<li value="29">See Christian Borch, "Urban Imitations: Tarde's Sociology Revisited", Theory, Culture & Society 22(3) (2005), 81–100, here 96.</li>
<li value="30">Tarde, L'opinion et la foule, 41.</li>
<li value="31">The following draws on Borch, The Politics of Crowds, 150–7.</li>
</ol>

around sentiments in ways compatible with a free society.[32] Yet Blumer also stressed that the mass media were not simply innocent mediators of news or entertainment. They could also be utilized for dangerous political purposes. Contrary to Tarde, therefore, Blumer did not see the media as a public, i.e. as a balancing means, capable of holding crowd impulses in check; rather, the new media public itself could very well work as a manipulating instrument. Consequently, the Tardean distinction between the irrational crowd and the rational public could no longer be taken for granted.

Blumer's reflections echoed a wider problematization of mass media and how they might be used to manipulate the masses. In the American context this problematization revolved around the notion of public opinion. While this notion had a positive valence in the beginning of the twentieth century, being a kind of American equivalent to Tarde's concept of publics, things gradually changed (due in part to the Wilson administration's use of propaganda during the First World War), meaning that a new and much more skeptical framing evolved in the 1920s. In this reconfiguration, public opinion was no longer lauded as a rational alternative to the irrational crowd. Rather, public opinion was seen as being embedded in machinery which was anything but rational; in fact, public opinion was seen as an additional cogwheel in the repression of rationality. This idea was put forward, for instance, in Walter Lippmann's *Public Opinion* of 1922, in which Lippmann examined how public opinion was governed through propaganda and how stereotypes, prejudices, etc. allegedly dominated public opinion.[33] Lippmann's critical interrogation of the new media reality zeroed in on a basic socio-epistemological challenge, namely that in modern life people do not have direct access to the world. What they know is mediated by the mass media and public opinion.[34] In Lippmann's words:

> the mass is constantly exposed to suggestion. It reads not the news, but the news with an aura of suggestion about it, indicating the line of action to be taken. It hears reports, not objective as the facts are, but already stereotyped to a certain pattern of behavior.[35]

As the quote intimates, Lippmann drew on crowd-theoretical resources (such as Le Bon) to explain how propaganda purportedly worked as a filter separating the reality from people's conception of it. Lippmann basically asserted that the media endow people with a warped picture of the world, a kind of mass hypnosis, as it were. This filtering operation of public opinion, newspapers and the media practically eliminated the individual's free judgment and enhanced the irrationality of modern society – rather than forming a bulwark again it such as Tarde believed. Given that this was the central problem, public opinion and the stereotypes it produced should be restrained. One way of achieving this was, according to Lippmann, to insert an elite, or more precisely 'some form of expertness between the

---

32   Herbert Blumer, "Moulding of Mass Behavior through the Motion Picture", *The American Sociologial Society* 29 (1935), 115–27, 127.

33   Walter Lippmann, *Public Opinion* (New Brunswick: Transaction Publishers, 1991).

34   Ibid., 26–8.

35   Ibid., 243.

private citizen and the vast environment in which he [*sic*] is entangled'.[36] This, Lippmann believed, would prepare the way for more rationality in politics and hence for a democracy worthy of its name, one that was not distorted by the prejudices produced by the press, but which permitted individuals to make up their own mind on a more independent basis.

There are two key points to be made here. First, the problematization articulated by Blumer and Lippmann (and many others) basically focused on how the mass media had assumed the role of the hypnotizing leader, being able to mould the minds and actions of their followers, i.e. the dispersed masses (rather than singular co-present crowds). This problematization was gloomier than that of Le Bon. While he was concerned with the alleged fact that all could potentially become a crowd (including, and that was for Le Bon the scariest part, the well-educated elite), the problematization of the mass media's manipulating powers suggested that Le Bon's fears had become true on a much larger scale than he had ever imagined: in the mass-mediated society, there was no longer any outside. The occasional, if ever more frequent, eruption of crowds had been replaced by the incessant and widespread manipulation of the masses.[37]

Second, Lippmann's wish to give individuals a better chance of making up their own minds, independently of mediated manipulation, provides an indication of a concern with the individual subject that would become still more central to subsequent discussions of crowd-related phenomena. To be sure, Lippmann was not the first to suggest that the individual was subjected to mass mediation. This idea was at the heart of Le Bon's work, too, where it took the form of a problematization of the de-individualizing force of crowds. Still, as I have argued elsewhere,[38] the US adoption of the French crowd semantics was framed almost from the outset in a more liberal tone where the problem attributed to crowds was not simply that of their alleged destructive nature, but more importantly that they put into question the notion of the liberal subject: in the crowd, the autonomous, self-contained subject was seemingly transformed into an automaton. This is further discussed in the following.

The dissolution of crowd mediation

Without going into too much detail, it can be stated that some of the central ideas propagated by early crowd psychology came under heavy fire from historians and sociologists

---

[36] Ibid., 378.

[37] As indicated, this problematization had a wide resonance in the 1920s. It therefore seems slightly misleading when Peter Sloterdijk refers to Hermann Broch's *Massenwahntheorie* (written between 1939 and 1948) and its emphasis on mass poisoning of the mind as being emblematic of an important turn in atmospheric politics in the twentieth century. While Broch was certainly concerned with atmospheric politics in the form of media propaganda, he was far from the only one and far from the first to articulate and discuss this concern. See Hermann Borch, *Massenwahntheorie. Beiträge zu einer Psychologie der Politik* (Frankfurt am Main: Suhrkamp, 1979); Peter Sloterdijk, *Sphären III. Schäume* (Frankfurt am Main: Suhrkamp, 2004), 182–90.

[38] Borch, *The Politics of Crowds*.

especially in the 1960s and 1970s. Two aspects of early crowd psychology in particular were questioned. One was the irrationality attributed to crowds by Le Bon and many others. Against the notion of inherently irrational crowds, scholars began to argue that, upon closer inspection, crowds were better understood if attention was paid to how they were organized and mobilized as responses to specific problems (e.g. famine) or perceived injustices. Put differently, it was claimed that, rather than being irrational eruptions, crowd behavior was actually enthused by quite reasonable motives. The second aspect of classical crowd psychology that was severely contested related to the first point; thus, a fundamental critique was voiced of the explanatory potential ascribed to the notion of suggestion. Rather than seeing suggestion as a key concept in analyses of crowd behavior, sociologists and social psychologists now argued that suggestion was entirely lacking in explanatory capacity and therefore should be dismissed from any attempt at proper analysis. Instead of seeing crowd members as hypnotized automatons, they should rather be conceived of as capable subjects well aware of the situations and collective formations they entered, it was argued.

For present purposes, the most important thing to note is not so much the critiques themselves, but rather how they gave rise to a radically new concept of crowds within sociology. Thus key ideas in classical notions of crowds were eventually turned upside-down. From seeing crowds as incarnations of irrationality and de-individualization, an image emerged in which crowds were depicted as entities composed of rational individuals pursuing rational interests. The most radical example of this reconfiguration of crowd discourse appeared in the work of the American sociologist Richard Berk who proposed a rational-choice model of crowd behavior. According to Berk, 'crowd participants (1) exercise a substantial degree of rational decision-making and (2) are not defined a priori as less rational than in other contexts'.[39] Furthermore, he stated, in his conception 'the gathering of a crowd is viewed as an *opportunity* in which individuals can experience certain rewards and certain costs'.[40] What Berk did, in other words, echoing a widespread movement within American sociology, was to suggest that the individual, rational actor should form the starting point for the analysis of crowd dynamics.

Now, why is this important for a discussion of crowd mediation? It is important because this rationalist-individualist account essentially annulled the notion that the crowd could exercise a mediating power over the crowd members. Put differently, when the crowd was reduced to a play of rational individuals pursuing rational individual goals, one of the key features of classical crowd psychology, namely the interest in crowd dynamics per se – i.e. the emergent order of crowds, their *Eigenlogik* – was entirely ignored. Consequently, it became impossible within this rationalist paradigm to account for any emergent, over-individual level that might have a mediating effect on the behavior taking place in the crowds.

---

[39]   Richard A. Berk, "A Gaming Approach to Crowd Behavior", *American Sociological Review* 39 (June 1974), 355–73, here 356.

[40]   Richard A. Berk, *Collective Behavior* (Dubuque, IA: Brown, 1974), 67, italics in the original.

Conclusion

I have tried in this chapter to provide a brief account of a theoretical-historical foundation on which contemporary debates on transformations in relations between crowds
and media/mediation might build. The claim is not that current debates on these issues
necessarily need to follow directly in the footsteps of classical crowd theory, but rather
that this tradition of theorization actually does address the relation(s) between crowds and
media(tion) in various ways, and that contemporary articulations of crowds/mediation
may be better understood when analyzed against the background of how the tradition of
sociological crowd theory has addressed these issues.

At least two lines of inquiry can be followed here. One is to examine how present forms
of crowd mediation express continuity rather than discontinuity with past configurations.
One example of this approach is offered by Carsten Stage who has argued that blogging
can be fruitfully analyzed on the basis of Le Bon's framework.[41] Drawing on empirical
research, Stage demonstrates how blogging can generate an online crowd, defined as '*the
affective unification and relative synchronization of a public in relation to a specific online
site*'.[42] The fundamental point in this approach is that rather than signifying a qualitative
transformation in crowd mediation – i.e. rather than suggesting, for instance, that new
media render old modes of crowd formation obsolete – new media simply intensify particular forms of crowd formation that have been thoroughly analyzed in classical crowd
theory. That is, what appears to be new phenomena can in fact be appropriately conceived
on the basis of more classical conceptions.

A second line of inquiry focuses more on qualitative changes. One example of this is
Sloterdijk's analysis of the transformation from a Führer to a program principle. Another
example, which is more radical in its media perspective, is Jean Baudrillard's work on
postmodern, mass-mediated simulation and how it entails a shift from active, noisy crowds
to passive, absorbing and above all silent masses.[43] The crucial point here is not whether
Baudrillard's analysis is adequate or not, but rather that the transformation he diagnoses
can only be fully understood against the backdrop of insights into more classical forms
of crowd mediation. That is, the reservoir of classical crowd thinking offers a framework
for assessing and discussing the possible emergence of new types of masses today and
how they relate to mediating practices.

***

---

[41] See Carsten Stage, "The online crowd: a contradiction in terms? On the potentials of Gustave Le
Bon's crowd psychology in an analysis of affective blogging", *Distinktion: Scandinavian Journal
of Social Theory* 14(2) (2013), 221–26.

[42] Ibid., 216, italics in the original.

[43] Jean Baudrillard, *In the Shadow of the Silent Majorities* (New York: Columbia University Press,
1983).

Christiane Heibach

From Masses to Collectives
Dimensions of a Discursive Paradigm Shift

"But *feeling, motion, action* – even if they should prove inconsequential (for what has *timeless* consequence on the stage of mankind?), if there will be *knocks* and *revolutions*, if these feelings will at times turn *fanatical, violent*, even *detestable* – as *instruments in the hands of time*, how great their *power* and *effect!* How they nourish the *heart*, not the *head!* How they bind everything together with *inclinations* and *drives*, not with *sickly thoughts!* [...] Nothing could be further from my mind than to defend the endless mass-migrations and devastations, the vassals' wars and feuds, the armies of monks, the pilgrimages and crusades: I only wish to explain them, [to show] how *spirit* breathes in everything, after all! The fermentation of *human forces*, the *great cure* of the whole species by *forced movement* [...]!"[1]

Johann Gottfried Herder's spirited praise of revolutions and their agents, quoted above, was published in 1774 and thus long before the so-called "masses" were to become a recognized feature of society. Nevertheless, the passage contains a number of elements that would reverberate a century later in the foundational studies of crowd psychology. Gustav Le Bon and Gabriel Tarde, not to mention Sigmund Freud and Elias Canetti, each used similar language to define the crowd, but their overall assessment was pejorative. Their negative evaluations can be explained by a single historical event that served as the backdrop for their investigations, namely the storming of the Bastille. The latter incident was regarded as a sort of "prototype" for a phenomenon that is neither individual nor collective, one that manifests itself as an unmistakable yet amorphous conglomeration that is simultaneously organic in its physical and psychological synchronicity. It is this phenomenon that the concept of the "crowd" or "masses" would later come to designate.[2]

The anti-Enlightenment triumvirate of "feeling," "motion," and "action" alongside the emphasis on the "heart" (over the "head") and on "inclinations and drives" (over "sickly

---

[1] Johann Gottfried Herder, "Another Philosophy of History for the Education of Mankind," in *Another Philosophy of History and Selected Political Writings*, trans. Ioannis D. Evrigenis and Daniel Pellerin (Indianapolis: Hackett, 2004), 3–98, at 42 (the emphasis is original).

[2] See Susanne Lüdemann and Uwe Hebekus, "Einleitung," in *Massenverfassungen: Beiträge zur Diskurs- und Mediengeschichte der Menschenmenge*, ed. Lüdemann et al. (Munich: Fink, 2010), 7–23, at 8.

thoughts"), all which still represented to Herder the basis of a collective spirit with positive connotations, later struck the criminologist and social theorist Tarde and the physician and sociologist Le Bon as Janus-faced characteristics that oscillated precariously between the heroic and the horrifying. That a singular word, "the crowd," was used to label this phenomenon led to the notion of a "collective specter" whose forces could no longer be explained by individual characteristics, because it possessed a genuine character of its own.[3] Thus was born the demon of the masses, which, analogous to Herder's description, was characterized above all by its particular forms of feeling, motion, and action. A discourse was thus initiated that has persisted to the present day, though noteworthy paradigm shifts have taken place that, as I would like to argue, are closely associated with media structures. The manner in which crowds and collectives are described and characterized is correlated to the prevailing media constellations of a given time and to the way in which such constellations are used. Some of the implications of these discursive and reciprocal effects will be discussed in greater detail below.

I. Feeling

According to Le Bon and Tarde, crowds function affectively, impulsively, and in an instinctively imitative manner. Neither author differentiated between affect, impulses, or instincts, and thus they created a conceptual synthesis that is grounded in the (ever-recurring) ideas of genetics and biology. Within such a framework, a "natural" genesis is attributed to the masses, which are regarded as something distinct from the social. The synonymous use of these three terms would appear again, though somewhat indirectly, in Canetti's typology of crowds, according to which the "prevailing emotion" (or affect) of a given social group will yield one of the following classifications:

a) The baiting crowd (*Hetzmasse*): a short-lived gathering assembled to kill an object;
b) The flight crowd: a group that flees from a common danger;
c) The prohibition crowd: protest movements, strikes, etc.;
d) The reversal crowd: revolutions as a reversal of power relations;
e) The feast crowd: a harmless group gathered for the sake of hedonistic celebration.[4]

A closer look at this typology reveals that it is based much more on action than it is on affect or emotion and that its origin, in turn, lies in instincts: baiting and killing, fleeing, resisting, revolting, celebrating. In some of these cases it can even be said that feelings, instincts, and actions converge into one. Of course, structural heterogeneity is inherent

---

[3]   See Michael Gamper and Peter Schnyder, "Kollektive Gespenster: Eine Einleitung," in *Kollektive Gespenster: Die Masse, der Zeitgeist und andere unfassbare Körper*, ed. Gamper and Schnyder (Berlin: Rombach, 2006), 7–26, at 16.

[4]   Elias Canetti, *Crowds and Power*, trans. Carol Stewart (New York: Farrar, Straus and Giroux, 1984), 49–63.

to all types of crowds, but they are united in their affective "synchronization" (*"Gleich-schaltung"*), which forms each of them into an independent and active organism. This organic unity enables the diametric opposition between crowds and individuals, who are believed to act rationally (and therefore ethically and morally).[5] It is in this way that a crowd can be treated as a subject – in the dual sense of the word: On the one hand, the crowd is identified as "a provisional being formed of heterogeneous elements, which for a moment are combined, exactly as the cells which constitute a living body form by their reunion a new being which displays characteristics very different from those possessed by each of the cells singly."[6] As a "sentient being," on the other hand, its affective or emotional orientation is such that it is prone to being subjected to the will of a charismatic and genial leader.[7] What crowds lack is the dimension of reflection, and especially that of self-reflection. Beyond their affects and impulses, crowds are hardly aware of their own situation, a fact that is reflected in their particular forms of motion.

II. Motion

The crowd is always a crowd in motion; as a "physical convention," it is never static.[8] Its process of formation is simultaneously its identity, for this is what reveals its purpose (as Canetti's typology suggests). Crowds are set in motion above all by forms of transmission (*Übertragung*) that have roots in biological and physical processes and that are thus suggestive of the original concept of "mass" in physics.[9]

Even Herder's use of the word "fermentation" suggests such an analogy. The metaphors used by Le Bon, Tarde, and Canetti to describe the communication that takes place within crowds or between a crowd and its leader are drawn either from the natural sciences or from the then nascent field of individual psychology: "radiation" and "contagion" (Tarde),[10] "magnetic influence" (Le Bon),[11] and "discharge" (Canetti)[12] are each analogies based on "natural" (i.e., physical) processes, whereas the "hypnotized subject" and "suggestion"

---

[5]   See Gustave Le Bon, *The Crowd: A Study of the Popular Mind* (New York: Macmillan, 1896), 8; and Canetti, *Crowds and Power*, 18.

[6]   Le Bon, *The Crowd: A Study of the Popular Mind*, 6.

[7]   See ibid., 117–45 ("The Leaders of Crowds and Their Means of Persuasion"); and also Gabriel Tarde, *The Laws of Imitation*, trans. Elsie Clews Parsons (New York: Henry Holt, 1903), xxii. Tarde's principle of imitation as a driving force behind social and biological behavior presupposes that there is someone who can be imitated, namely an innovative genius who guides the social community.

[8]   Peter Sloterdijk, *Die Verachtung der Massen: Versuch über Kulturkämpfe in der modernen Gesell-schaft* (Frankfurt am Main: Suhrkamp, 2007), 16.

[9]   See Joseph Vogl, "Über soziale Fassungslosigkeit," in *Kollektive Gespenster: Die Masse, der Zeitgeist und andere unfassbare Körper*, ed. Michael Gamper and Peter Schnyder (Berlin: Rombach, 2006), 171–89, at 179.

[10]   Tarde, *The Laws of Imitation*, 17.

[11]   Le Bon, *The Crowd: A Study of the Popular Mind*, 11.

[12]   Canetti, *Crowds and Power*, 17.

(Le Bon) were borrowed from the realm of individual psychology.[13] The notion of unintentional, involuntary, and uncontrollable behavior is latent in all of these terms; such "impetuosity," according to Le Bon, will cause one to lose "his conscious personality" and to become "the slave of [...] unconscious activity."[14] Tarde's conception of society was not much different. He considered imitative processes to be "elementary social acts"[15] that spread "like a wave of light, or like a family of termites"[16] and ultimately functioned like any number of epidemics or "contagions."[17] Regarding the extent to which crowds are dominated by unconscious impulses, Tarde unequivocally concluded: *Society is imitation and imitation is a kind of somnambulism.*"[18] Canetti, for his part, believed that the constitutive element of any crowd – its "most important occurrence" – is the discharge: "Before this the crowd does not actually exist; it is the discharge which creates it. This is the moment when all who belong to the crowd get rid of their differences and feel equal."[19] Accordingly, the principle behind these unconscious forms of transmission lies in the synchronization of individuals. Crowds are based on resonance, synchronicity, and common motion in two respects: as a physical rhythm that manifests itself in marching, clapping, yelling, and singing – on the one hand – and as a coordinated generator of affect on the other.

Around the beginning of the twentieth century, these psycho-physical processes were also an expression of the extent to which the enlightened individual had been deconstructed; they brought to mind positive connotations of ecstatic collective experiences, especially in the context of aesthetic cultures of celebration, which had largely been reinvented. The visions of mass theater by the likes of Max Reinhardt, Georg Fuchs, and the post-revolutionary Vsesvolod Meyerhold aimed to mobilize the masses not only for political purposes but above all for the sake of intensifying a common aesthetic experience. Reinhardt described the dynamic between actors and the audience as a "mutual influence of atmospheres" in which "naïve and spontaneous impulses" are dominant:

> It is always the case that a decisive and guiding majority is formed extremely quickly – without a vote, without negotiations, and without any deliberations at all. Once part of a crowd, the individual and his essence undergo a significant change. The most quiet of people will abruptly and frantically begin to yell, as though carried away by the explosions that have suddenly been discharged.[20]

---

[13]   Le Bon, *The Crowd: A Study of the Popular Mind*, 12.

[14]   Ibid., 12, 11.

[15]   Tarde, *The Laws of Imitation*, 144.

[16]   Ibid., 3.

[17]   Ibid., 145–46n1.

[18]   Ibid., 87 (the emphasis is original).

[19]   Canetti, *Crowds and Power*, 17.

[20]   Max Reinhardt, *Ich bin nichts als Theatermann: Briefe, Reden, Aufsätze, Interviews, Gespräche, Auszüge aus Regiebüchern*, ed. Hugo Fetting (Berlin: Henschel, 1989), 440–41.

The ecstasy of common experience, the emotional "discharge," is conceived here as being unconscious and divorced from all media, exactly as it is in the theories proposed by crowd psychologists. Here, however, it is reinterpreted positively (and in aesthetic terms) as a resonating sensation and intensive experience between the individual ensemble of actors and the anonymous crowd that is the audience. Georg Fuchs had a similar vision for the "stage of the future," the purpose of which would be to "arouse and discharge an effusive sense of excitement," an excitement that will arise organically "from the orgiastic and effusive motion of a festive crowd."[21] In this case, it is rhythm itself that generates communal excitement; it is a transmedial structure that intertwines *physis* and *psyche*.[22]

Somatic synchronizations of this sort reached an ignominious climax in the "narco-political alliances"[23] of National Socialism and Stalinism, which went above and beyond to master the unconscious by harnessing the contagious powers of affect, hypnosis, and suggestion. The paradigmatic staging of the masses, whereby the masses are first experienced as such, requires a highly sophisticated and media-based production strategy, a coordinated effort that is best exemplified in Leni Riefenstahl's propaganda film *Triumph of the Will* (1935). By giving such order to the crowds, a feat accomplished to perfection both aesthetically and cinematically, the film represents both a confirmation and repudiation of crowd psychology. It corroborated the *Führer* principle, according to which the order-bestowing hand of a leader can restrain the masses but nevertheless needs them in order to create, by means of mass media, a self-representation of and for the masses themselves.[24] *Triumph of the Will*, whose intended audience was the very masses shown in the film, relies on the conflation of two types of crowd. In Peter Sloterdijk's terms (which derive from Canetti's), it depends on a "discharge crowd," which is an organism present in time and space, and on an "entertainment crowd," which is the result of mass-media programming.[25] The latter type was ultimately the result of the now-obsolescing age of television, whereas the totalitarian staging or representation of both types (in unison) required something more. Characterized by its receptive passivity, the entertainment crowd ultimately had to be programmed by suggestion processes into a discharge crowd that acted in a homogeneous manner.

III. Action

It is one thing for crowds to lose themselves in a communal present by means of psycho-physically synchronized motion. It is another matter, however, that their activity might

---

21   Georg Fuchs, *Die Schaubühne der Zukunft* (Leipzig: Schuster & Loeffler, 1905), 34, 38.

22   See Inge Baxmann, *Mythos – Gemeinschaft: Körper und Tanzkulturen der Moderne* (Munich: Fink, 2000), 35–62.

23   Sloterdijk, *Die Verachtung der Massen*, 23.

24   For further discussion, see Christiane Heibach, "Manipulative Atmosphäre: Zwischen unmittelbarem Erleben und medialer Konstruktion," in *Atmosphären: Dimensionen eines diffusen Phänomens*, ed. Heibach (Munich: Fink, 2012), 262–82.

25   Sloterdijk, *Die Verachtung der Massen*, 25.

have grave consequences for those who are not members of the group. As Canetti's typology suggests, a crowd can even represent a sort of demonic threat for those who are outside of it (or believe that they are). As a catalyst for revolutions and "destructiveness" (in Canetti's terms), crowds are unpredictable, and they are so despite the *Führer* principle and despite their receptiveness to intellectual suggestion. According to Le Bon, crowds can be manipulated by excessive and sentimental rhetoric – "[t]o exaggerate, to affirm, to resort to repetitions […] are methods of argument well known to speakers at public meetings" – and such manipulation does not require a speaker to prove his or her point by rational means.[26] If Le Bon located the suggestion of presence in the rhetorical forms of his time, the totalitarian regimes of the first half of the twentieth century were able to amplify this by means of technical mass media, above all by the radio. With the radio, the voice became the suggestive medium of the totalitarian masses. Through it, affective messages could be delivered to the masses more adeptly than ever before, as Rudolf Arnheim argued as early as 1936 in his book *Radio: An Art of Sound*. There he developed an ontology of sound by claiming that the combination of music, noise, and language into a unitary piece of sonic material represented a genuine form of expression particular to the radio.[27] He also claimed that the effects of non-verbal acoustic elements were more powerful than the contents of any speech. In the early theories of the radio, but also in recent studies, the cultural significance of the voice is generally discussed in terms of its immediacy and affective potential, characteristics that function beyond language and create space for suggestion and manipulation.[28]

The high affective potential of the radio – as well as that of film, the other new mass medium of the time[29] – was received rather ambivalently. Thus the opinions about the masses outlined above were more or less transferred into the characterizations of the (potential) radio audience. At one end of the spectrum, the radio was expected to cross cultural borders and enable friendly relations between different nationalities; at the other end, radio waves were believed to exert a sort of mind control over people in the form of electromagnetic telepathy (much like the concepts of magnetic influence and contagion

---

[26]   Le Bon, *The Crowd: A Study of the Popular Mind*, 36–37.

[27]   See Rudolf Arnheim, *Radio: An Art of Sound*, trans. Margaret Ludwig and Herbert Read (1936; repr. New York: Da Capo Press, 1972), 15: "[T]he artist was given the exciting possibility of making an amazing new unity out of pure form and physical reality with the combined help of three means – sound and voice; music; words."

[28]   See Sigrid Weigel, "Die Stimme als Medium des Nachlebens: Pathosformel, Nachhall, Phantom," in *Stimme: Annäherung an ein Phänomen*, ed. Dorish Kolesch and Sybille Krämer (Frankfurt am Main: Suhrkamp, 2006), 16–39. The example of the voice is especially interesting, however, because its complex nature can cause a variety of effects. It is just as suitable for expressing emotions as it is for articulating intellectual ideas, and thus it functions in such a way that is not always and necessarily affective.

[29]   For early discussions of film in Germany, see Anton Kaes, ed., *Kino-Debatte: Texte zum Verhältnis von Literatur und Film, 1909–1929* (Munich: dtv, 1978).

in crowd psychology).[30] The range of arguments presented in such theories of the radio discloses the ambivalent nature of medial effects, an ambivalence that seems to define cultural debates whenever a new medium is introduced: Whereas utopian-minded thinkers tend to focus on the possible enlightening effects and social cohesion that a new medium might engender, the dystopian-minded will underscore the suggestive and manipulative potential of an invisible force.

In his analysis of Orson Welles's radio drama *The War of the Worlds* (1938), Werner Faulstich referred to the radio as the "medium of anxiety" *par excellence* and stressed its affective and collective influence over a crowd that, as an "individualized" audience, is present only temporally (not spatially).[31] In this techno-medialized form, too, crowds still managed to induce certain fears about the uncontrollable nature of commonly experienced emotions, even though the synchronization of such crowds did not occur in a common space. Nevertheless, the theories of the time did maintain a sharp distinction between crowds as spatio-temporally present phenomena and crowds as techno-medial conglomerates of recipients: Whereas "discharge crowds" are destructively active, "entertainment crowds" are passive to the point of being anaesthetized and at most *re*active (for instance as a "flight crowd" threatened by an invasion from Mars). The latter type of crowd is, first and foremost, a product of its media, whereas the physically and spatially present "discharge crowd" is only defined as such by its own activity. Thus the two types are distinguished less by the matter of affective synchronization than by the possibility for psycho-physical and somatic synchronization and the corresponding predisposition for communal action.

Again, technical mass media were no longer directed at a spatio-temporally present crowd but rather at a public or audience that was only temporally present. To this physical shift of location can be traced the origins of the mass-medial production of the audience, a concept that would be discussed with the same ambivalence that had characterized earlier theories of the crowd. Paradoxically, negative opinions of the dispersed audience seem to be most pronounced in texts that stress the positive aspects of mass media. In Walter Benjamin's canonical essay "The Work of Art in the Age of Mechanical Reproduction," despite its enthusiasm for deconstructing the bourgeois and auratic concept of art, there is an implicit sense of unease about the burgeoning mass-media culture, and this discomfort is not only manifest in Benjamin's criticism of the manipulative potential of National-

---

[30]   For representative texts from the period, see A. K. Fiala, "Elektrophysiologische Zukunftsprobleme," in *Medientheorien, 1888–1933: Texte und Kommentare*, ed. Albert Kümmel-Schnur and Petra Löffler (Frankfurt am Main: Suhrkamp, 2002), 177–203; and Johannes Maria Verweyen, "Radioitis!" in ibid., 454–61.

[31]   Werner Faulstich, *Radiotheorie: Eine Studie zum Hörspiel "The War of the Worlds" (1938) von Orson Welles* (Tübingen: Narr, 1981), 89. According to Faulstich's analysis, *The War of the Worlds* manipulated the cultural notions of authenticity and fictionality quite masterfully and thus exploited the ambivalence of the radio in a paradigmatic manner (see ibid., 102).

Socialist media practices.[32] It is rather the case that film generates certain manners of behavior that, though typically diagnosed as negative by crowd psychologists, Benjamin regards as positive. The audience of a film appropriates what it is watching by assimilating the film into itself and evaluating it intimately. It does not do this, however, on the basis of rational or normative aesthetic values, but rather in a way that exalts entertainment and distraction as its standards.[33]

In his text "The Mass Ornament" (1927),[34] Siegfried Kracauer focused on a different aspect of mass culture, an aspect that would be addressed again in the cultural criticism of the 1960s. According to Kracauer, an industrial mass of workers was created by synchronized and collective manners of behavior, and such behavior was not motivated by politics but rather by economic factors. These masses emerged from assembly-line work and from the Tayloristic fragmentation of manufacturing processes associated with it. As Charlie Chaplin illustrated so clearly in the film *Modern Times* (1936), this faction of society consisted of people whose existence was defined simply by repetitive physical activity and whose experience was thus fragmentary. Because production processes had been broken down into individual elements of motion, workers on an assembly line had no notion of such processes as a whole.

Whereas, in Kracauer's work, a distinction existed between the Tayloristically structured masses of assembly-line workers and the businesses that employed them,[35] this distinction would vanish in the post-industrial "society of the spectacle" (as Guy Debord called it). In the latter society, the proletariat went from being a victim to being a ben-

---

[32] Walter Benjamin, "The Work of Art in the Age of Mechanical Reproduction," in *Illuminations*, trans. Harry Zohn (New York: Schocken Books, 1968), 217–52, at 240–42.

[33] See ibid., 240: "The film makes the cult value recede into the background not only by putting the public in the position of the critic, but also by the fact that at the movies this position requires no attention. The public is an examiner, but an absent-minded one." In the epilogue that immediately follows this passage, Benjamin argues that the central strategy of fascism is to aestheticize politics, and in this light he associates film's distractive potential with the affective manipulation techniques so characteristic of the National-Socialist use of the media.

[34] Siegfried Kracauer, "The Mass Ornament," in *The Mass Ornament: Weimar Essays*, trans. Thomas Y. Levin (Cambridge, MA: Harvard University Press, 1995), 75–88. See also the essays by Roland Meyer and Sascha Simons in this volume.

[35] Unlike Marx's diagnosis of the accumulation of capital by business owners, Kracauer regarded the shift toward increased profits as an effort to keep production processes running: "[T]he capitalist production process is an end in itself. The commodities that it spews forth are not actually produced to be possessed; rather, they are made for the sake of profit that knows no limit. Its growth is tied to that of business. The producer does not labor for private gains whose benefits he can enjoy only to a limited extent (in America surplus profits are directed to spiritual shelters such as libraries and universities, which cultivate intellectuals whose later endeavors repay with interest the previously advanced capital). No: the producer labors in order to expand the business. Value is not produced for the sake of value. Though labor may well have once served to produce and consume values up to a certain point, these have now become side effects in the service of production processes" (Kracauer, "The Mass Ornament," 78).

eficiary of its own powers of production. Producers and consumers became one and the same, whereby the economic cycle became inherently self-referential.[36] This is a process that would recur, though in a slightly different manner, at the level of the mass media, which came to create its own audience.

IV. From Masses to Audiences

In his anthropological examination of cyberspace, Pierre Lévy distinguishes three cultural-historical stages of community formation. The first stage consists of "organic groups," which are small and informal collectives based on physical proximity; the second consists of "molar groups,"[37] the density of which is so great as to require the establishment of regulatory structures such as hierarchies, institutions, and organizations; and the third consists of "molecular groups," which respect and cultivate the diversity of individuals in order to create new forms of collectivity by means of networked media.[38] Despite their regulated social structures, which are based on hierarchies and the centrality of the mass media, Lévy's "molar groups" resemble Tarde's, Le Bon's, and Canetti's characterization of crowds. Their formation takes place under the aegis of technologies that "manage objects in bulk, in the mass, blindly, entropically" – technologies that communicate unilaterally and are centrally controlled.[39] Even when such groups are formed with a particular aim in mind (to demonstrate for a cause, for instance), the result of such collectivization is a corresponding reduction of complexity (in the case of demonstrations, an example would be simplified slogans).[40]

This characterization is a classical topos of intellectual media criticism. In *Amusing Ourselves to Death*, a book published in 1985, Neil Postman portrayed the general public as being uncritical and anaesthetized by television, as an audience that is not defined by its collective activity but by its remote-controlled and synchronized passivity in response to colorful images and dumbed-down language. Peter Sloterdijk has echoed this in his diagnosis of "entertainment crowds" that are programmed by their "participation in the mass media." For Postman and Sloterdijk, the transition from crowds to public audiences is characterized by "irrelevance, incoherence, and impotence"[41] As a reflection of its own mediocrity, the mass-media "culture of the uninteresting" (*Kultur des Uninteressanten*, in Sloterdijk's words) concentrates its affects on the trivial and indulges in irrelevancies.

---

[36] See Guy Debord, *The Society of the Spectacle*, trans. Donald Nicholson-Smith (New York: Zone Books, 1994).

[37] "Molarity" is a concept used in physics to denote the concentration of solution (moles per liter). By using this term, Lévy indirectly perpetuates the analogy between physics and crowds (masses).

[38] Pierre Lévy, *Collective Intelligence: Mankind's Emerging World in Cyberspace*, trans. Robert Bononno (New York: Plenum Trade, 1997), 39–56.

[39] Ibid., 40.

[40] Ibid., 66.

[41] Neil Postman, *Amusing Ourselves to Death: Public Discourse in the Age of Showbusiness* (1985; repr. New York: Penguin, 2005), 76.

Unlike the concept of the masses during the first six decades of the twentieth century – which at least involved charismatic leaders who, though perhaps no more intelligent than the general mob, certainly demonstrated greater willpower – the focus by now has shifted squarely onto the idea of the average person. The latter idea has proven to be an important instrument for cementing the role of the mass media, which now design their programming to satisfy the desires of the "average Joe." Throughout this process, it is insinuated that this "average person" is first and foremost a construct of quantitative methods that have been applied to evaluate the supposed behavior of media consumers.

It is no coincidence that the origins of this idea go back to the nineteenth century, during which the development of statistics (and the creation of the so-called *homme moyen*) served to reduce the diverse character of the masses by introducing the idea of "normality."[42] The establishment of statistical methods and their mathematical analysis entailed abstraction and concretization at the same time. A fictitious average person was invented whose presumed behavior continues to dominate the media landscape and to provide society with its self-image. Statistics, however, was more than a mere "scientification" of the masses; it established a new ethical standard beyond the normative, a standard according to which such things as virtue, truth, and beauty were replaced by normality, which in turn dictated how one ought to behave so as not to be out of the ordinary. Instead of exceptionality, it is now mediocrity that best defines the masses, while also serving as a measure of the extent to which the masses have been disciplined. At the level of scientific methods, this supports the thesis that society has been trivialized, and it does so in two ways. First, it elevates mathematically determined averages to the norm and treats statistics as a transcendental *Ersatz*. Second, this process contributes to the development of empirical methods for collecting data that are largely value-free, and these data are used to co-create mass audiences.[43]

In light of these mass-media structures, it is no surprise that media critics often implicitly use the term "mediocracy" to refer to two phenomena, namely domination by the media and the domination of mediocrity. Here, however, there is a degree of self-referentiality that must be taken into account, for it is ultimately unclear whether the mass media create their audience or whether the audience creates the mass media. This circularity is indicative of a general structural dynamic that is manifest not only in the realm of the media but also on political, social, and especially economic levels.

Since the 1960s, as criticism of globalization has become widespread, self-referential processes of this sort have been cited as a hallmark of the power relations that happen to be prevalent at a given time. In 1967, Debord argued that "vicious circles" were one of

---

[42]   See Jürgen Link, "Tendenz Denormalisierung oder Tendenz Normalität? Zur Massensymbolik im 19. Jahrhundert," in *Kollektive Gespenster: Die Masse, der Zeitgeist und andere unfassbare Körper*, ed. Gamper and Schnyder (Berlin: Rombach, 2006), 157–69; and Michael Gamper, "Das Gespenst des Kollektiven: Fiktive Figuren des Sozialen von Quetelet bis Freytag," in ibid., 217–44.

[43]   For a historical analysis of the methods used in the communication sciences, see Isabell Otto, *Aggressive Medien: Zur Geschichte des Wissens über Mediengewalt* (Bielefeld: Transcript, 2008).

the telltale characteristics of the "society of the spectacle." Contrary to Marx's diagnosis of social tensions, according to which the perception of imbalances is skewed by distance-generating processes (such as alienation), the society of the spectacle inhibits its own self-awareness by means of integrative movements. The reigning forces of excess and abundance lead to the generation of fictional values, be it in the form of "pseudo-needs" or in the predominance of exchange value over use value in the circulation of commodities.[44] Because, in the meantime, everyone has profited from this luxury-generating fictionalization and even the proletariat can lead lives of relative prosperity, there is no longer anything that exists beyond or outside of economic processes – even dissatisfaction itself can become a marketed commodity.[45] Moreover, the society of the spectacle is fundamentally media-based and, as such, it has devised comprehensive strategies for enforcing attention in order to celebrate its own triviality.[46] The assessments of Debord, Postman, and Sloterdijk are thus generally in agreement, though none of the authors had been aware of the others' work.

As regards the discourse concerning crowds or the masses, the cultural-theoretical implications of this discursive shift from the political to the economic should, for a variety of reasons, not be underestimated. First, this development pushed aside Le Bon's, Tarde's, and Canetti's political conception of the crowd and replaced it with the audience of mass media.[47] Second, however, a crucial paradigm shift took place in the prevailing theories of society. This involved the transition from differential and/or competing systems (crowd – crowd, leader – individual) to the dominance of circular processes in which such distinctions disappear. Moreover, these processes are all-encompassing; one cannot stand outside of them, and this is because any opposition to the circumstances will immediately be integrated and used to increase the productivity of the processes themselves.

Thus it could be claimed today that society is dominated by "omnivorous circles" (to coin a phrase), processes that operate in a radically integrative manner and that will sooner or later subject everything to their mechanisms. A third issue is the question that this situation raises about the possibility of criticism. If critics can no longer set themselves apart from the objects of their critique, because any effort to create such distance will immediately initiate one reintegrative process or another, then it must be asked whether opposition is possible at all. Michael Hardt and Antonio Negri have discussed such problems, though largely without reference to media developments, as they pertain to the presently unfolding processes of globalization, but they could not offer any viable solutions. According to their argument, the dissolution of national power structures has brought about the new form of sovereignty that is Empire, which is characterized by globalization processes controlled by transnational complexes of corporations that oper-

---

[44]   Debord, *The Society of the Spectacle*, 31–34.

[45]   Ibid., 38.

[46]   Sloterdijk, *Die Verachtung der Massen*, 46.

[47]   On Tarde's later distinction between the masses and the public, and on the relationship between the latter and the mass media, see Christian Borch's contribution in this volume.

ate in an opaque manner. This new hegemonic form yields "biopower" and thus creates the living conditions in which crowds and multitudes are formed. Such is the result of Empire (which the authors prefer to spell with a capital letter). In the relationship between Empire and the multitude, a new form of anti-dialectical tension will ultimately manifest itself. Although the multitude will admittedly remain an effect of transnational Empire's opaque, power-generating, and power-stabilizing processes, it will nevertheless be able to turn such mechanisms against themselves:

> Our political task, we will argue, is not simply to resist these processes [of imperial globalization] but to reorganize them and redirect them toward new ends. The creative forces of the multitude that sustain Empire are also capable of autonomously constructing a counter-Empire, and alternative political organization of global flows and exchanges.[48]

The impetus behind Hardt and Negri's Enlightenment-esque appeal is based less on a conscious retreat from hegemonic mechanisms as it is on the internal application of these very strategies in an effort to subvert the prevailing tendencies of our time.[49] Regarding what is supposed to happen after this inversion or reversal takes places, the authors are strangely vague and idealistic. For if it is assumed that the "omnivorous circle," which has been diagnosed by many other theorists under a different name, is in fact the dominant mechanism of post-industrial society, then it must also be assumed that this circular process will continue to function just as it did before Hardt and Negri's hopeful revolution, the only difference being that those who might profit from the situation will have changed.

V. The Power of Collectives

It remains to ask how or whether this vicious circle of economic and medial self-referentiality can be broken. Many thinkers have expressed their faith in the salvational powers of new networking technologies. Ever since the World Wide Web commenced its triumphal march in 1993, there have been utopian fantasies – as is always the case after breakthroughs in media technology – about new and grass-roots-democratic forms of society, such as the notion of "collective intelligence" imagined by Pierre Lévy. There has been much talk about "smart mobs" (Howard Rheingold) and "swarming intelligence," and even the multitude discussed by Hardt and Negri is just a variant of these new concepts of collectivity, according to which the masses will adapt to a bilaterally functioning network structure that is anti-hierarchical and fundamentally flexible. This convergence of networking media and social structure is inspired by the nature of the computer itself, which programs its users through its application but at the same time can be programmed by them. That is, it allows for feedback and interaction. The idea of collective creativity or intelligence is thus based on a specific technological foundation, and it is upon this

---

[48] Michael Hardt and Antonio Negri, *Empire* (Cambridge, MA: Harvard University Press, 2000), xv.

[49] See Michael Hardt and Antonio Negri, *Multitude: War and Democracy in the Age of Empire* (New York: Penguin, 2004).

foundation that Lévy set up his anthropological step ladder, which leads from organic groups, past molar groups, all the way to molecular collectives. In terms of media, he draws a line from face-to-face interactions to centrally controlled and unilateral mass media, and from there to the electronically networked, placeless, and digital Bohemia of real-time communication. And it is there that he locates the future of new, self-programming collectives. By self-referentially creating their own values, such collectives will not be based on the synchronization of affects for the sake of engaging in homogeneous activity; rather, they will be based on an orchestration of differences. In terms of action theory, these collectives will be no less defined than previous groups, but unlike others they will cultivate individual abilities and competencies.[50] In their fluidity, in their perpetual metamorphosis in tandem with networked communication technologies, molecular collectives can no longer be compared with the homogeneous "discharge crowds" or "entertainment crowds." They are not based on the homogenization of individuals as much as they are on project-specific (and thus always temporally limited) combinations of individuals whose diversity is appreciated as a positive quality.

In fact, the dualistically structured concepts of the crowd (or masses) and the audience (or public), which were formulated on the basis of the enlightened and rationally acting individual, are entirely incompatible with the complexity of complementary worlds of communication. The antitheses that have long been at the heart of any discussion of the masses – namely active vs. passive, emotional vs. intellectual, uncontrollable vs. controlled, etc. – are no longer applicable given that the fundamental dualism of the masses and the individual has dissolved. In this context, it is therefore no longer possible to speak of the masses at all. The term "collectives" (in the plural) seems to be more adequate in this regard, though it will need to be delineated somewhat further.

Collectives possess, in several respects, a rather ambivalent character. It is striking, first of all, that one of the main features attributed to them – in the works of Hardt and Negri, Lévy, Rheingold, and many others – is their project-specificity and goal-orientation. They are discussed, that is, in terms of being efficient and creative, characteristics that happen to be a result of their economic rationality. Despite their potential for social criticism, it thus seems as though these discourses themselves were unable to escape from the omnivorous circle of economization, given that they define collectives primarily in terms of their efficiency and creativity (even if this evaluation was induced by the very same things).

Second, collectives are not only creative but can also have synchronizing effects, as is clear from the success of social platforms. This is based not least on a synchronization of behavior that ennobles self-presentation and permanent communication as a paradigm and rewards activity for its own sake. As the sociologist Hannelore Bublitz has claimed, this leads to a constant oscillation between "hyper-individualization" on the one hand and, on the other hand, the tendency to join prominent groups in various social contexts. It follows, therefore, that the construction of norms takes place through the presentation and communication of an individual's own way of life, which, in its representation, is in

---

[50] Lévy, *Collective Intelligence*, 18.

turn oriented toward externally constituted values (especially as far as consumption is concerned).[51] The effect of this is so-called "massively staged individuality," something that Gerhard Schulze had analyzed as early as 1992 in his book *The Experience Society.*[52] There he critiqued "prosperity and hedonism" as signs of a society that has come to prefer individualized experiences and pleasures over collaborative political engagement. Schulze identified "experience-orientation" to be the main purpose behind activity, which is characterized by subjectivity/internalization and involuntariness, and which is simultaneously presented in entirely apolitical terms.[53]

So it is that the groups of individuals presenting themselves and communicating in social networks tend in large part to focus self-referentially on their own banalities and to be based on highly superficial relations. As social formations they are therefore extremely unstable, but as economic factors they are extremely productive. Because communication, as the example of Facebook has shown, has become rather lucrative in itself, these collectives have essentially economized their productivity on their own, a reality that lends further support to my thesis of the omnivorous circle.[54]

VI. From the Collective to the Individual

If collectives are temporary and project-specific associations of individuals, this raises questions about the nature and role of individuals themselves within these medial and social constellations. Hardt and Negri have referred to the "symbiotic" relationship between the collective and the subject: "Subjectivity, in other words, is produced through cooperation and communication and, in turn, this produced subjectivity itself produces new forms of cooperation and communication, which in turn produce new subjectivity, and so forth."[55] If the collective and the individual now behave in a manner that is complementary to one another, then the former cannot be properly understood without a closer examination of the latter.

The arguments of crowd psychology were founded on a concept of the individual that was closely tied up with Enlightenment ideas. A self-aware subject controlled by reason

---

[51]   See Hannelore Bublitz, *Im Beichtstuhl der Medien: Die Produktion des Selbst im öffentlichen Bekenntnis* (Bielefeld: Transcript, 2010), 55.

[52]   Gerhard Schulze, *Die Erlebnisgesellschaft: Kultursoziologie der Gegenwart* (Frankfurt am Main: Campus, 1992), 19.

[53]   Ibid., 44–46.

[54]   If examples such as Google, Facebook, and YouTube are any indication of things to come, it must generally be supposed that the network of commercialization will not go away any time soon. Accordingly, every successful endeavor on the part of DIY culture will inevitably – and sooner than later – be treated as marketable capital. This in turn raises the question of how the relationship among capitalism, new media, and democracy will be configured under the assumption that every successful platform will eventually be commercialized and/or instrumentalized, if only to generate enough money to pay for its further development.

[55]   Hardt and Negri, *Multitude: War and Democracy in the Age of Empire*, 189.

represented the antipode to the crowd, which was held to be unpredictable and governed by emotion. Now that the individual is conceived as a complementary part of the collective, however, this contradiction seems no longer to exist. As alternative formations, collectives are formed today in light of the organizational configurations of industrial society: Collectives are informal communities that come together at a particular time in order to pursue a particular goal. They are "projective" communities, made up of "projective" existences,[56] to which creativity represents one among other leading paradigms.

Given their "monadic" structure as gatherings of individuals, collectives can hardly be described in an adequate manner with the terminology of crowd psychology; it is far more appropriate to define them according to the processes that they initiate and engage in (communication or cooperative creation, for instance). The fact that these "molecular collectives" (to return to Lévy's term) are now attributed a high degree of rationality and keen critical faculties certainly has much to do with their medium, a medium that precludes the immediate and impetuous occurrence of "discharge" or "contagion." Communication on the internet is based primarily on written and spoken interactions, which are necessarily dependent on moments of reflection. At least for now, in other words, rhythmically induced moments of collective ecstasy cannot really be achieved online.

At the same time, however, social-media applications rely quite heavily on emotional needs. As Alexander Pschera has written, they are "intuitive and supple," given that they are easily accessible and offer the promise of instant recognition.[57] Perhaps no symbol captures this better than the "like button" on Facebook.[58] Networking media are therefore also emotional media, and thus they represent the dissolution of yet another dualism from the Enlightenment, namely that between *ratio* and *emotio*.

This is evident not only in the social interactions enabled by networked communication but also in the formulation of new epistemological concepts of individuality. With recourse to the phenomenological idea of "total-body" (*gesamtleiblich*) sensations, Anglo-American media theorists have developed the concept of "pure experience," which immediately affects the somatic condition of the recipient.[59] Brian Massumi and Mark Hansen, for instance, have drawn upon Maurice Merleau-Ponty's phenomenology and Henri Bergson's

---

[56] Vilém Flusser introduced the idea of "projective" existence as an ontological hallmark of the digital age and set it in contrast to "subjective" existence, which underlies traditionally hierarchical power structures. See Vilém Flusser, *Into the Universe of Technical Images*, trans. Nancy Ann Roth (Minneapolis: University of Minnesota Press, 2011); and idem, *Vom Subjekt zum Projekt: Menschwerdung* (Frankfurt am Main: Fischer, 1998).

[57] Alexander Pschera, *800 Millionen: Apologie der sozialen Medien* (Berlin: Matthes & Seitz, 2011), 14.

[58] For further discussion of this topic, see the chapter by Irina Kaldrack and Theo Röhle in this book.

[59] The term "pure experience" was coined at the beginning of the twentieth century by the psychologist William James, who was also in contact with Henri Bergson. See William James, "A World of Pure Experience," *Journal of Philosophy, Psychology, and Scientific Methods* 1 (1904), 561–70. James and Bergson would in turn influence Gilles Deleuze, whose theories were warmly embraced by the majority of American film scholars.

philosophy of perception in order to model a total psycho-physical experience that is inherently compatible with the functional operations of interactive digital technologies.[60] A reception of this sort is thus primarily affective, and it is precisely this emotional orientation that levels out the medial experience of difference: "In short, affectivity is *the* privileged modality for confronting technologies that are fundamentally heterogeneous to our already constituted embodiment, our contracted habits and rhythms."[61] That which Hermann Schmitz, the founder of "new phenomenology," had conceived of as "affective concern" and "total-body communication" for experiencing daily life has here been transferred to the new (and old) world of media, whereby mediality itself has paradoxically been made to disappear or at least to fade into the background.[62] Foregrounded instead is the idea of "immediate" experience, an experience that excludes any form of distancing. It is just such an immersively integrated and affectively concerned individual that has become a component part of the collectives described above. In the media habits of such an individual, intuition and the intellect have become inseparably entwined, as have emotions and rationality.

It is hoped that this cursory outline of the constitution of the individual, a topic that warrants a far more detailed discussion, has at least managed to demonstrate that classical dualisms, such as "uniformity vs. individuality," "affect vs. rationality," or "mind vs. body," which have long been integral to the discourse about the masses, have by now reached their limits. Faced now with digital networking media, we are clearly dealing with

---

[60] See Joel McKim, "Of Microperception and Micropolitics: An Interview with Brian Massumi," *Inflexions* 3 (2009), 1–20, at 4; and Mark B. N. Hansen, *New Philosophy for New Media* (Cambridge, MA: MIT Press, 2004).

[61] Hansen, *New Philosophy for New Media*, 132. Hans-Ulrich Gumbrecht has proposed something similar with respect to poetry, namely a type of reading that treats moods and atmospheres as a completely physical "encounter" with the "physical reality" of literature that should be experienced in an immediately sensual manner. See Hans-Ulrich Gumbrecht, *Atmosphere, Mood, Stimmung: On a Hidden Potential of Literature*, trans. Erik Butler (Stanford: Stanford University Press, 2012), 4. Gumbrecht argues for a new understanding of reading on the basis of a concept of presence, according to which "things always already – and simultaneously with our unreflective habitus of positing significations they are supposed to hold – stand in a necessary relationship to our bodies" (ibid., 6) Out of this presence, according to Gumbrecht, an "immediacy in the experience of past presents occurs" (ibid., 14), and this immediacy is accompanied by the stipulation of "giving oneself over to [textual artifacts] affectively and bodily – yielding to them and gesturing toward them" (ibid., 18).

[62] Based on his observations of everyday experience, Hermann Schmitz identified a stage of human perception that far precedes the process of conscious perception by one specific sense or another. He referred to this phenomenon as an affective feeling that brings about instinctive behaviors, such as the ability to avoid obstacles in dangerous situations. See Hermann Schmitz, *Der Leib, der Raum und die Gefühle* (Ostfildern: Edition Tertium, 1998), 31–45. Although Schmitz did not discuss this preconscious and entirely physical feeling in terms of media theory, innumerable sensed and perceived signals need to be processed before a body can react to any situation. In general, the relationship between mediality and such forms of perception, which undoubtedly exist, certainly warrants a thorough investigation of its own.

an entirely different situation, one that requires a type of thinking that is inclusive ("both-and") instead of analytically exclusive ("either-or"). This, however, poses new challenges of its own, and particularly for the sciences, which still operate in large part according to a modality of thought that is analytical and isolating. The sciences now have to concern themselves with a world of which they are a part and in which circular processes operate inherently, so much so that nothing can be external to it. Where, then, will there be room for criticism? And if yes, what could it look like, given that it can no longer be produced in a distanced and analytical manner? These are some of the more pressing questions that media studies and cultural studies will have to address.

FLORIAN SPRENGER

Inertia, Acceleration, and Media/Theory

I. Introduction

From the eighteenth century up to the present day, a variety of historiographical narratives, concerned with topics ranging from philosophy to sociology and media theory, have attempted to draw a connection between the comprehensive transformation known as globalization and the increases in speed that have been brought about by electric media. This transformation has largely been attributed to acceleration, and acceleration has in turn come to be regarded as a defining feature of modernity. Distance could (and can) no longer be considered a limiting factor of human exchange, a fact that is underscored all the more today by the ubiquity of so-called "smart" communication. In what follows, I would like to locate this idea historically and discuss it as a model that recurs whenever a new transmission medium has been introduced. The thesis that distance has been eliminated by electric communication has been expressed repeatedly, and therefore my goal below will not be to situate each of its historical iterations. My focus will rather be on the productivity of this thesis within various debates and on "coherence in contradiction," which, according to Jacques Derrida, "expresses the force of a desire."[1] On the basis of this notion, it will be possible to reach a better understanding of how these discourses are relevant to the current theoretical debates that are taking place in the field of media studies.

By citing the connection between the processes of globalization and the technological acceleration of communication, however, more is meant than simply the coincidence of global changes and the media of the changes in question. Acceleration is accompanied by the self-perception of a new "community," one that now considers itself to be globally connected by electric or electronic media – by the fact that distances can be overcome in little or no time at all, by the fact that a sense of presence can be achieved *in absentia*, and by the fact that people can be brought together from remote places.[2] Ever since the

---

[1]   Jacques Derrida, "Structure, Sign, and Play in the Discourse of the Human Sciences," in *Writing and Difference*, trans. Alan Bass (London: Routledge, 2001), 351–70, at 352.

[2]   In a political study published in 1887, Ferdinand Tönnies was the first to draw a firm distinction between *society* and *community*. The latter notion, as its etymology suggests, is closer to the concept

establishment of these media (and the development of various theories about them), *community* has been understood as an effect of media and as the *common* element that is inherent to concept itself. This element has always remained somewhat imaginary in that it can only be said to exist in the connectivity that is achieved through communication, and yet this communication appears as though it is immediate.[3]

By looking briefly at the genealogy of electric connectivity – which is just as concerned with the material infrastructures of distribution, connection, and addressing (*Adressierung*) as it is with the discursive fixation of these techniques in the imagination of their time – it will be possible to draw attention to an apocalyptic motif of modernity, namely electric acceleration and the elimination of space and time that is attributed to it. These self-descriptions have proposed concepts and economies that have defined the media of community as accelerated or immediate. In the twentieth century (whether intentionally or not), these same concepts and economies were adopted and perpetuated by a tradition of media theory whose most prominent representative was Marshall McLuhan.[4] By means of its imaginary and genealogical basis, this tradition was involved with the formation of community, and it attempted to explain this community with media-theoretical concepts that were products of the very history that they were supposed to explain.

---

of communication and lends itself particularly well to the perspective that I have adopted in this essay. This is especially so because the concept of community, from its very beginning, has suggested a sense of immediacy that the concept of society is lacking. For a recent translation of Tönnies's work, see Ferdinand Tönnies, *Community and Civil Society*, trans. José Harris and Margaret Hollis (Cambridge: Cambridge University Press, 2001).

[3]   Despite what is often thought, *community* remains merely imaginary even when the imaginary idea of it happens to be political reality. In this sense, the concept of community, the problematic nature of which I will address later on, should be used as a descriptive tool that also has a history of its own within the discourses being described. Here it should be kept in mind that community implies something slightly different from the concept of the crowd, though crowds (or the "masses") have likewise been described with the metaphor of electricity. See Joseph Vogl, "Masse und Kraft," in *Zeichen der Kraft: Wissenformationen, 1800–1900*, ed. Thomas Brandstetter et al. (Berlin: Kadmos, 2008), 187–97.

[4]   For the sake of streamlining my argument, my remarks below will concentrate predominantly on McLuhan, though several other thinkers could just as well have been brought into the discussion. Lewis Mumford, Derrick de Kerckhove, Paul Virilio, Peter Weibel, and Götz Großklaus – to name a few – have all operated within the theoretical territory that had been staked out by McLuhan. Worthy of mention, too, is Stephen Kern, whose authoritative study of acceleration was based on the concept of instantaneity. See Stephen Kern, *The Culture of Time and Space, 1880–1918*, 2nd ed. (Cambridge, MA: Harvard University Press, 2003). Here I will also have to neglect the discourses concerned with the internet in the 1990s and the many recent histories of electric or electronic media. In this regard, see especially Clara Völker, *Mobile Medien: Zur Genealogie des Mobilfunks und zur Ideengeschichte von Virtualität* (Bielefeld: Transcript, 2010); and Frank Hartmann, *Globale Medienkultur: Technik, Geschichte, Theorien* (Vienna: WUV, 2006). It would also take me too far afield to address the many sociological theories that have been formulated about globalization, though I will have occasion toward the end of this essay to comment on a few of them.

In short, my thesis is as follows: There is an obstacle that forces acceleration-oriented media theories to adopt an essentialist and therefore politically and epistemologically precarious notion of community. Through the immediacy inaugurated by these theories – the immediacy of presumably instantaneous electricity – they are in danger of overlooking both the specific nature of the media in question as well as the manner in which the conditions for "community" are produced. Historically, such theories may have been among the first to point out the significance of media and yet, as I hope to show, they also serve to undermine the potential of this new point of view. If, in the genealogy of electric acceleration, media and communication can be described as "mediators of human ubiquity"[5] that are "transmitted instantaneously by electricity"[6] to a "brand-new world of all-at-onceness"[7] – if, that is, communication in electric or electronic media is supposed to be always already omnipresent – then neither the materiality of communication, with all of its delays and interruptions, nor the differences that are necessary for "community" are being taken into consideration.[8]

Since the early-modern era, as the German historian Reinhart Koselleck has shown, the acceleration of historical sequences and cultural developments has changed from an extra-historical category (in the sense of God) into an intra-historical axiom.[9] Technology has admittedly provided this notion of acceleration with a new field of operation, but it

---

[5] Ernst Kapp, *Grundlinien einer Philosophie der Technik: Zur Entstehungsgeschichte der Cultur aus neuen Gesichtspunkten* (Braunschweig: Georg Westermann, 1877), 135.

[6] Edward Lind Morse, ed., *Samuel F. B. Morse: His Letters and Journals*, 2 vols. (Boston: Houghton Mifflin, 1914), 2:6.

[7] Marshall McLuhan and Quentin Fiore, *The Medium is the Massage: An Inventory of Effects* (Corte Madera: Gingko Press, 2001), 63.

[8] The sociologist John Tomlinson has described transmission in terms of its production of immediacy, but he does so with the assumption of there being a "space-time-convergence," which itself is a product of this discourse. See John Tomlinson, *The Culture of Speed: The Coming of Immediacy* (London: SAGE, 2007), 11.

[9] See Reinhart Koselleck, "Zeitverkürzung und Beschleunigung," in *Zeitschichten: Studien zur Historik* (Frankfurt am Main: Suhrkamp, 2003), 177–202, at 195. Building upon Koselleck's work, Hartmut Rosa has differentiated between technological acceleration, the acceleration of the pace of life, and the acceleration of social change. On the basis of these distinctions, he identifies a temporal crisis with origins in the late twentieth century, a crisis whose foundations, however, had already been laid as early as the nineteenth century. To decelerate identity, according to Rosa, would thus be equivalent to abandoning the "project of modernity." See Hartmut Rosa, *Social Acceleration: A New Theory of Modernity*, trans. Jonathan Trejo-Mathys (New York: Columbia University Press, 2013). Kay Kirchmann has pointed out two main aspects of our self-situating "new era" of acceleration, namely a "substantialization and semanticization of history as a mobilizing force" and a "relativization of historical epochs according to the parameter of speed." Quoted from Kay Kirchmann, *Verdichtung, Weltverlust und Zeitdruck: Grundzüge einer Theorie der Interdependenz von Medien, Zeit und Geschwindigkeit im neuzeitlichen Zivilisationsprozess* (Opladen: Leske + Budrich, 1998), 304. In this regard, see also Thomas Sutherland, "Liquid Networks and the Metaphysics of Flux: Ontologies of Flow in an Age of Speed and Mobility," *Theory, Culture & Society* 30 (2002), 3–23.

has not been its catalyst. Rather, it has always been dependent on existing discourses, outside of which it cannot be effective. Within the context of the French Revolution and the processes related to it, as well as within the context of the Industrial Revolution, technology functioned as a "historical concept of hope." A crucial aspect to this, according to Koselleck, was a difference between expectation and experience that allowed modernity (*die Neuzeit*) to designate itself as a new era (*neue Zeit*) – a denotation that has also been applied ever since to media and reflects the influence of the latter on spatio-temporal relations. Koselleck contends that, a few vestiges aside, the discursive figure of acceleration can no longer be derived from the premises of the Judeo-Christian tradition of apocalyptic thinking, according to which time is cut short, and that this is all the more true in the case of technological acceleration. And yet it can be demonstrated how the metaphysical content of this tradition has been perpetuated in its infatuation with physical contact or touch.

In what follows, I will be less concerned with suggesting alternative approaches than with outlining a history of media theory as a history of the negation of media. This is a history of immediacies that, physically concerned with high speeds or minimal amounts of time, nonetheless phantasmatically fashion no speed or time whatsoever. By ignoring technological delays and social differences, such immediacies consign media to oblivion and ultimately relate their communities to a principle of unity.[10] As effects of media and as engines of historical development, acceleration and speed not only possess a function for the communities that they bind together or separate; they also possess a function for the media theories that attempt to explain them. The latter theories, however, build upon these concepts, and therefore explanations and the explained blend into one. The following considerations are meant to contrast the inner side of these narratives – that is, the stories or histories told by them – with the outer side of their historicity, and the goal is to reach a firmer understanding of the way in which these two sides reflect and distort one another. My argument can be summarized as follows: Media theories, media of transmission, and communities cannot – from a historical perspective – be uncoupled from one another. They are enmeshed.

The two most important driving forces behind processes of acceleration, as implemented in the nineteenth century, were electricity and the railroad. Frequently associated with one another, they influenced many aspects of daily life, from industrial production to the nature of warfare.[11] They were responsible for the increased speeds in transportation and transmission that made space disappear, eliminated time, and brought remote places close together. In the 1990s, Frances Cairncross referred to this process as "the

---

[10]   I have discussed this at greater length in Florian Sprenger, *Medien des Immediaten: Elektrizität, Telegraphie, McLuhan* (Berlin: Kadmos, 2012).

[11]   The specific effects of these processes have been studied in great deal. Among other works, see James R. Beniger, *The Control Revolution: Technological and Economic Origins of the Information Society* (Cambridge, MA: Harvard University Press, 1986); James W. Carey, "Technology and Ideology: The Case of the Telegraph," in *Communication as Culture: Essays on Media and Society*, 2nd ed. (New York: Routledge, 2009), 155–77; and Carolyn Marvin, *When Old Technologies Were New: Thinking about Communication in the Late Nineteenth Century* (Oxford: Oxford University Press, 1988).

death of distance,"[12] but the concept would have fit just as nicely in the discourses of the time; Cairncross simply advanced an idea that had already been established. In fact, this discursive figure has recurred again and again since the middle of the nineteenth century and the advent of electric communications media.

Primarily in the form of telegraphs, which were at first implemented through cables and then later wirelessly, electricity exceeded the speed of the railroad in that, as many contemporary authors were quick to note, it separated the medium from the message and therefore liberated speed from the burdens of inertia (or slowness in general). Acceleration can thus be regarded not only as a force that brings things closer together; with electricity, and the immediate instantaneity attributed to it, acceleration also abolishes separations and differences and inaugurates something that could be called electric unity – a "gigantic auditorium,"[13] as one writer put it, or "electric nowness," in the words of another.[14] Both during the nineteenth century and in a specific media-theoretical discourse that emerged later on, this argument was generalized in historical and philosophical terms. For if electric immediacy entails a sort of timelessness, then, as Paul Virilio aptly observed, "in our ordinary everyday life, *we are passing from the extensive time of history to the intensive time of instantaneity without history* made possible by the technologies of the hour."[15]

To put it simply, acceleration allows for a teleological orientation. For such theories, it functions as an impetus behind a sort of history whose results happen to be the very positions that enable this same history to be narrated, regardless of whether this narration is one of decadence or redemption. They establish their own origin and thus bring it into being. This goes hand in hand, moreover, with the evocation of communities whose individuals are connected with one another in a simultaneous manner:

---

[12] Frances Cairncross, *The Death of Distance: How the Communications Revolution is Changing Our Lives* (Boston: Harvard Business School Press, 1997). In this sense, McLuhan's idea of implosion can be regarded as a counterpoint to Heidegger's concept of "de-distancing" (*Ent-Fernung*), for implosion does not allow there to be any distance in that which is far away. For Heidegger, distance only becomes apparent in the proximity that is produced by technology. Wherever there is only proximity, no one can really be near anyone else. In contrast, the process of distancing creates a sort of distance that prevents proximity. Heidegger characterized the concept of de-distancing as the sublation of distance into a type of proximity that no longer exists. This he did under the impression of the communication media of his time and with an implicit high regard for physical contact. He stressed, however, that this proximity can never be near because it is de-distanced. That is, it is simultaneously not-near and not-far, for which reason that which is far away loses its distance. See Martin Heidegger, "The Thing," in *Poetry, Language, Thought*, trans. Albert Hofstader (New York: Harper & Row, 1971), 164–80, at 175: "Today everything present is equally near and equally far. The distanceless prevails."

[13] Karl Knies, *Der Telegraph als Verkehrsmittel: Mit Erörterungen über den Nachrichtenverkehr überhaupt* (Leipzig: H. Laupp, 1857), 242.

[14] Marshall McLuhan and Barrington Nevitt, "The Argument: Causality in the Electric World," *Technology and Culture* 14 (1973), 1–18, at 2.

[15] Paul Virilio, *Polar Inertia*, trans. Patrick Camiller (London: SAGE, 2000), 24–25 (the emphasis is original).

> After three thousand years of explosion, by means of fragmentary and mechanical technologies, the Western world is imploding. During the mechanical ages we had extended our bodies in space. Today, after more than a century of electric technology, we have extended our central nervous system itself in a global embrace, abolishing both space and time as far as our planet is concerned.[16]

McLuhan, who has become a model figure in this context, explained the transition from mechanical to electric transmission as a change from an explosion, an expansion of space into ever greater distances, to an implosion. In the latter case, the presumably instantaneous speed of electromagnetic oscillations, as manifested above all in satellites, eliminates spatial limitations and the notion of centers in favor of a worldwide, borderless space – the "simultaneous field of relations," as he called it, borrowing the concept of the field from physics.[17] Yet even this formulation already contains a contradiction or divide: Simultaneously connected locations can hardly be thought of as relations; they rather entail the abolishment of relations, although they remain separated. This space of community, the so-called "global village," has only an interior – not an exterior – into which it is capable of expanding. In this space, that is, the distances of communication are eliminated, and it is therefore susceptible to essentializations that require an internal connection between all locations: the immediacy of their media.

II. Connecting One and All with a "Vital Cord"

The discursive field upon which McLuhan, with his notion of the global village, erected what might be the most influential concept of community in all of media theory, was pre-established by the fantasy that electromagnetic telegraphy might serve as a medium to connect the entire world.[18] This fantasy operated with a broad repertoire of metaphors and narratives that linked together multiple areas of knowledge in order to make sense of the paradoxical new relations between the near and the far, the local and the global, and to seek the cohesion of a community in the media of its connection. The "intimate connection between nations, with race and race," which had been anticipated in 1858 with the installation of the first transatlantic telegraph cable, and which was expected to

---

[16]   Marshall McLuhan, *Understanding Media: The Extensions of Man* (New York: McGraw-Hill, 1964), 19.

[17]   Marshall McLuhan, "The Electronic Revolution in North America," *International Literary Annual* 1 (1959), 165–69, at 169.

[18]   In such a fantasy or *rêverie*, as Gaston Bachelard referred to it, the poetic power of imagination is driven by its object, and so it is also, as he demonstrated in his *Psychoanalysis of Fire*, in the case of electricity. See Gaston Bachelard, *The Psychoanalysis of Fire*, trans. Alan C. M. Ross (Boston: Beacon Press, 1964). Thus it is possible to understand this concept, in Erich Hörl's words, "as a sort of self-generating knowledge that creates images of itself, images that are partially an expression of the difficulty of breaking from what had come before and partially a sign of the uncertainty that its arrival necessarily entails." Quoted from Erich Hörl, *Die heiligen Kanäle: Über die archaische Illusion der Kommunikation* (Berlin: Diaphanes, 2005), 18.

reveal the traditional (local) politics of exclusion and border-enforcement to be a politics of "stagnation and death," came with the implication, both during the middle of the nineteenth century and the middle of the twentieth, that there could be a "vital cord" of "free and unobstructed interchange of each with all."[19] Two aspects are noteworthy about these remarks, which were so typical of the time.

First, the connection of individuals is considered to be "vital," especially given that it takes place through a "cable soul" (*"Kabelseele"*), as the core of a cable is known in German. The connecting cable, according to one author, is "the mightiest bond in all of living creation."[20] If taken seriously, these expressions imply that there is life in being connected and death in being separated, for, as McLuhan would remark a century later in very similar language, "electricity is organic in character and confirms the organic social *bond* by its technological use in telegraph and telephone, radio and other forms."[21] The abolishment of distance by means of electricity, and therefore the commonness of community, bestows life, and it does so in a way that calls to mind the Platonic paradigm of truth in unity. Difference is a vacuum; it is emptiness, forlornness, and loneliness. Separated elements, separated people, and separated continents can only become alive as a unity – be it as an audience of live television. The abolishment of separation by means of communication is prized above all else. Life comes into play from two sides: through the association of the cable with nerves, formulated as an analogy between the cable network and the nervous system,[22] and through the presence of physical contact and proximity, which is life (that is, the opposite of supplementary absence and death). It is in the cables, and later in television or satellites, that there is life and a connection between one and all: "The cities and their people 'experience' the events simultaneously – precisely as though a sensation were searing through a single body."[23] In 1857, and thus still before the installment of the transatlantic cable, the economist Karl Knies formulated on this basis what would be the first systematic theory regarding the economy of communication. For him, too, the connectivity of electricity encompasses everything and is omnipresent, though he considered it to be immaterial, vital, and not bound to the material inertia of lifeless bodies and cables. No one, he thought, could escape from this bodiless life. According to this sort of logic, technology cannot be conceived in terms of its materiality and community cannot be conceived in terms of its divisions, both of which entail interruptions and delays.

Second, it is symptomatic of these formulations to merge individuals together into an "each with all." This indicates the specific nature of those communities that, now describable, are formed by means of electric communication and media, spatial divi-

---

[19] Charles Briggs and Augustus Maverick, *The Story of the Telegraph, and a History of the Great Atlantic Cable* (New York: Rudd & Carleton, 1858), 21–22.

[20] Carl August von Steinheil, *Ueber Telegraphie, insbesonders durch galvanische Kräfte* (Munich: Carl Wolf, 1838), 3–4.

[21] McLuhan, *Understanding Media*, 219 (my emphasis).

[22] Laura Otis, *Networking: Communicating with Bodies and Machines in the Nineteenth Century* (Ann Arbor: University of Michigan Press, 2001).

[23] Knies, *Der Telegraph als Verkehrsmittel*, 244.

sions notwithstanding. The connections exist not only between individual people; as a network, they rather connect everyone with everyone else. The innovation of technological transmission networks and binary coding procedures, such as Morse code, is that they enable a transmission to be sent from one person to many or, in the case of broadcasting, to everyone. If everyone is vitally connected to everyone else, then there is nothing exterior to this network – there is no outside. The "everyone" in question, communicating through a wire, "is a proponent of Volapük, an exceedingly clever fellow who can relay all the languages of the world precisely and impeccably."[24] The telegraph, in other words, "reproduces in one what is given to all."[25] It is precisely this connection of the individual with the global that McLuhan endeavored to describe. In doing so, he revisited a notion that, a century before his time, had been referred to as a new order: "The globe is now in electric union."[26] The world received a new image of itself – of its globality – and could now address itself as a world in an entirely different manner. And yet, again, if everyone is vitally connected to everyone else, then there is no outside. No one can be unconnected, and the consequence of this is an essentialist concept of community that is based on medial immediacy.

From McLuhan's perspective, too, the idea of "each with all" began with the implementation of electricity. Admittedly, the telegraphic globe of the nineteenth century could not yet be understood as a global village, for the separation of local and global orders was still too manifest at the time. And yet its self-image as the imaginary household of a self-forming community persisted until the conceptual formulation of the global village at the beginning of the 1960s. In this light, instantaneity also became a constantly renewed promise of economic progress. It motivated newspapers to disseminate the news as quickly as possible and it became a strategic instrument of war.[27] Communication provided ways to deal with the uncertainties that lie between separated and remote communication partners; in its production of certainties, however, it obscured the fact that it, too, had originated in uncertainty. On account of their instantaneous communication, the communities that were established in this context could at least be certain about the technological foundations of its success.

The possibility of medially expanding communities resulted from the negotiations that took place regarding the new status of proximity and distance, a status engendered by the advent of electronic transmission. All of the debates concerned with electricity were pervaded by anxieties and expectations about the observation that, as one writer

---

[24] This remark was made in a presentation delivered in 1899 by a member of the American wire industry; it is quoted here from O. G. Döhner, *Geschichte der Eisendrahtindustrie* (Berlin: Springer, 1925), 3. Regarding Volapük and universal languages in general, see the chapter by Michael Andreas in this volume.

[25] Steinheil, *Ueber Telegraphie*, 3–4.

[26] Cortlandt van Rensselaer, *Signals from the Atlantic Cable: An Address Delivered at the Telegraphic Celebration* (Philadelphia: J. M. Wilson, 1858), 5.

[27] See Stefan Kaufmann, *Kommunikationstechnik und Kriegführung, 1815–1945: Stufen telemedialer Rüstung* (Munich: Fink, 1996).

succinctly noted, "time and space are annihilated."[28] The contemporary observer Artur Fürst expressed these sentiments as follows:

> No genuine obstacles, only economic deterrents and the lack of practical need, have prevented every place on earth from being immediately and telegraphically connected to every other. If so desired, this bridge, which annihilates time and space, can be built at any moment. This thought is now truly free. It has become so on account of the telegraph, which has liberated it from the bondage of sundering space. [...] The telegraph overcomes distance in the blink of an eye; beneath its beating wings, the earth dwindles into a mere extensionless point.[29]

Even if distances remained geographically identical and the earth neither dwindled nor disappeared materially, the time needed for transmission was indeed reduced to such an extent as to approach zero. However, transmission can never eliminate time altogether but can only be phantasmatically charged (*phantasmatisch aufgeladen*). And if there is no time between connected places, people, or addresses, they are accordingly sublated in the unity of a community whose essence is sought in its connection. A divide between phantasms of immediacy and the techno-physical knowledge that forbids such immediacy thus becomes productive, and this is because every transmission requires a certain amount of time. This tension is characteristic of early electricity research and can be detected in McLuhan's media theories as well.

Whereas animal-based or mechanical means of locomotion, in which the medium and the message are intertwined, still exhibited the tendencies of expansion or explosion that characterized the way in which human beings occupied space, in the case of electricity it is implosion that is omnipresent. It is with the concepts of explosion and implosion that McLuhan, writing in the 1960s, updated the discourses concerning the establishment of telegraphy. Explosion, he thought, accelerated speed, and yet the space on earth is finite. With electricity, its worldwide network, and the dissolution of the message from its material medium, he argued, it is no longer necessary to expand space. Electricity is everywhere; it cannot be further accelerated, moreover, because it is instantaneous: "Electric is always instantaneous; there is no delay. [...] The telegraph also has that built-in dimension of the instantaneous and it completely transformed news and information. The mere speed. Didn't matter what was written; the fact that it went at the speed of light transformed everything."[30] For the Sputnik satellite, an emblem of global ubiquity, every place on earth is within

---

28 Marshall Lefferts, "The Electric Telegraph: Its Influence and Geographical Distribution," *Bulletin of the American Geographical and Statistical Society* 1 (1856), 242–64, at 260. On the prevalence of this idea in Great Britain during the last half of the nineteenth century, see Iwan Rhys Morus, "'The Nervous System of Britain': Space, Time, and the Electric Telegraph in the Victorian Age," *British Journal for the History of Science* 4 (2000), 455–75. A similar response was incited by the railroad; see Wolfgang Schivelbusch, *The Railway Journey: The Industrialization of Time and Space in the Nineteenth Century* (Berkeley: University of California Press, 1986).

29 Artur Fürst, *Das Weltreich der Technik: Entwicklung und Gegenwart* (Berlin: Ullstein, 1923), 3.

30 Quoted from an interview conducted with McLuhan on July 17, 1978. The audio recording is preserved on the following CD-ROM: *Understanding McLuhan – "In the Electric World, Change is*

reach; there is no more "outside" or externality. Electricity is everywhere simultaneously. Electricity is even faster than light, or so McLuhan claimed in his delusional disregard for relativistic physics.[31] With speeds faster than light, connections are not delayed at all. The places within this space are connected to one another without interruption, every place to every other. The local becomes the global. Distances continue to exist, but it no longer matters how vast they are because, for electricity, large and small distances are one and the same. Therefore it is also irrelevant that the global village is home to billions of people. Total speed entails the total involvement of everyone in everything that is happening everywhere else. Within the village, everyone participates every day in everything and hears every piece of news as quickly as possible because the word is spread acoustically, announced by tribal drumbeats, or broadcast on the radio or television.

McLuhan at one point dismissed the common misunderstanding that he had envisioned the global village to be a harmonious community or a sort of jolly get-together:

> There is more diversity, less conformity under a single roof in any family than there is with the thousands of families in the same city. The more you create village conditions, the more discontinuity and division and diversity. The global village absolutely insures maximal disagreement on all points. It never occurred to me that uniformity and tranquility were the properties of the global village. It has more spite and envy. [...] I don't approve of the global village. I say we live in it.[32]

Nevertheless, it is *one* village, and only as such does it allow for tensions and thus the possibility of integration. It is an ongoing matter of negotiation, of course, whether this will take place with cudgels and axes or with words and arguments. Systematically speaking, even a conflict-laden village is a unity. The emphasis of such conflict lies on the inner side of the distinction between unity and difference, that is, on the side of unity. The conflict is not a conflict derived from an ineradicable confrontation or from an unexcludable outside; at best, it is rather a necessary evil that the unity is ultimately unable to call into question. The discord arises from the unity itself and is a result of its imploding consolidation or fusion. The global village exists only in the singular.[33]

This village is admittedly well acquainted with conflict and discord, but it knows of no outside or foreign entity. It is by no means totalitarian on the inside, but to the outside it presents a totality without any alternative, just as the continents, by virtue of being telegraphically connected, were expected to guarantee global peace. In 1858, a sermon was

---

the Only Stable Factor": A CD-ROM on the Ideas of Media Guru Marshall McLuhan (New York: Voyager, 1996).

[31] See Marshall McLuhan, "Probleme der Kommunikation mit Menschen mittels Medien," in *Wohin steuert die Welt? Massenmedien und Gesellschaftsstruktur*, trans. Heinrich Jelinek (Vienna: Europa Verlag, 1978), 42–73. This essay is not available in English.

[32] Marshall McLuhan, "The Hot and Cold Interview," in *Media Research: Technology, Art, Communication*, ed. Michel A. Moos (Amsterdam: G & B Arts, 1997), 45–78, at 58.

[33] See Hartmut Winkler, *Docuverse: Zur Medientheorie der Computer* (Regensburg: Boer, 1997), 71

delivered to commemorate the installment of the first transatlantic cable, and it touched upon this very theme:

> At the present day, all tendencies of the world's advancement are towards intercourse, unity, and peace. The swift communication of thought is the best harbinger of universal concord. As the original dispersion of mankind was accomplished by the confusion of language at the tower of Babel, so its reunion in the bonds of peace is promoted by the creation of a new, universal language, outstripping the resources of combined human tongues.[34]

In all of its universality, the global village, like the telegraphically connected world with its universal code, does not allow for any alternative beyond itself. My critique of the global village is not that it failed to account for social practices. McLuhan referred extensively to the conflict and turmoil that prevail there. Harmony, such as that imagined by the internet discourses of the 1990s, is not a necessary feature within the village. After the events of the Second World War, McLuhan had little faith in any sort of "bond of peace,"[35] preferring instead to speak of an "organic social bond."[36] The utopia of the global village is not totalitarian but rather an essentialist and vitalized community of "each with all." Its interior, which lacks an exterior, is constituted by electricity. The global village is universal. It cannot question itself because there is no alternative to it. Thus the conflict that takes place within the village is certainly relevant, but the idea of the global village is problematic because it is only capable of acknowledging the difference or otherness that already exists within the village itself.

McLuhan based the abstract universality of community – the origins of which can likewise be found in the *fraternité*, *egalité*, and *liberté* of the French Revolution – on the technical networks of electricity. As early as 1790, and thus long before electricity was first implemented, the idea of overcoming social divisions was associated metaphorically with sparks flickering through crowds of revolutionaries. Even at this time, the formation of community was thought of in terms of electricity, and in retrospect this insight explains a good deal about its earliest applications. Electricity allowed for crackling, spark-flying, and flashing communication to take place between the subjects of the Enlightenment, whose hearts were also thought to be connected by a "vital cord" that would bring about the unification of nations. Thus Madame de Staël could report the following about the meeting of the Consituent Assembly on July 14, 1789: "Thoughts were communicated there with electric rapidity, because the action of man on man is irresistible, and because nothing appealed more strongly to the imagination than that unarmed will bursting the ancient chains, forged originally conquest and now suddenly disappearing before the simplicity of reason."[37] "The populace," she noted later on, "in a state of insurrection, are,

---

34 Rensselaer, *Signals from the Atlantic Cable*, 14.

35 Ibid.

36 McLuhan, *Understanding Media*, 219.

37 Germaine de Staël, *Considerations of the Principal Events of the French Revolution: Newly Revised Translation of the 1818 English Edition*, ed. Aurelian Craiutu (Indianapolis: Liberty Fund, 2008),

in general, inaccessible to reasoning, and are to be acted on only by sensations rapid as electricity, and communicated in a similar manner."[38] It was the dense gathering of people and their mutual friction, she believed, that provided the Assembly with an electric charge and bound all of the present bodies into an inseparable community. Had they been sitting in separate seats and not rubbing together, all of this tension or voltage would have been lost. The crowd has to stand and move around in order to merge into a vital and electrically charged unity. Its notion of "each with all" is the nation itself, in which everyone is supposed to be equal. Multiple transmissions are at play here: the transmission from body to body, from person to person, from person to spirit (*Geist*), and ultimately to the collective, that is, to the unified community.

McLuhan shared the nineteenth-century fantasies about the animism of networks and the capacity for everyone to merge with everyone else. Electricity, its universal language of telegraphy, and the arbitrariness of its code were thought even then to have put an end to Babylonian confusion and to the general sluggishness of human communication. Such problems lamentably persisted, however, and McLuhan would seek to resolve them a century later. In the nineteenth century, the vital bond of "each with all" became a bond of peace to be achieved by means of communication. In 1870, the author Hermann Grimm wrote the following telling lines in his diary:

> The telegraph and the railroad have become the organs of human existence. We are no longer conceivable without them, and we have come to rely on them as much as we rely on our own arms and legs. And yet all of this is just the beginning. The time will come when every person will share something like a single brain, which at any given moment will be thinking the same thoughts. I see no end to this development.[39]

According to this diagnosis, which treats the infusion of instantaneity into society as a common good, the question of distance has become a matter of politics.

III. Unprecedented Desires

The function of this discourse, which converges with McLuhan's media theory, is first and foremost to create a self-image of community that perceives itself as being accelerated and is therefore forced to redefine its cohesion and relations in response to the introduction of any new acceleration-inducing medium. If the ends of the world, or colonies and cities, are temporally adjacent to one another, and if distant relatives, merchants, and factories can be connected in little or no time at all, then their social or economic organization

---

    178.

[38] Ibid., 229.

[39] This diary entry, which was made on July 30, 1870, is quoted from Alexander C. T. Geppert et al., "Verräumlichung: Kommunikative Praktiken in historischer Perspektive, 1840–1930," in *Ortsgespräche: Raum und Kommunikation im 19. und 20. Jahrhundert*, ed. Uffa Jensen et al. (Bielefeld: Transcript, 2005), 15–49, at 36.

must necessarily change in reflection of this situation. By way of the mid-nineteenth-century discourse concerning the establishment of electromagnetic telegraphy, an image of community became widespread, according to which community is no longer related to a previous essence but rather – no less essentialistically – seeks cohesion in the "substance" of its medial connection.

By articulating descriptive models, metaphors, or images for communities and their configuration, media theories have participated in the formulation of this substance. Because community can always and only be composed in an imaginary manner – given that it can only appear in utterances, representations, or imaginations – its link to media theories can serve as a point of departure for identifying its constitution, as an approach that goes beyond the mere connection of individuals to a group.[40] Every description or theory of a community forms the latter according to the likeness or image of its imaginary nature. Whenever it is occupied with instantaneous electricity or worldwide computer networks, essentialism substantializes medial contacts as the cohesion of a unity, one that forms community by means of acceleration. In order to institutionalize this connection, an additional unity is introduced as a sort of higher-order category in which individuals can be reclassified yet again – something like the global village or the "electric union."[41]

If transmission media, enabled by the speed of electricity, are able to cause a distant place to be present simultaneously in the here and now, that is, if they are able to transform distance into proximity and eliminate the materiality at their basis, then their relation becomes one of oscillation. If, moreover, the possibilities for connection become more and more comprehensive, because nearly every household owns a radio or because satellites are orbiting the earth, then decentralization – the phenomenon of being in multiple places simultaneously – is transformed into a decentralized centralization, into the unity of the global village, and not only as a metaphor. This new unity entails a fundamental change in the way that community is formed as imaginary. The divisions at the base of such contacts are negated in favor of immediacy and the world becomes a project of transmission, something prefigured to some extent by the character of Robin Goodfellow (Puck) in Shakespeare's *Midsummer Night's Dream*. The latter is depicted holding both ends of a cable (or "girdle") that is encircling the earth; when one end is pulled, the other moves as well, and thus the character is acting as a transmitter and receiver at the same time. In this case, he is less concerned with connecting individual places with one another than he is with forming a connection that ends where it begins: "I'll put a girdle round about the earth in forty minutes." The image recurs in Alexander Jones's *Historical Sketch of the Electric Telegraph*, which, though published more than a decade before the transatlantic cable was laid, already anticipated that such a cable would soon wrap around

---

40 See Cornelius Castoriadis, *The Imaginary Institution of Society*, trans. Kathleen Blamey (Cambridge, MA: MIT Press, 1987); and the articles collected in Albrecht Koschorke et al., eds., *Der fiktive Staat: Konstruktionen des politischen Körpers in der Geschichte Europas* (Frankfurt am Main: Fischer, 2007).

41 Rensselaer, *Signals from the Atlantic Cable*, 5.

Fig. 1: The frontispiece of Alexander Jones's Historical Sketch of the Electric Telegraph (1852)

the entire globe. The actual achievement simply fulfilled what had been imagined.

Acceleration has also had effects on historiography. In particular, it has caused historiography to advance teleologically and in faster and faster steps in the direction of unity. This goal was stylized with the introduction of telegraphy and the emergence of an "unprecedented desire" for proximity and acceleration.[42] Such desire was not only promoted by the history of media as a destroyer of time and space from one epoch to the next; it can also be regarded as a breeding ground for engaging with media and communication in theoretical terms.[43] "It is undoubtedly true," wrote the political economist Ernst Gottfried Fischer in 1795, "that every invention that has enabled faster and easier communication among men (such as the invention of writing, the compass, the postal service, and the printing press) can also be said to have inaugurated a new epoch in the history of culture."[44] The effects of this desire are no less apparent in the McLuhanesque theories that were developed during the 1980s and 1990s: "Wireless telegraphy, on the contrary, is a bodiless and immaterial form of transmission. The transmission and reception of a message occur at the same time, thus achieving the ultimate goal of acceleration, which is instantaneity."[45] Immediacy is treated as the backdrop of history especially in those cases where the line of argumentation is more or less explicitly Catholic.[46] Such immediacy is used to various ends: It eliminates the uncertainties and contingencies that exist in division or separation by promising to replace multiplicity with unity; it aims to create an undivided community by means of immediate media; metaphysically, it reverts back to an origin from which all differences can be derived; and it aspires for a sort of transmission that is always already transmitted, a transmission in which mediation or loss plays no role at all.

---

[42] Ernst Gottfried Fischer, "Ueber Telegraphie," *Deutsche Monatschrift* 2 (1795), 85–95, at 85.

[43] In this sense, the discourses of immediacy create their own descriptive language. The risk of describing any culture of description lies in being deceived by this culture into regarding it as it wants to be regarded. To counteract this inclination, every descriptive language has to be historicized and interrogated in terms of the conditions in which it appeared.

[44] Fischer, "Ueber Telegraphie," 88.

[45] Peter Weibel, *Die Beschleunigung der Bilder in der Chronokratie* (Bern: Benteli, 1987), 102.

[46] In this light, McLuhan's Catholicism, which despite many assertions to the contrary played an important role in his thinking, warrants a thorough philosophical and media-historical examination. His religiosity allowed him to draw connections to numerous discourses; far from being a mere addendum to be brushed aside, it is rather an essential component of his intellectual framework.

A narrative of desire for communication and for contact in communication, as has been unfolding since the early nineteenth century, may seem all too appealing (it still, in fact, entices those who write about the history of media), but it goes some way to explain the overcoming of distance and the fact that the technologies involved have served as the impetus for historical processes. The phantasms of electricity and the renewal of this "praise of touch" (*"Lob des Berührens"*) are improbable. As an agent of history, however, their appearance would be probable, and this is the effect of the narrative of desire. An anthropological approach to this need, which can still be seen in the narratives concerned with the global village, characterizes media as a necessary step toward an approximation of immediacy and undermines the contingencies of technology and its dependence on discursive constellations or materialities of communication. It would be misleading to consign the phantasms of instantaneity to such an anthropological need and to use it in order to discuss their history. To do so would be to discredit all too rashly the historicity of discourses and the technologies used to produce proximity and distance and thus to lose sight of the productivity of delays or postponements. It is not a desire for proximity that inspired the technological development of telegraphs or the fusion of society; it was rather the detailed and physical work on synchronization processes, which, instead of real time (*Echtzeit*), produced instances of timeliness or punctuality (*Rechtzeitigkeiten*). Any theory or history of media that would take as its starting point a constellation oriented toward unity would necessarily depict media as agents of immediacy and thus embed itself into the very imaginary that it intends to describe.

These considerations indicate how, with the instantancity of electricity and the acceleration of its community, immediacies are systematically produced wherever the intent is to describe the difference of media. In the telegraph wire, according to Frank Hartmann, the receiver is "remotely present or telepresent under the conditions of real-time transmission."[47] Theories of globalization, not least those advanced by the prominent sociologists Anthony Giddens and Manuel Castells, belong to this tradition as well. In these cases, acceleration occupies the same systematic place as it does in the media theories under discussion. Because they are part of this genealogy, their attempts to theorize about the communities of globalization are focused on accelerated immediacy and thus on essentialization.

In this regard it will be worthwhile to examine some of the sociological approaches to globalization that have treated acceleration as an agent of modernity. In such approaches, the "annihilation of space and time" has been developed into a model for explaining global transformations. During the 1970s, sociologists concocted utopian ideas about a "wired society" or an "electronic cottage" to describe the phenomenon of masses of people being immediately connected with one another. In doing so, they borrowed a good deal from McLuhan's work, though they were often quick to disparage his scientific

---

[47]   Hartmann, *Globale Medienkultur*, 42.

credibility.[48] Conceptually, the guiding premise of these works was that of a "time-space convergence," and thus electric instantaneity was fundamental to these sociologies. The term was coined by Donald Janelle with reference to the railroad, after which it was used (quite influentially) by David Harvey to describe the operations of global finance. Even more recently, Anthony Giddens molded the idea into a general theory of sociology and Manuel Castells adopted it as a model for the so-called network society.[49] Evidence for the power of this discourse is especially clear in Castells's work when, after providing an extensive analysis of the synchronization processes of social times and flows in light of networks and global interdependency, he makes mention of the "annihilation of space and time by electronic means."[50] Castells describes a real-time interaction that creates space for social connections when locations share the same time and actors can act within the same space even though distances lie between them. The conclusion that he draws from this, namely that the network society is "without reference to either past or future,"[51] seems analogous to McLuhan's idea of "electric nowness."[52] In the final pages of his work, Castells thus contradicts everything that he has described in such painstaking detail and neglects the contingencies of globalization just as much as he overlooks the effects of the convergence of technologies and social practices. The global communities that Castells wishes to describe as redistributions of society are regarded as a new unity of exchange even though he had already described them as complex organizations of social differentiation.

Any media theory that treats this "addiction to communication,"[53] a phenomenon discussed by Ernst Gottfried Fischer as early as 1795, as an agent is inherently problematic because it has taken its analytic tool from the history of the tool itself. The remarks that have been made about the inner side of these histories can be expanded to include the historicity that exists outside of them. They, too, are products of the historical processes that they are describing. It is precisely this issue that prevented McLuhan from recognizing the potential of his own theory: "All means of interchange and human interassociation tend to improve by acceleration. Speed, in turn, accentuates problems of form and structure."[54] These questions of form constitute the epistemological utility of his media theory. In short, McLuhan believed that electric acceleration had brought about the media-

---

[48]   See James Martin, *The Wired Society* (Englewood Cliffs: Prentice-Hall, 1978); and Thomas Forester, "The Myth of the Electronic Cottage," in *Computers in the Human Context: Information Technology, Productivity, and People*, ed. Forester (Oxford: Blackwell, 1989), 213–27.

[49]   See Donald Janelle, "Measuring Human Extensibility," *Journal of Geography* 5 (1973), 8–15; David Harvey, *The Condition of Postmodernity: An Enquiry into the Origins of Cultural Change* (Oxford: Blackwell, 1990); Anthony Giddens, *The Consequences of Modernity* (Stanford: Stanford University Press, 1990); and Manuel Castells, *End of Millenium*, 2nd ed. (Cambridge, MA: Blackwell, 2000).

[50]   Ibid., 379.

[51]   Ibid., 386.

[52]   McLuhan and Nevitt, "The Argument: Causality in the Electric World," 2.

[53]   Fischer, "Ueber Telegraphie," 85–95.

[54]   McLuhan, *Understanding Media*, 95.

theoretical shift from analyzing content to analyzing its medium. By means of electricity, in McLuhan's estimation, familiar forms of thinking and knowing – those oriented toward linearity, rationality, and content – have become obsolete and should be replaced by pattern recognition, Gestalt theory, and media theory. McLuhan was looking for tools to explain the "simultaneous field of relations"[55] without having to rely on linear and rationalistic models, for such models obscure the fact that the medium is the message. For him, the global simultaneity of electricity, which is the end point of acceleration, was what made media theory intelligible, and this is because media (understood in terms of Gestalt theory) lie in the background and can only be recognized as media if figure and background appear simultaneously. Simply put, this simultaneity is provided by electricity. It is electricity that makes the message recognizable in the medium and yet, as an instantaneous force, it also does away with the medium at the same time: "Before the electric speed and total field, it was not obvious that the medium is the message."[56]

IV. Gaps in the Community

Like the notion of "each with all," the vitalization of the (cable) connection is based on a failure to acknowledge the exclusion entailed by the all-encompassing and vital inclusion of the telegraph network. This presence does not recognize any difference. The white areas on the map, which are not included in the cable network, or those places that lack access to radio and television are simply omitted. A space of this sort necessarily has a blind spot: an outside that can no longer be recognized. In the process of differentiation, however, the inside identifies the outside and therefore necessarily constitutes it. One's own identity cannot exist without that of the Other, and yet the global village, like the telegraphic "electric union,"[57] makes everything its own by means of inclusion. If everything is included, there can be no Other. McLuhan, however, did not emphasize the collective to such an extent as to believe that it transcended the individual and could lead to a totalitarian or even fascist position. Far from being tempted by the error of political exclusion, McLuhan was sure to stress the role of the individual. Nevertheless, in the global village there exists only a plurality, composed of individuals who are connected together into a unity, and there is no outside. The blind spot of exclusion is structurally integrated as an enclosure of connections.

With reference to more recent, difference-oriented theories of community, it is possible to critique McLuhan's idea and to situate it more accurately within its historical context. It would be too simplistic to regard it as a fundamentalist utopia, especially if the goal is to understand it on the basis of its media and communication (which stubbornly resist understanding). Recent theories of community – such as those presented by Jean-Luc Nancy, Roberto Esposito, Jacques Derrida, or Jacques Rancière – insist that community

---

55 McLuhan, "The Electronic Revolution in North America," 169.
56 McLuhan, *Understanding Media*, 28.
57 Rensselaer, *Signals from the Atlantic Cable*, 5.

should only be thought about in terms of connection to the extent that it is not unified. The communities described here, which view themselves as being connected by means of media, seem to be especially susceptible to this danger when they seek their community in the form of unity. In recent years, and especially in France, a lively debate has taken place about how to go beyond a (historically problematic) concept of community that, in essentialistic terms, understands it as a collection of individuals who are all related in a similar way to a common unity.[58] Two strategies of community formation, which the Austrian philosopher Matthias Flatscher has identified as ideal-typical, warrant criticism because their essentializing dual function consists of creating homogeneity on the inside and creating boundaries to exclude the outside. On the one hand, unity or connectivity can be created retroactively, in a political act, by establishing a definition of shared qualities. In this way, everyone is afforded something essential – a political orientation, for instance – that unites him or her with everyone else. This feature constitutes the essence of the community, and those who lack this feature are excluded from it. On the other hand, community can be ascribed to a common and *a priori* affiliation, be it religious, familial, or geographical (in the sense of churches, tribes, or nations). In this case, every person is subordinated to a higher order – be it race, religion, or the global village – and from this they are thought to derive regardless of whether they are amenable or threatening to it.[59]

By McLuhan's time, the genealogy of electricity had opened up a third approach to the formation of community. The results of this approach, however, were similar to those of the other two, for it imagined that community could be developed out of an ontology, in particular an ontology of media-based connectivity. The bond in question is neither antecedent nor subsequent to this community but is rather attributed to the (immediate) media that connect separate entities. The acceleration of electricity thus offered an exclusive option for forming community in which a central role was assigned to media whose phantasm or self-delusion happened to be that of a unity of divided or separate elements.[60] Yet without remoteness and difference there can be no communication, transmission, or

---

[58]   For an overview of this debate, in which media and technology happen to be treated as mere ancillary phenomena in the formation of communities, see Oliver Marchart, *Post-Foundational Political Thought: Political Difference in Nancy, Lefort, Badiou and Laclau* (Edinburgh: Edinburgh University Press, 2007).

[59]   See Matthias Flatscher, "'And there is nihil nuder under the clothing moon': Rekonzeptionen von 'Bild' und 'Gemeinschaft' nach Jacques Derrida," in *Bilder und Gemeinschaften: Studien zur Konvergenz von Politik und Ästhetik in Kunst, Literatur und Theorie*, ed. Beate Fricke et al. (Munich: Fink, 2011), 492–520.

[60]   This dimension of community formation has received only scant attention from theorists. Even in those cases where the media of community have been addressed, the focus has been restricted to such things as its representation in film. The infrastructures of connection, that is, have largely been ignored. In this regard, see Lars Gertenbach and Dorothee Richter, "Das Imaginäre und die Gemeinschaft," in *Mit-Sein – Gemeinschaft: Ontologische und politische Perspetivierungen*, ed. Elke Bippus et al. (Zurich: Springer, 2010), 119–36. For this reason it seems necessary to encourage a different perspective. For an approach that is similar to what I have in mind, see Erich Hörl's discussion of the connection between community and technology in his article "Die künstliche Intelligenz des

community. They are preconditions for the very distance that they are meant to overcome. Within unity, the anteriority of distance is erased in order to make the unity conceivable – a gesture that can be likened to pulling the rug out from under one's own feet. In contrast to more recent concepts of community, which embrace its difficulties and tend to associate universality with individuality, McLuhan's resembles that of a Christian *communitas*, in which conflicts are set aside in the name of achieving a higher union. The classification into the unity imagined by McLuhan does not entail a general standardization or unification, but it certainly does entail the lionization of a common feature that is condensed into an essence, namely the inevitable connection forged by electricity.

Only against the background of an Other, which has not been sublated into the Same, is it possible to conceive of a non-essentialist community and to displace or shift this concept, which has been defined by logics of identity and mechanisms of exclusion, in a deconstructive manner. An open community, which is neither exclusive nor inclusive, must retain its outside. One possible way of achieving this has been suggested by Jean-Luc Nancy, who, so as to avoid the ideas of inclusion and exclusion, has conceptualized community in terms of difference and communication and not in terms of identity.[61] The establishment of identity should not entail the establishment of boundaries. Nancy considers separation or division to be a formative aspect of community and as something that cannot be neglected if essentialism is to be averted. It is not to be understood as a utopian and conciliatory counter-model for a fragmented society. In this way it is possible to sustain the peculiar tension that exists between closure (*Schließung*), which always remains imaginary (regardless of all the practical attempts that have been made to close things off), and the necessary differences among individuals – a tension that has shaped the politics of communities and needs to be understood in terms of its media, history, and the media theories that it has inspired.

A recurring idea in Western thought is that of an original, undivided community that is always a long-lost thing of the past. In the Platonic sense, this is a community whose truth is thought to lie in its immediacy. In contrast to such an idea, we should conceive of a community in which difference is not only tolerated but is fundamental – despite the risk of fragmentation and, as Flatscher has urged, in opposition to the substantialism of a predetermined sense of togetherness and in opposition to the immanence of a normative ideal of community. The preservation of difference is not only politically relevant in the sense of an operative space of exchange that cannot be occupied by essences. The issue is to think of this connectivity without unification, to think of relations without the unity of difference, and not to impose on them any notion of presence or consistency. As far as the essentialism of medial connections is concerned, these challenges can only be met if attention is paid to the technological networks that distribute

---

Sinns: Sinngeschichte und Technologie im Anschluss an Jean-Luc Nancy," *Zeitschrift für Medien- und Kulturforschung* 2 (2010), 129–47.

[61] See Jean-Luc Nancy, *Being Singular Plural*, trans. R. D. Richardson (Stanford: Stanford University Press, 2000).

presence and absence, that overcome space by synchronizing distant locations, and that connect separate entities. Here I have in mind such things as the cables that create a circuit between continents, the switches that alter the state of things, the relays that, at various nodes, split cable connections into networks, or the protocols that rule over connection and disconnection.[62]

The concept of the global village and all of the ideas about global interconnectedness, which can have religious connotations, consequently exclude difference both in regard to transmission and in regard to the diversity of the individuals that have been unified. Difference can play no part in this unity, even though unity is preceded by it. The global village is contact without tact, without time, without distance, and perhaps without propriety or decency. Even if it lacks coordination, conformity, or synchronization (*Gleichschaltung*), it is still characterized by simultaneous and immediate touching, by a tact that is caught up in the act of touching. In the instantaneous medium of electricity, the separation bridged by this medium is erased. The global village conceals the spatio-temporal relations – the spaces and moments of interruption – that are generated by electric media and thus it also conceals the ways in which such media have reconfigured the social. If there is no difference within the unity and yet still a degree of variability (simply because the inhabitants of the global village are not all identical), then these distinctions are themselves simply derivations from the unity. There can then be nothing like an Other or outside that is not encompassed by the unity. Within the global village, it is structurally impossible to regard the Other as something autonomous, as something that is not a component of the village itself. The idea of the global village thus neglects the complex and ruptured (because interrupted) forms of electric or electronic distributions, networks, and protocols that not only globalize the small-scale coordinates of the social but also continue to reconfigure them in a radical manner.[63]

Instead, it is possible to engage with the genealogy of media theories and media concepts that constitutes the history of their communities and will likely continue to do so. If understood in terms of difference, the connectivity sought by such theories and concepts can be regarded as having a historical index that can be analyzed on the basis of the techniques and technologies of connection and direct address. If, along with these theories and their media, the community and history in question are allowed to converge into unity, then we will find ourselves caught in the paradoxical position of having to imagine immediate media or we will end up in a dubious political utopia like the global village, which lacks both an Other and an outside. If they continue to be preoccupied with such phantasms, which cannot be resolved logically but only historically, media theories

---

[62]   See Hugo Theodor Horwitz, "Das Relais-Prinzip," in *Das Relais-Prinzip: Schriften zur Technikge-schichte* (Vienna: Löcker, 2008), 77–117; and Bernhard Siegert, *Relays: Literature as an Epoch of the Postal System*, trans. Kevin Repp (Stanford: Stanford University Press, 1999).

[63]   To cite one example, Alexander Galloway has described how protocols do not function as a disciplinary force but rather exert control in the form of modulation and distribution. See Alexander R. Galloway, *Protocol: How Control Exists after Decentralization* (Cambridge, MA: MIT Press, 2004).

and media histories will remain untenable. Among the effects of this untenability are those theories and histories that treat media as media of immediacy and serve to accelerate community even though their intention is to do precisely the opposite.

Irina Kaldrack and Theo Röhle

Creating Subsets of the Masses
Taxonomies, Orders, and Crowds in Facebook's Open Graph Protocol

I. Introduction

The German version of Facebook's homepage greets its visitors with the following euphemistic self-description: "Facebook enables you to connect with the people in your life and to share content with them."[1] If this motto is taken seriously (and there seems to be no reason not to do so, given the platform's 1.5 billion users), this raises the question of how this connecting and sharing is designed to take place under the conditions of digital technologies and algorithms. What sort of relationship between media and the masses manifests itself in the interaction between formalization, staging (*Inszenierung*), and user activity on Facebook?

In an effort to answer this question, we direct our attention to one of the central features of Facebook's technical infrastructure, namely its Open Graph protocol and the various applications, such as the "Like" button, that are based on it. Within a few years, the Like button has become a ubiquitous element of the World Wide Web. It is now possible to "Like" everything from individual texts, videos, and photographs to entire websites. At first glance, the main function of this button is seemingly to rank the popularity of online content by counting the number of times such content has been "Liked." Upon closer inspection, however, it becomes clear that the growing prevalence of the Like button – and the Open Graph protocol with which it is associated – is establishing a new paradigm of order on the web.

Here we would like to investigate how the use of Open Graph generates a sort of interaction between organization and communication in which the media and the masses mutually (re)configure one another. In this regard, we are especially interested in the technical details of the markup protocol as well as its medial staging and types of use. We hope to focus above all on how the masses are currently ordered and classified by a stratification of algorithmical and staging processes. In historical terms, such processes can be associated with particular medial and phantasmatic conceptions of oversight and

---

[1]   See https://de-de.facebook.com/ (accessed on August 15, 2014): "Facebook ermöglicht es dir, mit den Menschen in deinem Leben in Verbindung zu treten und Inhalte mit diesen zu teilen."

emergence. The reconstruction of these historical genealogies will allow us to provide a more precise definition of the interaction between the characteristics of the media and our understanding of the masses.

II. From Like Buttons to Profiles: The Technical Infrastructure of Open Graph

Open Graph is a protocol that enables content on the web to be tagged with metadata and connected to Facebook, the company that developed the procedure. The protocol forms the basis of most of Facebook's user functions, including clicking on the Like button or using other social plugins. Its central role within Facebook's infrastructure will only become evident, however, if a look is taken behind the graphical interface. The special feature of the protocol is that it makes content, both from within Facebook and outside of it, ascertainable in a manner that is formally describable and automated. This can be illustrated, for instance, by its treatment of the content on the film website imdb.com. Here, if someone looks up information about a given film, the corresponding page is furnished with a Like button. If the person in question clicks on this button, the movie is automatically incorporated into his or her user profile under the category "movies." Moreover, this "Like" will also appear on the person's own Facebook timeline and in the newsfeed of his or her "friends." Both the user and the movie are thus saved as so-called *objects* in Open Graph, and the "Like" specifies at what time and in what manner these objects were connected with one another.

On the one hand, Open Graph constitutes the format used internally by Facebook to save "semantic"[2] information and user data. On the other hand, it can also be used by external providers as a basis for making personalized recommendations. The metadata remain hidden from the users themselves; they are expressed only during the automatic categorization of content. Nevertheless, Open Graph also plays a role in the activity of users. Its features and its staging suggest which objects should be integrated into one's own profile; users collect "finds," present them to one another, and write comments about them. The automatic incorporation of objects into a newsfeed will direct the attention of "friends" toward one's own activity and stimulate them to comment on it, share it with others, or post their own recommendations in response.

In order for content from websites outside of Facebook to be integrated as objects into Open Graph, this content has to be equipped with metadata by the website operators in question. As an address, every object contains an individual identification number that makes its connections comprehensible to Facebook. By integrating their own content into Facebook's Open Graph, website operators gain the advantage of being able to know with greater precision who has been using their website and exactly what they have been look-ing at. Facebook marks and records every time an Open-Graph object has been clicked

---

2   Obviously, "semantic" can only be understood here in the sense of formal semantics; see Max
     Creswell, "Formal Semantics," in *The Blackwell Guide to the Philosophy of Language*, ed. Michael
     Devitt and Richard Hanley (Malden, MA: Blackwell, 2006), 131–46.

on as well as whatever interaction with content or plugins might subsequently take place. This information is made available to the operators of the corresponding websites in two forms. First, they are able to look at various statistics via a function called "Facebook Insights." These statistics consist of frequency data that can be filtered and sorted according temporal, geographic, and demographic criteria.[3] Second, each Open-Graph object has its own Facebook profile where, among other things, the comments of individual users can be recorded.[4]

The analytic tools made available by Facebook, however, are only a rudimentary variant of other possible ways to evaluate web traffic via the Open Graph. By means of an application program interface (API), the operators of websites can also access Open Graph directly and automatically in order to find far more comprehensive statistics about the use of their content. In this way it is possible to determine, for instance, how many users were directed to certain content by the recommendation of a friend. The restrictions that are supposed to accompany evaluations of this sort (for instance, the protection of personal information such as gender, age, and location) can be circumvented by encouraging users to download certain apps. When apps are installed, their operators are granted access to personal information that can include everything from the names of a user's friends to the contents of his or her inbox.[5] As soon as these rights are granted to the operator of a given app, the corresponding information is also made automatically accessible through the API.

This method of evaluating web traffic is used primarily by large content providers that want to have a precise idea of how and where their content is being circulated on social media. In fact, technical measures can be implemented to automate the dissemination of content and thus to promote its circulation on social networks. An example of this is an app for the eReading device Kobo. This app registers when Facebook users (if they are logged in) start reading a book, when they highlight a passage, take notes, and when they finish reading a book. It subsequently informs the user's circle of friends through the newsfeed that "user X started reading [finished reading/highlighted a passage/wrote a note in] book Y." Following the same schema, Tumblr, for example, informs a user's circle of friends about which elements where posted or reblogged. Moreover, the entire chain of comments, "Likes," and other interaction can also be monitored in real time by the employees of Kobo or Tumblr.

Of special interest are the technical conditions that need to be satisfied for a message such as "user X is reading article Y" to appear on someone's Facebook newsfeed. The first condition is that a definition has to exist in Open Graph of what an "article" is and what "reading" means. In order for developers to establish definitions of this sort, Facebook provides a form with which app programmers can define such things as "cooking" a "meal"

---

[3]   See Facebook's "Insights for Websites: Product Guide" (2011): http://developers.facebook/com/attachment/Insights_for_websites.pdf (accessed on August 18, 2014).

[4]   See https://developers.facebook.com/docs/reference/api/page (accessed on August 18, 2014).

[5]   See https://developers.facebook.com/docs/reference/api/permissions (accessed on August 18, 2014)

or "staying" in a "hotel."[6] The criteria for establishing such facts include interactions that leave a trace in Facebook's database, such as clicking on a link or a person's location as reported by a smart phone.

Here it seems important to take note of the convergence of interests that occurs during this process. The spread of Open Graph's presence throughout the entire web (in the rudimentary form of the Like button) has enabled Facebook to be made aware of the structures of links and user activity that exist outside of its own platform. The definitions of activities (such as cooking) and concepts (such as recipes) have provided Facebook with an unprecedented synoptic view of the semantic dimensions of the web.[7] This has become possible because Open Graph creates a considerable amount of incentive for website and app operators to mark their content with metadata. This it does by offering them essentially more comprehensive and detailed ways to monitor and evaluate their web traffic and by contributing to the broader and faster circulation of their content.

III. Communication and Copresence: The Use and Staging of Open Graph

Participants in Facebook use Open Graph primarily by clicking on Like buttons and by installing apps on their own profiles, as in the case of the Kobo app mentioned above. The act of "Liking" something links content to users' profiles and timelines and appears in the newsfeeds of their "friends." Beyond this, apps also generate information about the way people interact with the content that they have been linked to. What is more, Facebook users also receive content that was generated by Open Graph when they log in to the site and look at their newsfeed, which shows what their "friends" have "Liked" as well as the comments that others have posted about such things.

In this regard, the use of Open Graph creates a particular form of visibility.[8] On the one hand, Open Graph can be used to manage one's own profile and to present one's own preferences with links to categorized content. On the other hand, the Like button and other Open-Graph apps are used to refer to other web content while on Facebook. The links appear simultaneously in one's own timeline and in the newsfeed of one's "friends." Conversely, the links of one's "friends" and their various comments appear in one's own newsfeed.

Such use thus generates a visibility of showing and telling. What can be seen are links to content that has been seen by one's "friends," partial information about how they have

---

[6]   See https://developers.facebook.com/docs/opengraph/tutorial (accessed on August 18, 2014).

[7]   On the controversial relationship between the Open Graph protocol and other approaches to dealing with the "semantic web," see Yuk Hui and Harry Halpin, "Collective Individuation: The Future of the Social Web," in *Unlike Us Reader: Social Media Monopolies and Their Alternatives*, ed. Geert Lovink and Miriam Rasch (Amsterdam: Institute of Network Cultures, 2013), 103–16.

[8]   Crucial to this visibility are the privacy settings that allow users to determine exactly what should be visible to their "friends." For an insightful overview these settings, see Guilbert Gates, "Facebook Privacy: A Bewildering Tangle of Options," *The New York Times* (May 12, 2010), http://nytimes. com/interactive/2010/05/12/ business/facebook-privacy.html (accessed on August 18, 2014).

interacted with this content, and comments about the content itself. This visibility is based on one's list of friends and privacy settings, and it takes place as a sort of automatic distribution. By managing addresses based on lists of friends, Facebook gives order to the profiles, timelines, apps, and newsfeeds of its participants. The aim of the visibility created by this activity is for "friends" to follow the links of others and to repeat and comment about their perceptions and interactions. In this way, Open Graph produces a space of copresence (mainly in the form of the newsfeed) in which individual users can come into contact with their "friends," see what these "friends" have seen and done, and express their opinions about such things. Perceptions are shared and evaluations are exchanged.

Similar observations have been made in studies devoted to the use of new media by American adolescents. In the book *Hanging Out, Messing Around, Geeking Out*, Mizuko Ito and her colleagues aggregated the findings of various studies conducted between 2005 and 2008. Regarding communication media, which encompasses Facebook use and the Like button, the authors claim that the aim of young men and women is "to construct spaces of copresence where they can engage in ongoing, lightweight social contact that moves fluidly between online and offline contact."[9] Bernadette Kneidiger has made a similar argument about the Facebook users in German-speaking countries. A large majority of the 295 users that she surveyed (eighty-nine percent) stated that they had met most of their Facebook friends offline.[10] For ninety percent of her sample, the motive for using Facebook consisted of keeping in touch with old friends. Eighty percent claimed to be interested in "finding out what [their] circle of acquaintances is up to," and fifty-four percent agreed with the statement that they are more inclined to use the site "to share experiences with friends and acquaintances who live nearby."[11]

Open Graph produces a type of visibility that invites people to repeat the perceptions of others and to exchange opinions about these perceptions. With regard to the relationship between the individual and the crowd, Facebook creates a space of copresence for a collective. It forms groups in which everyone looks at similar content and exchanges and compares opinions about it. Upon closer inspection, however, this rather seems to be an imaginary concept of a collective. Every individual user of Facebook can imagine himself or herself as being part of a group with his or her "friends." However, one person's "friends" are not necessarily "friends" with one another. If the situation arises, they become visible to their common "friends" through their comments made about certain content, but otherwise they do not perceive any content from one another. If, as far as users are concerned, Facebook's Open Graph thus seems to be a medium of copresence, this observation needs to be modified at the structural level: It is rather an overlapping space of copresence, the overlapping nature of which also becomes somewhat porous when,

---

[9]   Mizuko Ito et al., *Hanging Out, Messing Around, and Geeking Out: Kids Living and Learning with New Media* (Cambridge, MA: MIT Press, 2010), 38.

[10]   Bernadette Kneidiger, *Facebook und Co.: Eine soziologische Analyse von Interaktionsformen in Online Social Networks* (Wiesbaden: Verlag für Sozialwissenschaften, 2010), 38.

[11]   Ibid., 95–96.

within this space, certain "friends" become visible to other "friends" whose address lists do not contain their names.

IV. Crowds and Their Forms of Knowledge

Facebook's Open Graph protocol is the basis of a conglomerate in which the technical functionalities of addressing and distribution go hand in hand with categorization, staging (*Inszenierung*), and user activity. A fundamental aspect to all of this is the fact that Open Graph can only be thought about in terms of crowds. An effective circulation of content requires an exceedingly large number of users; the semantic definition of content depends on the large-scale mobilization of website operators; and at the social level, the formation of "subsets" requires users to interact with online elements and with one another on a large scale. Open Graph produces a level of mediation between these crowds. It integrates organization and communication in such a way that crowds are rearranged; in the same way, it simultaneously organizes the classification of users in terms of content and thus gains, through the staging of its interfaces as well, its medial character.

As regards the classification or ordering of crowds, which is achieved by means of technical infrastructure, two points need to be made. *First*, Open Graph has brought about a massive expansion of addressability. Web content is no longer exclusively retrievable via a URL that belongs to an entire site or to part of one; it is also retrievable via an ID that is managed by Facebook and can thus reveal to website operators which elements of their sites attract the most interest from Facebook's users. This expansion has punctured the boundaries of observational space, but it has also caused differences to be leveled out. The integration of heterogeneous elements – user profiles, text-based communication, photos, descriptions of films, cooking recipes, etc. – into a common space of observation requires a severely reduced model. Here this is achieved by a type of network analysis that reduces objects and connections to the vertices and edges of a graph. *Second*, it is not in this reduced model – but rather in the data material – that organizations are made and thus that new categorizations are created. Categories are either determined by Facebook itself, as when a film from an internet movie database appears in a Facebook profile under the category "movies." Or they are defined, like the "read" books in the Kobo app by app operators on the basis of the Open Graph protocol.

Open Graph thus provides an infrastructure that is based on the expansion of observational space (by means of addressing and levelling) and offers the possibility of semantic categorization.[12] In its staging and user offerings, Open Graph is also seemingly meant to generate traffic that is then made available as data or metadata for further evaluation. At the user level, Facebook's Open Graph does not initially address crowds but rather the

---

[12]   The sequence of addressing, levelling, and categorization does not, however, necessarily result in a consistent semantic designation of web content, and this is because individual definitions can and often do conflict with one another.

constitution of groups. It promises a communal sense of being present and participating in the life of one's "friends" by circulating perceptions and opinions among them.

At the technical level, the main characteristics of Facebook's Open Graph are thus addressing, levelling, categorizing, and the generation of large-scale web traffic. This protocol, along with the large-scale data storage by Facebook and app providers, thus provides the basis for mathematical analysis. The protocol enables the use of statistical methods, the methods of data mining, as well as methods of network analysis that are based on graph theory.[13] Below we will summarize the fundamental concepts behind these types of analysis and offer a sketch of their inherent forms of knowledge. Above all, this will allow us to characterize and underscore the connections that exist between them.

The basis of "statistical knowledge" is the data collected about actors or events. These data correspond, for instance, to features such as gender, age, or other profile information of Facebook users. In this manner, every Facebook object can be classified according to a list of characteristics. In light of these collected characteristics, a crowd or group of Facebook objects can now be classified by means of a certain metric and by various calculation procedures. The metric determines in which manner the collected data can be made comparable to a given characteristic and thus provides a measure for proximity or similarity.[14] For instance, deviation from the mean can be used to classify or order a given Facebook object with respect to a particular characteristic.

It is also determined, moreover, whether there are any connections between various characteristics, and this too is a form of ordering the group of objects under consideration. Two of the most important methods for determining such connections are correlation and (linear) regression. The method of correlation considers the extent to which two features of a data set (that is, two different characteristics of an object) simultaneously deviate from the mean value of these features. Simultaneous anomality indicates that there is a relation between the two features. By means of regression, efforts are made to determine relations in the form of a function and to make them calculable (that is, to determine dependencies). Statistical knowledge is thus based on collections of features and on a measure of similarity. On this basis, elements can be ordered according to their proximity or similarity, and the features in question can be classified according to their degree of interdependence.

The type of network analysis that is modelled on graph theory takes as its starting point the relations between pairs of vertices (that is, the edges of a graph). A graph consists of a given number of vertices (also called "nodes") and a given number of edges that connect the vertices with one another. The vertices that are connected by an edge are known as neighboring vertices. A path consists of a sequence of neighboring vertices and

---

[13] Because the analytical methods that are actually used by Facebook and app providers are not public, we have to rely here on some degree of speculation. However, this speculation is informed by the current discourses that are taking place among software engineers and scientists.

[14] To each pair of elements in the set under consideration, a metric or distance function assigns a real number that is greater than or equal to zero. A metric must satisfy the following conditions: The distance of two elements is exactly zero if the two elements are identical; the distance between x and y corresponds to the distance between y and x; and the theorem of triangle inequality holds.

the edges that connect them. If the edges of a graph are associated with a direction (like arrows in a diagram), the graph is "directed"; otherwise, it is "undirected." The degree of a vertex corresponds to the number of edges that are incident to it. In directed graphs, a distinction is made between a vertex's indegree (the number of edges directed toward the vertex) and its outdegree (the number of edges directed away from it). Mathematical graph theory analyzes graphs with respect to their structures. On the basis of the relations between pairs of vertices and on conditions such as the total number of edges or the smallest degree that exists in a graph, graph theorists determine such things as whether a graph contains certain subgraphs, the length of a graph's paths, or how many vertices (or edges) have to be removed for a graph to "disintegrate" (that is, for subgraphs to be created that are not connected by any paths). In addition to being concerned with the existence of subgraphs and with the cohesion of graphs, graph theory is also concerned, for instance, with combinatory problems (the number of possible graphs or subgraphs within a certain structure) and with questions of optimization (determining the shortest path in a graph).[15]

Graph theory is thus interested in determining which structures can be deduced from the presence of pairwise relations between the elements of a given multitude. In doing so, it is less concerned with making statements about specific vertices than with generally establishing the existence of certain (sub)structures within networks. Network analysis, however, shifts this focus to some extent. Admittedly, it also uses the model of the graph to deduce the existence of structures in the empirical networks under investigation, and is thus likewise concerned with subgraphs, the issue of network cohesion, and so on. Crucial to network analysis, however, are the graph-theoretical methods for measuring the "importance" of a vertex, above all by means of various centrality measures. These are meant to determine how "central" a given vertex is, which depends (for example) on the extent to which a vertex has an especially high number of neighbors relative to the amount of edges in the graph or on the extent to which a vertex is connected to all the other vertices via especially short paths. By means of performing matrix operations on adjacency matrices, moreover, it is possible to make calculations concerning the relations between neighboring vertices (to some extent, these calculations are concerned with the logical connections that define the relations between and among vertices that are not necessarily direct neighbors).[16]

In this perspective, the knowledge of network analysis is based on the relations between actors. Network analysis distinguishes itself explicitly from the sort of sociology that hopes to describe actors by means of their attributes and to measure them statistically: "As regards network research, the actor is primarily interesting as an abstract concept in

---

[15]   For textbooks on the subject, see J. A. Bondy and U. S. R. Murty, *Graph Theory* (London: Springer, 2008); and Jonathan L. Gross and Jay Yellen, *Graph Theory and its Applications* (Boca Raton, Fla.: CRC Press, 1999).

[16]   A matrix is a tabular arrangement of symbols in rows and columns. Matrices can be added, subtracted, and – by means of a specific procedure – multiplied. In an adjacency matrix, the rows and columns designate the respective vertices of a graph. If two vertices i and j are neighboring, the entry of the ith row and j^{th} column will be a 1. Otherwise the entry there will be a 0.

which various relations can be established and observed."[17] Although the focus of network analysis, based as it is on graph theory, is on individual vertices, it is chiefly concerned with the function or importance of these vertices in relation to the network as a whole. From the perspective of network analysis, such importance is generated neither by personal attributes nor exclusively by a vertex's direct relations to others. Rather, it is based on a vertex's neighboring relations in the interaction with the relations between other actors.

The fundamental logic of network analysis is also quite relevant to Open Graph. The expansion of address space has made it possible to understand data traffic as a product of the relations (or edges) between addresses (or vertices). In this way (or so it is claimed), structures can be comprehended that have developed out of the activity and interrelations of a vast number of web users.

In its evaluation of profile information, Open Graph offers the possibility of drawing connections between the activity of an actor (in the sense of traffic between vertices) and the frequency of such activity. The features of a vertex exist in the form of a profile and its activity exists in the form of data saved by Open Graph, and the two can be analyzed together. Moreover, Open Graph also offers the opportunity to categorize, in terms of their features, the relations between edges (that is, the traffic between vertices). Such features can include, for instance, the time that something was communicated, the geographic location of those participating, as well as the semantic evaluation or the "weight" (importance) of certain acts of communication.[18] On the basis of these data, profile information can be combined with statistical methods, network analysis can be combined with profile information, or all three methods can be combined.

The statistical analysis of profile information allows for different types of profiles to be determined and subsequently classified. If certain profile information is associated with web traffic, the importance or function of the vertex within the network can be ascertained by means of network analysis.[19] If this analysis is conducted with an extensive number of vertices and subnetworks, statistical methods can be applied to determine how the network-analytical importance of a vertex correlates with its profile or profile types. Even without the intermediary step of network analysis, it is possible to investigate whether and how certain profiles and interactions correlate with one another on the basis of the connections that exist between profile information and interaction data (along with an extensive amount of comparative data). In addition, Open Graph makes it possible to bundle together certain constellations of vertices and edges into a single vertex. For instance, the profile of a user can be examined as a network of vertices and edges and can thus be analyzed in terms of the relations that exist between these elements. It is also

---

[17] Steffen Albrecht, "Knoten im Netzwerk," in *Handbuch Netzwerkforschung*, ed. Christian Stegbauer and Roger Häußling (Wiesbaden: Verlag für Sozialwissenschaften, 2010), 125–34, at 129.

[18] See Matthias Trier, "Struktur und Dynamik in der Netzwerkanalyse," in ibid., 205–17, esp. 214–16. The type of event-based network analysis described by Trier seems to be perfectly suited for Open Graph's data model. Its aim is to analyze changes in networks and thus to determine the effects of short-term changes on the importance of vertices.

[19] Logically enough, only subnetworks are analyzed in this process, not all of Facebook.

possible to treat the entire profile of a user as a single vertex and to analyze it, with the methods of network analysis, in light of its relations to other profiles. In this same way, profiles can be bundled together into a group that, in turn, can be analyzed with respect to its relations to other such groups.

By now it should be clear that the different analyses of various levels can be combined to draw conclusions about different profile types, vertex functions, and web traffic. Network-analytical measures thus allow statements to be made about the value of individual vertices (or groups of vertices) to the structure or topology of the network under consideration. For their part, statistical methods provide insight into the similarities, normalities, deviations, and connections of characteristics, which have been collected according to their semantic evaluations. It is also possible, in turn, to zoom in and out between the structures and types (the macro level) and the individual vertices pertaining to addresses and profile data. In this way, there is an inherent promise in these methods to be able to observe and explain structural developments that take place from the bottom up.

Semantic information and statistical analysis thus fill in the gaps that network analysis leaves open. Such information enables edges to be determined qualitatively and networks to be hierarchized. If, for example, preferences for certain movies are defined as *part* of given profile, this creates a tree structure in which the profile is placed at a higher level that subsumes the level of movie preferences. By means of statistical analysis, statements can be made at each of these levels about the position of a given vertex within a network and the thematic orientation of its content.

A variant of network analysis that is especially well suited to deal with Open Graph's database is known as "semantic social network analysis." With the traditional forms of analysis, vertices and edges are often reduced in such a way that causes the influence of certain vertices to be overestimated, and this is because the measures applied take into account only the number of connections from one vertex to another. Semantic social network analysis thus seeks to overcome this shortcoming:

> The betweenness value mainly depends on the graph topology, and the knowledge shared between vertices is not taken into account. Thus, in an ordinary graph, a vertex can own a high betweenness value while sharing no knowledge or endogenous content with the members of the social graphs, just getting connected with people who belong to various communities within the social graph. For instance, a recruiter aided by SNA metrics, seeking the most efficient profiles related to some specific knowledge communities (e.g., a gas turbines engineer), would only obtain the most active and connected individuals, i.e., community managers, famous or media-friendly people.[20]

As a way out of this dilemma, the authors propose a statistical analysis that examines a somewhat different set of properties that can be assigned to the vertices within a network. If agreements can be identified between these properties that can be assigned to a certain category, this is regarded as an indication that these properties belong to a group

---

20   Christophe Thovex and Francky Trichet, "Semantic Social Networks Analysis: Towards a Sociophysical Knowledge Analysis," *Social Network Analysis and Mining* 3 (2013), 35–49, at 42.

that might escape detection in traditional network analysis. The integration of statistical and graph-theoretical methods allows for groups, types, and topologies to be ordered or stratified out of a large quantity of heterogeneous elements, and such or similar methods are conceivably employed by Open Graph to achieve its results.

Whereas the taxonomy based on statistics employs types as representations of groups and thus limits its analysis of connections to the micro level, network analysis at least allows the topological structure of groups to remain theoretically visible. By combining these two approaches toward creating order, the distinction between micro and macro levels is resolved as a matter of projection. The projection methods used by network analysis determine whether a phenomenon is perceived as a micro phenomenon or as a macro phenomenon, whether (for example) a complete group is regarded as a single vertex within a network or whether the members of the group are themselves analyzed as individual vertices. Statistical aggregations can then be applied to classify the characteristics of a group into particular types.

V. Crowds and Organization

For website operators, Open Graph represents a medium for observing and analyzing a self-organizing or self-ordering crowd, and this medium is meant to enable operators to zoom in and out between individuals, types, and groups. These new forms of scalability are compatible with the promise of media to make the emergent phenomena of structural formation observable within a crowd. In what follows, we will take a closer look at the genealogy of this medial promise, which lies at the intersection of figures of thought, formalization (as visualization and calculability), and their operationality. In our historical reconstruction, Open Graph is seen to belong to a specific epistemic tradition whose oppositional nature has incited a steady expansion of observational space and medial representation. Here we hope to clarify this development by considering certain focal points from the history of statistics, sociology, and network analysis.

As regards the development of statistics, we have chosen as our starting point the works of Adolphe Quetelet (1796–1874), which have served both as an inspiration and as a foil to subsequent studies. In his book *Physique sociale* (1835), Quetelet adopted the approach of so-called error theory, which was then prominent in the field of astronomy. This is based on the assumption that measurement errors when observing planetary orbits follow a particular distribution and that the true orbit of a planet can be calculated on the basis of this distribution. Quetelet transferred this idea to social processes and systematized it into a law of deviation. According to this law, human characteristics (such as size, for instance) likewise follow a fixed distribution curve. He considered the mean value of this distribution – the average man – to be both an abstract law, which was substantiated by empirical observations of crowds, as well as an ideal that could be applied as a normative standard to individuals and to society at large.

In Quetelet's work, the act of observing and the law that derived from this act exist on two different levels. The macrostructure of law precedes the deviating micro-phenomena:

Quetelet sought to discover the laws of association between statistically defined social facts. The interdependence of social facts, he argued, could be studied through the systems of equations that define these laws. This basic insight was elaborated in economics and in social demography by those who applied concepts of "force" and "gravity" in their studies of the social world.[21]

It is only possible to infer a law from a large quantity of observations on account of the reductive moment that is inherent to statistical analysis. The variability of individual activity is ultimately uninteresting because it always converges toward the mean, which is the only relevant factor. The movement also entails a specific conception of government: A well-governed society is distinguished by its orientation toward the mean, for it is this that represents "all which is grand, beautiful, and excellent."[22] As Jürgen Link has noted:

> Quetelet elevated his "average man" [...] into an ideal type that is both *aesthetic and political*, and he did this by associating the "average man" with the collective symbolism of *balance, stability, beauty*, and *the optimal*. [...] Quetelet's emphasis on invariant normalities tended toward a purely proto-normalistic strategy: Empirical and mathematical statistics were expected to discover the "natural" normalities toward which politics could then orient itself.[23]

This normative orientation toward the mean was problematized by subsequent thinkers, above all by Francis Galton (1822–1911). Although he accepted Quetelet's ideas about normal distribution, Galton increasingly distanced himself from error theory. As a proponent of eugenics, he thought it was less and less possible to interpret certain deviations from the mean, namely those deviations that he considered desirable for society, as errors.[24] Whereas Quetelet regarded variability as a problem that needed to be overcome, in Galton's case it was considered a phenomenon that needed to be measured more accurately and even promoted (in certain instances). Thus, in itself, it was not the idea of

---

[21]   John Scott, "Social Physics and Social Networks," in *The SAGE Handbook of Social Network Analysis*, ed. John Scott and Peter J. Carrington (London: SAGE, 2011), 55–66, at 56.

[22]   Adolphe Quetelet, *A Treatise on Man and the Development of His Faculties*, trans. Robert Knox (Edinburgh: W. and R. Chambers, 1842), 100.

[23]   Jürgen Link, *Versuch über den Normalismus: Wie Normalität produziert wird*, 3rd ed. (Göttingen: Vandenhoeck & Ruprecht, 2006), 195. For an English introduction to Link's concept of normalism, see Jürgen Link, "From the 'Power of the Norm' to 'Flexible Normalism': Considerations after Foucault," *Cultural Critique* 57 (2004), 14–32. The question of why any controls are needed at all if nature, on its own accord, is always moving toward a mean has been discussed in recent debates in terms of "statistical determinism." Ian Hacking has suggested that the goal of reformatory movements was rather concerned with an indirect level of control: "to reorganize 'boundary conditions' under which a population was governed by statistical law." See Ian Hacking, "How Should We Do the History of Statistics?" in *The Foucault Effect: Studies in Governmentality*, ed. Graham Burchell et al. (Chicago: University of Chicago Press, 1991), 181–95, at 188.

[24]   See Donald A. MacKenzie, *Statistics in Britain, 1865–1930: The Social Construction of Scientific Knowledge* (Edinburgh: Edinburgh University Press, 1981), 58.

distribution that Galton called into question but rather Quetelet's normative judgment of distribution.[25] Instead of regarding the mean or average as a sort of ideal, he considered deviations from the mean to be the basis for defining "group-specific types": "Average size and average weight are no longer thought to represent the dimensions of the well-built individual in a well-governed society; rather, such averages enable individuals to be organized into different groups."[26]

Instead of focusing on a universal average, Galton embraced the idea of "relative rank,"[27] which allows individuals to be placed into narrowly defined groups. Of course, averages continued to play a central role in the definition of such groups,[28] but the idea of averages was expanded to include other aspects and thus allowed a broader range of variability to be covered: "It is difficult to understand why statisticians commonly limit their inquiries to Averages, and do not revel in more comprehensive views. [...] An Average is but a solitary fact, whereas if a single other fact be added to it, an entire Normal Scheme, which nearly corresponds to the observed one, starts potentially into existence."[29] According to Jürgen Link, Galton's more pronounced focus on variability can be understood as a transition from a "fixed" to a "dynamic" form of normality.[30] Instead of postulating a quasi-natural law of universal norms, which could be enforced with control mechanisms, Galton located optimization processes within groups that (at least to some extent) were placed in relation to one another. Parallel to his rejection of universal norms, he also cast doubt on the prevailing macro-perspective that Quetelet had relied on. Galton's process of regression, for instance, can be seen as an effort to make the dependencies between various attributes comprehensible and analyzable. However, a total renunciation of Quetelet's reductionist approach did not seem to be achievable.[31] Then again, the field of sociology, which was just developing at the time, has been dominated by statistical surveys that are aimed at comprehending the attributes of actors. The basis of such processes – even if they are not concerned with establishing averages but rather with finding correlations – has been the selection of which characteristics should be examined and thus the organization of these characteristics into categories. The inevitable result of this has been the creation

---

25 See Link, *Versuch über den Normalismus*, 239.

26 François Ewald, *Der Vorsorgestaat* (Frankfurt am Main: Suhrkamp, 1993), 193.

27 See MacKenzie, *Statistics in Britain, 1865–1930*, 58.

28 In his studies motivated by eugenics, for instance, Galton relied on one of Booth's classifications for defining "civic worth," which falls on the X-axis of a normal distribution. See Alain Desrosières, *The Politics of Large Numbers: A History of Statistical Reasoning*, trans. Camille Naish (Cambridge, MA: Harvard University Press, 1998), 114–15.

29 Francis Galton, *Natural Inheritance* (London: Macmillan, 1899), 62.

30 Link, *Versuch über den Normalismus*, 157.

31 For a discussion of the opposition between a "living inventory" and "dead statistics" in the work of Hans Zeisel, see Isabell Otto, "Massenmedien wirken: Zur Aporie einer Evidenzlist," in *Die Listen der Evidenz*, ed. Michael Cuntz (Cologne: DuMont, 2006), 221–38, esp. 225–26.

of group definitions that Rom Harré refers to as "taxonomic collectives."[32] These are collectives whose coherence is endowed exclusively by an external observer and in which there have been no internal processes of structural formation.[33]

From the turn of the last century, two names are closely associated with the effort to analyze such processes from the bottom up: Gabriel Tarde and Georg Simmel. Today, both of these thinkers are regarded as pioneers in the development of network theory.[34] Tarde (1843–1904) devised an understanding of sociology according to which society is based on the interactions between individuals. Central among these interactions is imitation, which is primarily the repetition of ideas and opinions but can also find expression in fashions or trends.[35] By means of imitation, a complex network of influences is created between individuals, and it is this network that ultimately constitutes society. Tarde conceived of imitation in terms of suggestion and transference, and thus his work can be associated with the discourses of his time concerned with electricity, magnetism, hypnosis, and contagion.[36]

Simmel (1858–1918) likewise focused to a large extent on the reciprocal effects and interactions between actors. It was only by analyzing such interactions, he thought, that we would be able to explain the development of stable social structures: "[U]nity in an empirical sense is nothing other than the interaction of elements; an organic body is a unity because its organs are in a closer interchange of their energies than with any outside entity."[37] What is crucial here is that the concentration has shifted from the attributes of individual actors to the processes that operate between them. It is the intertwining of such micro-processes that is understood to form structures. The theoretical turn has since been radicalized and systematized by network research. Here the point of departure is no longer

---

[32] Rom Harré, "Philosophical Aspects of the Micro-Macro Problem," in *Advances in Social Theory and Methodology: Toward an Integration of Micro- and Macro-Sociologies*, ed. Karin D. Knorr-Cetina and Aaron V. Cicourel (Boston: Routledge & Kegan Paul, 1981), 139–60.

[33] As regards the process of measuring television viewers as opposed to measuring internet users, see the discussions in Ien Ang, *Desperately Seeking the Audience* (London: Routledge, 1991); and Josef Wehner, "'Taxonomische Kollektive' – Zur Vermessung des Internets," in Herbert Willems, ed., *Weltweite Welten: Internet-Figurationen aus wissenssoziologischer Perspektive* (Wiesbaden: Verlag für Sozialwissenschaften, 2008), p. 363–82.

[34] See Scott, "Social Physics and Social Networks," 55–66; Linton C. Freeman, *The Development of Social Network Analysis: A Study in the Sociology of Science* (Vancouver: Empirical Press, 2004); and Elihu Katz, "Rediscovering Gabriel Tarde," *Political Communication* 23 (2006), 263–70.

[35] Another central concept in Tarde's theory is innovation or discovery, which defines moments of novelty in society.

[36] See Michael Gamper, *Masse lesen, Masse schreiben: Eine Diskurs- und Imaginationsgeschichte der Menschenmenge, 1765–1930* (Munich: W. Fink, 2007), 412; and idem, "Charisma, Hypnose, Nachahmung: Massenpsychologie und Medientheorie," in *Trancemedien und neue Medien um 1900: Ein anderer Blick auf die Moderne*, ed. Marcus Hahn and Erhard Schüttpelz (Bielefeld: Transcript, 2009), 351–73, at 354–55.

[37] Georg Simmel, *Sociology: Inquiries into the Construction of Social Forms*, trans. Anthony J. Blasi et al., 2 vols. (Leiden: Brill, 2009), 1:22.

actors, who have been described and statistically measured according to their attributes, but rather the relations between these actors. One of the founders of network research was Jacob Moreno (1892–1974), who coined the term "sociometry" during the 1930s. At the heart of his approach was the representational form of the sociogram, which he developed in order to make certain patterns visible that, in turn, provide insight into the hidden dynamics of a group.

Moreno's explicit goal was for sociometry to be an alternative to the traditional application of macro-sociological categories.[38] The micro-sociological analysis of networks was at first limited to smaller and closely defined groups, the members of which were asked about their preferences and distastes. The results of these surveys were then recorded as points and lines on a sociogram. It was only in the visual formalization of the sociogram that the decisive structures of a given group became recognizable. In this regard, Moreno expressly distinguished structural analysis, as based on a sociogram, from quantitative analysis, which is based on the statistical evaluation of the frequencies with which certain choices are made within a group. In the case of structural analysis, according to Moreno, "[t]he sociometric status of an individual is defined by the quantitative index of choices, rejections and indifferences received in the particular group studied."[39] With his sociograms, moreover, Moreno also made use of certain forms of projection by representing networks of "cottage groups" as vertices (the respective importance of which were weighted, to some extent, with plus or minus signs).[40]

The most decisive aspects for Moreno were thus the addressability and legibility of sociograms, the purpose of which is to make structures visible.[41] The goal of this visualization was to change the structures of groups in such a way that the preferences and distastes of its members would come to align with one another. Basing his work on a social-psychological approach, Moreno was concerned with identifying blockades or impasses that could be resolved in group therapy sessions. As this process became more methodologically advanced, network research also came to be applied to larger groups. Even these investigations, however, remained faithful to a fundamental principle, a principle that was theoretically formulated in the work of Tarde and Simmel and methodologically implemented in Moreno's sociograms. With respect to the organization of groups, that is, the main issue at stake was not individual attributes such as age or gender but rather the ability to identify certain patterns in the relations *between* the individual actors in question.

In this regard, it is noteworthy that the early stages of network research took place around the same time that graph theory was being developed into a mathematical discipline of its own. At first, however, these two types of analysis adopted different perspectives.

---

[38] See Katja Mayer, "On the Sociometry of Search Engines: A Historical Review of Methods," in *Deep Search: The Politics of Search Beyond Google*, ed. Felix Stalder and Konrad Becker (Innsbruck: Studienverlag, 2009), 54–72.

[39] J. L. Moreno, *Who Shall Survive? Foundations of Sociometry, Group Psychotherapy and Sociodrama* (Beacon, NY: Beacon House, 1953), 704.

[40] Ibid., 435.

[41] See ibid., 141: "A readable sociogram is a good sociogram."

A look at the early textbooks devoted to graph theory reveals quite clearly the traditions to which the young field belonged as well as its perspectives and areas of applications.[42] Many of the problems addressed by graph theory, for instance, happened to originate as a sort of mathematical entertainment, that is, as mental games or brain teasers. They were concerned with the possibility of such things as walking across all the bridges in Königsberg without walking across any of the bridges twice (Euler formulated his famous problem regarding the seven bridges of this city in 1735) or with making one's way through a labyrinth in an optimal manner. Around the middle of the nineteenth century, some of the problems to be faced by graph theory were introduced by the theory of electricity.[43] At the end of the same century, the terminology of trees and graphs was adopted by organic chemistry in order to determine the number of isomeric arrangements.[44] Beyond discussing different types of graphs and the various combinatory problems associated with them, the textbooks also provide extensive illustrations of how certain concepts from algebra and group theory, not to mention matrix calculations, could be made fruitful for graph theory. Conversely, they demonstrate how the methods of graph theory can be applied to the findings of other disciplines. It is apparent that, during the 1930s, graph theory was struggling to establish itself as a legitimate field of mathematics. Although the early developments of graph theory and network analysis were not connected – but rather took place in parallel with one another – the crucial factor is that both fields made use of the same sort of visualization, be it that of a graph or a network diagram.

In an article about visual models and network theory before 1900, Sebastian Gießmann has shown how graphs, as visual models, were adopted from the diagrammatic practices of chemistry into other scientific disciplines, most notably into the logical notation developed by Charles Sanders Peirce.[45] Florian Hoof has called attention to the trend of using diagrams and other visualizations in the field of business management between the years 1880 and 1925. As part of the so-called "visual management" of the 1910s, network diagrams were implemented as schematic abstractions for visualizing the relational structures of business processes for lending support to decision-making procedures.[46] Along

---

[42] See Dénes König, *Theory of Finite and Infinite Graphs*, trans. Richard McCourt (Basel: Birkhäuser, 1990). The original German version of this book was published in 1936.

[43] In this regard, König refers to the circuit laws that had been formulated by Gustav Robert Kirchhoff (1824–1887), especially to his loop rule (or mesh rule) and to his rule concerning nodes or vertices (see ibid., 241–42).

[44] See ibid., 62–72.

[45] Sebastian Gießmann, "Graphen können alles: Visuelle Modellierung und Netzwerktheorie vor 1900)," in *Visuelle Modelle*, ed. Ingeborh Reichle et al. (Munich: Wilhelm Fink, 2008), 269–84. On Peirce's use of so-called "existential graphs," see also Wolfang Schäffner, "Electric Graphs: Charles Sanders Peirce und die Medien," in *Electric Laokoon: Zeichen und Medien, von der Lochkarte zur Grammatologie*, ed. Michael Franz (Berlin: Akademie Verlag, 2007), 313–26.

[46] Florian Hoof, "Vertraute Oberflächen: Möglichkeitsbedingungen der Systemkrise," a presentation delivered at the Annual Conference of the Society for Media Studies (*Jahrestagung der Gesellschaft für Medienwissenschaft*) on October 4, 2012.

with the forms of calculability employed by graph theory, especially by means of matrix representations and calculations, these forms of visualization were the preconditions that enabled the merger of the micro-sociological and macro-sociological concepts of the network, a convergence that took place in the 1950s, if not somewhat earlier: "In this translatability – between matrix tables with 1/0 conditions, on the one hand, and the topological network diagram on the other – lies an extremely reductive but nevertheless stable foundation for the isomorphism of social, electrical, and telecommunications networks, and for a general theory as well."[47] What is decisive about the network diagram is thus reduction, formalization, calculability, and the "continuous intersection of calculability and iconicity – the acts of writing and imaging converge."[48]

In light of the lineages outlined above, it is apparent that two different and contrary traditions of knowledge, each with the operative practices of visualization and calculability, intersect with one another in Facebook's Open Graph protocol. The opposition of statistical approaches and the approach of network analysis reveals two epistemic constellations that, viewed historically, can be said to compete with each other. Statistics is concerned with the features of individual actors, but it leaves the relations among such actors undefined. Whereas statistics can claim to analyze structures at the macro level on the basis of the frequency of particular attributes, network research affords the possibility of ascertaining the processes of structural development from the bottom up. The reduction of phenomena to vertices and edges is the price that has to be paid in order to examine emergent structures. At the same time, it is this reduction that also enables different networks to be managed and compared with one another. The promise of visibility and manageability is thus closely connected to the visualization of sociograms. The most prominent characteristic of the latter (at least in contemporary practices and discourses) is that they make visible and legible, by means of visual formulations and the "top views" that such visualizations entail, something that would otherwise remain hidden from the individual. It is precisely this that enables the formation of structures to be managed and even controlled. This possibility becomes more and more achievable as visual formulations merge more and more with calculable formulations.

In addition to the medial intersection of formalistic practices and traditions of knowledge, there is something else that deserves our attention. This is the use of metaphors from the field of physics that allowed different theoretical traditions to be compatible with one another before the mathematical formalization of graphs and matrix calculations could guarantee the translatability of fields of knowledge. Quetelet, Simmel, Tarde, and (later) Moreno all relied to some extent on physical terminology and thus drew analogies between physics and society. What is instructive in this regard is the different nature of these analogies. Whereas Quetelet sought to demonstrate the general validity of laws in

---

47 Erhard Schüttelpelz, "Ein absoluter Begriff: Zur Genealogie und Karriere des Netzwerkkonzepts," in *Vernetzte Steuerung: Soziale Prozesse im Zeitalter technischer Netzwerke*, ed. Stefan Kaufmann (Zurich: Chronos, 2007), 25–46, at 35.
48 Gießmann, "Graphen können alles," 284.

the social realm, Simmel, Tarde, and Moreno were concerned with describing the interactions that exist beyond the directly observable connections between individuals. Moreno, for instance, refers to the vertices in a network as atoms; accordingly, he discusses the connections between them in terms of the forces of attraction and repulsion, the effects of which are then used to explain the cohesion of the atoms. Elsewhere he discusses connections as "channels," which serve to represent flows of communication as well as various types of influence.[49]

It is in these contradictory references to physical terminology that the two aforementioned epistemic traditions find expression: the search for universal natural laws, on the one hand, and the search for emergent structures on the other. Such physical terminology, however, has another side to it, one that is more normative-oriented than epistemic. Just as Quetelet hoped to understand "social physics" as the basis for governance, Moreno's sociometry also contains an aspect of control. In his *Foundations of Sociometry*, Moreno notes: "[J]ust as we have been able to correct the direction of rivers and torrents, we may be able to correct the direction in which psychological currents flow."[50] Despite being used to different ends, these physical metaphors seem to be associated with the idea of making existing forces (in the sense employed by the natural sciences) explicable or at least calculable – and thus also with the idea of being able to affect these forces in a formative manner. The references to physical concepts thus function to make contradictory conceptions of the social compatible with one another and to ennoble them in scientific terms. Although the individual actor is therefore subjected to a sort natural law, this same actor (or his or her preferences and rejections) only becomes operable within the social. This conglomerate now promises to be controllable.

This manner of thinking has advanced in network research as the analogies between physics and society have become less metaphorical and more and more technological and methodological. As more comprehensive means have become available for collecting and processing data, models from physics and graph theory have become increasingly more effective at identifying universal laws that apply to any type of network.[51] This reliance on the natural sciences has helped network models to gain greater acceptance, and it has also led to a "hardening" of the formalizations that are associated with them.

If network theory, as the basis of automated data analysis, has infiltrated the media-technological infrastructure of our time, this has not taken place without the accompanying phantasms of natural laws, emergence, and controllability. Physical models are actualized within an infrastructure that has been conceived of in "hard" and graph-theoretical terms, and they are used to cast our materials and technology.[52] As a sort of undercurrent, these

---

[49]   See Martin Donner, "Rekursion und Wissen: Zur Emergenz technosozialer Netze," in *Rekursionen*, ed. Philipp von Hilgers and Ana Ofak (Munich: Wilhelm Fink, 2009), 77–115, esp. 92.

[50]   Moreno, *Who Shall Survive? Foundations of Sociometry*, 439.

[51]   Scott, "Social Physics and Social Networks," 57–58.

[52]   For a critique of the application of "hard" physical models to social phenomena, as currently practiced in the field of "social physics," see ibid. At the same time, however, Scott also stresses the

models are simultaneously accompanied by the inconsistency of the fields of knowledge that enabled them to exist in the first place. They almost seem to be prompting yet another gesture of "physicalization."

This can be demonstrated by that fact that analogies to physics continue to pervade the present discourse. Whereas network theory, especially as it is practiced by Barabási, has embraced the "objectification" of networks to such an extent that mathematical proofs (such as the development of the "power law") have come to approximate natural laws,[53] the current discussion held by engineers and computer scientists about semantic social network analysis contains references to physics yet again. These references are concerned with forces that govern phenomena beyond their observable relations:

> The experiment of E. Branly on radio-construction (1890) has demonstrated that some flows can circulate between points without specific connections. On the radio-construction principle, we emit the hypothesis that in the social graphs, significant and invisible information flow exists between certain individuals, connected or not by visible arcs. We study our hypothesis, comparing the arcs of the skills graph to solid conductors transporting electrical flows, in the purpose to represent the invisible flows within the graph and to quantify the reactance conditioning the social network structure and evolution.[54]

On the one hand, then, there is a deterministic macro force, while on the other hand there is a multiplicity of interacting micro forces. The oscillation between these contradictory physical analogies seems less to be a symptom of the developments under discussion than their driving force. Whenever the moment of reduction seems all too apparent in the processes being applied, the analogy tips in the other direction, as a sort of compensatory gesture, and suggests that it is possible to fill in the respective empty spaces with a mere methodological adjustment. This dynamic of tipping back and forth generates a continuous "impulse to fill things in" (*"Drang zum Auffüllen"*), the backdrop to which seems to be the promise of loss-free scalability. If this compensation were in fact to succeed, then it would be possible at every point in a network to take both viewpoints into account and to organize the participants in a network both on the basis of their interrelations as well as on the basis of their attributes.

The overlapping nature of these types of organization, as identified in the case of Open Graph and in the case of current processes of analysis, can be understood as a direct result of this "impulse to fill things in." An aspect that Markus Krajewski has referred to as being fundamental to the use of tables as instruments of knowledge, for instance, recurs here in a potent form:

---

productivity of these analogies on a metaphorical level, as they have been used by social theorists since the time of Comte.

[53] See Albert-László Barabási and James Fowler, "Social Networks," in *Science is Culture: Conversations at the New Intersection of Science + Technology*, ed. Adam Bly (New York: Harper Perennial, 2010), 297–312.

[54] Thovex and Trichet, "Semantic Social Networks Analysis," 44.

> The grid of a table is consequently oriented toward the completeness of that which it is designed
> to include. Neatly selected categorial subdivisions into columns and rows not only allow for
> all of the present elements to be classified; they also generate anticipation for the empty spaces
> that result from a strict combinatorics of categories. [...] In this sense, a table can serve as an
> instrument of knowledge because its blank spaces immediately expose acute gaps in our under-
> standing and other desiderata.[55]

In the case of Open Graph, as opposed to tables produced manually, categories are created automatically out of the data material at hand and are dynamically made to suit the respective state of information. At the same time, the overlapping processes of analysis in the technical infrastructure increase, many times over, the number of empty spaces and desiderata. Thus an ongoing sensation of shortage is produced that calls for being filled in with more and more data and metadata on the part of users. This infrastructure not only gains its medial quality as a tool of analysis in the hands of its operators but also by means of the specific staging of its empty spaces and by the way in which users deal with them. Here it seems important to note that the orderings of crowds and categories are neither determined *a priori* in the technical infrastructure and merely applied, nor do they arise exclusively from the interaction of users on a terrain that is quasi-technically neutral. It is therefore necessary to take into account technical preconditions, manners of use, and the interaction between them.

In our discussion of the ways in which Open Graph is used, we emphasized that, as a medium, it is a space of copresence that simulates communal presence and promises participation. A closer inspection indicated, however, that Open Graph in fact produces an overlapping of copresent spaces instead of individual spheres that are sealed off from one another. These groups are generated because their members engage with each other as a collective to share similar online content, to exchange opinions about it, and to create a feeling of togetherness by means of such interactions.[56] Their visibility is based on public

---

55   Markus Krajewski, "In Formation: Aufstieg und Fall der Tabelle als Paradigma der Datenverarbei-
     tung," *Nach Feierabend: Zürcher Jahrbuch für Wissensgeschichte* 3 (2007), 37–55, at 45.

56   This figure of thought is also discussed in the social sciences. For an overview of the treatment of
     virtual groups by social and media theorists, see Karin Dollhausen and Josef Wehner, "Virtuelle
     Gruppen: Integration durch Netzkommunikation? Gesellschafts- und medientheoretische Überle-
     gungen," in *Virtuelle Gruppen: Charakteristika und Problemdimensionen*, ed. Udo Thiedeke (Wi-
     esbaden: Westdeutscher Verlag, 2000), 68–87. From their social-scientific perspective, they discuss
     the relationship among social connections, communication, and technology in terms of changes in
     the constitution of society. Thus they maintain that modern forms of society entail an increase in
     individualization and the dissolution of traditional social forms. In this light, the technical infrastruc-
     ture of social networks and the interactions that such networks enable are thought to correspond to
     the need for "flexible" people to create non-binding, fluid, but temporarily stable social forms in
     which to situate their identities. Open Graph would thus be the medium of fluid social groups that
     exchange experiences and opinions and that enable their members to orient themselves both flexibly
     and with mobility. Such groups, however, are no longer to be understood as "social groups" in the
     strict sense, which are defined by their diffuse (though narrow) and above all stable interrelations.

forms of distribution and reception in which what is seen is comprehended and commented upon. The decisive moments consist in the comprehension of others' perceptions and in the circulation of opinions about them. It remains to be asked how the medial character of Facebook's Open Graph and the manner in which it is used correlate with organizations or orders of crowds. In order to pursue this question, it will be necessary to provide a historical examination of the ways in which media, the masses, and their arrangements or orders have been connected.

VI. Communication and the Masses: Gabriel Tarde and Crowd Psychology

Gabriel Tarde understood the public as a dispersed mass of physically separated individuals. On a mental level, however, these individuals are nevertheless capable of forming a collective. The mutual influence of individuals over one another, which Tarde referred to as "suggestion," results in a common opinion that is unified by the collective. By distributing and circulating opinions, the newspaper thus served (and serves) as a decisive medium for influencing people remotely.[57] According to Tarde, suggestion nevertheless takes place between readers, who unknowingly imitate the opinions expressed in the newspapers and share them with other readers. Crucial to all of this is that opinions or thoughts can circulate within a crowd so that the crowd can differentiate itself into collectives. Michael Gamper has summarized this process as follows: "The world of 'public spheres' was thus first of all the world of mechanical transmission media, then of thermodynamic transmission media, and finally of electromagnetic transmission media. Within the social units in question, these media were the actual bearers of suggestive exchange."[58]

Tarde's notion of the public (or public sphere) was based on his understanding of crowd psychology. Toward the end of the nineteenth century, a decisive question about crowds was how a mass of people – a disorderly congregation of individuals – could suddenly coalesce into a unit that, on the one hand, would function as something like a subject of activity and, on the other hand, would integrate individuals into itself in such a way that their individuality (and rationality) would dissolve. It is crucial to Tarde's understanding that, in a crowd, the normal social interrelations of imitation and suggestion increase in their intensity and speed. In such a way, the individual is transferred into a sort of common psychic condition, and it is this condition that gives unity to a crowd. Within the concept of public spheres, this common psychic condition is diminished to common opinion, but

---

On the concept of flexibility in modern society, see Richard Sennett, *The Corrosion of Character: The Personal Consequences of Work in the New Capitalism* (New York: Norton, 1998).

[57] For a discussion of Tarde's idea of the newspaper as a "social organism," see John Durham Peters, "Satan and Savior: Mass Communication in Progressive Thought," *Critical Studies in Mass Communication* 6 (1989), 247–63.

[58] Michael Gamper, "Charisma, Hypnose, Nachahmung: Massenpsychologie und Medientheorie," in *Trancemedien und neue Medien um 1900: Ein anderer Blick auf die Moderne*, ed. Marcus Hahn and Erhard Schüttpelz (Bielefeld: Transcript, 2009), 351–73, at 368.

such remote effects are based on the same principle as that which governs the influence of individuals over others in their presence.

As formulated by the likes of Tarde, Gustave Le Bon, and Scipio Sighele, early crowd psychology was concerned above all with the supposed irrationality that appears in crowds and that was thus assumed to be constitutive of them. At the moment of transference – something which is also integral to the knowledge of electromagnetism, hypnosis, and contagion – this irrationality is encapsulated in a certain way and thus made operational. Gamper has pointed out that the early theories of the cinema also relied on this type of knowledge. Perception, hypnosis, and transference became the *modus operandi* of these theories and were used to explain how an audience or public could become a community. Thus the formation of crowds is explained by a type of knowledge that is being attributed to the leadership of crowds. The irrationality of transference can now be implemented to turn a crowd into a unit.[59]

The early discourse about the interaction of media, the masses, and the public is thus characterized by three figures of thought. Fundamental to this discourse is the notion of transference, which is what brings individuals together in the first place and orders them into a commonality. On the one hand, this is associated with an idea of perception according to which it is common perception that initiates the process of transference (and is controllable by means of one apparatus or another). One the other hand, Tarde's notion of the public encompasses a concept of communication (or at least of distribution and circulation) that entails the formation of common opinion.

In considering Facebook's Open Graph as a space of copresence, it is important to understand the developments that have taken place in the crowd-psychological conception of media. Christina Bartz has investigated how the discourse about television in the 1950s and 1960s relied on the theories of crowd psychology and how it was in such terms that television first came to be discussed as a mass medium. Accordingly, the mass-medium theory of television correlates the dispersed or scattered masses with the discourse about perception and hypnosis that had defined early theories concerned with crowds and the cinema. Television is designed to be a medium of perception instead of a medium of communication and can thus function as a simulator of presence.[60]

Facebook's Open Graph protocol has reconfigured this mixture of transference, perception, and communication. With its form of visibility, which prompts users to see the same things that their "friends" have seen, Open Graph is thus associated with the discourse that regards television as a medium of collectivization based on perception. At the same time, Open Graph is presented as a medium of communication that not only displays links to content and to the interactions of others with this content but also circulates opinions and comments about it. In this regard, Open Graph is thus also associated with the understanding of public spheres in Tarde's sense of the concept. It is crucial that, in

---

[59]   See ibid., 366.

[60]   See Christina Bartz, *MassenMedium Fernsehen: Die Semantik der Masse in der Medienbeschreibung* (Bielefeld: Transcript, 2007), 15–16.

both of these traditions, the idea of transference serves as a sort of basis or undercurrent. It lies at the heart of the discourse and generates the sense of belonging together – the actual connectivity in question.

By now, transference has itself been transmuted into the technical realm and is realized as distribution and in the address management of friend lists. At the same time, it remains a crucial figure of thought for being able to imagine the staging of overlapping micro-publics as existing groups within a space of copresence. Open Graph thus reconfigures the constellation of transference, perception, and communication into a technical infrastructure that is staged as a simulator of presence. In line with the historical tradition outlined above, presence and participation are medially configured, even if they remain unoccupied in terms of content. Whereas communication and transference have been consolidated into a technological infrastructure, the level of perceptual content remains empty and demands to be filled in.

As a form of use, sharing one's perceptions on the internet may indeed comply with this demand, but it does not necessarily do so in accordance with the dictates of technological structure. In light of recent work by Ralf Adelmann and Hartmut Winkler, it is possible to understand the relationship between use and infrastructure in a more differentiated manner.[61] The concept of the "doubled subject" makes it clear that, as far as digital media are concerned, it is impossible to distinguish an unambiguous development with respect to the positions of the subject. Whereas postmodern critiques of the digital subject tend to stress the disempowerment of the subject's autonomy, the prevailing forms of the subject in computer games, for instance, happen to be coherent and capable of action. Adelmann and Winker have explained this "paradoxical" phenomenon by noting that there is a degree of interaction between real and imaginary levels. Thus the subject is able to compensate for its fragmentation (for instance, in the form of multiple individual bits of information that are stored in a database) by means of an imaginary coherence and thereby to maintain its capability to act. Crucial to this is precisely the interaction between both levels: "In metaphorical terms, the reenactment of the civil subject requires the *real* stage of the mediation and distribution of the subject in databases."[62]

Corresponding tendencies can also be identified in the case of belonging to groups on Facebook. The real fragmentation of the subject, which on the internet or in Open Graph only exists in the form of disparate database entries, is compensated for by the imagination of a group that shares common perceptions and opinions. When Adelmann and Winker speak of the pleasure that accompanies the change from being incapable of action to being capable of it, this is precisely the main characteristic of Facebook as a medium of col-

---

[61] See Ralf Adelmann and Hartmut Winker, "Kurze Ketten: Handeln und Subjektkonstitution in Computerspielen," *Ästhetik & Kommunikation* 148 (2010), 99–107; and Ralf Adelmann, "'There Is No Correct Way to Use the System': Datenbanklogiken und mediale Formen," in *Sortieren, Sammeln, Suchen, Spielen: Die Datenbank als mediale Praxis*, ed. Stefan Böhme et al. (Berlin: LIT Verlag, 2012), 253–67.

[62] Ibid., 255.

lectivization. In the act of fragmentation, the process of transference is given a degree of "free rein" – the subject finds itself once again within a cascade of impressions, and this situation is suggestive of openness, of a lack of limitations, and even of freedom. These impressions are given order within the context of a group. First, one's own newsfeed can serve as a sort of filter, something that must be taken into account because the group considers it to be "relevant." Second, the web content on the newsfeed has already been evaluated with regard to its ability to attract attention within the group. Third, the assembly of the newsfeed – the presentation of one's own online discoveries – can somewhat be regarded as a chain of action on the level of self-representation: The comments of "friends" concerning one's own "Likes" serve to confirm one's choices, generate attention, and enable the formation of common opinion. The circulation of one's "Likes" and the reaction to them mirror the individual as a perceiving, opinion-forming, and active subject. Thus there appear moments of causal effectiveness; the impression of copresence is felt; and the decentralized, fragmented subject regains its bearings. The copresent space of a communally perceiving group therefore supports the conception of an active and non-fragmented subject that is in control of its perception and action.

In this regard, the concept of the doubled subject goes beyond approaches that regard social media as belonging to a history of loss, according to which the postmodern potential of digital media was supposedly squandered.[63] Moreover, the integration of real and imaginary levels can be understood as a supplement to those philosophical and anthropological approaches whose point of departure is the "pleasure of self-fragmentation" or the demands for self-interrogation that are imposed by so-called technologies of the self.[64]

VII. The New Masses?

Our discussion of Facebook's Open Graph protocol has raised questions about the referent of a concept of the crowd that, on the one hand, is always already medially preconfigured and yet, on the other hand, is reflected in the medial. Our bipartite approach to the historical development of "organization" and to the idea of "communication" has made it clear that, in principle, Open Graph is not a novel phenomenon. Rather, it appears to be a tentative high point in the sociological practice of taking surveys, here based on an extremely expansive space of observation, a long-term outlook, and a medial infrastructure.

---

[63] This seems to be the position, for instance, of Geert Lovink, who complains that social media "are not postmodern machines but straightforward modernist products of the 1990s wave of digital globalization turned mass culture." Quoted from his introductory article "A World Beyond Facebook," in *Unlike Us Reader: Social Media Monopolies and Their Alternatives*, ed. Geert Lovink and Miriam Rasch (Amsterdam: Institute of Network Cultures, 2013), 9–15, at 12.

[64] See Gerald Raunig, "Dividuen des Facebook: Das neue Begehren nach Selbstzerteilung," in *Generation Facebook: Über das Leben im Social Net*, ed. Oliver Leistert and Theo Röhle (Bielefeld: Transcript, 2011), 145–60; Carolin Wiedemann, "Facebook: Das Assessment-Center der alltäglichen Lebensführung," in ibid., 161–82; and Hannelore Bublitz, *Im Beichtstuhl der Medien: Die Produktion des Selbst im öffentlichen Bekenntnis* (Bielefeld: Transcript, 2010).

That said, a new understanding the crowd or the masses has seemed to emerge from these constellations. The main contributor to this understanding is the interaction between technical infrastructure and user practices, both of which entail new forms of phantasmatic excess. In the case of infrastructure, what is at stake is the ability to comprehend emergence *in actu* by means of technical processes and thus the ability to overcome the reductive moment of traditional methodological approaches. Loss-free scalability should ultimately enable forms of control that recur in the momentum and self-organization of the masses being investigated. In the case of user practices, on the contrary, the main idea is to constitute a space of copresence by "sharing" content and circulating opinions about it. At the same time, this space represents a common sphere of activity and thus enables a degree of alternation between fragmentation and coherence.

In both cases, the phantasmatic excesses are associated with the change between various modes, an act of alternation that initiates a process of "filling things in" that is both continuous and compensatory. At the level of analysis, this process manifested itself in an increasingly dense sequence of methodological adjustments, which led to the conflation or layering of orders and forms of knowledge that were originally contradictory. Each of these adjustments has generated new empty spaces that demand to be filled in and has thus specifically contributed, by making various sorts of data available, to the enrichment of Open Graph. The meagerness or reduction that, despite such large amounts of data, is inherent to this conflation or layering is concealed by an elaborate form of staging. However, it is in no way guaranteed that users will necessarily "fall for" this staging. As our discussion of the "doubled subject" has made clear, it is rather the case that the users' imagination of belonging to a group can be understood as a gesture of compensation and thus as a form of actively "filling in" the reduction in question.

Our efforts suggest that the connection between empty spaces and phantasmatic excesses, which allow these spaces to be filled in, should be regarded as one of the decisive *medial* characteristics of social media. Paradoxically, however, it is precisely this view that is systematically obscured by the repeated references to the masses of people who use social media and by the massive amounts of collected data. When dealing with the masses, as our sketches of historical genealogies suggest, the need for infinite reduction seems to be immediately connected to the need for infinite inclusion.

Roland Meyer

Augmented Crowds
Identity Management, Face Recognition, and Crowd Monitoring

"The free citizen will show his face, say his name, and have an address." – Thomas de Maizière (German Minister of the Interior), *14 Thesen zu den Grundlagen einer gemeinsamen Netzpolitik der Zukunft* ["14 Theses on the Fundamentals of a Common Internet Policy for the Future"] (2009)

"Biometric face recognition has seen a number of advances since 2006, driven by the trend and popularity of social networking sites, the prevalence of mobile smart phone applications, and successful implementation in visa applications and in criminal and military investigations. Media giants such as Google, Apple, and Facebook now include face recognition in their products, and the commercial development of low-cost 'face sensors' (cameras with built-in face detection) is underway." – National Science and Technology Council (NSTC), Subcommittee on Biometrics and Identity Management, *The National Biometrics Challenge* (2011)

I. Augmented ID

He must have had a long night. Now, at a quarter past eight in the morning, the young man is standing in front of the mirror with disheveled hair and a crooked tie and preparing himself for another day at the office. Beyond typical bathroom activity, however, this routine also entails that the man has to turn on his smart phone and switch his public profile from "party mode" to "work mode." Once this has been done, whoever wants to learn any information about him will not be directed to his Facebook profile or Twitter feed but rather to his business card or to his latest professional presentation. This is a scene from a promotional video made by the Swedish company TAT, which designs user interfaces for smart phones. The concept being promoted is called "Augmented ID," and TAT advertises the idea with the slogan "Adding a digital layer to the real world to present yourself."[1] The video goes on: While the young man is clicking through a PowerPoint presentation at a meeting, his audience members are able point their phone cameras at him, and a face-recognition program calls up his profile onto their screens. With one of

---

[1] The video can be seen at http://www.tat.se/videos or on You Tube (http://www.youtube.com/watch?v=tbop Meg1UNo). Unless otherwise noted, the web addresses cited in this chapter were last accessed on March 9, 2013.

the icons that is floating around his face on the touchscreens, whoever so desires can look up his contact information and even rate and comment on his presentation. One member of the audience decides to give it four stars (even though the presentation has not even ended). In the final scene, a panoramic view of the room shows how Augmented ID will surround everyone there with a halo of icons. In other words, everyone present will be able to learn as much as they want about each other – business contacts, favorite songs on Last.fm, current Facebook statuses, and so on – without even having to ask. Of course, this also means that everyone gathered in the room will have to go through same identity management routine that the protagonist has performed in his bathroom. Everyone will have to decide, again and again, which digital mask to put on and which digital mask to take off.

Even though Augmented ID has not yet been fully developed, its promotional video offers a rather credible illustration of the convergence of social networks, mobile technologies, and face recognition. Essentially, the vision is one of an "augmented reality" in which every individual is constantly surrounded by a cloud of profile information and every social interaction can be linked to data operations. In this situation, every face is technologically recognizable and functions as a link to a public or semi-public profile that, for its part, is composed of various individual profiles on various social networks.

It is clear from several examples that there is a market for such applications and, moreover, that the necessary technology is largely available. In the summer of 2011, Facebook activated a highly controversial new feature that involved automatic face recognition. Previously, users of the social network themselves had to tag and identify pictures of their friends in order to assign names and profiles to one image or another, but now this process was supposed to take place (semi-)automatically. The new software compared pictures, grouped them together, and made suggestions about which recurring faces should be associated with which names.

More than two-hundred million pictures are uploaded onto Facebook every day, and thus the social network has become the largest database of images in the world. To the extent that more and more pictures are being tagged, and thus more and more people can be identified by name, Facebook has developed into the "registration office of the web," as Konrad Lischka has written for *Spiegel-Online*.[2] As more and more clearly identified photographs become available, face recognition software accordingly becomes more and more reliable. The company Face.com, which developed such software for web applications before being purchased by Facebook in 2012, claims that the probability of correctly identifying someone will increase considerably if at least ten pictures of this person have already been tagged.[3]

---

[2] Konrad Lischka, "Bilderkennung: Ich weiß, wer du bist," *Spiegel-Online* (August 2011), http://www.spiegel.de/netzwelt/netzpolitik/0,1518,777814,00.html.

[3] Face.com, "Documentation: Recognition How-To" (2011), http://developers.face.com/docs/recognition-howto/. I last accessed this page on December 1, 2011. It is no longer active.

Facebook was compelled to deactivate the feature after users had mounted large-scale protests and after data protection agencies had applied a considerable amount of legal pressure, at least in Europe. Yet the sheer number of pictures posted on social networks, which are relatively easy to access (not only due to inadequate security settings), has made them a valuable resource for automated identification programs that are unaffiliated with the networks themselves. In 2011, in fact, a research team at Carnegie Mellon University demonstrated quite clearly how easily the data on Facebook and other sites could be exploited by external systems. With commercial smart phones, web cams, and software from the company Pitt Patt, which was bought out by Google in the summer of that year, the researchers were able to identify the personal Facebook pages of a great number of people who were supposedly using a certain dating site "anonymously." From a representative sample of students on their campus, they were able to identify a third of them, using only unprotected and accessible profiles on social networks, and in several cases they were even able to access social security numbers and other sensitive data. The researchers summarized their findings as follows: "Your face is the veritable link between your offline identity and your online identit(ies). Data about your face and your name is, most likely, already publicly available online."[4] Faces have become the key to associating scattered and even anonymous profiles with one another.

It is thus no surprise that this form of cloud-powered face recognition has also been tested by the police. Since 2009, the European Union has supported a research project with the title INDECT, which stands for "Intelligent Information System Supporting Observation, Searching, and Detection for the Security of Citizens in Urban Environments." One goal of the project is to develop processes for connecting publicly accessible internet profiles with data from security cameras and police databases. In the near future, it is possible that face recognition techniques and behavioral pattern analysis will be implemented in drones and security cameras to identify suspicious people and potentially criminal behavior in urban areas.[5] It had been rumored that such technology

---

4   Alessandro Acquisti et al., "Faces of Facebook: Privacy in the Age of Augmented Reality" (2011), http://www.heinz.cmu.edu/~acquisti/face-recognition-study-FAQ. See also Jared Keller, "Cloud-Powered Facial Recognition Is Terrifying," *The Atlantic Monthly* (September 2011), http://www. theatlantic.com/ technology/archive/2011/09/cloud-powered-facial-recognition-is-terrifying/245867/.

5   See, for example, Kai Biermann, "Indect – der Traum der EU vom Polizeistaat," *ZEIT Online* (September 2009), http://www.zeit.de/digital/datenschutz/2009-09/indect-ueberwachung; and Jörg Thoma, "Indect – Bundesregierung finanziert Überwachungsprojekt mit," *Golem.de* (October 2011), www.golem.de/1110/87058.html. Similar steps are being taken in the United States, where the FBI has initiated a program called "Next Generation Identification." Its purpose is to supplement automated fingerprint recognition, which is already in place, with data from face and iris recognition, and presumably to allow all of this information to be compared with publicly available data from social networks. For the FBI's own description of this program, see http://www.fbi.gov/about-us/ cjis/fingerprints_biometrics/ngi. For criticism of these developments, see Jennifer Lynch, "FBI's Facial Recognition is Coming to a State Near You," *Electronic Frontier Foundation* (August 2012), https://www.eff.org/deeplinks/2012/07/fbis_facial_recognition_coming_state_ near_you.

was already to be used as early as 2012 at the European Championship games in Poland and the Ukraine, but this has been denied by authorities.[6] Of course, this does not mean that the European Championship did not serve as a testing ground for advanced security systems. Upon entering the National Stadium in Warsaw, for instance, all of the attendees were recorded on camera, and images of their faces were compared with the information on their personalized admission tickets. Throughout the game, 370 surveillance cameras monitored the stands, and face-recognition software was supposedly able to identify each and every fan unambiguously at any given time.[7]

The use of face-recognition software at large sporting events has a prehistory. One of the largest tests of face recognition in a public (or semi-public) space was conducted at Super Bowl XXXV in Tampa, which took place in January of 2001. Without their knowledge or consent, more than seventy thousand attendees were recorded by security cameras as they entered the stadium. A program known as Viisage then compared their facial features – the width of their mouths, the position of their eyes and nostrils, and so on – with mug shots collected in police databases. The result at the time was somewhat sobering for the authorities: The software raised several alarms, mostly false, and no arrests were made on the basis of its findings.[8]

The year 2001 was important to the history of biometric recognition for another reason as well. In response to the attacks on 9/11, the United States and Europe instituted new security measures for air travel and border crossings, and these measures included the mandated use of electronically scannable passports for the sake of biometric identification. As early as January of 2001, the *MIT Technology Review* named biometrics one of the "top ten technologies that will change the world."[9] The introduction of biometric-compatible passports in the European Union, which occurred in 2005, can be understood as a form of state investment in the development of a promising branch of industry; according to Otto Schily, who was the German Minister of the Interior at the time, "The passports will

---

[6] Konrad Lischka and Ole Reissmann, "EU-Überwachungsprojekt Indect: Die volle Kontrolle," *Spiegel-Online* (November 2012), http://www.spiegel.de/netzwelt/netzpolitik/eu-ueberwachungsprojekt-indect-die-volle-kontrolle-a-866785.html.

[7] Rafael Buschmann, "Fans in Polens Fußballstadien: Kontrolliert, gefilmt, überwacht," *Spiegel-Online* (2012), http://www.spiegel.de/wissen/schaft/technik/fussball-em-polen-installiert-hunderte-kameras-in-stadien-a-837380.html.

[8] See John D. Woodward, *Super Bowl Surveillance: Facing Up to Biometrics* (Santa Monica: Rand, 2001). For a detailed and critical history of biometric face recognition, especially in the United States, see Kelly Gates, *Our Biometric Future: Facial Recognition Technology and the Culture of Surveillance* (New York: New York University Press, 2011). On the topic of video surveillance and face recognition, see also Dietmar Kammerer, *Bilder der Überwachung* (Frankfurt am Main: Suhrkamp, 2008).

[9] Quoted from Woodward, *Super Bowl Surveillance*, 4

be economically important as well. We will be able to show that Germany has the know-how and innovative capabilities to set the standards in the new sector of biometrics."[10]

Given that biometric identification techniques have broken into the mass market, these investments seem to have paid off. What was at first developed and advanced by police forces, militaries, and secret services is now being used for purposes quite different from identifying criminals, monitoring the streets, and securing borders. Such technology has rather become an increasingly marketable aspect of consumer electronics: USB fingerprint readers are now used to secure access to sensitive data on laptops; Picasa, an image organizer owned by Google, allows users to browse through their private pictures with a face-recognition program; and game consoles equipped with 3-D cameras are able to distinguish between the various players standing in front of the television screen.

A more recent phenomenon known as "gigatagging" is predicated on the fact that, in certain cases, the desire of users to identify themselves in pictures is so strong that automatic face recognition is not even necessary. In addition to panoramic views of landscapes, the website gigapixel.com also contains photographs of sporting events and urban crowds. Thousands of hockey fans who watched game seven of the Stanley Cup finals in Vancouver can be seen in a photograph taken on June 15, 2011. The picture, which at first resembles a chaotic blur, can be enlarged like the images on Google Earth until each individual face is clearly distinguishable.[11] This mass panorama is in fact not a singular image but rather a composite of more than two hundred individual photographs that were taken over the course of about fifteen minutes. Yet it is only when the picture is fully enlarged – and under close inspection – that one can see the "seams" where the individual pictures have been sewn together. Visitors to the site are encouraged to tag themselves and their friends, that is, to provide each face with a link to a corresponding Facebook profile. Hundreds of people have already participated, and in doing so they have probably also identified a number of acquaintances who were not even with them at the event in question (Thomas Thiel has referred to this phenomenon a "manhunt among friends").[12] The company Orange Mobile had done something similar for the Glastonbury

---

10   Quoted from a press report issued by the Federal Ministry of the Interior on June 1, 2005. The report can be read online at http://www.pressrelations.de/new/standard/result_main.cfm?aktion=jour_ pm&r=192039. Regarding electronic passports, see also Roland Meyer, "Bildbesprechung: Lichtbildbelehrungen. Bilder im Grenzbereich. Die e-Pass-Fotomustertafeln der Bundesdruckerei," in *Bildwelten des Wissens. Kunsthistorisches Jahrbuch für Bildkritik 4.2: Bilder ohne Betrachter*, ed. Horst Bredekamp et al. (Berlin: Akadamie Verlag, 2006), 64–68.

11   See http://www.gigapixel.com/image/gigatag-canucks-g7.html.

12   Thomas Thiel, "Die tausend Augen der Biometrie," *Frankfurter Allgemeine Zeitung* (July 2011), http://www.faz.net/aktuell/feuilleton/debatten/digitales-denken/gesichtserkennung-die-tausend-augen-der-biometrie-11111864.htm. A closer look at gigapixel.com, however, reveals that the number of falsely identified faces seems to be rather high.

Festival in 2010. According to their website, nearly ten thousand faces were tagged in crowd photographs, which was supposedly a world record at the time.[13]

In theses cases, the crowd identifies itself – though retrospectively, after it has dissolved. The virtual gathering of festival-goers consists of hundreds of individual profiles, while the crowd photographs serve as the interface with which the individuals in question can subsequently locate themselves within a mass experience. The commercial value of this for Orange Mobile lies in so-called post-event marketing and in prolonging the consumer experience and its associations with the sponsoring company. However, the fact that such large-scale instances of self-identification might also be of interest to security forces is made clear by a somewhat off-putting caption above the crowd picture taken in Vancouver: "Before the riot." After the home team had lost – to recall – the peaceful and joyful scene captured in the image gave way to massive riots in the streets. During the subsequent police investigations, digital images of the crowds happened to be quite useful to law enforcement agencies. In order to identify offenders, the authorities scoured through vast amounts of video material that fans and passers-by had recorded on their mobile phones and made available to the police.[14]

II. Unlikely Repetitions

Since the onset of modernity, crowds and the act of identification have been closely associated with one another. Identification has always been a means to cope with contingency. It serves to filter out the repetition of significant patterns from streams of people, data, and images, and it makes use of such recurrences to differentiate and address individual subjects. Essentially, biometrics is thus a means to filter and select on the basis of repetitions and probabilities. It identifies configurations of features that repeat themselves and allows for such features to be associated with a name, a profile and a person. Since the nineteenth century, the process of identifying people for police records has been concerned with masses and crowds – with anonymous urban throngs, with real or imaginary masses of undetected repeat offenders, but also with the increasingly expansive amounts of data collected by the police itself.

From the perspective of security forces and the apparatuses of control, masses and crowds have been a problem of assigning correct addresses, and this is as true today as it was then. In this regard, the *crowd* is something like the opposite of the *archive*, namely a disorderly gathering in physical space. Identification, on the contrary, means isolation, registration, and designation, and it is based on the production of standardized conditions that allow for the comparison of repeating features. Such was the case as early as 1882,

---

[13]   This information was taken from http://glastonbury.orange.co.uk/glastotag/, which I accessed on December 1, 2011. Although the particular site is no longer active, a video can be seen at http://vimeo.com/19790160.

[14]   The Vancouver Police Department even set up a website where people could post information about possible suspects: https://riot2011.vpd.ca.

when, in Paris, Alphonse Bertillon developed the method of Bertillonage or anthropometric identification. Instead of relying on vague information about a suspect's stature, hair color, and physique, Bertillon based his technique on measurable data that could be recorded alongside photographs on standardized index cards. This required an anthropological approach to identification that was grounded in statistics. He would begin his measurements of a suspect by recording the length of his head, which he would then sort into three categories: average, above average, or below average. The methodological basis of this classification was the statistical notion of normal distribution (each of the three segments of a bell curve represents a subset of equal size). These categories were further classified according to the width of a suspect's head, the length of his (or her) middle finger and forearm, and so on. With such a system in place, it was possible to organize an archive of thousands of index cards into manageable sections with no more than a dozen entries per drawer.[15]

Today, four categories are used to classify biometric features: universality, distinctiveness, robustness, and measurability. In order to serve as a distinguishing trait, a physical characteristic therefore has to be present in all people, slightly different in everyone, unchanging over time, and quantifiable by means of one technology or another. The biometric criteria of distinctiveness and robustness, however, are relative quantities. Instead of a certain feature being understood as entirely unique and absolutely permanent, the quantitative extents to which a physical characteristic varies within a given population or changes over time become the "criteria to distinguish the qualities of biometric systems."[16] Bertillon's measuring procedures were insufficient in both of these respects, and at the beginning of the twentieth century his methods were therefore superseded by fingerprint identification. Although Bertillon was able to narrow down his searches quite well with his archive, his final proof for identifying someone still depended on photographs and the special "discriminating features" of the suspects. With fingerprints, however, identities could be determined with remarkable certitude, and Francis Galton and the other founders of dactyloscopy were able to provide statistical evidence for the uniqueness of papillary ridges. The arrangement and distribution of so-called "minutiae," which are the characteristic points at which individual ridges come to an end or branch off, show such a high

---

[15] See Allan Sekula, "The Body and the Archive," in *Contest of Meaning: Critical Histories of Photography*, ed. Richard Bolton (Cambridge, MA: MIT Press, 1992), 344–89; Milos Vec, *Die Spur des Täters: Methoden der Identifikation in der Kriminalistik (1870–1933)* (Baden-Baden: Nomos, 2002); and Roland Meyer, "Detailfragen: Zur Lektüre erkennungsdienstlicher Bilder," in *Verwandte Bilder: Die Fragen der Bildwissenschaft*, ed. Ingeborg Reichle et al. (Berlin: Kadmos, 2007), 191–208.

[16] John D. Woodward et al., *Biometrics: A Look at Facial Recognition* (Santa Monica: Rand, 2003), 1.

level of variance that their recurrence in nature is supposed to be extremely unlikely.[17] To this day, "nature does not repeat itself" serves as an axiom of biometric identification.[18]

III. Identity Without the Person

Over the past few years, one of the most vocal critics of biometric identification has been Giorgio Agamben. In response to the stringent entry requirements initiated by the United States after 9/11, he wrote a widely publicized short essay in 2004 with the title "Bodies Without Words: Against the Biopolitical Tattoo." Because of his refusal to have his fingerprints taken, which foreign visitors to the country are now obligated to do, Agamben resigned from his faculty position at New York University. In his essay, he objected to "the appropriation and registration of the most private and unsheltered element, that is the biological life of bodies." Through this reduction to "bare life," to a mute "body without words," he believed that individuals would be politically incapacitated, and he did not hesitate to compare this practice to the compulsory tattoos given at concentration camps.[19]

In a later essay, Agamben took it upon himself to elaborate upon his critique of biometric registration. At the heart of his discussion is the concept of the person. His diagnosis is that an "identity without the person" has come to replace personal identity, a process that began with the police records taken around the year 1900 and has culminated in the biometric systems of the present day. Agamben argues that the goal of biometrics is not the recognition (*Anerkennung*) of the person – which is always a social act – but rather the mechanical recognition (*Wiedererkennung*) of features and data records. The word *persona* originally denoted a "mask," and the person is thus a social role whose identity is produced by society. People become persons when they are recognized as such by others, and recognition as a person comes with certain rights and privileges. As a moral person, my relationship to this role is ambivalent, in that I can choose to adopt it or I can distance myself from it. First developed in the nineteenth century, police methods of identification have served to disconnect identity from the person and its recognition; the societal mask has been set aside, and identity has been fused with the biological features and characteristics of the body. To Agamben, this "identity without the person" is no longer engendered by society and adopted by individuals; it is rather defined in terms of biology and specified by means of technology. Instead of identifying myself with a social mask, which I can wear without being reduced to it, I have been reduced to impersonal data, data about my biological existence that is technologically recorded and processed.[20]

---

[17]   See Francis Galton, *Finger Prints*, 2nd ed. (New York: Da Capo Press, 1965); and Simon A. Cole, *Suspect Identities: A History of Fingerprinting and Criminal Identification* (Cambridge, MA: Harvard University Press, 2001).

[18]   Vec, *Die Spur des Täters*, 61.

[19]   Giorgio Agamben, "Bodies Without Words: Against the Biopolitical Tattoo," trans. Peer Zumbansen, *German Law Review* 5 (2004), 168–69.

[20]   Giorgio Agamben, "Identity Without the Person," in *Nudities*, trans. David Kishik and Stefan Pedatella (Stanford: Stanford University Press, 2011), 46–54.

There is a literary precedent to Agamben's notion of "identity without the person." In *The Man Without Qualities*, Robert Musil has his protagonist Ulrich experience something quite similar, namely the "statistical disenchantment of his person."[21] Ulrich, the man without qualities, happens to be arrested in the fortieth chapter of the novel. The occasion for the arrest is almost as trivial as it is random, and yet before Ulrich is able to explain matters, he finds himself at the police station. The arrest resembles an encounter with a *Doppelgänger*, for the description of himself that Ulrich confronts at the station is unquestionably a description of *him*. However, although this description may be proof of his identity, it is in no way identical to him – on the contrary: "His face counted only from the point of view of 'description.' He had the feeling that he had never before thought about the fact that his eyes were grey eyes, belonging to one of the four officially recognized kinds of eyes in existence of which there were millions of specimens. His hair was fair, his build tall, his face oval, and his special peculiarities were none, although he himself was of a different opinion on this score."[22] Interestingly enough, Ulrich is able to derive a good deal of fascination from the disenchantment of his person: "The most wonderful thing about it was that the police could not only dismantle a human being in this way so that nothing remained of him, but they would also put him together again out of these trifling components, unmistakably himself, and recognize him by them."[23]

What happens at the police station could be called a transformation of characteristics into features. Characteristics lose their intrinsic qualities and become generally available. Identification does not operate with singular peculiarities, for such things cannot be compared. Isolated details such as one's eye color and body size, which "mean" nothing in themselves, become identifying features when their combination with other impersonal traits is highly unlikely to be confused with another person's combination of features. The "impersonal" aspect of identity is not the body reduced to its bare biological factuality, as Agamben supposed; it is rather the mass existence of the features with which it can be identified. As probable or improbable differentiators, these features always exist outside of the individual persons whom they make recognizable. They represent repetitions or deviations within statistically normalized multitudes. Every act of identification entails the conjuring of virtual and latent masses of people, the inestimable masses of other bodies. The crowd is not only the counter-image of biometric databases and identity indexes; it is also their prerequisite, and this is because biometric identity is always relational, based as it is on significant differences within large-scale distributions. The statistical disenchantment of the person locates these differences within pre-recorded sets of comparative data, and its most impersonal element is not the biological body but rather the masses of other bodies with which the latter is compared.

---

21   Robert Musil, *The Man Without Qualities*, trans. Eithne Wilkins and Ernst Kaiser, vol. 1 (London: Secker & Warburg, 1966), 186.
22   Ibid., 185.
23   Ibid., 186.

IV. Anonymous Masses

Urban crowds have engendered fascination and horror since the nineteenth century, if not before. They are a particular product of the modern city, of acceleration, anonymity, and the fragmentation of all aspects of life.[24] While the masses can simply be regarded as a quantitatively determinable multitude of each and everyone, from a bourgeois perspective they have long represented the "other" – the rabble, hoi polloi, the "dangerous classes." The discourse of crowd psychology, which reached its zenith in the last decades of the nineteenth century, is an expression of bourgeois anxiety about the unpredictability of such masses.[25] According to this discipline, the masses are the milieu in which human beings revert to a violent natural condition that was thought to have been overcome. In this light, crowd psychology is not so distantly related to criminal anthropology, and thus it was above all the potentially criminal and seditious masses that interested the likes of Scipio Sighele and Gustave Le Bon during the 1880s and 1890s. To them, the masses are anonymous and in fact cannot be named. They have no identity of their own; individual identities dissolve in them. For Le Bon, crowds seem to be a force of nature that causes personality to disappear, allows unconscious instincts to have the upper hand, and hypnotizes or infects individuals to move in a common direction.[26] As revenants of a prehistoric era, Le Bon's crowds collectively revert to an atavistic and primitive stage, and thus the discourse of crowd psychology is closely connected to the general fear of degeneration that prevailed during the late nineteenth century.[27] More than anything else, crowd psychology is the psychopathology of crowds.[28] Then again, not a few of its ascriptions seem like the phantasmatic opposite of police efforts to maintain order and identify wrongdoers. Crowds were thought to be formless and indistinguishable, and their prevailing logic was believed to be one of similarity, imitation, and infection. This logic seemed to make it nearly impossible to differentiate individuals with distinguishable characteristics, and thus it seemed likewise impossible to ascribe individual blame to any of these individuals or to hold any one of them responsible for any given act.

The threatening and disorderly masses of the nineteenth century lost a good deal of their abhorrence by the 1920s. During the years between the wars, authors as various as Siegfried Kracauer and Ernst Jünger noticed the emergence of new, disciplined, and Fordistic mass formations. To them, such formations no longer represent the opposite of

---

[24] For a comprehensive discourse history of crowds, see Michael Gamper, *Masse lesen, Masse schreiben: Eine Diskurs-und Imaginationsgeschichte der Menschenmenge, 1765–1930* (Munich: W. Fink, 2007).

[25] See Christiane Heilbach's chapter in the present book.

[26] Gustave Le Bon, *The Crowd: A Study of the Popular Mind* (New York: Macmillan, 1896), 1–15.

[27] See Daniel Pick, *Faces of Degeneration: A European Disorder, c. 1848–c. 1918* (Cambridge: Cambridge University Press, 1989), 93.

[28] See Stefan Johnson, "The Invention of the Masses: The Crowd in French Culture from the Revolution to the Commune," in *Crowds*, ed. Jeffrey T. Schnapp and Matthew Thiews (Stanford: Stanford University Press, 2006), 47–75, at 73.

order but rather the indispensable bearer of orderliness itself. Published in 1927, Kracauer's essay "The Mass Ornament" begins with a discussion of the staged and synchronized mass formations of gymnasts in a stadium and dancers on a stage. In mass ornaments such as these, individuals are merely building blocks – exchangeable elements or "fractions of a figure."[29] Kracauer regards the impression of abstract figures onto living bodies as a visible expression of the capitalist production process: "[I]t is only as a tiny piece of the mass that the individual can clamber up charts and can service machines without any friction. A system oblivious to differences in form leads on its own to the blurring of national characteristics and to the production of worker masses that can be employed equally well at any point on the globe."[30] In his book *Der Arbeiter* (1932), Ernst Jünger similarly remarks that modern technology has transformed the potentially dangerous masses of the nineteenth century into a disciplined army of workers. This was accomplished, he thought, by means of the Tayloristic optimization of the work process as well as by the complex networks and infrastructures of bureaucracy, technology, and transportation.[31] The new, Fordistic mass formations of the 1920s are not defined by a common desire; they are rather an expression of an external and rigid order. In Jünger's description, such masses are made to resemble a cinematographic sequence of shocks and sensations. The masses, he writes, "are perceived as interlaced ribbons and concatenated streaks of faces that rush by in a flash, and also as ant-like colonies whose forward motion is no longer subject to rampant desire but rather to an automatic form of discipline."[32]

To Le Bon and others, the dreaded masses of the nineteenth century evinced the raw and uncontrollable animal nature of human beings. To Kracauer and Jünger, on the contrary, the masses of the 1920s called to mind a higher and abstract level of order. In both cases, however, the masses in question consist of homogeneous, indistinguishable, and faceless elements that are fully subordinate to the crowd itself, regardless of whether it is compulsive or disciplined.

V. Crowds in Augmented Space

Police identification was and remains an attempt to differentiate these seemingly faceless mobs, namely by finding statistically significant features that enable individuals to be addressed unequivocally. However, it is not only the job of the police records department to differentiate the masses on a statistical basis. This is rather a central concern of the social sciences as well, including their commercial applications in the fields of advertising, public relations, and marketing. Whenever these fields turn their attention from determining target groups or market segments to establishing individualized client relations, the primary

---

29   Siegfried Kracauer, "The Mass Ornament," in *The Mass Ornament: Weimar Essays*, trans. Thomas Y. Levin (Cambridge, MA: Harvard University Press, 1995), 75–88, at 76.

30   Ibid., 78.

31   See Anton Kaes, "Movies and Masses," in *Crowds*, ed. Jeffrey T. Schnapp and Matthew Thiews (Stanford: Stanford University Press, 2006), 149–57, at 152.

32   Ernst Jünger, *Der Arbeiter: Herrschaft und Gestalt* (Stuttgart: Klett-Cotta, 1982), 101–02.

issue becomes the proper attribution of consumer decisions. While the "salaried masses" of employees described by Kracauer in 1930 – not to mention the "other-directed" people that constituted David Riesman's "lonely crowd" in the 1950s – were already treated by advertisers and the culture industry as individual consumers, it was only in exceptional circumstances that they were addressed as identifiable economic agents.[33] Their individual preferences gained relevance only in the form of huge quantities: sales numbers, circulation rates, and radio or television ratings. Today, on the contrary, every single consumer decision creates added value; each decision contributes more information to a consumer's profile, which can in turn be treated like a commodity in itself. Consumer feedback, moreover, is now being processed more and more quickly and directly by distributors, marketers, and manufacturers.[34] Consumers are in fact rewarded for participating in such feedback loops – with product recommendations, rebates, and so on – and at the same time it is becoming more and more inconvenient *not* to participate in them.[35] Data collection has become strikingly excessive, and this is especially so because it has become more and more inexpensive to gather, save, process, and transfer information. No longer sporadic and partial, the collection of data is now taking place more or less continuously.[36]

If the person, in Agamben's sense of the word, had once been a stabile social mask whose statistical disenchantment was essentially experienced as a reduction to abstract and technologically detectable features, "identities without the person" have now been developed and expanded into complex profiles. Such profiles are the result of countless individual activities, decisions, transactions, and movements; and they define themselves against the immense background of data that can be statistically and sociometrically evaluated.[37] As David Joselit has written: "We are all profiles: data records collected from innumerable consumer decisions, about whose consequences we are scarcely aware."[38] Although profiles can easily be distinguished from one another, their form at any given time is dependent on the type of access that leads to them. The elements of a profile are weighted differently, that is, depending on the search terms that are used to find it and the interests (or profiles) of those wishing to access it. Profiles collect previous consumer decisions and expressions of interest in order to identify potential customers, and they collect previous examples of suspicious behavior in order to identify potential threats. Although they are open-ended collections of data that can be supplemented and expanded

---

[33] See Siegfried Kracauer, *The Salaried Masses: Duty and Distraction in Weimar Germany*, trans. Quintin Hoare (London: Verso, 1998); and David Riesman, *The Lonely Crowd: A Study of the Changing American Character* (New Haven: Yale University Press, 1961).

[34] Greg Elmer, *Profiling Machines: Mapping the Personal Information Economy* (Cambridge, MA: MIT Press, 2004), 71.

[35] Ibid., 49.

[36] Rob Kitchin and Martin Dodge, *Code/Space: Software and Everyday Life* (Cambridge, MA: MIT Press, 2011), 98–99.

[37] On the relationship between statistics and sociometrics, as they are used by Facebook, see Irina Kaldrack and Theo Röhle's contribution to this book.

[38] David Joselit, "Profile," in *Texte zur Kunst* 73 (2009), 75–81 (http://www.textezurkunst.de/73/profile).

in any given way, profiles can nevertheless be understood as definable unities, at least to the extent that only information that can be related to a single, identifiable person becomes part of his or her profile. Such profiles, therefore, are simultaneously open and closed quantities. Admittedly, individual profiles on Facebook or other sites are centrally managed, but even in this regard it is clear that the amount of data that is saved internally far exceeds the complex of data that appears on the user interface. In that users maintain multiple accounts and profiles on various sites, and in that these can be associated with one another and with other data complexes by means of a user's own links or by a third party's targeted search, volumes of data emerge that, as a whole, seem to have no fixed location and no fixed address even though each of their elements remains discretely addressable. Identity dissolves into a network of relations, a scattered and diffuse multitude with blurry boundaries. The result is that we have permanently lost control over the data that we produce and over the data that we collect. And yet, as "agents and authors" of our own profiles, we are nevertheless encouraged to keep this information up to date and even to associate ourselves with it.[39] The presumably clear separation of social recognition (*Anerkennung*) and technological identification (*Erkennung*), which has been the impetus behind Agamben's argument, is in fact becoming more and more blurry as social networks such as Facebook have begun to formalize, technologically, the very structures that underlie the rituals of social recognition.

Individual profiles now seem to be subsets of larger sets of data, while collective entities are treated as something that emerges from incessant operations of gathering and linking individual pieces of information. This is true not only for the latent and scattered masses that are brought together by social media networks; it also applies to the manifest and concentrated crowds of people who occupy seats in stadiums or who gather anywhere in urban spaces. One of the theses of this essay is that it has become more and more difficult to distinguish between these two types of crowds, let alone call them opposites. Rather, massive efforts are being made to establish stabile connections between latent and manifest crowds and to fuse them together into a single continuum. Throughout this process, the face is able to serve as one of several possible links that are used to connect physical bodies with digital profiles. It is generally more suitable for this than other biometric features because its digitally reproduced image is readily available in both spheres, assuming that such images are already circulating on the internet and have been recorded by security cameras in actual situations. The availability of facial images is opposed by the unavailability of the face itself, which is difficult to exchange, remove, or conceal – a fact that explains the immense interest in face-recognition systems.[40] Face recognition, however, is only one the possible ways to achieve such ends; mobile telephones, for instance, have been far more effective in this regard. Whereas the technological detection of faces

---

[39]   See Joselit's article, cited in the previous note, as well as Carolin Wiedemann, "Facebook: Das Assessment-Center der alltäglichen Lebensführung," in *Generation Facebook: Über das Leben im Social Net*, ed. Oliver Leistert and Theo Röhle (Bielefeld: Transcript, 2011), 161–82.

[40]   Here I should thank Hartmut Winkler for suggesting this line of thinking.

generates complex amounts of highly variable data that can only be made operational by means of rather error-prone algorithms, smart phones emit unambiguous address data.

As soon as each and every individual in a crowd can be recorded, identified, and associated with a data profile – by whatever means – a new mass formation will emerge that will have hardly anything in common with the anonymous crowds in modern cities. In Lev Manovich's terms, it might then be possible to speak of "augmented crowds" or of masses operating in an "augmented space," where physical gatherings are superimposed with huge amounts of digital information.[41] The descriptions of the masses in the nineteenth and twentieth centuries underscored the moment of homogeneity, the leveling of differences produced by human crowds; individuals, in other words, were thought to lose themselves in crowds and become indistinguishable. Augmented crowds, on the contrary, are highly differentiated and scalable masses. They are a product of the technologically realized possibility of shifting one's view from single elements of a crowd to the crowd as a whole, from individuals to nearly any given micro-gatherings, and from there to subgroups and immense multitudes. And they are product of being able to do all of this while ensuring that each level can be addressed and quantified. This new image of the crowd differs from previous conceptions in a second way as well. Because every physical gathering is limited by space and time, crowds were always regarded as fleeting and unstable formations. However, now that physical gatherings have become the object of comprehensive data processing, their temporality has changed accordingly; the information that refers to them can now be retrieved now or later, here or elsewhere. According to crowd psychology, the crowd was a collective without memory. Its members would literally forget themselves in order to act as though in a trance. With our new technological capabilities, the previously fleeting masses now seem to be archivable. What is more, today's crowds even make records of themselves.[42]

Whereas the process of gigatagging provides information about large gatherings after the fact, engineers working on crowd monitoring are attempting to analyze them in real time. In this case it is typically mobile phones – rather than faces – that are used to locate individuals in a crowd. During the summer of 2012, for instance, the German Research Center for Artificial Intelligence and the London Police Department collaborated on a project that enabled authorities to "follow the streams of visitors during the Olympic Games 'live' in their borough, […] recognize potentially hazardous situations early on, and inform the visitors directly."[43] For this to work, voluntary participants allowed the coordinates of their smart phones to be monitored. On the basis of this data, so-called "heat maps" were created that, like infrared images, used a scale of colors from light blue

---

[41]   See Lev Manovich, "The Poetics of Augmented Space," *Visual Communication* 5 (2006), 219–40.

[42]   I am grateful to Ute Holl for sharing this idea with me.

[43]   Quoted from a press release that the German Research Center for Artificial Intelligence posted on its own website: "Crowd-Monitoring Makes the Olympics Safer: Smartphone-Apps Support the Security Forces in London" (July 2012), http://www.dfki.de/web/presse/pressemitteilungen_intern/2012/crowd%20monitoring.

to red in order to indicate "in which direction and at what speed the crowds are moving and where conglomerations of people can reach critical dimensions."[44] The participants in this project seem to have played two strange roles at once. Their behavior was treated as being representative of the actual crowds, and projections and prognoses about overall crowd behavior were made on the basis of their activity. They were thus part of a potentially hazardous mass (and only as such were they of interest to the security forces), and yet at the same time they were addressed as responsible individuals who were actively participating in the circumvention of such dangerous situations: "For example, if the system shows congestion at an underground station, it will recommend people to go to the nearest alternative station via its built-in messaging function."[45]

This sort of ambivalence seems to be typical of such crowd monitoring systems, and perhaps of augmented crowds in general. Every action undertaken by a crowd as a whole, by its subsets, and by its individual components is continuously classified as more or less threatening or cooperative, whereby cooperation is often synonymous with consumption. So much can be made clear by citing a final example. Since 2011, the San Francisco-based company CrowdOptic has offered analytic tools to organizers of large sporting events that allow them to track where spectators are focusing their attention. The software tracks mobile phones, with which fans take pictures and videos of the event, and it uses GPS and compass data to monitor the position of the phones and the direction that they are pointing. By means of triangulation, moreover, the system is also able to determine the precise locations within a stadium that are attracting the most attention: "Location is good, focus is better," as CrowdOptic's slogan maintains. At the same time, the company also offers augmented-reality services for individual users: "CrowdOptic knows where all the mobile phones in the crowd are looking as they aim their phones; it can not only transmit this insight to the enterprise, but can also display relevant content on the phones according to the action each fan is watching, all in real time."[46] This overlaid information contributes to the appeal of participating in the data collection itself; it becomes part of the very pictures and videos that are being taken and can be tracked when they are posted online. The service promises to provide "hyper-targeted in-venue advertising, broadcast-

---

[44] Ibid. Another form of crowd monitoring, likewise implemented in London during 2012, relied on the MAC addresses of Bluetooth chips used in mobile devices, which could be monitored by city-wide scanners. According to the authorities responsible for the project, the monitoring was entirely anonymous. The system was able to determine how long a given visitor stayed in one place and how much time was required to move from one place to another, but the encryption of the MAC addresses prevented the system from being able to identify, say, the telephone numbers of the people under surveillance. See the report by the Olympic Delivery Authority: "Learning Legacy – Lessons Learned from the London 2012 Games Construction Project: Pedestrian and Crowd Monitoring" (January 2013), http://learninglegacy.independent.gov.uk/publications/pedestrian-and-crowd-monitoring.php.

[45] "Crowd Monitoring Makes the Olympics Safer" (cited above).

[46] See Bruce Sterling, "Augmented Reality: CrowdOptic Crowd Behavior Analytics," *Wired.com* (September 2011), http://www.wired.com/beyond_the_beyond/2011/09/augmented-reality-crowdoptic-crowd-behavior-analytics/.

ing, and security," and thus to offer several benefits for organizers and producers. First, they are able to receive live images of where the spectators are directing their focus, and this enables them to optimize the drama of a given event and to place advertisements in more strategic locations. Second, they are able to track the online circulation of videos after an event has concluded, which allows them to improve their post-event marketing and to monitor for potential copyright infringements. Finally there is the issue of safety and crowd control: "Using advanced algorithms, CrowdOptic alerts the enterprise in real-time to shifts in fan focus and momentum, as well as anomalous activity in the crowd." According to this line of thinking, safety risks manifest themselves first of all as anomalous shifts of attention. Danger looms, that is, as soon as the public ceases to focus on the game. At any given point, depending on the fluctuations of the incoming data produced by the crowd, a shift can thus take place from merely observing consumers to controlling the crowd. Here, to some extent, the crowd functions to govern itself with what could be called "crowd-sourced crowd control."

Such an augmented crowd is neither an atavistic force of nature nor an abstract mass ornament; it is rather a technologically enhanced and differentiable matrix of continuous data streams. Its consumption is productive to the extent that it incessantly provides more and more information about itself. Even its fluctuating attention and whimsical unpredictability can be statistically analyzed and exploited for profit. The responses of crowds are no longer thought to reflect the human instincts of times past; they are rather analyzed to make forecasts about the future. Impending disasters can supposedly be foretold by the teeming activity of the masses, whose behavioral patterns unwittingly anticipate future events.[47] Thus, too, the opposition has vanished between compulsive instincts and discipline, between life and form – the very opposition that, in one way or another, had characterized previous descriptions of the masses. In the end, augmented crowds are simultaneously spontaneous and predictable, passionate and controlled.

---

[47] This logic bears some resemblances to what Richard Grusin has termed "premediation." See Richard Grusin, *Premediation: Affect and Mediality after 9/11* (Houndmills/New York: Palgrave Macmillan, 2010); and Carolin Gerlitz, "Die *Like Economy*: Digitaler Raum, Daten und Wertschöpfungen," in *Generation Facebook: Über das Leben im Social Net*, ed. Oliver Leistert and Theo Röhle (Bielefeld: Transcript, 2011), 101–22, at 116–17.

II. Which Media?

Although the main topic of this section is the media of the social and of the (new) masses, it is less concerned with the social purposes of various media than it is with *which* media motivate and inform particular forms of sociality and crowds, *the extent to which* such media can be regarded as being constitutive of these forms, and *how* they have required us to shift our line of questioning, our methods, and our epistemology. Previously new media such as radio and film had prompted similar responses. In the works of Brecht of Vertov, for instance, the masses are not treated as an issue of content or images but rather as a question of medial infrastructures, forms of perception, and forms of organization. There have always been "old" media, moreover, which have enabled people to blame "new" media for whatever changes have occurred in the structure of society.

To draw a heuristic distinction, it is possible to claim that mediality is involved with such processes in at least two systemic places. On the one hand, it comes into play in the media-technological and material operations that are used to connect elements in such a way that a unity appears as an emergent effect. On the other hand, mediality is also relevant whenever such unities stabalize for instance social or cultural identities through symbolic processes. This distinction could be described as that between *connectivity* and *collectivity*. In this case, connectivity would thus denote operative and material functionality, while collectivity would invoke the representational and symbolic side of things. From an epistemological perspective, it is interesting how certain forms of connectivity and collectivity have a reciprocal relationship with the very media theories and social theories that have been used to describe them.

From a historical perspective, this calls to mind something like the distinction between the epistemological interests of sociology and media studies, that is, the distinction that exists to some extent between sciences of connectivity and those of collectivity. This distinction can perhaps best be summarized by relating one of Friedrich Kittler's anecdotes:

> Unlike social systems, flip-flops (that is, digital circuit elements) cannot exist without input and output. All of my attempts to explain this to Luhmann, while sharing one airport taxi or another, fell on deaf ears. "Mr. Kittler," he responded at the time, "so it has been since Babylonian times.

> A messenger rides through the gate. Some people (like you) will inquire about which horse he
> is riding, whereas other people (like me) will ask about the message that he is delivering."[1]

By focusing its attention on the operationality of media technology and thus on the "materiality of communication," and by making the pre-sensible and infrastructural level its true object of research, media studies (especially, though not exclusively, of the Kittlerian stripe) was able to achieve a high level of originality, produce a number of counterintuitive arguments, and develop an extensive archive of productive concepts. Sociology, on the contrary, has been characterized by its reliance on the two concepts of community and society.[2] In this regard, community has been treated as a pure figure of meaning, as a collective whose medial conditions are of hardly any interest at all. Technology might be visible, but its medial effects cannot be observed because they are hidden behind the transference of meaning that takes place within a meaningful domain. Hence the diagnosis that modernity has suffered a loss of community, a loss in which the material dimension of collectivity appears, at best, as a figure of fear – as an irrational and affective crowd that counteracts the structures of modernity while nevertheless originating at its very center. In a certain sense, this is also true of cultural studies, which has been interested in collectivity primarily as a phenomenon of symbolic, normative, and discursive identity formation. Such an approach has long been accompanied by the subordination, neglect, or outright exclusion of material and media-technological conditions.

From a systematic perspective, both figures of argumentation – that of media studies, which centers on technology (the horse), as well as that of sociology, which focuses on meaning (the message) – are of course stylizations insofar as the arguments that they hope to prove are, in their purest form, entirely untenable. On one side, the certainties expressed in constructivist diagnoses of social and cultural identities seem jaded. Instead the operationality of connectivity has been pushed into the foreground in order to focus – as in actor network theory or new materialism – on the hybridity and materiality of the social. On the other side, it is noticeable that the (once so provocative and productive) assertion that there is a "media-technological *a priori*" has yielded to more complex forms of argumentation that are precisely concerned with the reciprocal effects between (and the changes in) connectives and collectives and are thus interested in the interconnections between representational and media-technological structures. One could therefore say – and it is the aim of this section of the book to substantiate this claim – that sociology could gain a great deal by adopting media-theoretical approaches (by accepting, for instance, the significance of technological modes of networking), whereas media studies could profit from borrowing sociology's conceptual repertoire in order to gain perspec-

---

[1]   Friedrich Kittler, *Unsterbliche: Nachrufe, Erinnerungen, Geistergespräche* (Munich: Fink, 2004), 97.

[2]   My thoughts about the relationship between media studies and sociology have benefitted considerably from my conversations with Urs Stäheli, who kindly shared his ideas with me as we were making preparations to establish the graduate colloquium "Lose Verbindungen: Kollektivität im urbanen und digitalen Raum."

tives on the specific forms of representation and use that have come to characterize new collectivities. One of the main challenges of the articles collected here has been to bring about an exchange, one that is itself sensitive to the conditions of new social collectives and new technological connectives, between these historically and methodologically opposed ways of understanding connectivity and collectivity.

In this sense, Wolfgang Hagen maintains that the entire history of theorizing about the masses is itself only legible when accompanied by a history of media that seems to be lacking explicit terms and concepts for mass media. It is not only the case that the various styles of imagining the masses have been dictated by various media; just as the masses are always already medially constituted, our conceptions of the masses are also always already mediatized and formed on the basis of whatever media happen to be contemporary at the time. If, around the year 1900, it was the newspaper that stimulated socio-anthropological observations about the crowd (*Masse, foule*), and if, around the year 1930, it was (now explicitly) mass media such as the radio that caused the notion of the crowd to be reconceived ("New Masses"), today it is the World Wide Web and its applications that appear to be calling for the revision of these same concepts. However, if "actuality" or "up-to-dateness," that is, the fiction of large-scale participation engendered by sharing the same information simultaneously, is essential to the formation of crowds, then the World Wide Web, with its "social" services, is not a mass medium but rather, at best, a "networked sociability […] at the zero point of the social" and thus requires a different set of analytical tools and methods.

The argument presented in Michael Andreas's chapter is concerned with a level that lies somewhere in between media-technological and social functions. Here he has aimed to conceptualize social networks in terms of language and linguistic relations; in particular, he situates such networks within a genealogy of universal or artificial languages. Unlike the earlier designs of formal languages (such as Leibniz's), which disregarded the logical content of natural languages and have been studied intensively by technologically oriented media theorists, world auxiliary languages such as Volapük and Esperanto have received relatively little attention. Developed with the aim of effortless intelligibility, which was meant to facilitate economic transactions and improve international relations, these languages represent a sort of imperial gesture of connectivity – a purification of language (and thus also of possible relations) that leaves behind the historical "debris" associated with natural languages. It was hoped that their global application would expand the realm of what could be formalized and ensure an optimal standard of interaction and communication. From this perspective, certain protocols (or at least certain levels of protocol) come into light, as do the more recent trends of actor-oriented programming, which have taken on a similarly universalizing function and thus do much to define the scope of new collectivities.

As its title suggests, Dirk Baecker's "The Sociology of Media" offers a decidedly sociological perspective. Within his heuristic organization of media history into four communicative "catastrophes" (language, writing, book printing, electronic media), the internet does not represent a new media epoch. First of all, it is possible to understand any message that is not directly addressed as a message to the masses, for which reason Baecker maintains that the World Wide Web is indeed a mass medium and that all of the talk about functional loss or the end of mass media is unfounded. For although, on the technical level of digital networks, there is nothing that is ambiguously addressed, this fact is irrelevant. From the perspective of sociology and systems theory, mediality is not observable at the level of technology (connectivity) but rather only in the meaningful domain involved with the fulfillment of communicative functions (collectivity). It is also true of today's new media, according to Baecker, that they are still fundamentally engaged with managing the specific improbability of communication that was introduced by the epoch of electricity. Their challenge consists in the "taming" of instantaneity – that is, in negotiating the social rupture that was brought about by the ability of everyone to contact everyone else immediately about any state of affairs and that thus generated the possibility for communication to be rejected or accepted. In this case it is noteworthy that the traditional practices of distancing, hierarchizing, or networking have become problematic because the quantity of potential connections and the magnitude of uncertainty have increased considerably ("I know that I don't know how long I will be of interest to those network contacts who are of interest to me"). This situation requires a sociological diagnosis and theory of the present form of culture, which is capable of dealing with such excess.

In a sense, Sebastian Vehlken's comparative analysis of two monumental projects of social simulation starts off a step before the point from which the sociology of media might begin. As regards the epistemology of media history, his concern is to present neither a theory of society's media epochs nor a social theory of media but rather to focus on the connection between media technologies and the applications and experimentations of social theory itself. Vehlken interprets both Stafford Beer's "Project Cybersyn" and Dirk Helbing's "FuturICT" as practical attempts to realize "constructed" and "feasible" (and not simply written) system theories. First, these undertakings are efforts to integrate social analysis and social control; second, they rely on concepts and models that are not influenced by classical ideas of mass pathology but rather treat the masses as something that can be controlled and simulated; third, both of these social projects can be dated according to the particular state of hardware and software at their disposal. A comparison of the two projects requires precise historical delineations: Whereas Cybersyn depended on circuited, cybernetic feedback loops to model the systemic socio-economic dynamics of a rather data-poor world from the top down, FuturICT makes use of data mining and agent-based simulations, which benefit from the wealth of data produced by our highly networked world, in order to model it from the bottom up and presumably without the help of theory (that is, purely connectively). In the latter process, the new masses are treated as masses of data whose analysis and feedback create a situation in which the masses (much like the search machines described by Wolfgang Hagen) are circuited to themselves. In other words, society informs the very simulations that are meant to control society.

This new legibility of the social and its political implications are the focus of Christoph Engemann's chapter, which examines the use of social data to perform interventions in places where attempts to control society are not supported in advance by majority approval (as they were in the case of Beer's and Helbing's projects, however naively) and where data is not simply made available by incessant acts of online self-documentation. The example of the U.S. Army's "Human Terrain System," which is perhaps the most recent form of militarily implemented sociology and anthropology, illustrates the conflicting relationship that exists between social networks and political sovereignty. Whoever wishes to identify enemies and insurgents must – in short – be able to analyze their social networks under the conditions of new media in order to change such networks by means of (military) intervention. Wherever data of this sort (i.e., online data) is unavailable, the Human Terrain System endeavors to topologize the social by conducting interviews and gathering information on the ground. Social graphs thus become a means for distinguishing between allies and enemies under asymmetrical conditions: Those who do not make themselves legible (as so many people do on Facebook and other social media) must be made legible. Whereas enemy status is implied by illegibility, legibility itself is no guarantee of friendship or loyalty. This is not merely a matter of diagnosing the militarization of social networks or of updating the notorious problem of identifying enemies to account for present-day media. Rather, the question of the "governmedial situation" and the "legibility" of the social is pertinent to a key topic in the history of media studies, one that concerns both the role of secrecy in society as well as the long history of government documentation practices as they are related to sovereignty – neither of which, it seems, have been left unchanged by the current media-technological conditions.

Claus Pias

Wolfgang Hagen

Discharged Crowds
On the Crisis of a Concept

Elias Canetti spent more than three decades of his life studying the concept of the crowd. He began his research in Vienna shortly after the July Revolt of 1927, with which he had been unintentionally involved. *Crowds and Power* was not published until 1960, by which time people had grown quite accustomed to the term "mass media." A more significant study of crowds has not appeared since, with the possible exception of the posthumous work by Canetti's friend Hermann Broch.[1] Early on in *Crowds and Power*, Canetti makes the following observation:

> The most important occurrence within the crowd is the *discharge*. [...] This is the moment when all who belong to the crowd get rid of their differences and feel equal. [...] Only together can men free themselves from their burdens of distance; and this, precisely, is what happens in a crowd. During the discharge distinctions are thrown off and all feel *equal*. [...] It is for the sake of this blessed moment, when no-one is greater or better than another, that people become a crowd.[2]

I.

Canetti rejected any understanding of the masses that was based on social ontology, and thus he paid no attention to such things as the unconscious suggestibility of "collective souls," the idea of the "Führer nimbus," or ambivalent "popular fantasies." Such concepts had been prevalent in the studies written some fifty years before by Scipio Sighele, Gustave Le Bon, and Sigmund Freud.[3] For Canetti, the crowd (and the individual's "fear of

---

[1]   Hermann Broch, *Massenwahntheorie: Beiträge zu einer Psychologie der Politik* (Frankfurt am Main: Suhrkamp, 1979). This unfinished work is the twelfth volume of Broch's collected works (*Kommentierte Werkausgabe*).

[2]   Elias Canetti, *Crowds and Power*, trans. Carol Stewart (New York: Farrar, Straus and Giroux, 1984), 17–18. For the German original, see Elias Canetti, *Masse und Macht* (Hamburg: Claassen, 1960).

[3]   See Scipio Sighele, *La folla delinquente: Studio di psicologia collettiva* (Turin: Bocca, 1891); Gustave Le Bon, *The Crowd: A Study of the Popular Mind* (New York: Macmillan, 1896); and Sigmund Freud, *Group Psychology and the Analysis of the Ego*, trans. James Strachey (London: The International Psycho-Analytical Press, 1922). An English translation of Sighele's work is forthcoming in Nicoletta

being touched,"[4] which serves as its basis) is a sort of "zero point" for social phenomena; it does not represent, as writers from Le Bon to José Ortega y Gasset had maintained, an "unconscious" sociality or a second (archetypal) nature lurking in every individual.[5]

Which of these ascriptions, however, is valid in the case of "mass media"? The latter concept was formulated by American advertising agencies around the time when Canetti began his research in Europe. In the United States, ideas such as the "media of mass communication" or the "mass media" began to circulate toward the end of the 1920s within the context of the burgeoning advertising business.[6] Their implication is that the crowds of people who had previously been restricted to reading newspapers could now be medially addressed via new "channels" such as the radio, the cinema, and large billboards.[7] Interestingly enough, Canetti's work ignores the concept of the mass media altogether. Like the entire "psychological" discussion that had taken place before (by the likes of Gabriel Tarde and David Riesman),[8] *Crowds and Power* makes no reference to the mass media whatsoever. Neither the origination nor general procedure of the mass media possesses, as far as Canetti was concerned, the necessary mystique to qualify as a universal phenomenon that is "suddenly there where there was nothing before."[9] What is more, mass media clearly lack the ambivalence that is so specific to crowds, namely their simultaneously anarchic and egalitarian character. This feature of crowds, which has been observed from antiquity to today, manifests itself at stadiums and outdoor festivals, for instance, when particular activities are suddenly "discharged" in the form of collective jeering, yelling, clapping, whistling, and feet stamping. It also manifests itself when a crowd, as though following orders from an unknown source, begins to move in one common direction or another. "In order to understand how the colorless crowd of classical modernity is distinguished from the mediatized, fragmented, and colorful crowd of postmodernity," according to Peter Sloterdijk, it would be enough "to explain the difference between a leader (*Führer*) and an agenda (*Programm*)."[10]

Of course, things are not so straightforward. It is hardly a foregone conclusion that the "old" social-psychological crowd can simply be contrasted with a "postmodern" crowd defined by the experience of mass media. In fact, several factors suggest that the intrinsic effects of mass media could be felt as early as the year 1900, around the time

---

Pireddu, ed., *Scipio Sighele: The Criminal Crowd and Other Writings* (Toronto: University of Toronto Press, 2015).

4   Canetti, *Crowds and Power*, 15.

5   José Ortega y Gasset, *The Revolt of the Masses* (New York: W. W. Norton, 1932).

6   See Herman Strecker Hettinger, *A Decade of Radio Advertising* (Chicago: University of Chicago Press, 1934).

7   Ibid., 134.

8   See Gabriel Tarde, *L'opinion et la foule* (Paris: F. Alcan, 1901); and David Riesman, *The Lonely Crowd: A Study of the Changing American Character* (New Haven: Yale University Press, 1961).

9   Canetti, *Crowds and Power*, 16.

10   Peter Sloterdijk, *Die Verachtung der Massen: Versuch* über *Kulturkämpfe in der modernen Gesellschaft* (Frankfurt am Main: Suhrkamp, 2007), 20.

when Le Bon's best-selling book provided a "new" definition of the crowd phenomenon (before then, thinkers such as Kant and Hegel had treated the "crowd" as a mere material concept). Such effects were not only manifest in the "sensational" popularity of Le Bon's book itself, which was reprinted on multiple occasions and translated into ten languages before 1920, but also in the countless reviews of the book that appeared in the newspapers, which were often printed several times a day. Around the year 1900, incidentally, more than 3,400 independent daily newspapers were published in Germany alone.

As of 1896, when German industry was enjoying its final boom before the First World War and German voters came out by the millions in support of Social Democracy (without gaining much influence over the politics of the Empire), crowd theorists such as the Social Democrat Eduard Bernstein were quick to observe, for instance, "how crowds, in moments of great agitation, are prone to committing acts of wild cruelty."[11] They repeatedly cited the examples of 1789 and 1848: "Yet the majority of a crowd consists of easily excitable and weak-willed individuals who display all of the characteristics associated with women, namely acute irritability and an inclination toward extreme behavior: toward excessive sacrifice but also toward excessive wildness and cruelty."[12] Admonishing remarks such as these, made by eminent politicians, were widely printed and quoted in the more than ninety party-affiliated or party-run newspapers of the day.

In his *L'opinion et la foule*, which was published in 1901, Gabriel Tarde deviated from other early crowd theorists by discussing the obviously self-referential interdependence between the masses and the mass media. Tarde, for whom the fundamental mechanisms of crowd psychology were suggestion and hypnosis (phenomena that had been made fashionable by the spiritism of the nineteenth century),[13] attributed the tendency of "scattered masses" to become a singular community to the peculiar sensation of being up-to-date (*cette sensation de l'actualité*), which he famously regarded as an ever-renewing effect of mass media (*le propre de la presse périodique*).[14] "Both the somnambulist and the social man," he wrote elsewhere, "are possessed by the illusion that their ideas, all of which have been suggested to them, are spontaneous."[15] To feel up-to-date is to be convinced, according to Tarde, "that the information one receives is being shared by one's peers at the same moment."[16] Being up-to-date thus shares the same features that characterize the double contingency of communication, for its immanent collective cohesiveness implies that what is up-to-date is not only of interest to myself but rather to everyone, and therefore to myself as part of a larger conglomerate: "Everyone, not every one" (*"Alle, nicht jeder"*), as Elisabeth Noelle-Neumann and Thomas Peterson would later encapsulate their

---

[11]   Eduard Bernstein, "Die Menge und das Verbrechen," *Neue Zeit* 16 (1898), 229–37, at 235.

[12]   Ibid., 236.

[13]   See Wolfgang Hagen, *Radio Schreber: Der "moderne Spiritismus" und die elektrischen Medien* (Weimar: Verlag und Datenbank für Geisteswissenschaften, 2001).

[14]   Tarde, *L'opinion et la foule*, 4–5.

[15]   Gabriel Tarde, *The Laws of Imitation*, trans. Elsie Clews Parsons (New York: Henry Holt, 1903), 77.

[16]   Alexander Thomas, *Grundriss der Sozialpsychologie* (Göttingen: C. J. Hogrefe, 1992), 263.

demoscopic concept of the crowd.[17] In Tarde's estimation, this suggestive fiction of participation is constituted by the mass media, which in turn transform crowds into crowds.

Crowds are thus not formed out of the ontological and social existence of an unconscious "collective soul" that occasionally gives rise to acts of sedition or cruelty. Rather, this image of a social crowd – that is, the idea of its emancipated "soul" acting out in a criminal, feminine, or salutary manner – turns out to be a projection based on the possibility that crowds can be "up-to-date" at any given point in time. This is because crowds become crowds by referring to actuality or "up-to-dateness" on a massive scale. What remains beyond the construct of the "collective soul" is simply to observe the crowd as a social zero point, a practice performed by Canetti (with his own specific form of symbolism) and revisited in Klaus Theweleit's essays on crowd behavior.[18]

Perhaps it is even possible to say that, after the Second World War, the mass media served to perpetuate the legacy of the soulful "man of the masses," a concept often reiterated in the newspapers of the 1920s (when Canetti was first beginning to fumble into his research) and cited, however ambivalently, by nearly all of the crowd theorists of the time. For Le Bon, who inaugurated the sociological and psychological approach to the phenomenon in the 1890s, the crowd was pure depravation; to Spengler it represented the new "fourth estate"; the Social Democrats Karl Kautsky and Bernstein regarded the crowd as a dangerously unpredictable "woman" that had to be tamed by their political party;[19] while Rosa Luxemburg considered the revolutionary masses to be the one true hope for social change.[20] In her parable of the "Wij" – "a living, iron man hidden deep beneath the earth, with long eyelids hanging down to the floor" – she treated the crowd as a political subject (*wij* means 'we' in Dutch):

> Once upon a time there was a place inhabited by men in which evil spirits had settled. […] And there was no remedy or countermeasure against the evil spirits because they could not be seen or met with, even though their presence could be felt all around, their uncanny flight and their horrifying touch. It was said that only one could undo their power […]. The residents went in search of the Wij, found him, and brought the iron man with the heavy gait and closed eyes back to the dwelling place of the evil ones. "Lift my eyelids," said the Wij, and his voice creaked like rusted iron. With great effort they managed to lift his heavy iron eyelids, which were hanging to his feet. He looked around and pointed with his iron finger at the drove of evil spirits, who at that moment became visible and fell to the ground in terror, their wings beating in vain.

---

[17]   Elisabeth Noelle-Neumann and Thomas Peterson, *Alle, nicht jeder: Einführung in die Methoden der Demoskopie* (Munich: DTV, 1998).

[18]   Klaus Theweleit, "Vom Mauer, Schild, Schirm und Spalt," in *Das Land, das Ausland heißt: Essays, Reden, Interviews zu Politik und Kunst* (Munich: dtv, 1995), 11–39.

[19]   Karl Kautsky, *Der politische Massenstreik: Ein Beitrag zur Geschichte der Massenstreikdiskussionen innerhalb der deutschen Sozialdemokratie* (Berlin: Buchhandlung Vorwärts, 1914).

[20]   Rosa Luxemburg, *The Mass Strike, the Political Party, and the Trade Unions*, trans. Patrick Lavin (Detroit: Marxian Education Society, 1925). The original German version of this book appeared in 1906.

Luxemburg concluded this story, which appeared in 1899 as a newspaper column in the *Leipziger Volkszeitung*, as follows: "The 'iron man,' the man of iron muscles, of the iron plow, of the iron hammer, of the iron wheel – the man of work has been found. He has been lured out of the dark earth, where society had banned him, onto the bright surface. It is only necessary to lift his heavy eyelids, upon which he will see and extend his iron hand, for the invisible evil spirits, who have plagued humanity for ages, to fall powerless to the ground."[21]

From this point on, after Luxemburg had converted the fear of the masses into hopefulness and after Kautsky had reinterpreted the condemnation of "mass strikes" as a revolutionary force,[22] invocations of the new "man of the masses" spread widely and could even be heard in the literary works by American liberals during the 1930s. Such an invocation appears, for instance, in Brecht's legendary radio introduction to his play *Man Equals Man* (1927): "This new human type will not be as the old type imagines. It is my belief that he will not let himself be changed by machines but will himself change the machine." This new man is not an individualist, collectivist, or communist. He is a man of the masses who, in Brecht's words, "only becomes strong in the mass."[23] Brecht was not alone in his vision. His sentiments were shared by the progressive pioneers of early radio broadcasting, such as Alfred Döblin and Hans Flesch, and the penchant for the new "man of the masses," so detested by Adorno, likewise shone through Benjamin's ideas about secularizing the aura for the sake of its own salvation ("To make the enormous technical apparatus of our time an object of human innervation – this is the historical task in whose service film has its true meaning").[24] Around the same time, while American advertising agencies were coining the term "mass media," an American literary movement known as the "New Masses" was also beginning to take shape (its work was circulated in a journal of the same title). The authors participating in the movement – who included William Carlos Williams, John Dos Passos, Upton Sinclair, Dorothy Parker, Eugene O'Neill, and Ernest Hemingway – took it upon themselves to redefine American mass culture: "I want the New Masses to explore in this world, not the other. Both worlds exist in America, but one is dying, while the other is being born."[25]

Around the year 1930, among the cultural elite in the United States and Europe, yet another new concept of the crowd emerged, and this was defined by the rise of radio broadcasting. The radio brought about a new concept of political mass utopia. It was the first medium that could not only address thousands at large gatherings or millions of people at newspaper kiosks; rather, it was capable of addressing innumerable masses

---

21   Rosa Luxemburg, "Nur ein Menschenleben," *Leipziger Volkszeitung* 101 (May 4, 1899).

22   See Antonia Grunenberg, *Die Massenstreikdebatte* (Frankfurt am Main: Europäische Verlagsanstalt, 1970).

23   Bertolt Brecht, "A Radio Speech," in *Brecht on Theatre: The Development of an Aesthetic*, trans. John Willett (New York: Hill and Wang, 1964), 18–20, at 18–19.

24   Walter Benjamin, "The Work of Art in the Age of Its Technological Reproducibility [First Version]," trans. Michael W. Jennings, *Grey Room* 39 (2010), 11–37, at 19.

25   Michael Gold, "Let It Be Really New!" *New Masses* 2 (1926), 20–26, at 26.

at the same time. It was this new development, according to Brecht and Michael Gold, that would allow for the emergence of a "new human type." Brecht concluded his radio address with the following remarks: "And if the play finishes up with him conquering an entire fortress this is only because in doing so he is apparently carrying out the unqualified wish of a great mass of people who want to get through the narrow pass that the fortress guards."[26] The Left turned its attention to the masses around 1930, and within a few years it was forced to witness how, in Germany, racial hatred and the outright destruction of Europe were put into motion in the very name of the "man of the masses." All that was needed was for the Nazis to take the social utopia promised by the political concept of the masses and transform it into a dystopia of their own making.

Mass media, which Goebbels deactivated by means of *Gleichschaltung* or "synchronization," are not authoritarian systems. In the twentieth century, beginning with the Great Depression in the United States (1928–1934), they achieved a special sort of social amalgamation and thus also a special sort of pacification. "The masses of today," according to Sloterdijk, "have essentially ceased to be physical conventions of sundry people; they are now part of a system in which mass character is no longer expressed by physically congregating but rather by participating in the agendas of mass media."[27]

II.

For the past two decades or so, as internet-based media cultures have taken hold, the tendency has become clear that the concept of the masses is becoming more and more disassociated from the mass media. This is not simply the case because the mass media have been losing numbers and thus their claims over the public, though this is admittedly true enough. The situation for the oldest of mass media, namely newspapers, is especially dire. Whereas three-and-a-half thousand German newspapers were in daily circulation around the year 1900, approximately four thousand in 1932, and more than six hundred as late as 1954, that number today stands at 347 and will most likely continue to fall.[28] It is also the case that radio stations have lost a considerable amount of market share among younger listeners and that television stations have lost viewers to the rising number of online viewing options, especially in the United States. "Approximately 90% of American television programs," as Horst Stipp has reported, "reach no more than 1% of households."[29]

On top of this, there is the fact that the masses addressed by the mass media have become more difficult to define and measure. The number of people with mobile phones is continuing to increase (about a third of those between the ages of fourteen and twenty-

---

26   Brecht, "A Radio Speech," 19.

27   Sloterdijk, *Die Verachtung der Massen*, 16.

28   See "Die deutschen Zeitungen in Zahlen und Daten," a brochure edited by the Bundesverband Deutscher Zeitungsverleger (Berlin: Bundesverband Deutscher Zeitungsverleger e.V., 2012), 2.

29   Horst Stipp, "Media-Planung in den USA," *Media Perspektiven* 10 (2004), 483–88, at 488.

nine already use them), and thus it has become difficult to reach people for surveys. Telephone surveys conducted over mobile phones no longer provide any localized data, and this is because mobile-phone numbers are not tied to the location of their users (unlike the area codes associated with land-lines). Moreover, the reliability of surveys has been undermined to some extent by the socio-epistemological problem of the so-called Hawthorne Effect, whereby only those who are already susceptible to answering surveys are willing to participate in them ("normal people" simply hang up). The result of this, as Rainer Diaz-Bone has noted, is that empirical social research has come to rely more and more on self-referential data collected from within its own (closed) society.[30]

But this empirical data is not really the point. Far more important is the fact that mass media are losing more and more momentum as regards their central promise, which is to keep people "up-to-date." As late as 1997, Niklas Luhmann was still able to make the following remarks (apparently without any irritation):

> Every morning and every evening, an inexorable web of news settles over the earth and sets out what has happened and what one has to be ready for. Some events take place of their own accord, and society is so turbulent that something is always happening. Others are produced for the mass media. Above all, expressions of opinion can be treated as events, so that the media can allow their material to reenter itself reflexively. In all of this, the print media interact with television.[31]

What Luhmann is describing here is the classical definition of the mass media, as it had been established by newspaper theorists after the First World War. This definition includes "periodicity" (a regular publication schedule), "publicity" (availability to everyone), "universality" (coverage of a multitude of issues), and "currency" (enough up-to-date material to capture the attention of society as a whole).[32] With these four integrated functions, the mass media had long served to represent the social memory of modern, functionally differentiated society. As Gabriel Tarde was aware, this fourfold function also served to define the modern concept of the masses itself. Crowds, after all, were able to display the same universal "up-to-dateness" as their media, by which they were designed in such a way as to be directly addressed.

In this classical sense, the status of the internet as a mass medium is questionable, if that. Depending upon its accessibility, the internet could perhaps be said to possess the characteristics of "publicity" and "universality," but its services are altogether lacking in "periodicity" and "currency," features that are now simulated by software and "apps." Regarding the transactions that take place over the internet, it is not true that "no interaction among those co-present can take place," and thus Luhmann's fundamental definition of

---

³⁰ Rainer Diaz-Bone, "Die Performativität der Sozialforschung: Sozialforschung als Sozio-Epistemologie," *Historical Social Research* 36 (2011), 291–310, at 299.

³¹ Niklas Luhmann, *Theory of Society*, 2 vols., trans. Rhodes Barrett (Stanford: Stanford University Press, 2012–2013), 2:315.

³² Otto Groth, *Die Zeitung: Ein System der Zeitungskunde*, 4 vols. (Mannheim: J. Bensheimer, 1928–1930), 1:22.

the mass media does not apply in this case.[33] Notwithstanding the ever-growing "masses" of people who "use" it on a daily basis, the internet is even less of a mass medium than the book (which likewise lacks "periodicity," beyond the fact that new books are printed every day). Every interaction on the internet takes place via a point-to-point connection between a "server" and a "client" and is communicated across nodes that constitute a network of data. These interacting machines, at least, are all that have to be "co-present" in one way or another. Regardless, it is never the case that a "mass" of people is addressed.

During the innumerable internet connections that take place throughout a given day, "invisible machines" (in Luhmann's terms) "communicate" with automated agents. Millions of "users" (so long as they are not the programmers who program the agents) operate merely at the level of "interfaces." A crowd – that is, a temporally or spatially coherent gathering – cannot directly experience anything over the web. Search engines and the links provided by the software of so-called social networks can only "speak" with individual users, whose activity they aggregate, bundle, rank, monitor, and weigh. The internet addresses a mass of atomized and monitored individuals, but it does not address them with the same content. Internet search engines cannot be said to have any "agenda." Their semantics is rather based on a series of connected algorithmic operations whose existence depends on the operations of their "users." From their "back office," so to speak, search engines (of which there are more than a thousand; Google is but one) send out computer robots that scour the web around the clock (these are known as "crawlers," "spiders," or simply "robots"). These gather content; index websites according to their texts, images, audio recordings, or videos; and operate a highly complex system of "sorters," "barrels," and "repositories." From these, the "front office" of the search engines, which is the client interface, provides responses to their "users" within a fraction of a second. Search engines form the "interface" of the internet, which has no interface on its own, and deliver results that, in the words of Elena Esposito, "have never been thought of before."[34] If, in Deleuze's sense, crowds were once "molar," they have now disintegrated definitively into the "molecular."[35] The formlessness of today's masses of users, sitting as they are in front of their search engines, is made of atomic connections that are entirely unclear. Regardless of how seriously one should take Deleuze's metaphors, in analytic terms it can be claimed that the contingency of countless searches recurs in the form of the contingent lists of answers provided by search engines. After this has taken place, everything then depends on the ability of those engaged in a search to reconstruct the context of their inquiry and on their openness to changing their own context at any given time. Formally speaking,

---

[33]   Niklas Luhmann, *The Reality of the Mass Media*, trans. Kathleen Cross (Stanford: Stanford University Press, 2000), 2.

[34]   Elena Esposito, *Soziales Vergessen: Formen und Medien des Gedächtnisses der Gesellschaft*, trans. Alessandra Corti (Frankfurt am Main: Suhrkamp, 2002), 358.

[35]   Gilles Deleuze and Félix Guattari, *A Thousand Plateaus: Capitalism and Schizophrenia*, trans. Brian Massumi (Minneapolis: University of Minnesota Press, 1987), 57–63.

this structure applies equally to every search query, for it is only through this procedurally formalized informality that the "memory of the internet" reveals itself.

However, because an entirely random list of (often ten thousand) websites given in response to a search would be the same as offering no answer to the search at all, the truly decisive memory function of the internet is based on the ranking structure with which search engines construct their lists of answers. It is this act of ranking that corresponds, in its semantics, to the idea of "currency" or "up-to-dateness" that partially defines the traditional mass media, and yet it functions in an entirely different manner. Every individual site found during a search is assigned a degree of significance from the "back office" of the search engines, but this evaluation has nothing to do with the search itself. Nevertheless, it is this ranking that determines the order in which the search results are presented. Like the mechanism of "up-to-dateness" (though the latter operates according to collective associations), this generates a semblance of double contingency. With its weighted lists, the machine simulates "expectations of expectation,"[36] and it does so as though it knows that the person searching expects it to know what is most important to him or her.

In the process of simulating was is "really" important – or, in the terms of mass media, what is "up-to-date" – the decisive factor is thus the search robots that identify "links," save their forward and backward directions, count their "backlinks," and thereby assign a "page rank" to every website. At Google, for instance, this entire procedure is undertaken anew every three months. The rank, value, importance, and validity of a website are determined exclusively by the number and weight of the links that direct to it, whereby the most weight is given to those pages to which many other sites provide a link. The structure is recursive. Through its "backlinks," a site receives a ranking in popularity *qua* popularity, and thus this recursiveness is self-reinforcing. That which structures the memory of the internet, and thus replaces the traditional mass-media concept of being up-to-date, was developed at Stanford in 1998 by Sergey Brin and Lawrence Page, the founders of Google.[37] As such, their ranking process is not much of an innovation; epistemologically, it belongs to the classical twentieth-century tradition of sociometry, which for its part can be located within the radically anti-metaphysical tradition of Paul F. Lazarsfeld, one of the pioneers of empirical social research. Brin and Page refer specifically to studies on the formation of teenage cliques in 1950s America. With their lists of "likes of likes," Facebook and Twitter, which likewise form a "memory" interface of the internet, adhere to the same logic of ranking. It should be noted, too, that search engines rank books and other texts in the same manner (Brin and Page rely a good deal on bibliometrics). The page-rank algorithm allots greater value to a book when it has been cited by another book that itself has been frequently cited (a textbook, for instance) than it does to a book that has been cited by a lesser-known and thus less-frequently cited book. The result of this process is that the websites near the top of the list are those that mutually cite one another

---

36 Dirk Baecker, *Form und Formen der Kommunikation* (Frankfurt am Main: Suhrkamp, 2005), 85.
37 Sergey Brin and Lawrence Page, "The Anatomy of a Large-Scale Hypertextual Web Search Engine," *Computer Networks and ISDN Systems* 30 (1998), 107–17.

with high frequency, belong to the mainstream of scholarly or public opinion, and thereby lend further affirmation to the mainstream itself. Those who search the web in order to refresh their memory will be reaffirmed in what they already know; it is unlikely that they will be referred to something that is unfamiliar to them. With the implementation of "PageRank," as Brin and Page called their ranking system, networked structures therefore tend to be rather authoritarian, except that, in this case, a sort of networked "sociability" takes the place of personal authorities or classical leaders of the masses. Such information systems, however, are not exactly immune to the dangers of increasing segregation and social fragmentation.

Then again, only the World Wide Web is large and variable enough, diverse and comprehensive enough, fast and precise enough, and high-definition and differentiated enough to absorb, as a new form of social memory, the immense flood of data produced by a globalized world, a world that now supports twice the amount of biomass as it did in 1960. On their own, mass media are obviously no longer capable of managing and disseminating so much information, but the crisis of the mass media is not merely one of quantity. Rather, analyses of their *content* have long revealed signs of stress that complicate the situation even further. As Karl Otto Hondrich, Bernhard Pörksen, and Hanne Detel have recently demonstrated, television stations and the press have reacted to their ineluctable loss of influence by resorting to a "journalism of outrage" and by turning more and more issues into "scandals."[38] In doing so, they have narrowed, rather than expanded, the scope of themes with which they keep their audiences up-to-date. Accordingly, the crisis is not so much that young men and women no longer read the newspaper; or that they have ceased to regard the radio as their medium of choice; or that they have come to prefer online, on-demand viewing outlets over traditional television; or even that mass media have been unable to identify the very things that seriously endanger their business model. At the heart of the crisis is rather the fact that the flood of information, swollen immensely, can no longer fit through the linear needle eye of mass-media currency or up-to-dateness. The consequence of this, which affects every individual one of us, is that we are not being reached by the content that we desire.

And so we get it elsewhere, though we admittedly do so as part of a vast and atomized mass of individuals, at a new zero point of the social that corresponds somewhat to Canetti's notion of the crowd. The difference is that today, unlike Canetti's mobs at the Viennese Revolt of 1927, the discharge of a crowd takes place at the very moment of its genesis and is thus already taken care of. No one using Facebook, for instance, is bothered by the fear of being touched, and such is the successful model that has come to define new social media. In our present *Dasein*, an existence enabled by the smart phone, we – the new masses – live in the blissful condition of fearing to be touched by the fear of being

---

[38]   Karl Otto Hondrich, *Enthüllung und Entrüstung: Eine Phänomenologie des politischen Skandals* (Frankfurt am Main: Suhrkamp, 2002); Bernhard Pörksen and Hanne Detel, *The Unleashed Scandal: The End of Control in the Digital Age*, trans. Alison R. Koeck and Wolfram K. Koeck (Exeter: Imprint Academic, 2014).

touched (ostensibly, that is, without this fear at all). This must be the reason why we allow nearly everyone to read our personal information – to save it, analyze it, and evaluate it. Or, to put it differently: We are crowds without being crowds and thus we find ourselves, in Baudrillard's words, at "the zero point of the political."[39]

---

[39] Jean Baudrillard, *In the Shadow of the Silent Majorities ... or the End of the Social, and Other Essays*, trans. Paul Foss et al. (New York: semiotexte, 1983), 18. Foss's translation ("zero degree of the political") has been modified here.

Michael Andreas

"Open" and "Free"
On Two Programs of Social Media

"Naturally, no theory of communication can avoid the discussion of language. Language, in fact, is in one sense another name for communication itself, as well as a word used to describe the codes through which communication takes place."[1]

```
#!/usr/bin/perl
sub protest{
    reset $wall_street;
return our $future;
}
until($equality){
    protest;
}
```[2]

"Esperanto, eloquente Definition: / Schnellerlernter lingo zur Verständigung der Nationen / Basiert auf Romanisch, Deutsch, Jiddisch, Slawisch / Kein Sprachimperialismus oder Privileg des Bildungsadels / Esperanto – kein Manko, wenn ihr's nicht gleich versteht / Wichtiger ist, dass ihr zwischen den Zeilen lest, / Euch unser Style beseelt, fühlt, was mein Input ist / Ich sei Lyricist, internationaler Linguist."[3]

---

[1] Norbert Wiener, *The Human Use of Human Beings: Cybernetics and Society* (Boston: Houghton Mifflin, 1954), 75.

[2] A microcode, written in Perl and called "Protest," by Pall Thayer. The code was sent to the NetBehaviour mailing list on October 6, 2011. It is archived at http://www.netbehaviour.org/pipermail/ netbehaviour/20111006 /022999.html (accessed on February 19, 2013).

[3] Lyrics from the song "Esperanto" by the band Freundeskreis, *Esperanto* (Four Music, 1999), FOR 667103 6. The lines can roughly be translated as follows: "Esperanto, an eloquent definition: / An easy-to-learn lingo for international dialogue, / Based on the Romance languages, German, Yiddish, Slavic. / No linguistic imperialism or privilege of the educated classes. / Esperanto – there's no drawback if you don't understand it right away; / It's more important for you to read between the lines, / for our style to inspire you, / for you to feel what my input is. / I'll be a lyricist, and international linguist."

I.

The general conception of the acute role of "social media" is based on the possibility of individual expression. In this regard it is believed that their mere use is enough to emancipate the individual from a governmental apparatus. Such an understanding of media can be traced back to Brecht's argument in "The Radio as an Apparatus of Communication" and, above all, to Hans Magnus Enzensberger's in his "Constituents of a Theory of Media." It is the result of a conceptual shift that took as its starting point the democratization of the media and thus altered the fundamental notion of "mass media." According to this understanding, the masses are no longer simply the receivers of information; they are its transmitters as well. As early as the middle of the 1990s, when internet technology became more generally available, the idea began to attract renewed interest, especially in light of the revived attention that was being devoted to McLuhan's utopian fantasy of a "global village."[4] The later propagation and habitualization of "social media" rekindled the idea yet again, particularly from an economic perspective. Headline-grabbing concepts such as "the wisdom of crowds" or "Wikinomics" reconceived the relationship between the masses and mass media in such a way that the individual was placed at the center of all media activity.[5] In this arrangement, recipients were regarded as producers, and consumers were taken to be "prosumers." According to this understanding, not only the consumption of media content, but also its production, should come to take place *en masse*. Even during the early stages of "Web 2.0," Geert Lovink expressed reservations about conflating a political concept of freedom with the economic models of social networks and their open-source paradigms ("open" in the sense of "free," and "open source" in the sense of having "open programming codes"): "No dissidents have yet stood up to object to the hypocritical agenda behind 'free' and 'open' in broader public arenas. What, in fact, should be done is to demand from the Free gurus to come up with an innovative economic model every time they 'free up' the next cultural or social activity."[6]

My focus below will be on the *programs* of "social media" – on their software, for one, but above all on their programmatic agendas in the original sense of word *programma*, which in Greek denoted a written notice or a public announcement. The first goal will be to analyze the social-media concepts of "free" and "open" as spillover effects into the realm of politics. Attention will then be paid to the metaphor of the *programming*

---

4   For an influential study written during the early stages of the internet, see Derrick de Kerckhove, *The Skin of Culture: Investigating the New Electronic Reality* (Toronto: Somerville House, 1995).

5   See James Surowiecki, *The Wisdom of Crowds: Why the Many Are Smarter than the Few and How Collective Wisdom Shapes Business, Economies, Societies, and Nations* (New York: Doubleday, 2004); and Don Tapscott and Anthony D. Williams, *Wikinomics: How Mass Collaboration Changes Everything* (New York: Portfolio, 2006).

6   Geert Lovink, *Zero Comments: Blogging and Critical Internet Culture* (New York: Routledge, 2008), xiii.

language, the origins of which will be traced back to the prehistory of computer science.[7] Given the impossibility of avoiding this very metaphor, my second goal will be to describe "social media" as a result of the programmatic agendas of programming languages. The syntactical and semantic details of such languages will not be treated in great depth, and this is because the political effects of software and the ideologies of various programs only become visible in their invisibility, that is, as part a functionality that veils their underlying technicity and only comes to light as manipulations of an invisible code, as an interface on the surface of things.[8]

II.

The economic and media discourses of "open" and "free" recently infiltrated the realm of politics in the context of the viral political movements in North Africa, the Middle East, Southern Europe, Great Britain, and finally in association with the "Occupy Wall Street" movement in the United States and elsewhere.[9] During the anti-regime uprisings in North Africa and the Middle East, the Western press was especially eager to suggest that new forms of communication had been the driving force behind the protests. Multiple experts voiced the opinion that the efforts toward democratization, above all in Egypt, could be attributed to "social media."[10] This was so much the case that the events were discussed with labels borrowed from the leading social-networking enterprises and trends: "Facebook Revolution," "Twitter Revolution," "Revolution 2.0," and so on.[11] In February of 2011,

---

[7] On the early history of the metaphor of the *program* in computer science, see Hans Dieter Hellige, "Zur Genese des informatischen Programmbegriffs: Begriffsbildung, metaphorische Prozesse, Leitbilder und professionelle Kulturen," in *Algorithmik – Kunst – Semiotik: Hommage für Frieder Nake*, ed. Karl-Heinz Rödinger (Heidelberg: Synchron, 2003), 42–73. On the metaphorology of the internet in general, see Matthias Bickenbach and Harun Maye, *Metapher Internet: Literarische Bildung und Surfen* (Berlin: Kadmos, 2009).

[8] See Wendy Hui Kyong Chun, "On Software, or the Persistence of Visual Knowledge," *Grey Room* 18 (2004), 26–51, esp. 32.

[9] See Martin Doll, "Revolution 2.0: Über den Zusammenhang zwischen den Aufständen im 'arabischen Raum' und ihren medialen Bedingungen," *kultuRRevolution* 60 (2011), 64–71, esp. 64–66.

[10] It is interesting to note that, in their analyses of the protests, cultural and media theorists generally discounted the effectiveness of social networks and more or less regarded the phenomenon as a mere discourse of the mainstream media, whereas empirical and "big-data" approaches tended to presume that the "Revolution 2.0" in Egypt and Tunisia had been catalyzed by streams of information sent via Twitter. For a critical approach to these issues, see (in addition to Martin Doll's article cited above) Jon B. Alterman, "The Revolution Will Not Be Tweeted," *Washington Quarterly* 34 (2011), 103–16. For an empirical analysis, see Gilad Lotan et al., "The Revolutions Were Tweeted: Information Flows During the 2011 Tunisian and Egyptian Revolutions," *International Journal of Communication* 5 (2011), 1375–405.

[11] The term "Revolution 2.0" was recently adopted by the organizational psychologist Peter Kruse. See Peter Kruse and Philipp Meller, "Revolution 2.0: Facebook und die Mobilisierung von Gesell-

Al Jazeera even began to speak enthusiastically about a "social revolution," as though a revolution without society could somehow be imagined.[12]

The emphatic concept of freedom, with which the Egyptian events of early 2011 were so closely associated, lost some of its luster during the summer riots that took place in Great Britain. There, freedom came to be characterized by a "removal of political boundaries" such that the state was able to monitor its citizens – in real time – with electronic media.[13] The unrest began in London in August of 2011, only seven months after the incidents in Egypt had begun, and soon spread to other major British cities. The riots were instigated by the death of a man at the hands of the police in the London area of Tottenham. Two days later, a peaceful protest was staged outside of the police station, where demonstrators demanded an explanation for the death. The situation escalated to acts of arson and plundering, first in other parts of London but soon in cities such as Manchester and Liverpool as well. When the police began to suspect that the perpetrators were organizing their activity via "social media," they started to monitor conversations on Twitter and Facebook.[14] In addition to these open networks, however, Blackberry Messenger was also suspected to be a catalyst for the rioting, and its manufacturer, the company Research in Motion, soon declared its support for the authorities. Blackberry Messenger operates with proprietary but free software that comes preinstalled on the company's mobile devices. Like other short-message services, it enables users of the Blackberry system to send direct messages. Unlike other short-message services, however, Blackberry's functions with encryptions that prevent (or at least impede) unintended recipients from reading whatever messages have been sent. Thus, whereas the police were easily able to identify certain agitators on the public profiles of other networks, in the case of Blackberry Messenger they had to rely on corporate assistance to gain access. At first, Research in Motion agreed to suspend communication and briefly take its system offline, but then the company also promised to hand over its users' information for purposes of investigation. Oddly enough, this proposition did not incite any widespread outrage on the part of Blackberry's users. This is especially strange because Research in Motion had gone out its way to advertise the

---

schaften," *Cicero Online* (February 2011), http://www.cicero.de/salon/revolution-20-facebook-und-die-mobilisierung-von-gesellschaften /41577 (accessed on February 2, 2012).

[12] Al Jazeera, *Empire*. The broadcast of this program on February 17, 2011 was titled "Social Networks, Social Revolution."

[13] I have borrowed the term "removal of political boundaries" (*Entgrenzung des Politischen* 'unbordering of the political') from Claus Pias, "Der Auftrag: Kybernetik und Revolution in Chile," in *Politiken der Medien*, ed. Daniel Gethmann and Markus Stauff (Berlin: Diaphanes, 2004), 131–54, at 150.

[14] See the exemplary account by Josh Halliday, "David Cameron Considers Banning Suspected Rioters from Social Media," *Guardian Online* (August 2011), http://www.guardian.co.uk/media/2011/aug/11/david-cameron-rioters-social-media (accessed on February 2, 2012).

encryption technology of its devices and thus, by making private information available to the authorities, invalidated one of the main reasons for using its products in the first place.[15]

Along with their recent forms of dissemination and the manner in which they have become habituated, the uses of "social media" during the recent protest provide a good illustration of their ambivalent nature. The dual quality of this sort of mass communication came to light especially during the political protests in the "Arab world." On the one hand, the new media were perceived as instantiations of freedom – as the possibility of communicating independent information within the countries in question, as a channel for sending information to the outside world and coordinating protests internally, and as a forum for cultivating democratic opinions. On the other hand, this new information technology had also enabled governments to access information about their political subjects far more easily than before. In addition to monitoring protesters on centralized platforms such as Facebook and Twitter, of course, governments could also control internet access, bug telephone lines, and shut down domain name servers.[16]

So-called "Web 2.0" has served to augment the qualities that define its media's political mode of action. Such media can no longer be reduced to the mere technological possibility of inverting the relationship between transmitters and receivers, and thus to regarding the masses as simultaneous recipients and producers of information (according to Brecht, so much could already be achieved with the radio). Nor is it possible to regard them in terms of the repressive (bourgeois, according to Enzensberger; dictatorial, in the case of Egypt) intentions of a political apparatus "to hold on to the control of the means of production at any price, while being incapable of making the socially necessary use of them."[17] What defines such media is rather their increasing tendency to outsource communication to platforms, so much so that digital social media are controlled by the politics of the platforms themselves. This type of control is not the same as the censorship or surveillance of platforms such as Twitter or Facebook; rather, it is based on the political implications that arise from the discourses concerned with the technological condition of the very platforms in question.[18]

---

[15] See Adrian Sim, "Don't Shoot the (Blackberry) Messenger: The Technology of Riots," *Privacy & Data Protection Journal* 11 (2011), 18–20.

[16] See Doll, "Revolution 2.0," 66. On the materiality of protests under conditions of real-time communication, see also Tom Holert, "Der Akku der Kritik: Bildungsproteste und verteilte Handlungsfähigkeit," *Zeitschrift für Medienwissenschaft* 2 (2010), 131–34.

[17] Hans Magnus Enzensberger, "Constituents of a Theory of Media," trans. Stuart Hood, in *The New Media Reader*, ed. Noah Wardrip-Fruin and Nick Montfort (Cambridge, MA: MIT Press, 2003), 261–75, at 271.

[18] See Tarleton Gillespie, "The Politics of 'Platforms'," *New Media & Society* 12 (2010), 347–64.

III.

Having provided a few current examples of society's transformations under the conditions of "social media," I would now like to turn my attention to a historical matter, particularly to an activity that has been undertaken throughout all of modernity and whose lofty goal has been to rewrite and record everything that is and ever was. The history of artificial or universal languages begins with Descartes's letter to Father Marin Marsenne, if not with Ramon Llul's *Ars Magna*, Pedro Bermudo's *Arithmeticus Nomenclator*, or Francis Bacon's *De Dignitate et Augmentis Scientiarum* (Athanasius Kircher's *Polygraphia* and Johann Joachim Becher's *Character pro Notitia Linguarum Universali* also deserve to be mentioned).[19] Gottfried Wilhelm Leibniz and John Wilkins also concerned themselves with the issue of universal language, though they treated it as a sort of dual problem. For Leibniz, the problem straddled the ideas presented in his *Arte Combinatoria* and incomplete *Characteristica Universalis*, whereas for Wilkins it lay somewhere between his *Mercury*, a treatise on cryptography, and his far better-known *Essay Toward a Real Character and a Philosophical Language*. For both, the main question was how to formulate a universal language not as a taxonomy or code but rather as a language for everyday use.

The history of universal, artificial, or international auxiliary languages, of which more than five hundred have been devised, can be divided into two branches. Whereas the sixteenth- and seventeenth-century philosophers and authors of ideal languages were chiefly interested in the taxonomic and cryptographic possibilities of a *lingua universalis*, the nineteenth-century designers of *international auxiliary languages* hoped to create a language that could be used and understood by the general population. Artificial languages of this sort were thus essentially different from the universal languages of the Early Modern era, whose proponents regarded the universality of language in terms of coding and decoding the immanent nature of things. Inspired by the societal transformations brought about by an earlier wave of globalization (a boom in colonialism, more intensive international trade, etc.) and by corresponding changes in communication technology (the institutionalization of telegraphy and the post, new systems of signs such as Morse code and flag alphabets, etc.), more than one hundred artificial languages were developed during and following the last third of the nineteenth century, and the aim of these languages was no less than to address the entire world.[20]

---

[19]   For comprehensive historiographical studies of the subject, see Louis Couturat and Léopold Léau, *Histoire de la langue universelle* (Paris: Librairie Hachette, 1903); Umberto Eco, *The Search for the Perfect Language*, trans. James Fentress (Cambridge, MA: Blackwell, 1995); Alessandro Bausani, *Geheim- und Universalsprachen: Entwicklung und Typologie*, trans. Gustav Glaesser (Stuttgart: Kohlhammer, 1970); Gerhard F. Strasser, *Lingua Universalis: Kryptologie und Theorie der Universalsprachen im 16. und 17. Jahrhundert* (Wiesbaden: O. Harrassowitz, 1988); and Reinhardt Haupenthal, ed., *Plansprachen: Beiträge zur Interlinguistik* (Darmstadt: Wissenschaftliche Buchgesellschaft, 1976).

[20]   Regarding the fad of "global" ideas around the turn of the nineteenth century, see Markus Krajewski, *Restlosigkeit: Weltprojekte um 1900* (Frankfurt am Main: Fischer, 2006). An English translation of

Fig. 1: Addressing the world with a game of telephone: A letter sealer used by the Tobler chocolate company and written in "Ido," one of Esperanto's successors (ca. 1910). Österreichische Nationalbibliothek, Bildarchiv Austria, Digitale Sammlungen: Esperanto (Series 2, No. 18; inventory no. GmA 9, Ido 1,1,4)

Around the year 1900, the success of a given artificial language was determined by an agenda that was both political and based on the economy of knowledge. The nature of this agenda – and its rhetorical reliance on the terms "free" and "open" – can be seen anew under conditions of today's "social media." In this regard, the critical approaches to two of these international auxiliary languages should be mentioned. By now, technology-oriented scholars of media studies have delved into the depths of information coding and have succeeded in describing the economy of signals that accompanied the discourse surrounding universal languages in the seventeenth and eighteenth centuries.[21] In contrast, investigations of the artificial languages developed during the nineteenth century and beyond are few and far between, with the exception of certain studies that treat them as a curious side effect of a "universalizing" political project. Whereas Leibniz and his contemporaries associated universality with the idea of immanence, the *fin-de-siècle* idea of an international *auxiliary* language was pedagogical at heart: "The universal language degenerated into a secular version; the loftiest claim of all was reduced to a purely auxiliary instrument."[22]

As certain media theorists have pointed out in their reconstructions of the genealogy of the computer, the discourse about universal languages had been concerned with the societal effects of globalization since the seventeenth century. Reflections about the ap-

---

this book is forthcoming: *World Projects: Global Information Before World War I*, trans. Charles Marcrum (Minneapolis: University of Minnesota Press, 2014).

[21] See, for instance, Friedrich Kittler, "Ein Tigertier das Zeichen setzte: Gottfried Wilhelm Leibniz zum 350. Geburtstag" (1996), http://hydra.humanities.uci.edu/kittler/tiger.html (accessed on February 12, 2013); Stefan Rieger, *Speichern/Merken: Die künstliche Intelligenzen des Barock* (Munich: Fink, 1997); and Wolfgang Schäffner, "Medialität der Zeichen: Butet de la Sarthe und der Concours *Déterminer l'influence des signes sur la formation des idées*," in *Das Laokoon-Paradigma: Zeichenregime im 18. Jahrhundert*, ed. Inge Baxmann et al. (Berlin: Akademie, 2000), 274–90.

[22] Krajewski, *Restlosigkeit: Weltprojekte um 1900*, 316.

plicability of an abstract, scientific, taxonomic, and "pure" language appear as early as Descartes, who was interested in the possibility of communicating the *esprits vulgaires*, and in Wilkin's work they appear as efforts to ensure that even the *vulgus* – the common people – would be able to employ the "real character" of his taxonomic language.[23]

Discourses about the theories of coding have thus always overlapped with those about a "language for everyone." They intersect in Leibniz's work as well is in that of Louis Couturat (1868–1914), who was the leading figure in the movement devoted to international auxiliary languages. A mathematician and linguist, Couturat was not only the editor of Leibniz's unpublished writings on the problems of universal language; along with Léopold Léau, he was also the first historiographer of artificial languages in general. In their *Histoire de la langue universelle*, which was published in 1903, Couturat and Léau distinguished between *a priori* and *a posteriori* artificial languages. This distinction was above all a matter of theoretical approach. Among *a priori* artificial languages, on the one hand, were counted those philosophical and immanence-oriented languages that consisted of entirely invented grammars and whose vocabularies were intended to reflect the "essence" of things. On the other hand, they regarded as *a posteriori* those artificial languages whose grammar, vocabulary, and inflections were borrowed from existing languages and whose orientation was focused on the practice of speaking. In addition to this theoretical distinction, however, Couturat and Léau also maintained that there was a qualitative divide between the *a priori* languages of the sixteenth through eighteenth centuries, with their analytic precision, and the artificial languages of their own time, the *a posteriori* international auxiliary languages with pragmatic aims:

> The inadequate idea of a purely scientific language has to be abandoned. [...] The universal language [...] should not be a technical or aristocratic language that is only accessible to the initiated; rather, it should be an everyday language that is no less applicable at train stations and hotels than it is at the meetings of learned societies.[24]

As one of the most prominent linguists around the year 1900, Couturat could not have written otherwise. With such thoughts he encapsulated the agenda of an entire movement, one that began with Johann Martin Schleyer's invention of Volapük and whose most lasting contribution has been Esperanto, a language developed by Ludwik Zamenhof. By drawing a firm line between earlier efforts and those of his own time, however, he also unwittingly excluded international auxiliary languages from the present-day discourse of media studies that is concerned with the computer, an academic discipline that, in Friedrich Kittler's words, "would not exist had it not been for the triumphal advance of modern information technologies."[25] With its pronounced distance from the notion of coding, an idea promulgated

---

[23]   On Descartes, see Couturat and Léau, *Histoire de la langue universelle*, 11–14. On Descartes and Wilkins, see Bausani, *Geheim- und Universalsprachen*, 95–96, 101–04, respectively.

[24]   Louis Couturat, *Die internationale Hilfssprache* (Berlin: Möller & Borel, 1903), 5–6.

[25]   Friedrich Kittler, "The History of Communication Media," *CTheory.net* (July 1996), http://www.ctheory.net/ articles.aspx?id=45 (accessed on June 19, 2014).

by the likes of Leibniz and Wilkins, Couturat's agenda may indeed lie beyond the scope of such media theory, but it is also closely aligned with the social.[26] That said, the functionality of universal languages can likewise be used to describe the "social media" of our computer age. The latter should be understood less in terms of hardware or software, binary codes or programs, than as the result of a political program and an economic agenda.

IV.

Around the middle of the nineteenth century, thoughts about a *lingua universalis* gave way to ideas about an *international auxiliary language*. The latter were based on the hope of creating an international dialect for global communication, a linguistic means of eliminating, once and for all, many of the conflicts and misunderstandings that exist between people. Multiculturalism, though we tend to regard it as a recent phenomenon, was in fact an essential component of this nineteenth-century project. The linguistically and culturally heterogeneous backgrounds of two the leading designers of international auxiliary languages undoubtedly fueled their ambitions to prevent conflicts by abolishing miscommunication. Regarding Ludwik Lazarus Zamenhof, it has been said that his development of Esperanto was inspired by the mixture of Polish, Yiddish, Russian, and German that was spoken in his home town of Białystok. Johann Martin Schleyer, Zamenhof's most prominent competitor within the auxiliary-language movement, was a native of Konstanz.[27] Schleyer was moved to invent the language Volapük, according to his contemporary Ernst Beermann,

> without any knowledge that universal languages had already been created before him. [...] He arrived independently at the idea of inventing a language that could be understood throughout the entire globe, and he did so in response to the difficulty that his parishioners were experiencing in their correspondence to America. He came to think of how nice it would be if everyone in the world possessed a common alphabet, a uniform orthography, and a single language for correspondence. Thus he invented Volapük, in his words, "as a genuine friend to mankind who hoped at last, out of pure sympathy for our deeply divided and much-afflicted humanity, to redress with his invention the Babylonian linguistic confusion on earth, [...] the innumerable misunderstandings, disputes, quarrels, injustices, and costs; the sea of prejudices, hatred, and ambivalence, of ignorance, malice, fanaticism, and crises; as well as the many opinions of every sort that are by now obsolete or no longer tenable."[28]

---

[26]   On the expulsion of the social from media theory, see Geert Lovink, "What Is the Social in Social Media?" *e-flux* 40 (December 2012), http://www.e-flux.com/journal/what-is-the-social-in-social-media/ (accessed on February 15, 2012).

[27]   On the dialects in Konstanz and their reflection in Volapük, see Richard M. Meyer, "Künstliche Sprachen," *Indogermanische Forschungen: Zeitschrift für indogermanische Sprach- und Altertumskunde* 12 (1901), 33–91, 242–318, esp. 80.

[28]   Ernst Beermann, *Studien zu Schleyers Weltsprache Volapük* (Ratibor: Riedinger, 1890), 4–5. Beermann's quotation of Schleyer is from Johann Martin Schleyer, *Hauptgedanken meiner öffentlichen Vorträge über die von mir ersonnene Allsprache Volapük* (Konstanz: A. Moriell, 1885), 22.

A Catholic priest with missionary zeal, Schleyer named his invention *Volapük*, which means 'world language', and he derived most of its vocabulary from English (*vol*, for instance, is based on English *world*, *pük* on English *speak*). Despite the numerous auxiliary languages already in existence, about which Schleyer had supposedly been unaware (and wanted to remain as such), Volapük nevertheless turned out be a huge success. By 1890, twelve years after Schleyer's first publication on the language,

> the number of Volapük's speakers, supporters, and enthusiasts [was] 2,500,000, the number of Volapük associations 290, and the number of Volapük newspapers 3. [...] As of now, 300 companies (159 in Germany, 66 in France, 30 in Italy, 14 in England, 13 in Russia, and 9 in the United States) have adopted Volapük as their language of correspondence and have begun to restrict their hiring to people who have a command of this language.[29]

For all of its initial success, and despite Schleyer's polemical dismissals of other artificial languages, Volapük was able to remain a centerpiece in the debates over international auxiliary languages for no more than two decades. The main reason for this was the numerous critiques that targeted the artificiality of Schleyer's construct. Although derived from living languages, for instance, Volapük's lexicon was obscured to the point that the etymological origins of its words were no longer recognizable, a fact that made it difficult to learn. In general, the language was too cryptic. With their firm position against any form of artificiality, the proponents of the auxiliary-language movement soon exposed Volapük's vocabulary to be *a priori* in disguise. The mnemonic advantages that an anglophilic European would have enjoyed while learning the language, that is, were neutralized by the obscure manner in which English words were reformed (*vol* does not exactly look like *world*, and *pük* does not immediately call to mind the word *speak*).

That said, Schleyer's failure was not due to the competition offered by the other international auxiliary languages that were under development; rather, he failed to satisfy the democratic tendencies that came to define the community of Volapük enthusiasts. The latter hoped to optimize the language through public debate and to rely on multiple experts to test the applicability of the language's grammar and vocabulary, to make suggested revisions, and to turn Volapük into a living construct.[30] Schleyer, however, adamantly preferred to remain authoritarian. An irony of this story is that it was a cryptographer, of all things, that accelerated Volapük's downfall simply by encouraging its open use. The *Kadem Volapüka* ("Academy of the World Language") was founded in August of 1877 at the second annual Volapük Congress in Munich. The executive board of the academy consisted of a single member, namely the great inventor himself, who presided as the *cifal* 'chief' over all other Volapük associations. As the director of the academy, Schleyer named the French linguist and cryptographer Auguste Kerckhoffs. When, at a meeting of

---

[29]   Ibid., 3.

[30]   See Gustav Meyer, "Weltsprache und Weltsprachen," in *Essays und Studien zur Sprachgeschichte und Volkskunde*, by Meyer, 2 vols. (Strassburg: K. J. Trübner, 1885–1893), 2:23–46.

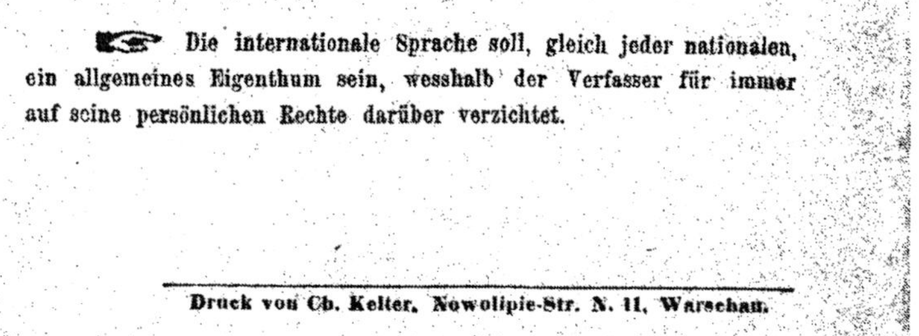

Fig. 2: Copyleft: Zamenhof's renouncement of any personal rights to Esperanto.

the Academy in Paris during the following year, Kerckhoffs suggested (without authorization) that a uniform grammar should be adopted, this clearly represented an attempt to democratize the new language. Schleyer, however, retorted at once that, from then on, no decision reached at any Volapük meeting would be valid without the approval of the *cifal*. In volume 107 of the journal *Volapük-Blatt*, Schleyer published an article ("The Academy and I") in which he demanded the Academy to comply with the established hierarchy, though he was not subtle about dismissing every position but his own:

> The Academy may serve as my advisor, but it is not my master or guardian, let alone something injurious to me. I do not stand within the Academy but rather above the Academy. For without me there would not even be an Academy of Volapuk. [...] Above all, the Academy should seek the medium with me, not flee from it. Yet I myself, in addition to my great idea, am at the center of Volapük; I am the originator and overseer of Volapük.[31]

If Volapük does not stay exactly as it is, in other words, the language should not exist at all. Although journals continued to be published in Schleyer's artificial language until 1956, it never really recovered from the authoritarianism of its founder. Despite Schleyer's apparent wish to address "all the inhabitants of the earth," Volapük more or less remained the pet project of its creator.

Another artificial language began its triumphant ascent around the end of the nineteenth century. Its design, which the physician Ludwik Lazarus Zamenhof published in 1887, remains to this day the most lasting contribution to the agenda of international auxiliary languages, and it is still known by the pseudonym of its inventor: Esperanto. Zamenhof worked on his language for fifteen years, all the while keeping a close eye on the events surrounding Volapük.[32] The 1887 publication, which was soon translated into English as *An Attempt Towards an International Language* (among other titles), was written in Russian

---

[31] Quoted from Beermann, *Studien zu Schleyers Weltsprache Volapük*, 13 (a German translation of the Volapük original).

[32] See Ulrich Lins, *Die gefährliche Sprache: Die Verfolgung der Esperantisten unter Hitler und Stalin* (Gerlingen: Bleichen, 1988), 16.

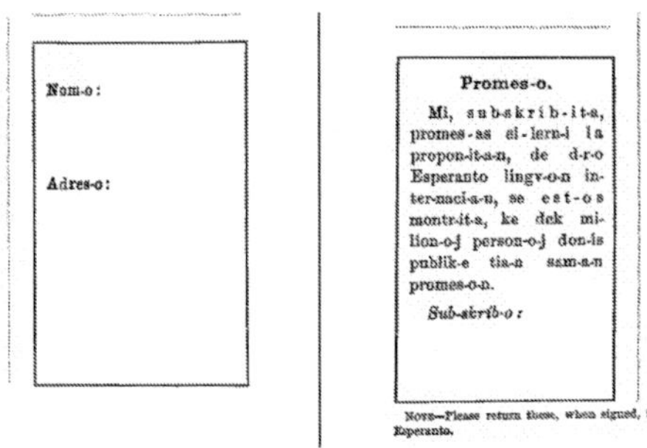

Fig 3: Language as a mass medium: Zamenhof's "mailbot"

and attributed to "Dr. Esperanto" (the hopeful one). In a mere thirty-nine pages, Zamenhof's manual, which is now commonly known as the *Unua Libro*, outlined the grammar of the language and provided a rudimentary dictionary. A quick perusal of the book makes clear, however, that Zamenhof intended Esperanto to serve as a "social medium." One of the three "principal problems" that needed to be solved, according to the author, was as follows: "Means must be found to overcome the indifference of the bulk of mankind, and to cause the masses to make use of the language offered as a living tongue."[33]

The appendix to Zamenhof's book contained a series of coupons that interested readers were encouraged to cut out and distribute to others after having signed one of their own and sent it to "Dr. Samenhof, Warsaw." The coupons consisted of a small contract, whereby the signatories were to announce their interest in Zamenhof's language and pledge their intention to learn it. The hopeful doctor imagined the formation of an Esperanto-speaking community of *dek milionoj personoj*; the contract would remain valid, that is, until ten million people had signed it.

Zamenhof remained true to his anti-authoritarian position, but nevertheless he had to wait eighteen years (ten more than Schleyer) before a commission was founded to supplement and refine his work. At the first World Congress of Esperanto, which was held in 1905 in Boulogne-sur-Mer, enthusiasts and experts finally came together to establish the *fundamento* of their language. Esperanto long remained the most significant legacy of the international-auxiliary-language movement, a movement that began around 1900 with the goal of providing transportation and communication technologies with a new social medium. Influenced by the economic, political, and technological conditions of their day, to which they made explicit references, authors such as Schleyer and Zamenhof (alongside hundreds of others) endeavored to prepare a mass medium for a global audience that was just beginning to take shape. Whereas one of the authors' reactions to these conditions resulted in failure, the other managed to devise an open structure for his language on the basis of the political and economic exigencies of his time.

---

[33] Dr. Esperanto (Ludwik Lazarus Zamenhof), *An Attempt Towards an International Language*, trans. Henry Phillips (New York: Henry Holt & Company, 1889), 9.

V.

It would be quite easy to compare the autocratic behavior of Johann Martin Schleyer with that of someone like Bill Gates.[34] In the figure of Ludwik Zamenhof, moreover, it would be just as easy to see an historical precedent to Steven Levy's hacker ethic,[35] Linus Torvalds's Linux kernel,[36] or Richard Stallman's GNU operating system.[37] Under the conditions of the computer, however, it did not take long for the discourse about open knowledge to shift from a technically-based logic regarding an open economy of knowledge to the neoliberal fantasy of the open-source movement.[38] The theoretical basis of interlinguistics, the field responsible for artificial languages, followed the example presented by Zamenhof. Its goal, in the words of one the discipline's founding documents, was "to study the natural laws for formulating a common auxiliary language."[39] Technology-oriented media studies, on the contrary, has treated artificial languages primarily as precursors to machine or computer languages. Within this context, two media-theoretical approaches are observable. The first, and more common, is a technical approach that understands these media-technological conditions and the history of combinatorics as the prehistory of the computer. The second concerns an economy of knowledge in which the *a posteriori* international auxiliary languages – developed around the year 1900 – serve as an origin story for open, "copyleft" programming codes. Speaking at the "Ars Electronica" symposium in 2003, Leo Findeisen maintained that Zamenhof's renouncement of any legal claims to Esperanto, which was expressed in his book from 1887, should be regarded "as the foundational act of the Free

---

[34]   In "An Open Letter to Hobbyists" (1976), Bill Gates imposed the authority of professional programmers over mere hobbyists: "As the majority of hobbyists must be aware, most of you steal your software. Hardware must be paid for, but software is something to share. Who cares if the people who worked on it get paid?" The letter, which was printed in several computer magazines, can be read in full at http://www.blinkenlights.com/ classiccmp/gateswhine.html (accessed on February 2, 2013).

[35]   The fundamental values of the hacker ethic are sharing, openness, decentralization, free access (to computers, in Levy's case), and world improvement. See Steven Levy, *Hackers: Heroes of the Computer Revolution* (Garden City, NY: Anchor Books, 1984).

[36]   See Linus Torvalds and David Diamond, *Just for Fun: The Story of an Accidental Revolutionary* (New York: Harper Business, 2001), 94–95: "I wanted people to be able to see it, and to make changes and improvements to their hearts' content. But I also wanted to make sure that what I got out of it was to see what they were doing. I wanted to always have access to the sources so that if they made improvements I could use those improvements myself."

[37]   The parallel between Zamenhof and Stallman has in fact already been drawn. See Leo Findeisen, "Some Code to Die For: On the Birth of the Free Software Movement in 1887," in *Code: The Language of Our Time*, ed. Gerfried Stocker et al. (Osterfildern-Ruit: Hatje Cantz Verlag, 2003), 73–87, esp. 86.

[38]   See Christopher M. Kelty, *Two Bits: The Cultural Significance of Free Software* (Durham, NC: Duke University Press, 2008), 112–15.

[39]   Jules Meysmans, "Eine neue Wissenschaft," in *Plansprachen: Beiträge zur Interlinguistik*, ed. Reinhardt Haupenthal (Darmstadt: Wissenschaftliche Buchgesellschaft, 1976), 111–12, at 111. This essay was originally published as "Une science nouvelle," *Lingua internationale* 1 (1911/1912), 14–16.

Software Movement."[40] Accordingly, Schleyer's Volapük would thus have to be interpreted as the failed strategy of an unyielding designer of proprietary code.

During the international protests against financial capitalism, the programmer Pall Thayer cast new light on the political potential of open codes. His "microcode," however, was less an instance of so-called "hacktivism" as it was an act of artistic intervention.[41] Thayer posted a small code, written in Perl and consisting of just a few lines, on Netbehaviour's mailing list and on his homepage, and he gave it the title "For Occupy Wall Street":

```
#!/usr/bin/perl
push(@rights, my $rights);[42]
```

The point of this intervention lies in the simple programmability of the code (Perl will even process through syntax errors) as well as in the emphatic visual message of its scripting language. Regardless of whether one knows what the prefixes @ and $ mean (beyond denoting addressability on the internet and a type of currency), it is clear to see that "For Occupy Wall Street" is concerned with the assertion of certain rights, namely "my $rights" – Thayer's rights and the rights of those who run the code. Then again, is the code "For Occupy Wall Street" truly about a political agenda? Or is it merely a linguistic manipulation that can only be executed within an interpreter, visualized with the help of a word processor, distributed by means of a mail client, and retrieved through a web browser? Wendy Hui Kyong Chun has pointed out that, of all things, the complex and alienating medium of the computer has paradoxically been accompanied by a narrative of transparency: "The history of computing is littered with moments of 'computer liberation.' [...] The narrative of the democratization of programming reveals the tension at the heart of programming and control systems: are they control systems or servomechanisms (Norbert Wiener's initial name for them)? Given that the machine takes care of 'programming proper' – the sequence of events during execution – is programming programming at all?"[43]

Proponents of the open-source movement – as well as supporters of net libertarian movements such as the burgeoning Pirate parties – continue to associate the origins of their cause with the democratic and libertarian metaphor of Esperanto.[44] Yet, already in one

---

[40] Findeisen, "Some Code to Die For," 82.

[41] On Pall Thayer, see Geoff Cox, *Speaking Code: Coding as Aesthetic and Political Expression* (Cambridge, MA: MIT Press, 2013), 70–72. On the notion of "hacktivism," see E. Gabriella Coleman, *Coding Freedom: the Ethics and Aesthetics of Hacking* (Princeton: Princeton University Press, 2013).

[42] This code, which was posted on October 5, 2011, is now archived at http://www.netbehaviour.org/pipermail/ netbehaviour/20111005/022975.html (accessed on February 19, 2013).

[43] Chun, "On Software, or the Persistence of Visual Knowledge," 32.

[44] See, for instance, Carsten Schnober and Martin Loschwitz, "Projects on the Move: An Up-To-Date Look at Free Software and Its Makers," *Linux Magazine* 72 (2004), 93–95; and the entry "Esperanto" in the wiki devoted to the German Pirate Party: http://wiki.piratenpartei.de/Esperanto (accessed on February 1, 2013).

of the foundational texts concerned with Web 2.0, Tim O'Reilly stressed the importance of "open" and "free" software to the success of future business models: "Lightweight business models are a natural concomitant of lightweight programming."[45] According to O'Reilly, Web 2.0 software models are characterized by the visuality of their interfaces and by simplified access to their source code. In order to present (new) users with the fewest possible obstacles, he believes that such software should be open enough to ensure that developers can make steady improvements to it: *release early, release often*. And thus the metaphor of language is ultimately unsuitable for this scenario, one in which the programs of Web 2.0, as well as its code and economic agenda, are chiefly concerned with the increasing number of interfaces that ensure the interoperability of machines and thereby facilitate communication between platforms, during which process the source text remains persistently hidden. In the case of such programs, the underlying code is not only meant to be looked over ("lightweight") but also *overlooked*.[46] Thinking again about Pall Thayer's intervention in the scripting language Perl, one has to wonder: How political could the use of platforms such as Twitter or Facebook really have been during the uprisings in the "Arab world"? The software of Web 2.0, designed as it is for mass markets, is grounded in the paradigm of interoperability, in the exchange between platforms and thus in their particular political and economic agenda. However, it is precisely this discursive coupling of the "open" and "free" codes of open-source software – this confusion of economic and informatic programs – that led to the emphatic statement made by the "Revolution 2.0."

---

[45] Tim O'Reilly, "What Is Web 2.0? Design Patterns and Business Models for the Next Generation of Software," in *The Social Media Reader*, ed. Michael Mandiberg (New York: New York University Press, 2012), 32–52, at 47. O'Reilly's article was originally published in 2005.

[46] On the invisibility of code, see Alexander R. Galloway, "Language Wants to Be Overlooked: On Software and Ideology," *Journal of Visual Culture* 5 (2006), 315–31, esp. 320.

Dirk Baecker

The Sociology of Media

"The task confronting contemporary man is to live with the hidden ground of his activities as our literate predecessors lived with the figure minus ground."[1]

Sociology is a product of modern society. By concentrating on issues of community, authority, status, the sacred, and alienation, it records and analyzes the uncertainties that have afflicted social order throughout society's transition from stratification to functional differentiation.[2] Its critical attention has focused especially on matters of power, social inequality, exploitation, and imperialism. With the help of concepts such as activity, norms, roles, groups, interaction, organization, systems, and networks, sociologists have developed theoretical foundations for observing the issues involved with the transition between various forms of societal differentiation and for identifying the problem of the social, a problem that remains the same both before and after any such transitions have taken place. Overarching ideas such as solidarity (Emile Durkheim), imitation (Gabriel Tarde), rationalization (Max Weber), or reciprocity (Georg Simmel) have allowed classical sociologists to make the societal dichotomy of order and disorder fruitful for theoretical and empirical investigations.

The discovery of media can be regarded as one of sociology's crowning achievements. No other phenomenon sheds a brighter light on the turbulent nature of modern society. Moreover, there has hardly been another concept within the field that has yielded more theoretical and empirical promise. At the same time, possibly no concept has been better suited to free sociology from the restrictions of examining the transition from traditional to modern society in order to focus on phenomena that allow it to treat even modern society in historical terms, that is, to assign modern society a beginning and an end.

---

[1]   Marshall McLuhan and Eric McLuhan, *Laws of Media: The New Science* (Toronto: University of Toronto Press, 1988), 114.

[2]   See Shmuel N. Eisenstadt and Miriam Curelaru, *The Form of Sociology: Paradigms and Crises* (New York: Wiley, 1976); and Robert A. Nisbet, *The Sociological Tradition* (New York: Basic Books, 1966).

My first aim below will be to revisit Talcott Parsons's discovery of media and to elucidate his understanding of the concept. My second concern will be to show how Niklas Luhmann refined Parsons's concept and supplemented it with his ideas of symbolically generalized communication media, dissemination media, and mass media. With such ideas, and with his engagement with the works of Fritz Heider and Marshall McLuhan, Luhmann was able to place the concept of media on theoretically and empirically firmer ground. My final section will draw upon one of Luhmann's cultural-theoretical hypotheses to propose a panoramic notion of media archaeology that allows us to observe various societal phenomena as the result of engaging with the dissemination media of communication. In light of such engagement, it will be possible to identify four media epochs of human society that can so far be ascertained and to describe them according to their various forms of culture, structure, integration, reflection, and negation.

I.

The discovery of symbolic media of interchange, as Parsons called them,[3] and the discovery of symbolically generalized communication media and success media, as they are referred to in Luhmann's work,[4] can both be attributed to a theoretical and structural problem. Parsons had developed his four-function differentiation of the social system inside the action system in the human – each of which in turn differentiated according to the basic functions of *a*daptation, *g*oal attainment, *i*ntegration, and *l*atent pattern-maintenance (AGIL) – to such an intricate extent that the question of how those different aspects of action can be "mediated" among each other could no longer be avoided.[5] Did each edge of this scheme that could be applied to itself ad libitum, or better, depending on need and availability of empirical research, correspond to a "medium", making sure that the calculated results of each box can be "exchanged" with all others? Parsons indeed embarked on a long journey to examine whether such an inquiry would be possible.

---

[3] See Talcott Parsons, "On the Concept of Political Power," *Proceedings of the American Philosophical Society* 107 (1963), 232–62; idem, "Some Problems of General Theory in Sociology," in *Theoretical Sociology: Perspectives and Developments*, ed. John C. McKinney and Edward A. Tiryakian (Englewood Cliffs: Prentice-Hall, 1970), 26–68; idem, "Social Structure and the Symbolic Media of Interchange," in *Approaches to the Study of Social Structure*, ed. Peter M. Blau (New York: Free Press, 1975), 94–120 [cited here from the reprint in Talcott Parsons, *Social Systems and the Evolution of Action Theory* (New York: Free Press, 1977), 204–28]; and idem, "A Paradigm of the Human Condition," in *Social Systems and the Evolution of Action Theory*, by Parsons (New York: Free Press, 1977), 352–433.

[4] See Niklas Luhmann, "Einführende Bemerkungen zu einer Theorie symbolisch generalisierter Kommunikationsmedien," *Zeitschrift für Soziologie* 3 (1974), 236–55; and idem, *Theory of Society*, 2 vols., trans. Rhodes Barrett (Stanford: Stanford University Press, 2012–2013), 1:113–250.

[5] The foundations of his theory are presented in Talcott Parsons and Neil J. Smelser, *Economy and Society: A Study in the Integration of Economic and Social Theory* (1956; repr. London: Routledge, 1984).

He referred to "boundary processes" that connected certain aspects of action between the different components of his system,[6] and it was on the basis of such processes that he ultimately came to develop the idea of symbolic media of interchange,[7] which can perhaps be regarded as one of the few truly significant discoveries of twentieth-century sociology.

Parsons's point of departure, as so often in his work, was not a deduction from his own scheme but an empirical observation. He realized that the same positions of social influence, which in traditional societies had been held by hereditary status groups such as the nobility or clergy, were taken over in modern society by groups associated with cultural prestige (academics, intellectuals, artists, lawyers, doctors), political prestige (politicians, businessmen, union leaders), or social prestige (leaders of civil rights movements or women's movements).[8] For "prestige" we would nowadays perhaps say "capital". He traced this shift to the appearance of media, which in modern society fulfilled the same ordering function that social stratification had served in traditional society, where the term "order" in both cases is related to matters of stability, mobility, and the division of labor. In modern society, according to his theory, the prestige of these groups results from their competency when dealing with various media such as influence, money, power, intelligence, and affect. At the same time, prestige is itself a medium, in that who possesses a given sort of prestige is a matter of negotiation.

What is it about these media that allows them to fulfill an ordering function in society even though they do not converge with any particular groups, social strata, norms, or cultural values? They select contributions to action not according to their coming from people of the same tribe or belonging to the same rank but according to functional solutions to problems of orientation of society. Functional solutions by appropriate action come first, people attached to those solutions and then possibly symbolizing them only appear in second place. Symbolic media of interchange came to be seen as highly dynamic ways to select and motivate that kind of action irrespective of people claiming to come first because of rights, power, or wealth. On the other hand, if certain people prove to make sensible use of those media they are awarded prestige and influence.

Due to an economic understanding of money and a linguistic description of language already at hand Parsons's primary model for investigating such media was money, to which he added the phenomenon of language in order to formulate the general characteristics of a medium. These he determined to be value, functions, institutionalization, specificity of meaning, circulability, and the fact that the medium should always have a non-zero-sum character.[9] To elaborate:

a. The *value* of a medium consists in its exchange value, not in its use value. A medium can only be appropriated individually to the extent that it is used to facilitate an exchange

---

[6]   Ibid.

[7]   Parsons, "Social Structure and the Symbolic Media of Interchange."

[8]   Ibid., 220–28.

[9]   Ibid., 204–07.

with other individuals.[10] A word for example, which we use may only match a reference if others are using it similarly.

b. As in the case of money, the *functions* of a medium are, in addition to its exchange function, its functions as a measure of value and as a store of value. Media enable the attribution of value (and its lack) or preference (and its lack) and they enable the cross-situational transportation of acquired values and demands through time and space. For example, investing successfully in the expression of love enables one to draw on the capital gained in later moments at perhaps lesser cost.

c. The characteristic of *institutionalization* means that a medium's terms of use are intuitively accessible and can taken for granted, just as money is embedded in the institution of property, power is embedded in the institution of the state, or language is embedded in the institution of grammar (subject, object, predicate, indexicality, and reflexivity).

d. The medium's *specificity of meaning* can be understood, on the one hand, as its reference and access to a particular sphere of society and, on the other hand, as its difference from other spheres. So it is that money pertains to the economy, power to politics, truth to science, faith to religion, and so on. However, efforts must be made to ensure that such media are not confused with one another. This is not to say that confusions are not continually made – quite the contrary – but that, if needed, such confusions can be recognized as such. Demarcation always entails one reference or another, such that possible interferences need to be taken into account when dealing with the concept of a medium's specificity of meaning. Again, to give an example, being able to pay does not lend a person power, because power consists in being able to force somebody to do something against his or her will. To distinguish between these two situations does not always come easily.

e. A medium has to be able to *circulate*, that is, its control must be transferable from one person or entity to another. It must be possible to distinguish between access and addressee, between occasion and object, in order to be able to identify which states of a situation have been influenced by the use of a medium and the manner in which such change has been accomplished. Paying a certain sum of money changes the property status of an object or service and enables the receiver of the payment to decide in his or her own way how to use the money thus gained.

f. Finally, a medium should always have a *non-zero-sum character* in that, no matter the medium, it must be possible for something like credit creation to take place. This is to say that units of media can be used repeatedly, so long as every use proves to be situational and individual and no single use excludes another. For example, one can evaluate the circumstances under which a declaration of love might be successful and use this declaration at the decisive time without taking any love away from the person whose own declaration you have imitated. This non-zero-sum nature of media is related to the societal possibilities of inflation and deflation (that is, to reductions and increases of

---

[10]   Otherwise its value would be like that of a fetish, which is not an individual phenomenon but rather a phenomenon of networks. It could perhaps be said that the circulation of fetishes in society paradoxically resembles the circulation of objects withdrawn from circulation.

value) as well as to the establishment of banks, which manage "deposits" in such media and grant "credit." One may notice that a certain formulation of declaring one's love has been overused and isn't credible any more, i.e. is not backed by real assets any more; vice versa, going from a love affair to a marriage might create a bank account for your love you may easily draw upon until all of a sudden the very ease of the transaction turns your love doubtful.

This conceptual catalogue of media characteristics has defined a research agenda that continues to be used by sociologists, if only in a rudimentary manner. Niklas Luhmann, for instance, published significant case studies on the media of power,[11] the media of love,[12] the media of money,[13] the media of truth,[14] and the media of art.[15] More recently, Peter Sloterdijk has interestingly enough argued that there are currently "banks" of rage in the political sphere.[16] Yet scholars have certainly not exhausted the possible applications of Parsons's fundamental ideas.

II.

Niklas Luhmann adopted Parsons's concept of symbolic media of interchange and modified it in four significant respects.[17] First, he abandoned Parsons's ideas of a general system of action and of a human condition and restricted the differentiation of symbolically generalized media to their role within the functional system.[18] Second, Luhmann no longer related the medium to exchange or action but rather to communication. In light of his understanding of the improbability of any form of communication, this move enabled

---

[11] Niklas Luhmann, *Trust and Power*, trans. Howard Davis et al. (New York: Wiley, 1979); idem, *Die Politik der Gesellschaft* (Frankfurt am Main: Suhrkamp, 2000).

[12] Niklas Luhmann, *Love as Passion: The Codification of Intimacy*, trans. Jeremy Gaines and Doris Jones (Cambridge, MA: Harvard University Press, 1986).

[13] Niklas Luhmann, *Die Wirtschaft der Gesellschaft* (Frankfurt am Main: Suhrkamp), 230–71.

[14] Niklas Luhmann, *Die Wissenschaft der Gesellschaft* (Frankfurt am Main: Suhrkamp, 1990), 122–270.

[15] Niklas Luhmann, *The Reality of the Mass Media*, trans. Kathleen Cross (Stanford: Stanford University Press, 2000), 15–22.

[16] Peter Sloterdijk, *Rage and Time: A Psychopolitical Investigation*, trans. Mario Wenning (New York: Columbia University Press, 2010). See also Dirk Baecker, "Ein Medium kommt selten allein," in *Die Vermessung des Ungeheuren: Philosophie nach Peter Sloterdijk*, ed. Marc Jongen et al. (Frankfurt am Main: Suhrkamp, 2009), 131–43.

[17] Luhmann, "Einführende Bemerkungen"; idem, *Theory of Society*, 1:113–250.

[18] Of course, he did not simply discard these ideas without acknowledging, as regards the analysis of social phenomena, the theoretical contribution of distinguishing between an objective dimension of differentiation and a temporal dimension of reproduction. See Niklas Luhmann, "Talcott Parsons: Zur Zukunft eines Theorieprogramms," *Zeitschrift für Soziologie* 9 (1980), 5–17. It might not be superfluous to note that this distinction is not very different from that between the static and the dynamic (existence and motion, order and development, consensus and reaction), a distinction that has been at the heart of every sociological theory since Auguste Comte.

him to analyze, more precisely than Parsons ever could, the motivational or selective role of media for each specific instance of communication. In this regard, too, he drew an important distinction between attributing communication to action and attributing it to experience. By considering the dimension of experience, he was able to treat the concept of meaning in a more differentiated manner than ever before,[19] and this allowed him to use, for instance, sensible observations of media use in literary fiction in a way that was sociologically fruitful. Third, Luhmann expanded the concept of the medium to include the dissemination media of writing, printing, and electronic media – which had previously been studied by economic historians, literary critics, and cultural theorists – and therefore, fourth, he sought (with the help of Fritz Heider's ideas) to establish the general concept of media so firmly as to encompass symbolically generalized media, dissemination media, and mass media.

Luhmann's formulation of the concept of symbolically generalized communication media supplemented every point on Parsons's list of media characteristics, with the one exception of the requirement of institutionalization, which Luhmann scaled back to some degree. His theoretical refinements were as follows:[20]

1. Every symbolically generalized communication medium requires a *binary code* that, within a functional system, distinguishes a preference value for desired communicative success from a reflection value for observing the possibility of failure. Within this framework, the binary code enables a considerable simplification (Luhmann speaks of "technization") of any communication's chances to connect to previous and next communication.[21] For instance, once having established, by successfully threatening the use of physical force, a communication by means of power it becomes much easier to continue a communication of the same type. The ease of the use of money, on the other hand, may lead one to overlook completely that there are things in the world which nobody can buy with money.

2. The code of a communication medium is accompanied by a *self-placing* of the code within its preference value. By such means the code is able to assert itself as an autonomous social value. To be able to love, for example, within the code of intimate communication,

---

19   Niklas Luhmann, "Sinn als Grundbegriff der Soziologie," in *Theorie der Gesellschaft oder Sozialtechnologie: Was leistet die Systemforschung?*, ed. Jürgen Habermas and Niklas Luhmann (Frankfurt am Main: Suhrkamp, 1971), 25–100. See also Alfred Schütz, *Der sinnhafte Aufbau der sozialen Welt: Eine Einleitung in die verstehende Soziologie* (1932; repr. Frankfurt am Main: Suhrkamp, 1974).

20   Luhmann, *Theory of Society*, 1:214–35.

21   Perhaps it is not superfluous to note that Luhmann proposes this form of binary code only for functional systems and (with some reservation) organizational systems, not for interaction systems. And even in the case of functional systems, their binary codes are paradoxically based on actually trivalent forms of code in that they have to make sure to hide the contingent, that is arbitrary nature of the very distinction (the third value) between the two sides, its first and second value, of the code. In academic literature, incidentally, it is too often presupposed that Luhmann's conception of social systems is based exclusively on binary logic.

is always preferred to not being able to love, such that the code asserts its value with respect to enabling love and not with respect to protecting from it.

3. All symbolically generalized communication media entail a *processual reflexivity*, so that it is possible to pursue truth by truthful methods and theories, to pay for money with money ("interest"), to love with love, to belief in faith, and to use power to gain power. Luhmann presumes that this is a precondition for formulating a special semantics with which to describe medial possibilities. Epistemologies in science, banking within the economy, love songs, love letters, and love stories, struggling with doubt in faith, or concepts of sovereign rights are examples of semantics produced by processual reflexivity.

4. Owing to its code, dealing with media enables a differentiation of *second-order observation*, that is, it enables the observation of observers as regards their success or failure at communication. Lovers observe lovers, researchers researchers, politicians politicians, priests priests, and so on, not only to imitate them, acquire self-confidence or gain subtlety, but also to modify them and carry the medium to previously unknown or uncharted terrain.

5. Because media are coded, they can also be *programmed*. That is, it is possible for organizations to append themselves to functional systems. By means of their programs, these organizations attempt to determine how the probability of communicative success can be increased and they are able to learn from their successes and failures. Thus in addition to the paradoxical unity of code, third values of communication also come into play. Businesses search for payments by offering products, political parties gain power by opting for a certain agenda, academic institutions profile the truth they are seeking by the benefits of the curricula and research programs they are offering, and so on. It is interesting to note that businesses will not succeed in just seeking profit, that political parties will not convince by just claiming power, or that academic institutions do not convince by calling for truth. They all have to offer something, which is not to be deduced from the values of the binary code but is to be judged by those values, as either success or failure. That something adds third (and more) values to the system that relies on a binary code.

6. Via *symbiotic mechanisms*, communication media secure connections to bodies and their perceptual capacities to allow for experiences in line with what the media have to offer. Physical force must threaten bodily invulnerability to have an effect of power. Love, at least passionate love in modern society, must appeal to sexuality to make sure what intimacy is about. Money, in fact, will only buy if needs are to be fulfilled, never mind how imaginary those needs may be. And even in science any kind of truth must relate to a world to be perceived differently when accepting that truth. Interestingly, the symbiotic mechanisms do not establish any straight and undeniable causality but create further ambiguities and call for cultural interpretation. The scope and range of invulner-ability, sexuality, needs, or empirical proof differ along with cultural development, such that the symbiotic mechanism in all these cases is to be understood more as a symbiotic symbol, which always has to reestablish its reference and demarcation. Not least the arts, i.e. society's way to communicate the variability of perception, make sure that no symbol stays unchallenged for too long, cultural criticism being only too happy to follow suit.

7. Finally, every medium requires a *zero method*, that is, a conception of its own conditions of impossibility. For instance, the supply of money by central banks cannot be purchased by the economy but rather must be guaranteed politically. Power thrives on the fact that it is not exhibited in certain situations. It must be possible to forget certain truths in order for researchers to pose alternative questions. One must be able to forego tokens of love so as not to overtax love's possibilities. By their zero methods media include their exclusion of certain possibilities and thus within their connective network produce empty places, which call for supplements by other means of communication.

One cannot, I suspect, present such a list without having substantial empirical experience in media research. In what follows, unfortunately, I will only be able to go into greater detail about the prominent examples of power, money, love, faith, and the law. The sketchy examples given above in explaining a little of the items on the list must suffice here.

Before moving on, however, it is essential to keep in mind that these media can only fulfill their function of transforming improbable communication into probable communication because each of them realizes specific constellations of action and experience and therefore excludes other such constellations.[22] Experience is bound by truth, while action is not. Inversely, action is bound by power, which sets experience free. Communication with the medium of money allows one person access to goods and services, while another must keep still, that is, must refrain from interfering even when being as hungry or needy as the first person is, limiting his or her communication to experience. Amazingly enough, art operates in the very same way. In this case, "autonomous" action is conceded to the artist, whereas only experience, though in the not entirely passive form of viewing, listening, and feeling is expected of the public audience. In the case of love, moreover, it can be imagined that the experience of one partner can bind the action of the other such that both behave in ways to confirm the world perceived by the one they love.

The power of these media to separate themselves is achieved in their motivation function by means of the exclusion of certain selections. Truths must *not* lead to action. Power must not also gain the appreciation of the other. Communication with the medium of money does not mean that an actor must simultaneously experience how an observer cannot satisfy his or her own needs. Artists must not expect that their art will have consequences for the actions of others. And even in the case of love, one need not experience one's own action as it is experienced by one's partner.

The consideration of dissemination media, in addition to the symbolically generalized media that can be referred to as success media, likewise owes itself to the introduction of a concept of improbable communication. Dissemination media such as writing, printing, and electronic media *reduce* the improbability of reaching the absent and the many (or even everyone) and of reaching them immediately. In doing so, however, they also increase the probability of rejection, given that the addressee might feel no pressure to respond, might not have any time, or the situation might not be right.

---

[22] Luhmann, *Theory of Society*, 1:199–213.

It remains conceptually unclear whether mass media can be considered part of the dissemination media or whether, in modern society, they have been differentiated as a functional system of their own.[23] Luhmann was inclined to believe the latter and thus accepted the possibility of ascribing to mass media – with its three agendas of news, entertainment, and advertising – the prominent role of distinguishing between information and non-information, which is relevant to all circumstances of society.[24] Though I cannot dwell on this point here, it should be pointed out that this form of distinguishing between information and non-information subsequently and complementarily directs the sociological inquiry also toward areas of society in which such a distinction has *not* taken hold, such as daily life, family life, or broader aspects of the work life.

More important in the present context is Luhmann's restructuring of the conceptual foundations of media sociology in order that they might able to encompass success media, dissemination media, and mass media. Admittedly, there is no need to unify certain concepts if it is no less elegant to keep their differing perspectives apart. Also, Luhmann placed no special value on designing a theoretical architecture whose every detail was in complete agreement, given that reality itself is hardly defined by consistency and coherence. Yet the proposal of a concept that is possibly suitable for coherently formulating media functions across a broad variety of individual cases is itself, in Luhmann's perspective, an empirical signal that can be taken to indicate a reality being met by that signal. This concept, as in our case, coming from a different discipline must not, then, be adopted on a one-to-one basis, for sociology is faced with problems of empirical access and phenomenological understanding that of course differ from those faced by other disciplines, but it is possible to vary the concept while remaining true to the established perspectives of one field or another.

One suggested concept of this sort is that of media proposed by Fritz Heider for the field of perceptual psychology, according to which media are understood as the condition of possibility for matters (things) of every sort.[25] Luhmann goes beyond this concept to the extent that he regards media as a condition of possibility for things of every sort and

---

[23] It usually seems as though the concept of the "masses" is often used to stress the expectability of unexpected effects of communication, whereas the concept of "dissemination" is used only to stress the solution of technical problems involved with overcoming distance. See Elias Canetti, *Crowds and Power*, trans. Carol Stewart (New York: Farrar, Straus & Giroux, 1984). If one postulates a functional system of mass media, as Luhmann does, it must be accepted that this system will display unexpected effects in the form of irritation, cultivation, and domestication (taming), including the possibility that manifestations of the mass media will take the place of latent "silent majorities." See Jean Baudrillard, *In the Shadow of the Silent Majorities ... or the End of the Social, and Other Essays*, trans. Paul Foss et al. (New York: Semiotext(e), 1983). However, a discussion of dissemination media requires one to look for other system references to serve as the basis for analyzing their effects, such things as interaction, organization, and society.

[24] Luhmann, *The Reality of the Mass Media*.

[25] Fritz Heider, *Ding und Medium* (1926; repr. Berlin: Kulturverlag Kadmos, 2005).

at the same time as circular products of the possibilities that are provided with them.[26] Communication media such as love, money, or power are not given by nature but the result of their own use; they evolve together with the uses they are put to and the disuse they may suffer. Undoubtedly influenced by the theoretical physics of his time, Heider rejected the possibility of remote perception. Dispensing with any philosophical *a priori* of space, time, and thing-in-itself, he formulated a theory of perception according to which the rigid coupling of certain elements to a thing is only possible if the very same elements exist also as loosely coupled elements of a medium. A thing thus becomes "imprinted" in its medium. Think of a footprint in the sand, an object in light, or a noise in the medium of sound.

At the latest, sociology came into contact with this conceptual understanding when, on the basis of constructivist epistemology, it began to ascribe to the observer, as someone who acts and experiences, an active role in the process of cognition. For even in Heider's work, an organism must actively move along the cycle of motor and sensory skills in order to be capable of perception and to be able to create and explore his or her world, so to speak, within the medium of this perception. And Heider's work comes especially close to Luhmann's systems theory in that his theory of perception, which acknowledges the uniformity of things and the diversity of media alike, approximates an operational theory of complexity, if "complexity" here means to allow for any event its constitution in at least two, possibly even contradictory, aspects of itself.[27]

Luhmann did not let this concept slip through his fingers, and he identified the general problem addressed by Parsons's and Heider's media theories to be the unity of the difference between unity and difference.[28] Luhmann was drawn to Parsons's work by the crucial idea that he, Parsons, regarded generality to be the specificity of a medium, which, thanks to this specificity, is able to transcend differences such as different situations, dif-

---

[26] Heider was possibly of the opinion, though Luhmann was certainly not, that media are "indifferent" with respect to their things or forms. The opposite would be to side with Luhmann and understand media as the byproduct of forms. See Sybille Krämer, "Das Medium als Spur und Apparat," in *Medien, Computer, Realität: Wirklichkeitsvorstellungen und neue Medien*, ed. Krämer (Frankfurt am Main: Suhrkamp, 1998), 73–94; and idem, "Form als Vollzug, oder: Was gewinnen wir mit Niklas Luhmanns Unterscheidung von Medium und Form?" *Rechtshistorisches Journal* 17 (1998), 558–73.

[27] It is no coincidence that Luhmann was introduced to Heider's concept of media through his engagement with Karl E. Weick's theory of organization, for it is in the "posts" (*"Stellen"*) of organization that the problem of practically and theoretically mediating between unity and multiplicity is especially apparent and observable. See Karl E. Weick, *The Social Psychology of Organizing*, 2nd ed. (Reading, MA: Addison-Wesley, 1979). Thus, a post is at the same time a fixed value defined both by hierarchy and workflow within the organization, as it is due to that important function an object of decision and reconsideration. A post is complex in that it is created in order to be dissolved – and everybody knows it.

[28] Luhmann, *Die Wissenschaft der Gesellschaft*, 181–89. See also Dirk Baecker, "Beobachtung mit Medien," in *Medien in Medien*, ed. Claudia Biebrand and Irmela Schneider (Cologne: DuMont, 2002), 12–24; and idem, "Medienforschung," in *Was ist ein Medium?*, ed. Alexander Roesler and Stefan Münker (Frankfurt am Main: Suhrkamp, 2008), 45–65.

ferent actors, or different times and thus "mediates" between them.[29] It is from this idea that the formulation of symbolically *generalized* media derives. The discovery of the usability of money or another medium in a *specific* situation with *specific* partners and at *specific* times is *generalized* to possibly and tentatively be of value in other situations with other partners at other times as well. This of course means that in any situation the use of a medium is to be established anew and may lead to conflict and become a subject of negotiation. It becomes become *generalized* as the *symbol* of exactly that possibility and thus to be of similar use in a different situation, which of course means that their loosely coupled elements in that new situation have to come up with a different rigid coupling in order to be distinguished as the use of the *same* medium in a *different* situation. Nothing repeats itself in the same way, even if repeated exactly over and over again.

That a potential conflict over the use of a specific medium in a specific situation has first to be solved before the medium can actually be used, and usually is solved in a matter of seconds, and as unobtrusively if not even invisibly as possible in the case of most media, is only rarely to be observed, as most media run smoothly in most the diverse situations of communication. This is proof of many structures of expectation being already firmly in place when the use of certain media is suggested. Most media in the case of success media, as in the case of dissemination media, would probably not even be used at all if lots of signs did not already indicate and assure their acceptability to actors, partners, and onlookers alike. On the other hand, it is often difficult to disentangle media from their structures of institutionalization to gain a fresh look at how they contribute to that institutionalization. Alluding to Immanuel Kant's understanding of critique we might term "critique of media" any procedure able to reconstruct how we use, and rely on, media to contribute to our construct. Newspapers turn us into newspaper readers, love makes us love our partner, truth attracts scientists searching the truth, and power changes the powerful into somebody we may just for that reason try to refuse to accept. This is only possible because we do not just use the things or forms impregnated in those media as instruments for certain purposes, but also move within the many loosely coupled elements describing and indeed bringing forth our space of possibilities for action, communication, and experience.

Heider's concept of medium in its sociological interpretation is able to show how media provide form (or *Dinglichkeit*, as Heider would say) to individual instances of communication. To the extent that communication is temporalized in terms of events,[30] this form then immediately disintegrates once again into multiplicity. A declaration of love, for instance, after being performed is remembered as not just this specific declara-

---

[29]   Talcott Parsons, *Action Theory and the Human Condition* (New York: Free Press, 1978), 395. It is typical of Parsons's empirical understanding that, immediately after making this suggestion, he mentions various "levels of generalization" (ibid.) and thereby introduces analytical variables to his own concept.

[30]   See Niklas Luhmann, *Social Systems*, trans. John Bednarz and Dirk Baecker (Stanford: Stanford University Press, 1995).

tion but as a selection out of a wealth of other possible ways to declare love. In another example, as soon as the buyer accepts a price, the seller asks him or herself whether a higher price would not have met with acceptance as well. The contingency, i.e. the possibility to appear differently as well (logically spoken the negation of both necessity and impossibility), prevailing in all media is only a sign of the permanent oscillation between actual form and potential alternative.

When comparing Parsons's and Heider's approach to media Luhmann noted that Parsons had followed Kant by thinking from multiplicity to unity, whereas Heider, adopting an approach of complexity theory, had moved from unity to multiplicity. This, however, made it all the more attractive "to bring their approaches together in order to formulate a general theory."[31] Beyond this, it would not be difficult to combine this general theory with Marshall McLuhan's distinction between "figure" and "ground,"[32] which also seems to oscillate between the two classifications of unity and multiplicity. This way we could propose a media theory in which media, which are intangible on account of their multiplicity, are understood as products of and preconditions for the circulation of re-dissolvable forms.[33]

III.

The project of media archaeology, which is associated with the sociology of media outlined above and in fact uses such sociology for the development of social theories, is quite conscious of the complexity of both the concept and phenomenon of media. Because of this complexity, however, it is forced to rely on a certain simplification. The project consists

---

[31] Luhmann, *Die Wissenschaft der Gesellschaft*, 186.

[32] See Marshall McLuhan and Eric McLuhan, *The Laws of Media: The New Science* (Toronto: University of Toronto Press, 1988), 91. A "figure" is a unit only in contrast to a "ground," though it becomes a multiplicity when this contrast is spelled out in greater detail. It is for this reason that Friedrich Kittler spoke of a "signal-to-noise ratio" (*Signal-Rausch-Abstand*) and argued that cultural theorists, media theorists, and social scientists ought to familiarize themselves with the possibilities of Fourier analysis. See Friedrich Kittler, "Signal-Rausch-Abstand," in *Materialität der Kommunikation*, ed. Hans Ulrich Gumbrecht and K. Ludwig Pfeiffer (Frankfurt am Main: Suhrkamp, 1988), 342–59 [this essay was replaced by another ("Unconditional Surrender") in the English translation of the book: *Materialities of Communication*, trans. William Whobrey (Stanford: Stanford University Press, 1994]; and Bernhard Siegert, *Passage des Digitalen: Zeichenpraktiken der neuzeitlichen Wissenschaften 1500–1900* (Berlin: Brinkmann & Bose, 2003). Here one is reminded of the attempt to reconcile the analysis of time series with signal processing, an effort that likewise relied on Fourier analysis. See Norbert Wiener, *Extrapolation, Interpolation, and Smoothing of Stationary Time Series with Engineering Applications* (Cambridge, MA: MIT Press, 1949). Fourier analysis is used to integrate complex (and therefore also imaginary) numbers and is thus seemingly applicable to the interpretation of intricate and convoluted relations that not only exhibit non-linear feedback and oscillation but also a certain *social* component in that independencies are increased within the medium of dependencies, and vice versa.

[33] See Elena Esposito, "Was man von den unsichtbaren Medien lernen kann," *Soziale Systeme* 12 (2006), 54–78.

in understanding social phenomena as forms that are realized in a specific medium of communication. This medium, for its part, remains in contact with all other media, which increase and reduce the probability of communication within a society and thereby maintain communication in a state of suspension. Society here becomes an intervening variable in the investigation of every social phenomenon, a variable whose reference is no longer institutions, norms, or social structures but rather operations of connection, convolution, confusion, exchange, and – as before – order, all of them, as Parsons suggested, relying on the dynamics of media at any moment possibly changing their range and scope.

The hypothesis of media archaeology that I would like to pursue here was expressed by Niklas Luhmann in the following terms:

> The combined effect of all communication media – language, dissemination media, and the symbolically generalized media – is to condense what we might overall call "culture." Condensation in this context means that the meaning used remains the same through reuse in various situations (otherwise there would be no reuse), but is also confirmed and enriched with implications that can no longer be reduced to a simple formula. This suggests that the overflow of meaning is itself the result of the condensation and confirmation of meaning, and that communication is the operation that thus creates its own medium.[34]

The complexities of this state of affairs, according to Luhmann, "leave us with a certain skepticism about the possibilities of a theory of culture,"[35] though such skepticism hardly prevented him formulating just such a theory. Luhmann proposes a theory of culture that takes seriously the combined effect of all communication media; keeping that combined effect in reserve for the analysis of an individual empirical phenomenon, however, he, like many previous scholars,[36] ascribes to the dissemination media of communication – such as writing, printing, and electronic media – a dominant role in the formation of society without venturing further into an analysis of the combined effect of those dissemination media together with success media and language.

Interestingly, the theory is not without signs that, in light of the complexity of the problem, point to the irony of the entire undertaking. One sign of this sort is the reduction of the investigation to dissemination media. Another such sign is the citation of authors to credit them with the identification, if not creation, of forms of culture able to relate the meaning overflow produced by the introduction of a new dissemination medium to a for-

---

[34] Luhmann, *Theory of Society*, 1:248

[35] Ibid.

[36] See Harold A. Innis, *Empire and Communication* (1950; repr. Victoria, BC: Peorcépic Press, 1986); idem, *A Bias of Communication* (Toronto: University of Toronto Press, 1951); Marshall McLuhan, *The Gutenberg Galaxy: The Making of Typographic Man* (Toronto: University of Toronto Press, 1962); idem, *Understanding Media: The Extension of Man* (New York: McGraw-Hill, 1964); Jack Goody and Ian Watt, "The Consequences of Literacy," *Comparative Studies in Society and History* 5 (1963), 304–45; and Eric A. Havelock, *Preface to Plato* (Oxford: Blackwell, 1963).

mula of comparison and control.[37] Those formulas or forms of culture become necessary
to provide a new societal situation with the possibility to both accept and to reject items
of that overflow. Otherwise, communication would be bound to reject the new medium
altogether or to be utterly dominated by it, which, of course, would be the end of communication. Communication demands decisions, decisions demand degrees of freedom,
and degrees of freedom consist in the possibility to either reject or accept a certain communication. To be sure, the hypothetical presentation of such a formula is without any
irony, but attributing them to great authors signals a certain parenthesis they are put in.

We could, of course, take the next step in constructing a theory of culture dealing with
media changes by proposing that the dissemination media, when newly introduced, may
be described as disruptive media, such that success media in contrast excel as integrative
media, but to this it must be added that dissemination media, once introduced, will also
integrate and success media, once introduced, will disintegrate. With regard to the latter
disintegration, if it does not suffer wholesale destructive effects, it may suffice to quote the
history and critique of money, power, truth, faith, and love offering numerous examples –
however tempting it might be to disregard those examples, which divert our attention from
the dominant role of the aforementioned media in the formation of societal complexity.

A theory of media epochs that is limited to the case of dissemination media can only
be justified by the fact that, when analyzing the present process of societal evolution, we
are simultaneously confronted with two problems. The first concerns the consequences
that the introduction of electronic media will produce on the structure and culture of
society. The second is the issue of whether, and if, any insight can be gained about our
present situation from observations that have been made about previous media changes.
The assumption that the appearance of new dissemination media not only reduces the
transaction costs of communication but also "catastrophically" (in the mathematical sense
of the word) overstrains society,[38] whose structure and culture are not prepared to process
meaning via these media, thus possesses a considerable amount of diagnostic value for
the present. This assumption distances itself from the prevalent thesis of "information
overkill" by providing it with historical parallels and thus allowing the present situation
to be compared to others.

Historically, we can identify four examples of media catastrophes, including that which
we are presently experiencing: the introduction of language (an overload of references),
the introduction of writing (an overload of symbols), the introduction of printing (an
overload of criticism), and the introduction of electronic media (an overload of control).
The social forms in which these catastrophes have been overcome correspond to tribal

---

[37]   To the eyes of sociologists, the names of "prominent" authors signal deviant cultural achievements,
       which by their very character cannot, of course, serve as a self-evident basis for society at large. Then
       again, in the case of catastrophes such as the media change we are referring to in the text below, a
       certain amount of deviance might be required to gain path-dependencies out of bifurcations.

[38]   See René Thom, *Mathematical Models of Morphogenesis*, trans. W. W. Brookes and D. Rand (New
       York: Halsted Press, 1983).

society, ancient society, modern society, and the so-called "next society."[39] In his work, Luhmann chiefly concerned himself with the cases of writing and book printing, while making a few observations about electronic media.[40] However, he left aside the issue of language, not least because it is conceptually undecided whether or not it belongs to the dissemination media of communication that allow communication to develop beyond certain thresholds of accessible addresses.[41] Looking at language in terms of a production of references, which are less easily controlled, that is to be assessed according to present situations and which even introduce an ease of lying which passes beyond the respective possibilities of mimicry and gesture, it may indeed be tempting to call language a medium disseminating those kinds of doubtful references. This would mean that we look at the culture and structure of tribal societies in terms of a means to control an overflow of language references. The territorial boundaries so pervasive for that kind of society both within its villages as well as outside between gardens and the wilderness could be interpreted as demarcations of zones of men and women, elders and young, hunters and planters, which all have their own unique language and who come together only during rites to be sure to control everybody's tongues.

The four catastrophes of the introduction of new media, the structure and culture of a society are not prepared for, can be summarized as follows: To language we owe the possibility of lying; to writing the tying down of time within an explosion of time horizons such as past and future now being imagined as to be remembered and to be envisioned; to printing the creation of an audience of readers all drawing opinions critical of their surroundings from articles, books, and calendar mottos they more or less uncritically consume; and to electronic media we owe instantaneous connectivity and the calculating power of computers at any moment surpassing the knowledge we nevertheless rely on to meet the moment.[42] Societies can survive these catastrophes only by developing the

---

[39] On the concept of the "next society," see Peter F. Drucker, "The Next Society: A Survey of the Near Future," *The Economist* (November 1, 2001), http://www.economist.com/node/770819 (accessed on August 13, 2014).

[40] Luhmann, *Theory of Society*, 245–50.

[41] For Luhmann it was more important to stress the role of language in the yes/no-coding of communication, which in fact goes beyond mere questions of dissemination (see ibid., 49–67). As a precaution, it should be added that language does not exhaust a form of communication that can also proceed gesturally, mimically, and silently.

[42] Like "language," "writing," and "printing," the "computer" is here simply an abbreviated formula for labeling a media change that, as McLuhan suggested in *Understanding Media*, can perhaps best be traced back to the introduction of electricity and thus to the introduction of the possibility of communicating all around the globe in a nearly instantaneous manner. This is because the possibility of instantaneous connection undermines all previous practices and techniques of distancing, hierarchizing, archiving, and networking communication. It also undermines the ordered and reflexive forms of the political, economic, legal, religious, artistic, and scientific calculus that serve as the basis of "European rationality," as divided and self-referential as it is. See Niklas Luhmann, *Observations on Modernity*, trans. William Whobrey (Stanford: Stanford University Press, 1998), 22–43. In place of this rationality we now find layers, flows, knots, and switches, the network logic of which of we

possibility of a rejection of communication as a precondition for being able to decide on an acception of it. In the case of the introduction of writing, Luhmann credits Aristotle for devising the cultural form of the *telos*; in the case of the introduction of printing, he credits Descartes for devising the cultural form of a self-referentially unsteady balance. As mentioned above, he did not cite anyone's breakthroughs in the case of language (all the more so because it would be difficult to name anyone). And he left the case of electronic media open-ended for the obvious reason that it was too early to recognize what sort of cultural form would emerge in the face of algorithms, data storage, internet platforms, and the overload of meaning that such things produce.[43]

These cultural forms could themselves be regarded as first potential subjects of a media archaeology that allows the conceptual achievements of philosophy to be read as social phenomena of engaging with the overload of meaning produced by communication within media of dissemination. As archaeology, this would designate a process that does not ontologically reconstruct individual phenomena with recourse to origins (*archē*) but rather ontogenetically in the medium of its own recourses to continuously newly-discovered origins.[44] To the extent that media epochs not only supplant one another but also overlap, this process is thus applicable to numerous social phenomena whose constitution can be described as points of orientation and as results of coordination with both the possibilities and restrictions of dissemination media.[45]

To elaborate this would take us too far afield. Here it is more important to focus on two consequences that would ensue if the sociology of media were to be further pursued in the form of media archaeology. The first involves Luhmann's speculative considerations about the cultural forms of individual media epochs, which raise the question of whether,

---

have only gradually come to recognize. See Michel Serres, *Hermès I – La communication* (Paris: Minuit, 1968), and Manuel Castells, *The Rise of the Network Society* (Oxford: Blackwell, 1996). In this light, the computer, the internet, and "social media" do not represent a new media epoch but rather forms of taming and exploitation; that is, they represent forms of reducing and increasing the objective, temporal, and social complexity that has accompanied the possibility of nearly instantaneous connectivity.

[43] Elsewhere I proposed a contest to determine which author might best exemplify the present media age. Of course, this was not meant to decide upon any one name in particular but rather to hear the reasoning that prompted the various suggestions. Nobody answered. Nevertheless, the list of possible candidates, as I imagine it, looks as follows (the concepts with which they are most closely associated are in parentheses): Claude E. Shannon ("message"), Norbert Wiener ("control"), John von Neumann ("automata"), George Spencer-Brown ("form"), Heinz von Foerster ("observing systems"), Gregory Bateson ("play"), Niklas Luhmann ("system"), and Harrison C. White ("identity"). At the moment, my favorite happens to be Bateson's concept of play, not least because it encompasses elements from many of the other concepts. For my original proposal, see Dirk Baecker, "Niklas Luhmann in der Gesellschaft der Computer," *Merkur* 55 (2001), 597–609.

[44] See Michel Foucault, *The Archaeology of Knowledge & The Discourse on Language*, trans. A. M. Sheridan Smith (New York: Pantheon Books, 1972); and Heinz von Foerster, *KybernEthik* (Berlin: Merve, 1993).

[45] See Dirk Baecker, *Studien zur nächsten Gesellschaft* (Frankfurt am Main: Suhrkamp, 2007).

in addition to the forms of comparison and control ("culture"), other forms – such as forms of securing distribution ("structure"), of reducing degrees of freedom ("integration"), of self-description ("reflection"), and of halting any expectation ("negation")[46] – can be identified and described with respect to their possibilities of communication in order to forge, out of this survey, a theory of the media epochs of society that would simultaneously be a social theory of media.

The second consequence is that the analytical requirements of such media archaeology, informed as it is by social theory, can presumably only be met if its conceptual means are refined and clarified to a greater extent than is typically the case in cultural studies, media studies, and the social sciences.[47] At least four of these conceptual means can be enumerated here. Beyond underpinning an approach to media archaeology, they are also independently able to facilitate a mediation between the sociology of media, as outlined above, and a type of media theory that is grounded in cultural studies:

1. First, there is the need to formulate a concept of *communication* that, from the perspective of a given *observer*, focuses on the selection of messages from within an endogenously co-constructed set of possible messages.[48]

---

[46] It makes sense to borrow this term   "expectation halt" (*Erwartungsstopp*) – from Harald Weinreich, but only if the halt is understood as being both "significantly total" and "confidently partial," in Raymond Williams's sense of the terms. See Harald Weinreich, *Textgrammatik der deutschen Sprache*, 4th ed. (Hildesheim: Olms, 2007), 864–77; and Raymond Williams, *The Sociology of Culture*, rev. ed. (Chicago: University of Chicago Press, 1995), 11. Here, again, we are faced with the desirability of a multi-value analysis to account for both the total and the partial, and for both the expectation and its halt. Cultural theorists and logicians have long emphasized the need to be able to conduct such analysis in a fruitful manner, but we seem no closer to figuring out how to do so and how to apply it to cultural theory, media studies, and the social sciences. See A. L. Kroeber and Clyde Kluckhohn, *Culture: A Critical Review of Concepts and Definitions* (Cambridge, MA: The Museum, 1952), 331–38; McLuhan and McLuhan, *Laws of Media*, 127–30; and Gotthard Günther, "Die Idee der 'mehrwertigen' Logik," in *Beiträge zur Grundlegung einer operationsfähigen Dialektik (Band II): Wirklichkeit als Poly-Kontexturalität* (Hamburg: Meiner, 1979), 181–202.

[47] This is simply an observation, not a rebuke. There is inherently nothing wrong with a concept of media that is kept just as vague as is heuristically needed to relate figures not only to backgrounds but to backgrounds that vary, interfere, and that are evasive and affected. There is nothing inherently wrong with the practice of analyzing media use without also inquiring about the functionality of both this use and this analysis. However, it should be made clear that this comes with the risk of fixing the object in such a way as to contradict a concept of media that makes use of the invisibility and undecideability of media to gain flexibility rather than rigidity. See Georg Christoph Tholen, "Die Zäsur der Medien," in *Schnittstelle: Medien und kulturelle Kommunikation*, ed. Georg Stanitzek and Wilhelm Voßkamp (Cologne: Du Mont, 2001), 32–50; and idem, *Die Zäsur der Medien: Kulturphilosophische Konturen* (Frankfurt am Main: Suhrkamp, 2002).

[48] See Dirk Baecker, *Form und Formen der Kommunikation* (Frankfurt am Main: Suhrkamp, 2005).

2. It is likewise helpful to have a concept of *systems* that allows the constitution of the observer to be formulated under the dual condition of his or her differentiation in an environment and reproduction in time.[49]

3. Furthermore, a productive concept of *networks* is required that provides a calculus for describing the uncertain constitution of the observer with respect to his or her dependence on addressable social partners and on a profilable identity.[50]

4. Not least, a corresponding concept of *form* can help to operationalize the complexity of certain contexts, and it can do so by delineating the operations involved with the constitution of units within a recursively explored space of unknown possibilities.[51]

Taken together, these two consequences yield one general and four specific formal equations of the reproduction of society under the conditions of four media epochs. These equations can be presented below without any further comment regarding their content.[52] Each "cross" represents the distinction encountered by an empirically substantiated observer that enables him or her to give value to a given variable depending on all other variables being numbered and ordered. The "re-entry" of the distinctions into the form of distinction constitutes the self-referential dependence of all variables contingent on all others, including the unmarked outside of the distinction to the right of the re-entry cross. The scaling of the space's "depth" indicates the degree of determination of each individual distinction in relation to all others, the variable in the deepest space at the left end of the form being the most determined:

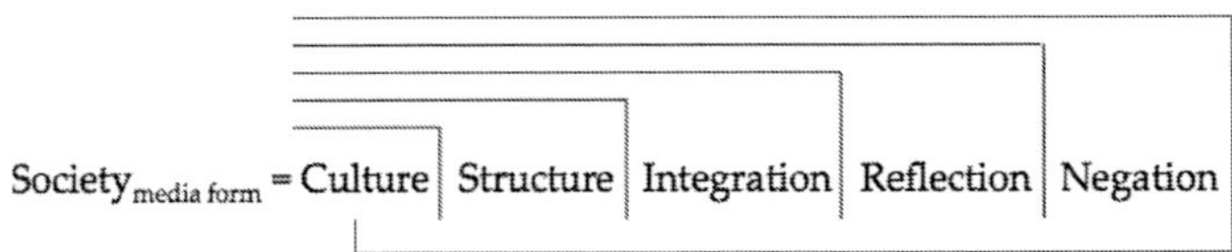

---

49   See Luhmann, "Talcott Parsons: Zur Zukunft eines Theorieprogramms," 5–17.

50   See Harrison C. White, *Identity and Control: The Structural Theory of Action*, 2nd ed. (Princeton: Princeton University Press, 2008).

51   See George Spencer-Brown, *Laws of Form* (London: Allen & Unwin, 1969).

52   For further discussion, see Dirk Baecker, "The Network Synthesis of Social Action I: Towards a Sociological Theory of Next Society," *Cybernetics and Human Knowing* 14 (2007), 9–42; idem, "The Network Synthesis of Social Action II: Understanding Catjets," *Cybernetics and Human Knowing* 15 (2008), 45–65; idem, *Studien zur nächsten Gesellschaft*; and idem, "What Is Holding Societies Together?" in *Criticism: A Quarterly for Literature and the Arts* 53 (2011), 1–22.

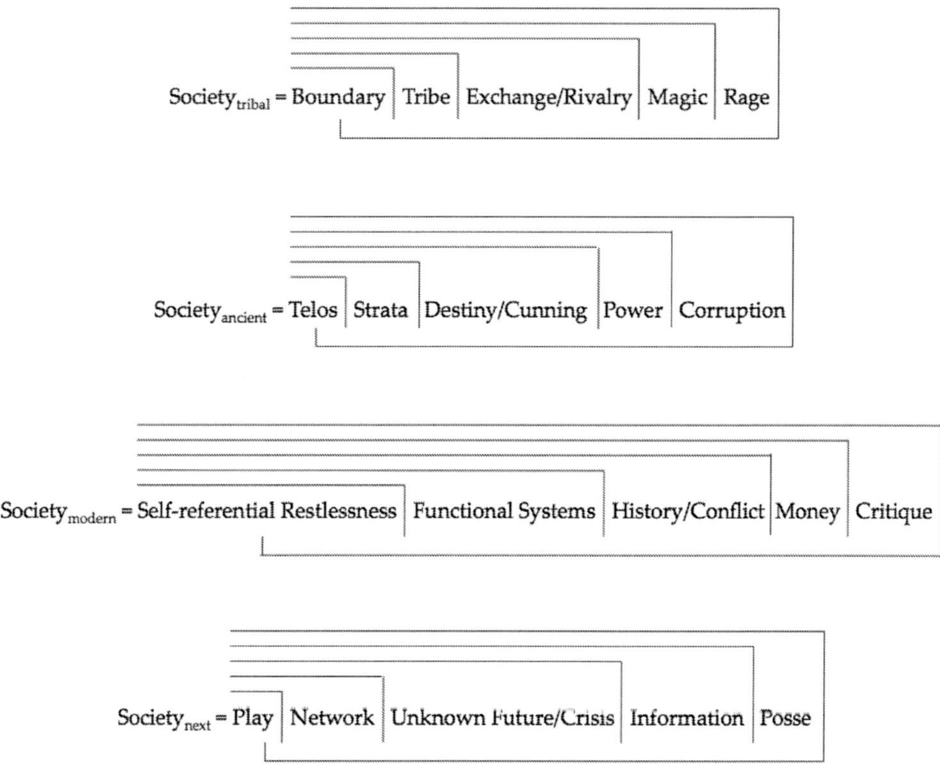

Each of these equations models the eigenvalue of a recursive function of the reproduction of communication in its respective society.[53] Each is thus to be understood as ideal-typical in the Weberian sense, that is, as a reference to the reproduction of units within a chaotic space of deviations.

Similar to Parsons's AGIL paradigm, the guiding idea when interpreting the eigenvalues of these recursive functions is that every instance of communication takes all of these variables into account and thereby redefines them while making locally and situationally specific determinations about matters of affairs, people involved, and time frames. As with Luhmann's concept of meaning and Harrison C. White's idea of a network, it is crucial to this process that every specific meaning can only be determined in light of its reference or switch to another meaning, and it is therefore in this form that it "potentializes" every other meaning (to borrow a term from Yves Barel).[54] Here the concept of media is also

---

[53] See Heinz von Foerster, "Epistemology of Communication," in The Myths of Information: Technology and Postindustrial Culture, ed. Kathleen Woodward (Madison: Coda Press, 1980), 18–27.

[54] Yves Barel, La paradoxe et le système: Essai sur le fantastique social, 2nd ed. (Grenoble: PUG, 1989). See also Luhmann, "Sinn als Grundbegriff der Soziologie"; Frédéric Godart and Harrison

indispensable because it underscores the latency of potentialized meaning while also, however, at the same time formulating the precise question of *which* observer, in this medium of latent potentialities, realizes and thereby manifests *which* form with the help of *which* distinction. It is only with recourse to such a concept of media that a sociological theory of communication can endeavor to unify, under a single concept of communication, such things as figure and ground, medium and form, systems and networks, indications and distinctions.

With the exception of the first equation, which puts forth the hypothesis followed by the others, these equations are already a result of the media archaeology sketched above. This is so because they identify the societal unity of an epoch – under the conditions of its forms of culture, structure, integration, reflection, and negation – with corresponding values for each variable. Moreover, they are also heuristics whose guidelines enable one to focus on individual phenomena within these media epochs.

The sociological concept of media remains central to all of this because it is able to conceive of the constitution of semantic and structural units within a diverse space of possibilities alongside the parallel phenomenon of improbable communication, which only therefore is subject to equally improbable motivation. Thus it offers a cultural-theoretically and media-theoretically attractive precondition for dealing, within a scientific framework, with the impenetrable complexity and recursivity of the social while also taking into account individual phenomena that are temporarily identical. Even with such an approach, however, Luhmann's warning still holds that repeated identity can only be understood as a condensation of differences, a neglect of variance that, at the moment of their effect, become unrecognizable yet again within their medium.

Every concept of medium entails a reference to observers. Media are that which allow observers, as those who act and experience within their environments, to seek and generate communicative connections. Media also necessitate, however, that this same insight applies to media theorists, who are themselves acting and experiencing observers within their environments. Each of these observers generates and practices his or her own typology, which is gained from his or her respective distinctions. For this reason it is especially important, both in practice as well as theoretically and methodologically, to pay close attention to the observer's performance of perception, decision-making, and activity. Media studies, too, is a medium, one that motivates certain observations while discouraging others. It is therefore co-responsible for the forms that become visible and then invisible in the medium of the discipline. Not least, media studies is thus also a participatory activity in the sensorimotor formation of the world.

In this sense, too, the hypothesis of an archaeology of four media epochs, as developed from the sociology of media, can be understood as a heuristic whose aim is to provide both

---

C. White, "Switchings Under Uncertainty: The Coming and Becoming of Meanings," *Poetics* 38 (2010), 567–86; and Harrison C. White et al., "Order at the Edge of Chaos: Meaning from Network Switchings Across Functional Systems," *Sociological Theory* 29 (2011), 178–98, esp. 191 (where the authors formulate their idea of "syncopated complexity").

a research agenda as well as a practical means of diagnosing the present. The hypothesis of a "next society" is integral to all of this and assumes the risk not only of making false scientific claims but also of drawing unsuitable distinctions in practice, leaving behind marks that lead astray, and making connections which prove unreliable. There is, however, no other way to proceed.

Sebastian Vehlken

Reality Mining
On New (and Former) Methods of Social Simulation

"Psychohistory dealt not with man but with man-masses. It was the science of mobs; mobs in their billions. It could forecast reactions to stimuli with something of the accuracy that a lesser science could bring to the forecast of a billiard ball. The reaction of one man could be forecast by no known mathematics; the reaction of a billion is something else again."[1]

"In the past, it was impossible to experiment with our future. This made social sciences different from the natural and engineering sciences, in which different options can be tried out before choosing one. In the future, we will also be able to make experiments with different socio-economic designs."[2]

On February 14, 1973, Stafford Beer – a cybernetician, self-proclaimed "old-fashioned" Marxist, and ex-Catholic yogi – officially introduced his latest project to an enthusiastic audience at Brighton Polytech. A month earlier, *The Observer* had dubbed it "Chile Run by Computer,"[3] and South American newspapers had run articles such as "The Command Center of Science Fiction" and "Mr. Beer's Big Brother."[4] What was it about the mysterious Project Cybersyn, as it had been called since its inauguration in November of 1971, that caused such a stir in the press? Stafford Beer, a "cross between Orson Welles and Socrates"[5] who, according to one obituary, was "larger than life,"[6] endeavored with his presentation to set the record straight and quell the journalistic frenzy, though the allitera-

---

[1]   Isaac Asimov, *Foundation and Empire* (1952; repr. New York: Alfred A. Knopf, 2010), 205.

[2]   Dirk Helbing and Stefano Balietti, "From Social Simulation to Integrative System Design," *European Physics Journal – Special Topics* 195 (2011), 69–100, at 85.

[3]   Nigel Hawkes, "Chile Run by Computer, *The Observer* (January 7, 1973).

[4]   See Hugo Palmarola, "Productos y socialismo: Diseno industrial estatal in Chile," in *1973: La vida cotidiana de un año crucial*, ed. César Albornoz and Claudio Rolle (Santiago: Planeta, 2003), 225–95, at 286; and the anonymous article "El 'hermano major' de Mr Beer," *Ercilla* (January 23, 1973).

[5]   Michael Becket, "Beer: The Hope of Chile," *The Daily Telegraph Magazine* (August 10, 1973), 7.

[6]   Dick Martin and Jonathan Rosenhead, "Stafford Beer: World Leader in the Development of Operational Research, Who Combined Management Systems with Cybernetics," *The Guardian* (September 4, 2002).

tive title of his lecture ("Fanfare for Effective Freedom") was more obfuscating than it was revealing. By that point, Beer had been the director and mastermind of Cybersyn, which stood for "Cybernetic Synergy," for eighteen months. The fundamental goal of the project was to install a sort of state control system that was based on cybernetic principles and information technology. It was Salvador Allende's Chile, of all places, that was chosen as the ideal nation for such an experiment, despite the facts that Chile was not exactly known for embracing new technology and that is was plagued at the time by supply shortages, anti-socialist strikes, and an international boycott on its exports.[7]

Beer faced criticism not only for his offensive application of modern information and computer technology, though Project Cybersyn was of course preceded by the unfortunate reputation of technocratic and dehumanized control structures. According to Beer, his system could not only serve to defuse ongoing social and economic crises; by means of a computer simulation system, it could also predict and help to prevent potential crises from occurring in the future. Such claims also struck his contemporaries as odd, if not outright laughable. Thirty years later, in any case, Cybersyn found itself again at the center of certain debates, and not only for the fact that its iconic management station, the so-called "operations room," could lightheartedly be referred to as the *Spaceship Social Enterprise.*[8] It was rather because Beer's cybernetic theory, which hoped to move state governance away from the (then) inadequate field of statistics toward a real-time control system based on computer hardware and software, transcended the prevailing dichotomies of the time. For Beer, cybernetics (or better: "cyBEERnetics"[9]) stood "beyond the dogmas of centralization or decentralization, beyond the doctrines of free-market or planned economies, and beyond the expertise of bureaucracy and cronyism."[10] Moreover, his blueprint for the operability of complex systems, the so-called "viable system model," was designed to be a grass-roots democratic feedback system. In the non-socialist West, however, hardly anyone was willing to believe this. Divulged only a year after the publication of *The Limits to Growth*, and thus at a time when computer-simulated models of the world

---

[7] Previous studies of this topic include Claus Pias, "Der Auftrag: Kybernetik und Revolution in Chile," in *Politiken der Medien*, ed. Daniel Gethmann and Markus Stauff (Berlin: Diaphanes, 2004), 131–54; Sebastian Vehlken, *Environment für Decision – Die Medialität einer kybernetischen Staatsverwaltung: Eine medienwissenschaftliche Untersuchung des Projekts Cybersyn in Chile 1971–73* (Master's Thesis: Ruhr-Universität Bochum, 2004), http://homepage.univie.ac.at/sebastian.vehlken/files/2007_04_04_Magisterarbeit%20Cybersyn%20Sebastian%20Vehlken.pdf (accessed on July 5, 2014); and Eden Medina, *Cybernetic Revolutionaries: Technology and Politics in Allende's Chile* (Cambridge, MA: MIT Press, 2011).

[8] Claus Pias, "Die Herrschaft der Sozialmaschine. Kurzschluß als Methode: Wie Chile einst zum kybernetischen Staat umgewandelt und seine Wirtschaft von einem einzigen Computer regiert werden sollte," *Frankfurter Allgemeine Zeitung* (March 13, 2004), 38.

[9] This neologism was allegedly coined by Martin Schaffernicht of the University of Talca in Chile. See Wolfgang Pircher, "Markt oder Plan? Zum Verhältnis von Kybernetik und Ökonomie," in *Cybernetics/Kybernetik: Die Macy-Konferenzen 1946–1953*, ed. Claus Pias, 2 vols. (Berlin: Diaphanes, 2003–2004), 2:95–110, at 104.

[10] Pias, "Der Auftrag: Kybernetik und Revolution in Chile," 140.

were a hot topic of discussion, Beer's project happened to be concerned with the most timely issue of them all, namely the question of the future and (more importantly) how to predict it. Of course, he repeatedly stressed that, as a cybernetician, he was not really concerned with predicting *the* future. As he often underscored, he was simply working with simulations in order to generate *potential* future scenarios and to compare them with one another, for it was only in this manner that viable and desirable scenarios could be identified. He claimed that everything else was out of his hands: "The future, I reckon, is only known to God, and it seems to me that the class of men who have always come nearest to perceiving his intentions are the science fiction writers."[11]

Yet it has been notoriously difficult to distinguish science fiction from fact within Cybersyn itself, and it has always been rather unclear exactly how the project intended to predict possible futures and decide which of them might be the most desirable. This situation was complicated even further when, six years later, the science-fiction writer Douglas Adams took inspiration from Beer's experiments and clarified, in *The Hitchhiker's Guide to the Galaxy*, the great extent to which our models of the world can be misguided:

> "Earthman, the planet you lived on was commissioned, paid for, and run by mice." [...]
> "Mice?" he said.
> "Indeed, Earthman."
> "Look, sorry – are we talking about the little white furry things with the cheese fixation and women standing on tables screaming in early-sixties sitcoms?"
> "These creatures you call mice, you see, they are not quite as they appear. They are merely the protrusion into our dimension of vast hyper-intelligent pan-dimensional beings. The whole business with the cheese and the squeaking is just a front. [...] They've been experimenting on you, I'm afraid."
> "Ah no," he said, "I see the source of the misunderstanding now. [...] [W]hat happened was that we used to do experiments on *them*. They were often used in behavioral research, Pavlov and all that sort of stuff." [...]
> "Such subtlety [...], one has to admire it. [...] How better to disguise their real natures, and how better to guide your thinking? [...] You see, Earthman, they really are particularly clever hyper-intelligent pan-dimensional beings. Your planet and people have formed the matrix of an organic computer running a ten-million-year research program [...]"[12]

As the hyper-intelligent and pan-dimensional beings were aware, and the science-fiction writer Adams had suspected by 1979, the future was to be forged out of computer simulation models on a global scale.

To what extent, however, are these bygone futures of the 1970s relevant to today's discussion about social media and the new masses? One could argue, first of all, that a

---

[11] Stafford Beer, "Fanfare for Effective Freedom: Cybernetic Praxis in Government," in *Platform for Change: A Message from Stafford Beer* (New York: J. Wiley, 1975), 422–52, at 444.

[12] Douglas Adams, *The Hitchhiker's Guide to the Galaxy: The Trilogy of Four* (1979; repr. London: Picador, 2002), 142–43. On the extent to which Adams was influenced by Beer, see Andrew Pickering, "Cybernetics and the Mangle: Ashby, Beer and Pask," *Social Studies of Science* 32 (2002), 413–37.

discourse is developing today that is highly similar to that of the early 1970s. In both of these discourses, crises, computer hardware and software, computer simulation techniques, and the management of complex socio-economic systems are entwined with one another in an intricate manner. Given that large research projects have recently been announced with catchwords such as "social meteorology," "social supercomputing," and "reality mining," and that such projects intend to produce computer simulations of the entire planet on the basis of whatever data is universally accessible, then headlines such as "Earth Project Aims to 'Simulate Everything'"[13] and "Living Earth Simulator Will Predict the Future of Everything"[14] are as unsurprising as a discussion about the epistemic and ethical implications of such projects. As far as social simulations are concerned, large-scale models have been rather highly advanced in the fields of traffic research (TRANSSIMS), epidemiology (GSAM, EPISIMS), and economics (EURACE, U-Mart) since the end of the 1990s. In past few years, however, one project in particular has come to sharpen and radicalize this dynamic more than any other. One of the recently proposed EU flagship initiatives bears the title "FuturICT" (ICT stands for "Information and Communications Technology"), and its goal was (and remains) nothing less than the comprehensive integration of all available social simulations. Taking a cue from large-scale physics research, its initiators were pleased to refer to their project as a "large knowledge collider." The funding committee, however, must not have been too impressed. As of 2013, the requested budget of one billion euros was allocated to other researchers.

*

Here my intention is not only to provide insight into the present discourse concerned with large-scale social simulations. By comparing such simulations with the socio-cybernetic layout of Stafford Beer's Cybersyn project, I also wish to outline the conspicuous similarities and differences between today's efforts and those of the 1970s, particularly in the problems that the projects sought to solve, in their conceptual designs, and in their media-technological implementation. Do the same urgent questions recur? Do similar conceptual problems encumber the operability of such systems? Did the different projects stimulate similar reservations from their critics? Why did the models from the 1970s lose significance, and what could this mean for the sustainability of today's efforts to produce models of the world? And are there perhaps fundamental objections to such projects that might have contributed to the negative evaluation of FuturICT?

Even if there has been a renaissance of similar reasons, goals, and reservations, it could also be argued that, as far as technology is concerned, a paradigm shift has taken place in the current approaches to simulation. These approaches no longer rely on cybernetic

---

[13]   Gareth Morgan, "Earth Project Aims to 'Simulate Everything'," *BBC News Online* (December 28, 2010), http://www.bbc.co.uk/news/technology-12012082 (accessed on July 5, 2014).

[14]   Evan Ackerman, "Living Earth Simulator Will Predict the Future of Everything" *Dvice* (December 31, 2010), http://www.dvice.com/archives/2010/12/living_earth_si.php (accessed on July 5, 2014).

feedback loops and equation-based modelling for their programming but rather on the techniques of agent-based modelling. It will be just as important below to address the reasons behind this transformation and its consequences. In this matter, too, it can be difficult to distinguish fact from science fiction, and this was true as early as the 1970s: Rainer Werner Fassbinder's *World on a Wire* (1973) concerns a social-computing system that is controlled and observed at the so-called "Institute for Cybernetics and Futurology." The nature of the system's program, however, is rather prescient of things to come; it functions with an artificial society, implemented on a supercomputer, that consists of ten thousand "agents." This theme, moreover, was taken up only two years after Thomas Schelling's famous checkerboard simulations, with which he was able to explore the processes of social segregation and ghetto formation – studies that have been regarded as a prominent step toward a paradigm of agent-based modelling.

And this leads to a third argument, according to which the *new masses* at the heart of this book are (or will be) interconnected by means of planned or already implemented global-scale agent models. For if the social behavior of individuals, accessible through social networks, is to inform agent-based computer simulations in order to generate scenarios of individual-based macro-developments, this will serve above all to alleviate the negative effects and pathologies that had traditionally been associated with the masses.

I. Santiago, 1971: Chile Run by Computer

"Project Cybersyn / OBJECTIVE: / To install a preliminary system / of information and regulation / for the industrial economy / that will demonstrate / the main features / of cybernetic management / and begin to help in the task / of actual decision-making / by 1ˢᵗ March 1972."[15]

It so happens that the media history of Cybersyn is a thrilling tale of interdisciplinary science and international politics. That said, it is also a utopian story of pan-societal happiness that lacks a happy ending. Unfortunately, no justice can be done to this media history in the present context. In order to compare Cybersyn with current social simulations, however, it will be necessary to devote some attention to its communications infrastructure and subsystems.

Its main component was a central computer that was meant to collect and link together all of the nation's economic data. It was hoped that such a device would allow necessary adjustments to be made in real time, adjustments toward targeted utilitarian goals. According to Beer's bio-cybernetic anamnesis, which he expounded in books such as *Brain of the Firm* (1972) and *The Heart of Enterprise* (1979), this "central brain" had to be connected to every individual economic element of the country. This was to be achieved by means of a "nervous system" known as Cybernet, which was essentially a telecommunication structure made of fax machines. The entire national economy – from the

---

[15]   Stafford Beer, *Brain of the Firm: The Managerial Cybernetics of Organization*, 2ⁿᵈ ed. (New York: J. Wiley, 1981), 251–52 (this passage is printed as a poem).

individual worker to groups of workers in factories, from foremen and managers all the way up to regional administrations and the relevant central ministries – was supposed to be "organismically" interconnected at all times and on all sides by means of rapid communication channels and transparent feedback mechanisms in place on all levels. All the elements of this network would be mutually controlled on the basis of current data and calibrated in a permanent condition of dynamic equilibrium. According to Beer, the viable system model (VSM) was not only meant to supersede, as regards the regulation of complex socio-economic systems, the well-known inadequacies of statistical data collection and classical bureaucracies. At the same time, the VSM was also intended to function as a time-critical and cybernetic-autoregulatory control system that would automatically keep the nation's economy and society in good order. In short, it was supposed to usher forth a cybernetic revolution that would simultaneously ensure that any other potential revolution would never occur.[16]

On its own, as Beer recognized, a networked communication system would not be enough to achieve these goals. It would also be necessary to create a media-technological "intelligence-amplifier" that could enable humans (as simply as possible) to make critical and relevant decisions regarding the future of an otherwise inestimably complex governmental system. For this reason, the data flowing into the "central brain" – namely into two Burroughs 3500 computers with a memory capacity of ten kilobytes (that could supposedly be expanded to a whopping five hundred kilobytes) – would not only be processed and saved by computer-technical means. Such data would also be presented on graphical displays and filtered by people in a lavishly designed "operations room." Created in collaboration with the Ulm School of Design, this room was meant to make data accessible to groups of human decision-makers according to the principles of user-friendliness, intuitive usability, and ergonomics. To this end they produced, as Beer noted, "a decision machine, in which men and equipment act in symbiotic relationship to amplify their respective powers in a new synergy of enhanced intelligence."[17] In order for people to deal with the mass of data being processed, the information displays in the operations room were equipped with "a sort of zoom function that, when necessary, would enable everything to be known, but would usually allow the majority of things to be overlooked."[18]

By means of an ingenious system composed of remotely operable rear projections through dia-slides, colored transparencies, stepper motors, cardboard, and colored lights, the designers managed to improvise an analog graphical interface whose fundamental approach to representation was not terribly different from that of the electronic graphical user interfaces developed much later. Dynamic flowcharts were projected onto the walls in order to visualize processes of exchange according to the VSM, and multi-colored bar graphs were displayed in order to compare, for instance, the actual production rate of a factory with its optimal potential. Like a stock-market index, a function known as "Cy-

---

[16]   See Pias, "Der Auftrag: Kybernetik und Revolution in Chile," 131.

[17]   Beer, "Fanfare for Effective Freedom," 449.

[18]   Pias, "Der Auftrag: Kybernetik und Revolution in Chile," 142.

berstride" summarized various series of data and automatically analyzed their deviations. It was hoped that such a feature would allow anomalous fluctuations in the system to be recognized early on, communicated to the responsible manager within the VSM system, and solved (if this proved unsuccessful, the next-highest authority would be informed, and so on). By analyzing indexes, moreover, the system was also expected to anticipate future trends.

However, the most advanced feature of all – and one that was only partially realized on account of technical problems – was the so-called "Futures System," which was conceived to generate interactive simulations of things such as trade relations, production processes, and transportation systems. It was meant to offer insight into the potential developments of socio-economic factors; Beer, after all, was a firm believer in the following dictum: "[I]f the government is not to be merely the management of perpetual crisis, it needs to look ahead."[19] The Futures System produced simulations by means of Jay W. Forrester's so-called Dynamo compiler, a system-dynamic application that calculated dynamic processes with the help of differential equations. Chile's economic data and processes were to be represented by an interactive flowchart. If the system of equations being used in the simulation were to be changed – something that could easily be done ("attendant scientist can change a few equations on request and produce a new read-out in a few minutes"[20]) – the appearance of the flowchart could be changed accordingly. The flowchart itself was constructed in such a way that flexible magnets could be attached to its surface. The magnets, for their part, held plastic strips of one color or another that could be arranged to represent, analogously, the animated lines in the viable system model. All of the other necessary symbols needed for the flowchart could likewise be positioned with magnets on the screen, and thus the chart could be modified quickly and according to any given specifications. As Beer had stressed in his lecture at Brighton Polytech (and this explains the plural form in the term *Futures System*), the concern was not to predict the one and only future but rather to manipulate data in order to simulate any number of possible futures and to determine which of these might be the most desirable: "The fact is that we need not to forecast, but to experiment."[21]

The longer Project Cybersyn progressed, the more its directors became convinced that the effective government of a nation could not primarily be achieved by effectively controlling its economy. They realized that political and social relations, and especially those between the government and its citizens, warranted special attention. In his *Brain of the Firm*, Beer wrote the following (the line-breaks are in the original text):

> [I]n March 1972, however, we addressed the basic issue of the organization of the state that
> is not economic, but societary. Parallel to the paper on Cybersyn, therefore, I wrote a second
> about a project to examine: "the systems dynamics / of the interaction / between government

---

[19]   Beer, "Fanfare for Effective Freedom," 444.

[20]   Ibid., 450.

[21]   Ibid., 445

and people / in the light of a newly available technology / such as TV / and discoveries in the realm / of psycho-cybernetics."[22]

By the term "psycho-cybernetics," Beer essentially meant that every individual citizen should be directly connected to one another by means of information technology. This direct link between the people and the government should take place by means of mass-media communication, sort of like a political television channel: "Government now communicates directly with the undifferentiated mass of the people, as if it were speaking to the individual, and creating the illusion in the home that it is."[23] Citizens would be able to provide direct feedback through their televisions by means of something like a remote control device, which Beer referred to as an "algedonic meter." In 1972, Beer's son Simon tested a prototype of this apparatus and it proved to be a remarkable success. Equipped with a multi-colored display screen for measuring happiness and unhappiness, the meter enabled users to indicate, by turning a knob, where they stood on a scale between "total disquiet and total satisfaction" while watching, say, a political speech on the television. This feedback would be aggregated in real time and displayed back as a bar graph both to the speaker at the television studio as well as on the audience's television screens.[24] This represented nothing less than the convergence of government and "instant market research."[25] Such a system, as Claus Pias has remarked,

> would organize entirely new relations between the individual and the whole, between personal and collective decisions, between freedom and functionality. Liberty, according to Beer, is not a normative question but rather "a computable function of effectiveness."[26] [...] The real time of electronic media that defines this new field of psycho-cybernetic government allows something like "statehood" to become fragile. It leads to a removal of political boundaries – an extensive, undulatory registration of the other and a will to knowledge that consumes everything and whose interests are boundless. [...] It is perhaps needless to stress that the happiness charts were supposed to be broadcast live to the "Opsroom," and that similar feedback loops were to be installed in factories so that workers could monitor themselves, bosses could monitor workers, workers could monitor their bosses, and bosses could monitor other bosses. This mirrored hall of surveillance, this perpetual control over relationships, which has elsewhere (though around the same time) been referred to as a "society of control,"[27] represented to Beer a promise of happiness.[28]

In sum, Stafford Beer's cybernetic vision for "viably" controlling socio-economic processes basically consisted of a sophisticated real-time network structure, the automated

---

22   Beer, *Brain of the Firm*, 278.

23   Ibid., 280.

24   See ibid., 278–83.

25   Ibid., 284.

26   Beer, "Fanfare for Effective Freedom," 428.

27   Gilles Deleuze, "Postscript on the Societies of Control," in *Cultural Theory: An Anthology*, ed. Imre Szeman and Timothy Kaposy (Chichester: Wiley-Blackwell, 2011), 139–42

28   Pias, "Der Auftrag: Kybernetik und Revolution in Chile," 149–50.

filtering and processing of data, a computer system for generating simulated "forecasts," and a direct connection between a government and its people relayed through "algedonic meters." Though laced with "economic" vocabulary, his project came to place more and more emphasis on "social" phenomena by measuring behavioral practices and preferences.

II. Zurich, 2011: A Large Knowledge Collider

"If crises are generally understood to be confusions of experiences and expectations, then the crisis-ridden dynamic of the finance economy is structured by a distortion of various orders of time. [...] Economic time is immeasurable, empty, undefined, proleptic, and abstract, whereas historical time periods are saturated, specific, defined, irreversible, and limited. As little as the vicissitudes of historical time periods are aligned with the regime of economic time, the infinite appetite for time inherent to capitalist processes has come all the more to encroach upon the existence of finite things and beings and to manifest itself there as a sort of imminent pressure."[29]

In light of Joseph Vogl's analysis of economic crises, it could be said that socio-economic computer simulations are media-technological attempts to align the disparate notions of economic and historical time. When I first read the position paper for the FuturICT project, which hopes to enact just such an alignment, I felt as though I was taking a trip back in time aboard Stafford Beer's *Spaceship Social Enterprise*. Directed by the physicist and sociologist Dirk Helbing, and (somewhat) ironically referred to as a "large knowledge collider," FuturICT was inspired by the fact – now so evident in light of ongoing financial crises – that we know more about the physical workings of the universe at large than we do about the interrelations of socio-economic systems. The position paper claims that society and technology are now changing at a speed that is unintelligible and beyond control; that it is high time for us to use information technologies to conduct more reliable research on socio-economic systems and to identify the best options for sustainable future developments; that these systems, as financial crises have indicated, are now unprecedentedly complex and are technologically, socially, and economically interconnected in unclear ways; and that, in response to positive feedback, this complexity can have highly problematic and counter-intuitive domino effects. In short:

Neither the precepts of traditional science, nor our collective experience from a simpler past, adequately prepare us for the future. It is simply impossible to understand and manage complex networks using conventional tools. We need to put systems in place that highlight, or prevent, conceivable failures and allow us to quickly recover from those that we cannot predict.[30]

---

[29] Joseph Vogl, *Das Gespenst des Kapitals* (Zurich: Diaphanes, 2011), 173. An English edition of this book is forthcoming: *The Specter of Capital*, trans. Robert Savage and Joachim Redner (Stanford: Stanford University Press, 2014).

[30] "FuturICT: Global Computing for our Complex World," http://www.futurict.eu/sites/default/files/docs/ newsletters/FuturICT_5p%20Project%20Summary.pdf (accessed on July 7, 2014).

Once established, such systems will enable risks and crises to be managed permanently by means of information technology – financial markets as much as epidemics, social instability, or criminal networks. By shifting the focus away from processing the characteristics of a system's components toward analyzing their *interactions,* it is thought that risks and crises can become self-modulating. If these concepts can be thought of as revolutionary, then the motto of the revolution could certainly be "Welcome Aboard the *Social Enterprise!*" Even the basic questions guiding this agenda sound like a eudemonic attempt to contrive the best of all possible worlds:

– How to avoid socio-economic crises, systemic instabilities, and other contagious cascade-spreading processes,
– how to design cooperative, efficient, and sustainable socio-technical and economic systems,
– how to cope with the increasing flow of information, and how to prevent dangers from malfunctions or misuse of information,
– how to improve social, economic, and political participation,
– how to avoid "pathological" collective behavior (panic, extremism, breakdown of trust, cooperation, solidarity, etc.),
– how avoid conflicts or minimize their destructive effects,
– how to cope with the increasing level of migration, heterogeneity, and complexity in our society,
– how to use environmental and other resources in a sustainable way and distribute them in the best possible way?[31]

Upon further analysis, however, it is clear that a few essential shifts have taken place. It is on the basis of these shifts, moreover, that the founders of FuturICT can rightfully argue that something fundamental has changed about the notoriously difficult process of modelling social and economic systems. Three of these transformations are particularly striking, each of which has come to be designated by a catchy term of its own: *reality mining, social supercomputing,* and something called *socioscope,* which is enabled by agent-based modelling and its corresponding visualization tools. Like other early computer simulation models of social and economic phenomena, Cybersyn had been designed around a rather clumsy and flimsy network infrastructure, and the effect of this was a highly porous database. In short, the main problem faced by Beer's research group was the following: *Get the right data.* FuturICT, on the contrary, hopes to profit from a highly connected world of information by extending its analysis beyond the "official" data provided by economic, climatological, and social indexes. That is, the project also intends to incorporate "individual" data from all available social networks into its control models (or "management models," as the authors more neutrally put it). In light of today's prodigious amounts continuously accruing data, the main problem is now somewhat different: *Get the data right.*

---

[31] Dirk Helbing and Stefano Balietti, "From Social Data Mining to Forecasting Socio-Economic Crises," *European Physics Journal – Special Topics* 195 (2011), 3–68, at 3–4.

A second way in which FuturICT's situation differs from that of Cybersyn has to do with the capabilities of computers. Although Seymour Cray, the "Evel Knievel of supercomputing,"[32] presented his Cray-1 as early as 1976, the team working on Cybersyn, with its Burroughs computers, could not even dream of having that capacity at their disposal. It goes without saying that any iPhone has more computing power than the Cray-1, and that current supercomputers, with their massively parallel systems, are close to achieving petaflop speeds.[33] FuturICT's proposal for collecting and processing data would require even more computing power than is presently available. The establishment of a "large knowledge collider" – especially in Europe, which is somewhat lagging behind the times – would entail a massive construction project together with the development of a highly sophisticated network of supercomputing capacities. And this may have been the primary reason why a variety of funding agencies opted not to support the project. Not surprisingly, the only precedent for storing and analyzing socio-economic "big data" of this sort happened to be set by Google.[34]

Third, FuturICT has stressed the central role of agent-based computer simulations for purposes of creating something called "social meteorology," a computer-generated forecast of potential developments and crises. With this paradigm (which has been available since the middle of the 1990s), it should be possible to create alternatives to the inadequate models of classical economics (such as the assumption that *homo economicus* behaves "rationally"). It could also help to close conceptual gaps between micro and macroeconomic theories. Crucial in this regard is its role as a "socioscope," which can make societal processes comprehensible and lead to a better understanding of "reality."[35] As was the case with Project Cybersyn, FuturICT's proposal entails a great deal of thinking about appropriate interfaces, about visualization techniques for complex and networked databases, and about so-called "decision arenas," in which relevant subsets of big data and agent-based models can be represented in such a way that this information can be used to predict potential activity. Below I intend to examine each of these three areas in greater detail, especially as regards their medial relations. Moreover, the extent to which "new

---

32   Charles J. Murray, *The Supermen: The Story of Seymour Cray and the Technical Wizards Behind the Supercomputer* (New York: John Wiley, 1997), 5.

33   See Sebastian Vehlken and Christoph Engemann, "Supercomputing," *Archiv für Mediengeschichte* 11 (2011), 143–61.

34   On the idea of "big data," see Douglas Laney, "3D Data Management: Controlling Data Volume, Velocity and Variety," *Meta Group* (February 6, 2001), http://blogs.gartner.com/doug-laney/files/2012/01/ad949-3D-Data-Management-Controlling-Data-Volume-Velocity-and-Variety.pdf (accessed on July 7, 2014); and Roger Magoulas and Ben Lorico, "Introduction to Big Data," *Release 2.0: Issue 11* (February 2009), 1–39. On Google's role in particular, see Helbing and Balietti, "From Social Data Mining to Forecasting," 10–11.

35   See Dirk Helbing and Stefano Balietti, "How to Do Agent-Based Simulations in the Future: From Modelling Social Mechanisms to Emergent Phenomena and Interactive System Design," *SFI Working Paper* 11-06-024 (June 16, 2011), 5. Available online at http://www.santafe.edu/media/workingpapers/11-06-024.pdf (accessed on July 8, 2014).

masses" of one sort (agent-based models) are constituted by "new masses" of another (reality mining) will also be investigated.

*

Reality Mining and "Nowcasting."[36] As the basis of its global-scale agent model, FuturICT has formulated a finely tuned "data-driven approach." Catchwords such as "data deluge"[37] or "information bonanza"[38] are telling indicators of the main problem faced by the project: Unlike previous situations such as Cybersyn's, which was characterized by small data samples and sparse networks, today's socio-economic research is data-heavy *in extremis*. Its very object of investigation, namely human social behavior, produces (as though on its own accord) immense sets of data through the ubiquitous dissemination of networked computer media and its sheer number of users. These data sets, moreover, pertain to nearly every aspect of social and economic life.[39] Some authors have been celebrating these effects as a new scientific paradigm, one that adds an epistemological component to theory, experimentation, and computer simulations.[40] This big data comprises, among other things, public registries of personal data, data from electronic services (telephones, flight information, monetary transactions, consumer information, behavioral analyses), data from interactivity, data from mobile media (smart phones, GPS, radio-frequency identification, electronic toll-collection systems, etc.), data from multimedia content (videos and pictures on social websites, Google Street View, public webcams), data from user-generated content (blogs, mailing-list archives, information from social-media networks), data from surveillance systems, and data from online multiplayer games. Some of the main challenges faced by such "reality mining" include the identification and filtering of *relevant* information, the integration of heterogeneous data formats, and ethical concerns about gaining access to private and sensitive data (such as trade secrets). In addition to the sources listed above, information can also be culled from "on-line repositories for the socio-economic sciences," among which can be counted all of the studies collected in public, government, scientific, and commercial databases.[41] "Reality," in this regard, is essentially conceived in terms of data. If data is to be filtered by sensitive search engines, stored in supercomputing centers (as is the case now with

---

36   See J. Vernon Henderson et al., "Measuring Economic Growth from Outer Space," *National Bureau of Economic Research – Working Paper* 15199 (July 2009), http://www.nber.org/papers/w15199.pdf (accessed on July 8, 2014).

37   "The Data Deluge," *The Economist* (February 25, 2010), http://www.economist.com/node/15579717 (accessed on July 8, 2014).

38   Simon Rogers, "Information is Power," *The Guardian* (May 23, 2010), http://www.theguardian.com/media/2010/may/24/data-journalism (accessed on July 8, 2014).

39   Helbing and Balietti, "From Social Data Mining to Forecasting," 4.

40   See Anthony J. G. Hey et al., eds., *The Fourth Paradigm: Data-Intensive Scientific Discovery* (Redmond: Microsoft Research, 2009).

41   Helbing and Balietti, "From Social Data Mining to Forecasting," 51–61.

private companies such as Facebook or Google), and structurally analyzed (as is the hope of the FuturICT initiative), then it should be possible to describe socio-economic systems from a scientific perspective (and not simply from the technical perspective or marketing). Ultimately, the analysis of large data sets should improve our understanding of collective dynamics by refining our models of social and cognitive behavior and by better preparing society and the individual to respond to future crises.[42]

Like Cybersyn before it, FuturICT considers the main source of inadequate government reactions to be the week-long or month-long delays involved with traditional forms of data collection and statistical analysis. Accordingly, the project's directors find it of the utmost importance to realize what they call "real-time knowledge mining," a new direction in data mining that is concerned with the following three themes:

> 1. *Continuous data analysis over streaming data*: Techniques for the on-line monitoring and analysis of high-rate data streams. Part of this theme is to develop mechanisms for handling uncertain and inexact data. 2. *On-line ingestion of semi-structured data and unstructured ones* (e.g. news items, product reviews, etc.) [...] 3. *Real-time correlation of streaming data (fast streams) with slowly accessible historical data repositories* [...] in order to deliver a contextualized and personalized information space. This adds considerable value to the data, by providing (historical) context to new data.[43]

Aside from the ethical and legal problems that the representatives of FuturICT have addressed in several publications (and will not be rehearsed here), there are other dangers to be considered when dealing with big data. It is believed that such dangers are best avoided through a combination of data-driven approaches in conjunction with "human intuition," an openness to experimentation, and computer simulations:

> Large data sets support the temptation to perform "blind" data mining, i.e. to apply pattern recognition tools and statistical methods without a deeper understanding of the underlying assumptions and implications of the results. [...] Typical problems are: 1. (mis-)interpreting correlations as causal relationships, 2. collinearity of variables [...], 3. underfitting or overfitting of mathematical models, 4. ignorance of underlying simplifications or critical approximations, 5. [...] the illusion of control over complex systems. This is quite dangerous and probably what happened during the recent financial crisis [...].[44]

All of this is compounded by what could be called "internet pollution" – by manipulated page ranks, viral or classical marketing, herd mentalities that can exaggerate the significance of certain data, or by the simple fact that the web is dominated by people who are "time-rich" (as the authors euphemistically put it) instead of by experts.[45] The sheer amount of accumulating data and the sheer difficulty of evaluating their relevance have

---

[42]   Ibid., 12
[43]   Ibid.
[44]   Ibid, 13.
[45]   Ibid.

presented data processing technologies with new challenges to overcome; it is in the face of such challenges that social supercomputing has come into play.

*

Social Supercomputing. Whereas the traditional applications of supercomputers have been in large-scale industrial research projects (e.g., predicting oil reserves or simulating airplane aerodynamics and atomic explosions), in meteorological research, and in large-scale projects in the hard sciences, for some years they have also been used in the social sciences, which have come to attract increasing attention from the leading centers of supercomputing.[46] Cluster computing and grid computing, which have been the prevailing supercomputing paradigms since the 1990s, happen to be especially well suited for implementing the agent-based computer simulations that are by now the paradigm for modelling social systems.[47] As is indicated, for instance, by the development of substantial supercomputing capacities by commercial firms such as Google or Facebook, supercomputers have also come to play a central role in the analysis of collected data (that is, data mining).

Like the data centers run by the global providers of internet services, the FuturICT system would like to increase the speed of its analysis by integrating data storage and data processing. Applications such as Hadoop (an open-source version of Google's MapReduce) are expected to automate, at least partially, the transformation of collected (and dispersedly stored) data into something like "knowledge."[48] Because the sheer amount of data makes it nearly impossible to load everything into a program in order to be processed, Hadoop shrewdly takes the opposite approach. In short, it brings the calculations to the data:

> [It] takes a computational problem and "maps" it to different nodes that will take care of solving a part of it. Moreover, since they are *also* running an instance of [the program], they can split their task into sub-tasks for distribution in the computer cluster as well, and so on. Once the single computational tasks are completed, they get "reduced" to a single output and returned back to the initial caller. [...] The advantage of its programming model is that it provides a powerful abstraction of *what* to do and *how* in the large-scale processing of data.[49]

Because bottlenecks occur in today's data processing during the transitions between storage systems and processors, it is hoped that such a hybrid arrangement of data storage and data processing might enable more effective analyses. By means of these measures,

---

[46]   Helbing and Balietti, "From Social Simulation to Integrative System Design," 74.

[47]   See G. Nigel Gilbert and Klaus G. Troitzsch, *Simulation for the Social Scientist* (New York: Open University Press, 2005).

[48]   See Tom White, *Hadoop: The Definitive Guide* (Sebastopol, CA: O'Reilly Media, 2009).

[49]   Helbing and Balietti, "From Social Data Mining to Forecasting," 11.

the "three V's" of big data – volume, variety, and velocity – might finally become manageable.[50]

*

Socioscope and Decision Arenas. For a variety of reasons, agent-based modelling is especially suitable for simulating socio-economic systems. It dispenses with global regularities and formalizations and instead models the behavior of a system on the basis of the individual features possessed by autonomous "agents," agents whose knowledge is limited ("bounded rationality") and whose interactions are governed by localized rules. With agent-based models it is possible to implement the potential reactions of individuals in accordance with the prior, present, and future expectations of other agents. The constitution and behavior of these agents enable heterogeneous activities to be represented far more accurately than was possible with the techniques of equation-based modelling. Moreover, system variations and coincidental occurrences can also be implemented rather easily. The great flexibility of agent-based models derives from the fact that data can be corrected or supplemented simply by adding or subtracting certain agents, and such modifications do not affect the general programming structure of the simulation. The spatial and temporal variations of a system can also be incorporated into the models, which are also well suited for parallel implementation, for instance on supercomputer clusters that make use of general-purpose computing on graphics processing units (GPGPU) and that, on account of their great computing capacities, can execute detailed simulations with several millions of agents.[51] Without much difficulty, agent-based models can also be combined with other simulation models. The global-scale agent model developed by the Brookings Institution, for instance, supplements an agent-based model, which simulates urban evacuation patterns, with another model that can simulate a dissipating plume of poisonous gas.[52] Last but not least, agent-based models have the advantage of being able to develop into unforeseen "emergent" (or "generative," in Joshua Epstein's terms) macro-processes that do not have to be programmed or specified in advance.[53]

---

[50] I have borrowed these terms from Laney's article "3D Data Management: Controlling Data Volume, Velocity and Variety" (cited above).

[51] See Sebastian Vehlken, "Epistemische Häufungen: Nicht-Dinge und Agentenbasierte Computersimulation," in *Jenseits des Labors: Transformationen von Wissen zwischen Entstehungs- und Anwendungskontext* (Bielefeld: Transcript, 2011), 63–85.

[52] Joshua M. Epstein et al., "Combining Computational Fluid Dynamics and Agent-Based Modeling: A New Approach to Evacuation Planning," *PLoS ONE* 6 (May 2011), http://www.plosone.org/article/info%3Adoi%2F10.1371%2Fjournal.pone.0020139 (accessed on July 9, 2014).

[53] See Joshua M. Epstein, *Generative Social Science: Studies in Agent-Based Computational Modeling* (Princeton: Princeton University Press, 2006), esp. 31–33. Epstein also provides an insightful discussion of possible epistemological objections to agent-based modelling. To enumerate these objections here, however, would take us too far afield.

Analogous to Cybersyn, the FuturICT project is mainly concerned with managing the *interrelations* among the data supplied by data mining and agent-based modelling. As is the case with weather forecasts, it hopes to integrate sensor data and historical patterns into computer simulations. These simulations, in turn, should generate "world patterns" that will allow socio-economic and political behavior to be predicted, but there is a twist: Unlike the weather, the systems to be simulated by FuturICT will react in response to these very "world patterns." In other words, as soon as a prediction becomes known to the public, the prediction becomes part of the very dynamic under investigation, and thus this sort of feedback has to be taken into account by the model that has instigated it.[54]

Such "world patterns" are supposed to be integrated in crisis-forecasting facilities or "decision arenas" in order to analyze such things as financial markets and the economy, crime, international conflicts, social unrest, transportation and logistics, healthcare, epidemics, and climate change. Advanced information-visualization techniques will allow these analyses to take place in a decentralized manner and on multiple levels of the system simultaneously (quite unlike Stafford Beer's centralized operations room).[55] By visualizing vast amounts of information, as the project leaders have written, it is possible to take advantage of the combined powers of the human eye and of expert intuition, which can be especially valuable at the early and hypothetical stages of analysis: "[T]he intuition of experts [...] can largely be stimulated by the great processing capacity of the human visual system, which can easily notice correlations and quickly recognize variations in colors, shapes, movements, etc."[56] This is especially important because data have been increasing not only in terms of quantity but also in terms of dimensionality: "What makes the data *Big* is repeated observations over time and/or space."[57] Accordingly, what is needed beyond the existing applications are more comprehensive visualization tools that will allow data to be filtered, viewed from a distance, and zoomed into focus. Such tools would have to provide access to particular details; to achieve this, it will be necessary for experts in scientific visualization to cooperate with graphic designers, artists, and communications specialists. In general, there is a democratic component to all of this that should not be forgotten:

> Finally, if the Information Seeking Mantra had been written more recently, it would probably have entailed a fourth directive in order to study data in a distributed way from different individual perspectives, namely *share*. [...] For example, people could explore new architectural designs (such as airports, railway stations, pedestrian zones, stadia, or shopping malls) before they are built, as interactive virtual multi-player environments would allow them to populate them in advance.[58]

---

54 Helbing and Balietti, "From Social Data Mining to Forecasting," 17–18.

55 Ibid., 20–23.

56 Helbing and Balietti, "From Social Simulation to Integrative System Design," 89.

57 Adam Jacobs, "The Pathologies of Big Data," *ACM Queue* 7 (2009) 1–12, at 5. Available online at http://queue.acm.org/detail.cfm?id=1563874 (accessed on July 8, 2014).

58 Helbing and Balietti, "From Social Simulation to Integrative System Design," 90.

The idea is that cases such as Stuttgart 21, a long-running and over-budget German railway project, would have been much easier to manage and keep afloat if it could have been simulated with something like a *Second Life* tool. It should be mentioned, too, that the overall vision for "decision arenas" reads as though it could been borrowed from a text by Stafford Beer:

> Combining suitable data, models, and visualization tools, the final goal would be to develop a *virtual observatory* of social, economic, and financial systems with the possibility to explore new scenarios and system designs through what is sometimes called a "policy wind tunnel." The corresponding ICT systems should be suited to craft policy options, contingency plans, and intelligent responses to emerging challenges and risks. They will allow one to develop concepts and institutional designs for a flexible, adaptive, and resource-efficient real-time management of complex socio-economic systems and organizations. Decision arenas visualizing, animating, and illustrating the acquired scientific insights will provide valuable decision-support to decision-makers, as they will make counter-intuitive feedback, cascading, and side effects understandable.[59]

Within this "virtual observatory," data mining, computer simulations, and the visualization of information are considered to be integrative and irreducible elements of managing the "new masses," which are the very object of global-scale agent models.

III. The Data Dust of Events

From what has been written so far, it is unclear whether the directors of FuturICT will devote as much attention to its informal design as Stafford Beer and his colleagues had accorded to such details in their operations room. The latter room made use of indirect lighting, built-in ashtrays, spaces for cocktail glasses, and an integrated mini-bar ("for pisco sours and so on") in order to create a pleasant "lounge atmosphere." Together with his team, the cigar-loving Beer wanted to "demystify" the work of management and economic planning.[60] The convenience of being able to pour oneself a stiff drink was just as much a part of this demystification as was the design of the human-machine interface, which was built to serve human needs above all others. Machines were no longer to dominate humans and require them to adapt; according to Beer's vision, on the contrary, machines should adapt to human beings, and the operations room should call to mind a "club house."[61]

Despite their similar vocabularies when discussing complex systems, which Cybersyn and FuturICT each borrowed from the idiom of management, there is a particular aspect of FuturICT that belongs to an entirely different media-technological genealogy. With terms such as "policy wind tunnel, "social meteorology," and "large knowledge collider," the

---

[59]   Ibid., 86.

[60]   The quotations in the last two sentences are from personal emails sent to me in February of 2004 by Gui Bonsiepe, who was the lead designer of Cybersyn's operations room.

[61]   Stafford Beer, *The Heart of Enterprise* (New York: J. Wiley, 1979), 243.

project's creators have evoked the technologies of the hard sciences in their descriptions of social systems. The complete absence of references to the socio-cybernetic approaches of the past, moreover, indicates the authors' intention to differentiate their work entirely from the "epoch of cybernetics," the epoch during which Beer's project was undertaken. In their attempts to characterize FuturICT's methods as integrative and distributive, however, they have perhaps exposed their efforts to design a sort of "ecological" approach, one meant to circumvent any objections to technocracy before such objections are even voiced.

The use of bold and trendy catchwords aside, it can certainly *not* be claimed that the project's participants have neglected to think about theoretical issues. Many critical objections to the practice of data mining and to the epistemological implications of agent-based modelling have already been formulated quite extensively, and from a transdisciplinary perspective, in the multiple reports and white papers that have been released by the participants themselves. It seems as though a media-theoretical and cultural-theoretical critique has already taken place internally and – what is more – that arguments have already been sought in anticipation of potential reservations.[62] Perhaps it should rather be asked what such a showcase of "enlightenment" and self-criticism implies with respect to FuturICT's communications strategy. Finally, it should also be noted that the articles by Helbing and Stefano Balietti, which I have cited so often here, not only present an extensive amount of material on the topic of social simulations; to some extent, they are also "about" the sort of instrumentalizing prose that might originate in a grant-writing workshop.

It is therefore no surprise that the authors stress to such a great extent that there are absolutely no alternatives to their project among the inadequate instruments of social management that are already in operation, and it is likewise no surprise that the articles are laced with a pronounced rhetoric of progress: Existing problems, such as those concerned with the "mining" and processing of relevant data sets, are simply presented as though they will ineluctably be solved over the course of the project. Nevertheless, the approaches adopted by the project are closely related to one of the central themes of this book. First of all, by means of network-based data mining, the management of big data, and the tracking of mobile communication devices, collective processes are to be formalized as a conglomerate of multivariate histories of activity and behavior. To this extent, today's new masses seem more and more to be an effect of perpetually linking together the increasing (data) dust of events. This implies nothing less than a major innovation over the tradition social-science approaches to studying mass phenomena, approaches such as empirical research and probability theory. Second, the new masses and their dynamics generate "measurable" data-events, at least in a certain sense, and this has resulted in a comprehensive de-psychologization of earlier efforts to explain collective dynamics (think of the traditional discipline of crowd psychology). Third, if agent-based computer simulations are developed on the basis of such data dust, and if these simulations allow the systemic behavior of human collectives to be "played around with" and enable their visualization in "decision arenas," then this interconnection between the new masses and

---

[62]   See Helbing and Balietti, "From Social Data Mining to Forecasting," 22–47.

the (simulated) new masses will do much to eradicate the pathologies – such as irrationality and animal-like unpredictability – that have traditionally been associated with large crowds of people. Such would be the case, for instance, if the evacuation plans in football stadiums were designed according to panic simulations, or if self-organizing transportation and logistical systems could be made to ensure a frictionless use of resources.[63]

Beyond the insoluble problem that social systems, unlike the weather, react to predictions about their own behavior and thereby render such predictions invalid, another fundamental misunderstanding on the part of FuturICT might lie in its incoherent approach to the evaluation of potential "decision-makers." For one, the project has vehemently insisted that rationalistic models of political agency are inadequate; it was this very inadequacy, in fact, that served as the inspiration for designing – by means of data mining, agent-based modelling, and visualization tools – models that are more complex, better-protected (as regards data), and more heterogeneous. It is just such "rational" decision makers, however, who are ultimately called upon to deal with the data generated by FuturICT's complex system, and it is assumed that such people will be capable of making "better," "more intelligent," or "more adequate" decisions with such information at their disposal. The authors are conveniently silent about the possibility that the translation of expert knowledge into political activity, which is always influenced by numerous complicated variables, might prove to be problematic. One of the general features of politicians, of course, is that they seldom do what might be best for the long term (not to mention the medium term). Understanding and modelling complex social systems is one thing; communicating and implementing this knowledge, for the benefit of society at large, is another thing altogether. If the unpredictable nature of everyday global politics is added to this equation, then the large knowledge collider – despite its good intentions – seems as though it might generate nothing more than a black hole, the gravitational pull of which will distort all potential futures to the point of being unrecognizable. This could be yet another reason why, at least for the time being, FuturICT's own future is as unclear as it is.

---

[63]   See Sebastian Vehlken, "Überleben rechnen: Biologically Inspired Computing zwischen Panik und Crowd Control," in *Informatik 2009: Im Fokus das Leben*, ed. Stefan Fischer et al. (Bonn: Gesellschaft für Informatik, 2009), 847–59 (CD-ROM).

Christoph Engemann

Human Terrain System
Social Networks and the Media
of Military Anthropology

The United States began its attack on Iraq in the evening of March 19, 2003. Donald Rumsfeld, the Secretary of Defense at the time, had already announced his doctrine of "shock and awe," according to which the American military would quickly demonstrate its superiority to the Iraqi troops and leadership with a show of force both in the air and on the ground. According to the military discourse at the time,[1] the enemy was supposed to be promptly defeated by a networked operation consisting of unprecedented intelligence, situational agility, and overwhelming firepower. American dominance of Iraqi airspace was in fact established within six hours. Stealth bombers flew undetected by Iraqi radar, and thus the Iraqi air defense was forced to shoot blindly into the dark sky – shots that appeared like fireworks on television screens being watched around the world. Only a single Iraqi fighter jet, moreover, was able to get off the ground. After it was shot down, the personnel stationed at Iraqi air force bases received the radio message "You Fly – You Die," which was also distributed on pamphlets throughout the country. From this point on, the American military was theoretically capable of controlling every location in Iraq with whatever firepower would be necessary.

Despite such capacities for locational positioning, the anticipated control was never established in Iraq, nor was any order whatsoever. My intention here is to conduct a media-theoretical analysis of the military discourses and media technologies that were current at the time; the goal will be to demonstrate how the American military reacted to this problem. I hope to show that, in the military debates and projects of the time, the problem of establishing local control and order shifted from metaphors of occupying territory to possible formats for ordering and governing social ensembles. New wars – or so the argument went – require social media and are to take place with and within such media. In what follows, the concept of social networks will thus not be sought in the usual places – Xing, Twitter, Google+, and Facebook – but rather where its logic has been implemented in an especially urgent manner, namely in contemporary international conflicts. A media-theoretical investigation of publicly accessible documents and projects

---

[1] See Stefan Kaufmann, "Network Centric Warfare: Den Krieg netzwerktechnisch denken," in *Politiken der Medien*, ed. Daniel Gethmann and Markus Stauff (Berlin: Diaphanes, 2005), 245–64.

will demonstrate that the American military in Iraq and Afghanistan has aimed to make the populations of these countries, even those segments that are on the other side of the digital divide, legible as social networks. It is on the basis of the data gathered with such methods, moreover, that the United States distinguished between enemies and allies. With its concept of "human terrain," the American military discourse managed to topologize the social in a rather peculiar manner. Human terrain is supposed to represent a novel and, according to several prominent war theorists, crucial area of operation for the military. As will be shown, the medial production of this area has simultaneously mobilized anthropologists (who in the case of colonialism and Vietnam had been concerned with "social media" well before the term was coined), networks, and the cultural techniques of social graphs. This has also entailed that societies be understood as quantities of relatable data – relations that can be represented as graphs, in terms of the frequency and intensity of their contact, and can thus serve the military as an operational means of establishing local control and order. My final questions will concern the relevance of social media and social graphs to the issue of sovereignty.

I. New Wars and the Transformation of the Network Concept

In 2003, Iraq was militarily defeated within two weeks. Along with the "coalition of the willing," the United States enforced a change in the Iraqi political system and in Iraqi institutions. At the end of 2003, after a brief period of relative peace, the Sunnis and Shiites recommenced their ongoing civil war, and northern Iraq became a Kurdish enclave. This civil war quickly nullified whatever success the American military had achieved. The operation known as "Enduring Freedom," which was not officially concluded until 2012, promptly began, as did the guerrilla war between the United States and various factions of the Iraqi population. Because their goal of liberalizing and democratizing the Middle East turned out to be mere fantasy, the neoconservative protagonists of the war went on the defensive and ultimately lost their positions during George W. Bush's second term in office. In the press, Rumsfeld's doctrine of "shock and awe" was treated as an obsolete way of thinking dating from the Cold War, one that was fixated on technological superiority. Rumsfeld was ousted from office at the end of 2005. As his next Secretary of Defense, Bush appointed Robert M. Gates, who changed the priorities for equipping the American military and struck down or cut back a whole series of large-scale projects, including outstanding orders for helicopters, tanks, and fighter jets. In light of the military's own recent losses and the general "collateral damage" from the war, a debate ensued at the time, both in public and within military circles, about neoconservative wars of occupation and their disregard for such things as insurgency warfare and nation building.

Over the course of these discussions, the concept of the network came to be perceived in an entirely different manner. During the first half of the last decade of the 20th century, networks were regarded as a condition of empowerment and as one of the particular advantages of the American military, which a number of publications characterized as a "network army" and discussed in terms of its advantageous network-based doctrine of swarming (such opinions were also expressed by German media theorists and in the books that caught their attention).[2] This perception began to shift around the second half of the 2000s. Instead of the idea that sovereignty could be imposed by the American military onto its poorly networked opponents, the focus of the discussion shifted to the networks of the opponents themselves, especially those of al-Qaeda, as being superior and generally threatening to sovereignty.[3] This shift in the understanding of networks was accompanied by an increased interest in anthropological discourses, whose reception began to dominate the doctrinal debates taking place within the American military. Digital infrastructures and technical media in general started to fade into the background. Instead, the concept of the network was derived from ethnological and sociological studies and the focus shifted to the necessity of understanding enemy cultures.[4] In a military-sponsored study by the anthropologist Sheila Miyoshi Jager, this shift is expressed as follows:

> In sharp contrast to former Secretary of Defense Donald Rumsfeld's heavy-handed approach to counterinsurgency, which emphasized aggressive military tactics, the post-Rumsfeld Pentagon has advocated a gentler approach, emphasizing cultural knowledge and ethnographic intelligence [...]. This "cultural turn" within the [Department of Defense] highlights efforts to understand adversary societies and to recruit "practitioners" of culture, notably anthropologists, to help in the war effort in both Iraq and Afghanistan.[5]

---

[2] In addition to Kaufmann's article cited in the previous note, see also Sebastian Vehlken, *Zootechnologien: Eine Mediengeschichte der Schwarmforschung* (Berlin: Diaphanes, 2012); Eva Horn, "Schwärme – Kollektive ohne Zentrum: Einleitung," in *Schwärme, Kollektive ohne Grenzen: Eine Wissensgeschichte zwischen Leben und Information*, ed. Eva Horn and Lucas Marco Gisi (Bielefeld: Transcript, 2009), 7–26; Sebastian Gießmann, "Netzwerkprotokolle und Schwarm-Intelligenz: Zur Konstruktion von Komplexität und Selbstorganisation," in ibid., 163–82; idem, "Netzwerk-Zeit, Zeit der Netzwerke: Fragmente zur Datenökonomie um 1960," in *Zeitkritische Medien*, ed. Axel Volmar (Berlin: Kadmos, 2009), 239–53; and Stefan Kaufmann, "Netzwerk-Zeit, Zeit der Netzwerke: Fragmente zur Datenökonomie um 1960," in *Vernetzte Steuerung: Soziale Prozesse im Zeitalter technischer Netzwerke*, ed. Stefan Kaufmann (Zurich: Chronos, 2007), 145–58. The latter works were influenced by John Arquilla and David F. Ronfeldt, *Swarming and the Future of Conflict* (Santa Monica: Rand, 2000); idem, *Networks and Netwars: The Future of Terror, Crime, and Militancy* (Santa Monica: Rand, 2001); and Sean J. Edwards, *Swarming and the Future of Warfare* (Santa Monica: Rand, 2005).

[3] See John Robb, *Brave New War: The Next Stage of Terrorism and the End of Globalization* (Hoboken: John Wiley & Sons, 2007).

[4] On the sociological origins of the network concept, see Irina Kaldrack and Theo Röhle's contribution to this volume as well as Erhard Schüttpelz, "Ein absoluter Begriff: Zur Genealogie und Karriere des Netzwerkkonzepts," in *Vernetzte Steuerung: Soziale Prozesse im Zeitalter technischer Netzwerke*, ed. Stefan Kaufmann (Zurich: Chronos, 2007), 25–46. Regarding the media-historical background of the concept, see Friedrich Kittler, "The City is a Medium," trans. Matthew Griffin, *New Literary History* 27 (1996), 717–29, esp. 718–19; and Claus Pias, *Computer Spiel Welten*, 2nd ed. (Zurich: Diaphanes, 2010), 170–71.

[5] Quoted from Roberto J. González, *American Counterinsurgency: Human Science and the Human Terrain* (Chicago: University of Chicago Press, 2009), 12.

The poster boy for this cultural turn was David Petraeus.[6] A touted general since the time of the Bush administration, Petraeus was made Director of the CIA by Barack Obama in 2010, though he soon had to resign from this position on account of an extramarital affair. Petraeus's prominence and ascent as a prototypical warrior-intellectual – he holds a doctoral degree in political science from Princeton and has taught at both West Point and Georgetown – were launched by his liberation of the city of Mosul, which had been a hotbed of the Iraqi civil war from 2003 to 2005. During these years, Petraeus was the commander of the 101st Airborne Division, which was stationed there:

> Petraeus and the 101st employed classic counterinsurgency methods to build security and stability, including conducting targeted kinetic operations and using force judiciously, jump-starting the economy, building local security forces, staging elections for the city council within weeks of their arrival, overseeing a program of public works, reinvigorating the political process, and launching 4,500 reconstruction projects in Iraq.[7]

In the wake of these efforts, Gates entrusted Petraeus with the task of revising and reformulating the U.S. Army's official *Counterinsurgency Field Manual*. The previous edition of this text, which had been prepared in 1982, largely reflected the experiences of the Vietnam War. The manual revised under Petraeus's supervision, which was published in 2006 with the title *U.S. Army Field Manual No. 3–24: Counterinsurgency (COIN)*, was treated as a public event by the American military and was accompanied by a large-scale media campaign. Unlike other documents of its sort, Petraeus's was furnished with a preface by Sarah Sewall, who was then the director of the Center for Human Rights at Harvard's Kennedy School of Government, and it was published by the University of Chicago Press. The back of the book is adorned with enthusiastic quotations from the American media. The *New York Times* lauded it as a "landmark, paradigm-shattering," the *Chicago Tribune* referred to it as "probably the most important piece of doctrine written over the last 20 years," while *Time Magazine* gushed that it was "revolutionary" and "Zen-tinged."[8] Bookstores ordered it *en masse* and displayed it prominently by their cash registers. Shortly after its publication, a number of anthropologists criticized the extensive amount of plagiarism that could be identified in the manual, but these accusations hardly made any ripples in public opinion.[9] Rather, a series of features in the press, not

---

[6]   For further discussion of this new approach, see Hugh Gusterson, "The Cultural Turn in the War on Terror," in *Anthropology and Global Counterinsurgency*, ed. John D. Kelley et al. (Chicago: University of Chicago Press, 2010), 279–98; and R. Brian Ferguson, "The Full Spectrum: The Military Invasion of Anthropology," in *Virtual War and Magical Death: Technologies and Imaginaries for Terror and Killing*, ed. Neil L. Whitehead and Sverker Finnstrom (Durham, NC: Duke University Press, 2011), 85–110.

[7]   Kirsten Lundberg, *The Accidental Statesman: General Petraeus and the City of Mosul, Iraq* (Cambridge, MA: Kennedy School of Government, 2006), http://www.case.hks.harvard.edu/casetitle. asp?caseNo=1834.0 (accessed on September 16, 2014; users must register to read the full text).

[8]   For an overview of the book's reception, see González, *American Counterinsurgency*, 10.

[9]   See ibid., 10–11.

to mention talk shows and television interviews, presented Petraeus and his co-authors as the intellectual leaders of the reoriented doctrines that were guiding the U.S. Army. In light of the shift that had taken place away from large-scale and swift wars of conquest against symmetrical or semi-symmetrical adversaries toward long-term efforts to occupy and stabilize asymmetrical opponents, which were expected to define American military operations in the present and foreseeable future, the *Field Manual No. 3–24* laid out strategies for engaging in "soft" forms of combating and pacifying insurgent groups.

II. The Counterinsurgency Field Manual and Human Terrain

In 2003 and 2004, the weapons preferred by such asymmetrical Iraqi insurgents were so-called "improvised explosive devices" (IEDs), which were self-made bombs set to detonate if American troops were on the streets or in public squares. Technological approaches to such devices, such as using strong radio signals to deactivate their detonation systems, proved to be more or less ineffective, and soon the number of casualties began to grow. In 2004, the U.S. Army's "Joint Improvised Explosive Devices Task Force" discouraged such "technological fixes" and instead recommended that soldiers should study the socio-cultural structures of the areas under occupation. The *Field Manual No. 3–24*, which appeared two years later, elaborated upon this recommendation and explained the new paradigm of counterinsurgency (COIN) operations in the following terms: "U.S. forces must understand the people of the host nation, the insurgents, and the host-nation (HN) government. Commanders and planners require insight into the cultures, perceptions, values, beliefs, interests and decision-making processes of individuals and groups."[10] In the works on counterinsurgency written during the Petraeus era, the word "understanding" is one of the most often used but little understood. It dominates the rhetoric employed by the Joint Improvised Explosive Devices Task Force, which expanded the idea to encompass a peculiar range of phenomena.[11] As far as counterinsurgency operations are concerned, the most important thing to control is the so-called human terrain.[12] The concept itself goes back to the well-known Un-American Activities Committee from the McCarthy era, which issued a report in 1968 with the title "Guerrilla Warfare Advocates in the United States." According to this report, militant groups within the Unites States, most notably the Black Panthers, had "the ability to seize and retain the initiative through a superior control of the human terrain."[13] In the year 2000, long after the idea of human terrain had been discussed in (obviously CIA-sponsored) publications concerning the 1970s revolu-

---

[10] The U.S. Army and U.S. Marine Corps, *Counterinsurgency Field Manual* (Chicago: University of Chicago Press, 2006), § 3-1.

[11] See Montgomery McFate et al., "What Do Commanders Really Want to Know? U.S. Army Human Terrain System Lessons Learned from Iraq and Afghanistan," in *The Oxford Handbook of Military Psychology*, ed. Janice H. Laurence and Michael D. Matthews (Oxford: Oxford University Press, 2012), 92–113, at 94.

[12] See González, *American Counterinsurgency*, 28.

[13] Quoted from ibid.

tionary movements in Latin America,[14] the former officer and conservative commentator Ralph Peters revived it yet again. In an article titled "The Human Terrain of Urban Operations," he argued that, unlike conventional warfare, it is not of the utmost importance when fighting against urban insurgents to conquer and control the territory itself; rather, it is paramount to control the "human terrain." It is these people, he goes on, "armed and dangerous, watching for exploitable opportunities, or begging to be protected, who will determine the success or failure of the intervention."[15] The article reads like a rather accurate prediction of the misunderstanding that would occur when, after Bagdad had been occupied and the statue of Saddam Hussein had been toppled in Firdos Square, the U.S. military declared the war to be over: "[T]he center of gravity in urban operations is never a presidential palace or a television studio or a bridge or a barracks. It is always human."[16]

The war against the Iraqi army, which at the time of the confrontation was considered to be the fifth largest army in the world, was over in a mere twenty-one days. Around the year 2000, it was obvious that geographic terrain no longer represented a problem for the American military. It had become clear by the time of this conflict that the United States had the ability to locate anything within a given geographical area and that, by means of GPS and geographic information systems, it could potentially gain control over any place on the globe. Nevertheless, victory in Iraq was evasive, and the population continued to act inimically toward its invaders. In light of the human terrain discourse that had been taking place, the American military regarded these facts as a new *terra incognita*; from then on, human beings and the relations between them were reconceived as the principal operative area that needed to be evaluated, navigated, and controlled.[17] From 2003 to 2006, a series of military reports were issued that, with reference to Peters's article about human terrain, encouraged a transformation within the military and called for the development of cultural competencies.[18] Although the term "human terrain" did not appear in the new *Counterinsurgency Field Manual*, Petraeus would nevertheless become one of its strongest proponents. From his various high-ranking positions in the military, and with the endorsement of Robert Gates and (later) Barack Obama, Petraeus promoted the development, systemization, and institutionalization of techniques and practices for managing the human terrain. In an often-repeated statement about his understanding of counterinsurgency and about the goals of the new field manual, he maintained the following: "You have to understand not just what we call the military terrain [...], the high ground and low ground.

---

[14] See Roberto J. González, "'Human Terrain': Past, Present, and Future Applications," *Anthropology Today* 24 (2008), 21–26, esp. 24; and idem, *American Counterinsurgency*, 29.

[15] Ralph Peters, "The Human Terrain of Urban Operations," *Parameters* 30 (2000), 4–12, at 4.

[16] Ibid., 12.

[17] See Fred Renzi, "Terra Incognita and the Case for Ethnographic Intelligence," *Military Review* 86 (2006), 16–23.

[18] For a summary of these reports, see González, *American Counterinsurgency*, 30–35.

It's about understanding the human terrain, really understanding it. Navigating cultural and human terrain is just as important as navigating geographic terrain."[19]

III. Anthropology and the Human Terrain System

It is rather difficult, for several reasons, to conduct a media-theoretical analysis of the discourses mentioned above. First, there is very little temporal distance between the present and the events under discussion, and second, it is possible only to cite the few sources that are currently available to the public. Even a superficial look at the material, moreover, reveals that the American military is not a monolithic entity. Within the army, between the various branches, and within the overall security apparatus of the United States, bitter disagreements exist regarding the methods and strategies that should be employed. This latter fact makes it especially difficult to develop a general overview of things because, just as there are proponents for the human-terrain approach, there are also alternative projects and competing interests – often economically motivated – that promote the implementation of entirely different systems. Like any attempt to formulate an "anthropology of the military,"[20] it is only with caution and reservations that a media-theoretical investigation of contemporary military discourses and media technologies can be undertaken. The materials that I have examined for this essay come from technical military journals, field manuals, budget reports on military purchases, and from PR reports published by contracted firms or by the military itself.[21] Moreover, numerous books and articles have since been published by anthropologists about the human terrain system and in response to the heated debates that this system has engendered.[22] And so anthropology – a discipline that, having undergone the difficult process of coming to terms with its colonial legacy and imperial past, has been committed since the 1970s to a post-imperial, post-colonial, and socially-embedded understanding of the world – was suddenly and unexpectedly called upon in 2007 to elucidate the operations of an ongoing war. "Over the long term," as Robert Gates observed in 2008, "we cannot kill or capture our way to victory."[23] In this light, the American military found itself needing and wanting to know, exactly, what a human being is, and subsequently realizing that any such generalization would be invalid. Rather, as the experiences in Iraq and Afghanistan revealed, it was

---

[19]   Quoted from Babak Dehghanpisheh and Evan Thomas, "Scions of the Surge," *Newsweek* (March 14, 2008).

[20]   See, for instance, Hugh Gusterson, *Nuclear Rites: A Weapons Laboratory at the End of the Cold War* (Berkeley: University of California Press, 1996).

[21]   On the nature of conducting research of this sort, see Roberto J. González, "Anthropology and the Covert: Methodological Notes on Researching Military and Intelligence Programmes," *Anthropology Today* 28 (2012), 11–25.

[22]   For a lengthy bibliography of such material (updated through 2010), see the website zeroanthropology.org.

[23]   Quoted from the Defense Science Board's report *Understanding Human Dynamics* (Washington, DC: Office of the Under Secretary of Defense for Acquisition, Technology, and Logistics, 2009), 1.

important to ascertain how local forms of producing knowledge, creating identity, and generating social cohesion come to define what humans are and how they interact with one another. In order to do this, Petraeus and his fellow military leaders looked to the field of anthropology for advice. As Gates stated in 2008:

> Throughout the Cold War, universities were vital centers of new research – often funded by the government [...]. [I]n the last few years, we have learned that the challenges facing the world require a much broader conception and application of national power than just military prowess. The government and the Department of Defense need to engage additional intellectual disciplines – such as history, anthropology, sociology, and evolutionary psychology.[24]

Although Robert Scales, a general, referred to the War on Terror as a "social science war," anthropologists such as David H. Price were not especially fond of the association. In 2011, Price made the following statement:

> [W]hile World War I was the Chemist's War and World War II the Physicist's War, the current wars with their heavy reliance on the cultural knowledge needed for counterinsurgency and occupation are envisioned by many Pentagon strategists as the Anthropologist's Wars; yet many in Washington seemed truly surprised at the push-back from anthropologists upon news of the formation of Human Terrain Teams and other efforts to adapt anthropology for counterinsurgency and asymmetrical warfare.[25]

The "push-back" mentioned by Price is the debate about the relationship between anthropology and the military that ensued after the publication, in October of 2007, of a front-page article in the *New York Times* with the title "Army Enlists Anthropology in War Zones."[26] The American Anthropological Association (AAA) issued an official reaction to this piece within four weeks. In a public statement, the association explained that the participation of anthropologists in the Human Terrain System (HTS) was incompatible with its ethical principles.[27] Among other concerns, the authors of the statement noted that

---

[24] Quoted from Shannon D. Beebe and Mary H. Kaldor, *The Ultimate Weapon Is No Weapon: Human Security and the New Rules of War and Peace* (New York: Public Affairs, 2010), 113.

[25] David H. Price, *Weaponizing Anthropology: Social Science in Service of the Militarized State* (Oakland: Counterpunch, 2001), 2. See also Hugh Gusterson, "The U.S. Military's Quest to Weaponize Culture," *Bulletin of the Atomic Scientists* (June 20, 2008), http://thebulletin.org/us-militarys-quest-weaponize-culture (accessed on September 18, 2014): "The Pentagon seems to have decided that anthropology is to the war on terror what physics was to the Cold War."

[26] David Rohde, "Army Enlists Anthropology in War Zones," *The New York Times* (October 5, 2007), http://www.nytimes.com/2007/10/05/world/asia/05afghan.html?pagewanted=all&_r=0 (accessed on September 18, 2014).

[27] See also the report that was issued two years later by the AAA Commission on the Engagement of Anthropology with the U.S. Security and Intelligence Communities (CEAUSSIC): "Final Report on the Army's Human Terrain System Proof of Concept Program" (October 14, 2009), http://www.aaanet.org/cmtes/commissions/ceaussic/ upload/ceaussic_hts_final_report.pdf (accessed on September 18, 2014).

the military could not guarantee the "voluntary informed consent" of the people subjected to HTS research and that the information gathered from such research might be used in whatever way the Pentagon saw fit: "[I]nformation provided by HTS anthropologists could be used to make decisions about identifying and selecting specific populations as targets of U.S. military operations either in the short or long term."[28] Moreover, the AAA stated that the Human Terrain System could lead to the general suspicion that anthropologists are potential collaborators with military forces. A number of anthropologists had especially harsh words for the program. According to Hugh Gusterson, for instance, the Human Terrain System is a "form of hit-man anthropology where anthropologists, working on contract to organizations that often care nothing for the welfare of our anthropological subjects, prostitute their craft by deliberately earning the trust of our subjects with the intent of betraying it."[29] Gusterson is a board member of the Network of Concerned Anthropologists, an organization that formed in the wake of the HTS debates and joined the discussion by releasing a series of publications, including *The Counter-Counterinsurgency Manual.*[30] According to the AAA, participation in the Human Terrain program was not a viable option for any anthropologist with academic ambitions. Nevertheless, anthropologists remained, as of 2006, the military's primary recruitment goal for the institutionalization of "cultural awareness" and "human terrain capacity," the two main elements that the IED Task Force hoped would characterize the so-called Human Terrain System. The initiator and original director of this system was the anthropologist and lawyer Montgomery McFate. Toward the end of 2006, she began to recruit anthropologists and social scientists to participate in a sixteen-week training program at the Human Terrain System Office, which was located at the Fort Leavenworth army base in Kansas. Having completed the program, these specialists were then sent as part of Human Terrain Teams to Afghanistan and later to Iraq:

> The Human Terrain System is a U.S. Army project intended to provide military decision makers in Iraq and Afghanistan with greater understanding of the local population's cultures and perspectives. HTS deploys Human Terrain Teams (HTTs) of five to nine civilian and military personnel to support brigade, division, and theater-level staffs and commanders with operationally relevant information. The program also provides training for deploying personnel, reachback analysis, and software tools developed by HTS to support socio-cultural analysis. HTS emphasizes the use of tools and approaches commonly associated with the academic disciplines of anthropology and sociology in its efforts to collect and analyze data about local populations.[31]

---

[28] Ibid., 70

[29] Quoted from Matthew B. Stannard, "Montgomery McFate's Mission: Can One Anthropologist Possibly Steer the Course in Iraq?" *San Francisco Chronicle* (April 29, 2007), http://www.sfgate.com/magazine/article/Montgomery-McFate-s-Mission-Can-one-2562681.php (accessed on September 18, 2014).

[30] The Network of Concerned Anthropologists, *The Counter-Counterinsurgency Manual: Or, Notes on Demilitarizing American Society* (Chicago: University of Chicago Press, 2009).

[31] Yvette Clinton et al., *Congressionally Directed Assessment of the Human Terrain System* (Alexandria, VA: Center for Naval Analyses, 2010), 1.

This summary comes from an investigation that was commissioned by the U.S. Congress in response to various accusations that the Human Terrain System was inefficient and a waste of public resources. On the one hand, the authors of the investigation concluded that "the HTS program has been, in many ways, a success."[32] On the other hand, they pointed out that one of the program's main problems has been the recruitment of qualified personnel. The number of HTS recruits who could speak a language spoken in Afghanistan, for instance, was in the single digits. Moreover, of the approximately five hundred HTS members who were active in 2009, only forty-two could speak Arabic. Even after the public had been made aware of sexual harassment charges within the Human Terrain program,[33] and despite the persistent criticism of the program in general (which was even documented in a film),[34] the U.S. Army nevertheless managed to develop it further and protect it from seemingly imminent budget cuts. Beyond the difficulties of establishing the Human Terrain System, the available documents indicate that the objective of the recruited anthropologists and social scientists has been to generate knowledge, data formats, and behavioral guidelines for counterinsurgency campaigns and to make such information available to the local units in which they are stationed. At the same time, the U.S. Army has used the program to give itself a humanitarian image and to change the prevailing culture within the armed forces. In the words of Robert Gates:

> The Human Terrain program [...] is leading to alternative thinking – coming up with job-training programs for widows, or inviting local power-brokers to bless a mosque restored with coalition funds. These kinds of actions are the key to long-term success, but they are not always intuitive in a military establishment that has long put a premium on firepower and technology.[35]

The military's fixation on firepower was expressed even more clearly by a member of the Special Forces. In an interview with the Human Terrain Office, which was attempting to evaluate the program, he made the following remark: "Had we understood the cultural role of celebratory gunfire, more than one wedding party would have been spared from fires conducted in self-defense against a perceived threat."[36]

Although documents of this sort are meant to legitimize the Human Terrain System to the public and thus have to be read with caution, it seems as though the program

---

[32] Ibid., 2.

[33] See John E. Sterling, "Findings and Recommendations: AR 15-6 Investigation Concerning Human Terrain System (HTS) Project Inspector General Complaints" (May 12, 2010), https://app.box.com/s/2mv0g54xsr41aegwbw9i; and Maximilian C. Forte, "Documents: Investigations into the U.S. Army's Human Terrain System," *Zero Anthropology* (February 19, 2013), http://zeroanthropology.net/2013/02/19/documents-investigations-into-the-u-s-armys-human-terrain-system/ (both sites accessed on September 18, 2014).

[34] James Der Derian et al., *Human Terrain: War Becomes Academic* (2010), http://humanterrainmovie.com/ (accessed on September 18, 2014).

[35] Quoted from Beebe and Kaldor, *The Ultimate Weapon Is No Weapon*, 122.

[36] Montgomery McFate and Steve Fondacaro, "Reflections on the Human Terrain System During the First 4 Years," *Prism* 2 (2011), 63–82, at 66.

Fig. 1: The Human Terrain System website
(http://hts.army.mil)

was first and foremost an instrument for providing the U.S. Army with modes of operation that do not involve violence. In the same text, an officer is quoted as saying that the Human Terrain Team stationed with his unit "has absolutely contributed to our operational mission. Some things we've looked at – solving problems in a lethal manner – we've changed to non-lethal options on the basis of the HTT information."[37]

IV. The Network of Others

What does the navigation of human terrain really entail? What systems are used to manage this terrain of people, that is, to spatialize cultures into a topology that is meant to be measurable and controllable? According to the U.S. Army's own description of the Human Terrain System, Human Terrain Teams in Iraq and Afghanistan were tasked with gathering

> information about the physical security, economic security, ideology and belief systems, authority figures, and organizations relevant to major social groups in the area under study. This information comes from open source, unclassified collections and is referenced geospatially, relationally, and temporally to enable the creation of various "maps" of the human dynamics in areas where the U.S. has committed forces or other U.S. government officials.[38]

From the available sources, it is clear that there have been competing approaches within the military on how to carry out the geospatial and dynamic process of mapping socio-cultural information.[39] Under the sustained pressure from political and military leaders to map human terrain, the specific cartographic procedures have remained in flux. Organizations such as the National Geospatial Agency, the U.S. Army's Civil Affairs Branch, the Human Terrain System itself, and various intelligence agencies are each committed to their own epistemic views and have accordingly used a variety of cultural techniques to represent what human terrain ought to be. For instance, the National Geospatial Agency,

---

[37] Ibid., 64.

[38] *Human Terrain System Concept of Operations (CONOP): Proof of Concept* (Fort Leavenworth, KS: U.S. Army Training and Doctrine Command, 2007), 2.

[39] See the Defense Science Board's report *Understanding Human Dynamics*; and Michael L. Wood, *Mapping Collective Identity: Territories and Boundaries of Human Terrain* (Master's Thesis: U.S. Army Command and General Staff College, 2011).

which is chiefly concerned with physical geography, has employed its technical media of "remote sensing" – satellites and airborne multispectral sensors – for gathering information about human dynamics and has developed mathematical procedures for integrating geospatial data with human-geographical and socio-cultural data.[40] Within the U.S. Army's Human Terrain System, which is dominated by anthropologists, the chosen approach is oriented largely toward qualitative methods, while Petraeus's counterinsurgency manual promotes the application of network analysis, as it has been used by intelligence services:

> Units gather information on these ties by analyzing historical documents and records, interviewing individuals, and studying photos and books. It is painstaking work, but there is really no alternative when trying to piece together a network that does not want to be identified. Charts and diagrams lead to understanding the insurgents' means of operation.[41]

The crucial point here, which is relevant both to the Human Terrain System as well as to the general relationship between social networks and statehood or sovereignty, is contained in one line: "… when trying to piece together a network that does not want to be identified." Insurgencies, social movements, and terrorism are thus conceived as networks, and both the *Counterinsurgency Manual* and the Human Terrain System, which is derived from it, rely heavily on concepts of social networks: "It's about human social networks and the way they operate," or: "People don't get pushed into rebellion by their ideology. They get pulled in by their social networks."[42] According to military anthropology, in other words, people are understood as networking beings who at the same time act according to the sanctioned activity of the networks to which they belong. Thus it is possible, either consciously or not, for certain networks to develop whose social activity can be recognized and for another type of network to develop that, in George Packer's words, "does not want to be identified." This latter type of network is typically more difficult to form because it requires conscious decisions to be made regarding its means and formats of communication in order to remain opaque and illegible to outsiders. Counterinsurgency is essentially an effort to make such networks legible; it is the continuation of an observation that the anthropologist and agriculturalist James C. Scott had made in his studies twentieth century colonialism: "Legibility [is] a central problem in statecraft."[43] In

---

[40]   See Richard Heimann, "The Future of Counterinsurgency: Altogether Quantitative, Scarcely Analytical …," *Imaging Notes* 27 (2012), http://www.imagingnotes.com/go/article.php?mp_id=313 (accessed on September 19, 2014); and the National Geospatial Intelligence College's *Incorporating Human Geography into GEOINT: Student Guide* (Fort Belvoir, VA: National Geospatial Intelligence Agency, 2011).

[41]   *Counterinsurgency Field Manual*, § B-15.

[42]   George Packer, "Knowing the Enemy: Can Social Scientists Redefine the 'War on Terror'?" *New Yorker* (December 18, 2006), http://www.newyorker.com/magazine/2006/12/18/knowing-the-enemy (accessed on September 22, 2014).

[43]   James C. Scott, *Seeing Like a State: How Certain Schemes to Improve the Human Condition Have Failed* (New Haven: Yale University Press, 1998), 2.

counterinsurgency campaigns, the distinction between friends and enemies thus hinges on the legibility of a given network's sphere of activity. People who make themselves legible might not necessarily be friendly, but those who attempt to make themselves illegible are almost certainly enemies. For one political philosopher, at least, the distinction between friends and enemies was relatively easy to draw. In his *Theory of the Partisan*, Carl Schmitt noted that the central feature of a regular soldier – the feature that distinguishes him from partisans or irregular soldiers – is the ability to be identified as such by a uniform: "The regular fighter is identified by a soldier's uniform, which is more of a professional garb, because it demonstrates the dominance of the public sphere. The weapon is displayed openly and demonstratively with the uniform."[44] Regular soldiers are legible. Their uniform is a sign that reveals them to be members of an army and thus representatives of a given state. In their case there is no need to gather and sort through documents, photographs, and interviews in order to establish, with the help of graphs and tables, the legibility of their networks. A major aspect of human terrain, namely the distinction between friends and enemies, is made instantly legible by uniforms. At the same time, however, Schmitt is quick to add that the symbolism of one's uniform can become rather problematic under the conditions of irregular conflict:

> In partisan warfare, a new, complicated, and structured sphere of action is created, because the partisan does not fight on an open battlefield, and does not fight on the same level of open fronts. He forces his enemy into another space. In other words, he displaces the space of regular, conventional theaters of war to a different, darker dimension – a dimension of the abyss, in which the proudly-worn uniform [of the conventional soldier] becomes a deadly target.[45]

In Iraq and Afghanistan, the American military, whose structures and organizations were still based on the doctrine of open confrontation, underwent this very experience and had to rely on forms of regular warfare, with its traditional distinctions between identification and surreptitiousness – uniforms and camouflage. In these new wars, however, the army's uniforms made the distinction between friend and enemy very clear to its opponents, who for their part remained opaque by avoiding the traditional media arsenals of legibility. The Human Terrain System can be regarded as an attempt to reestablish such arsenals and should be read in light of Schmitt's laconic assertion that the partisan "provokes nothing short of technocratic affect."[46] Even if the official representatives of the Human Terrain System never tired of stressing that their analyses and data were not used for "targeting,"[47] this information was nevertheless made available to other divisions within the mili-

---

[44] Carl Schmitt, *Theory of the Partisan: Intermediate Commentary on the Concept of the Political*, trans. G. L. Ulmen (New York: Telos, 2007), 14.

[45] Ibid., 69–70.

[46] Ibid., 76.

[47] McFate et al., "What Do Commanders Really Want to Know?"; McFate and Fondacaro, "Reflections on the Human Terrain System," 69–70. See also Nathan Finney, *Human Terrain Team Handbook* (Fort Leavenworth, KS: Human Terrain System, 2008), 56: "The results of our research provide

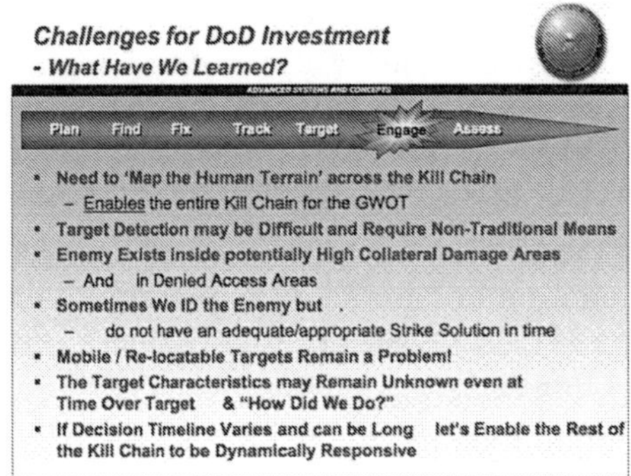

Fig. 2: Precision Strike: Winter Round Table (2007)[1]

tary.[48] For the military as a whole, network analysis serves as an important tool for illuminating and topologizing the "darker dimension" referenced by Schmitt; it is thus also helpful for targeting: "However acephalous or Janus-faced netwar may be, there must still be an *enemy* to be *targeted*: which is to say, located and subdued, either by being killed, destroyed, or rendered dysfunctional or dependent."[49]

V. Networks and Graphs in the Human Terrain System

In December of 2008, WikiLeaks published an internal training document that had been issued by the Human Terrain System.[50] The so-called *Human Terrain Team Handbook*, which became publicly accessible in September of the same year, explains what sort of data ought to be presented during briefings with military commanders. In addition to descriptions and images of local populations, their affiliations, religious convictions, socio-economic conditions, and history, the information to be passed along should also include so-called 'link charts': "Link Charts presenting any significant persons of influence who may be affected by the mission should be presented. These link charts should illustrate the relationship of the entity to the mission and his/her position within society (including ties to key political figures, threat organizations, etc."[51] Link charts are diagrams for representing social networks;

---

[1] John Wilcox, "Precision Engagement: Strategic Context for the Long War" (January 2007), http://www.dtic.mil/ndia/2007psa_winter/wilcox.pdf (accessed on September 22, 2014). For a critical discussion of this slide, which is taken from a PowerPoint presentation, see Ferguson, "Plowing the Human Terrain," 124.

non-target data that suggest Courses of Action to the commander and his staff." The latter book also stresses the goal of "non-lethal targeting."

[48] See R. Brian Ferguson, "Plowing the Human Terrain: Toward Global Ethnographic Surveillance," in *Dangerous Liaisons: Anthropologists and the National Security State*, ed. Laura A. McNamara and Robert A. Rubinstein (Santa Fe: School for Advanced Research Press, 2011), 121–22.

[49] Samuel Weber, *Targets of Opportunity: On the Militarization of Thinking* (New York: Fordham University Press, 2005), 101 (the emphasis is original).

[50] See David Price, "The Leaky Ship of Human Terrain Systems," *Counterpunch* (December 12–14, 2008), http://www.counterpunch.org/2008/12/12/the-leaky-ship-of-human-terrain-systems/ (accessed on September 22, 2014).

[51] Finney, *Human Terrain Team Handbook*, 37.

they consist of the following sort of information, which has to be gathered in the field by means of semi-structured interviews:

>   – What 5 people here have you known the longest?
>   – What 5 people here were you most recently in contact with?
>   – Who are the most important people here?
>   – Who are the most important people in Logar [a province in eastern Afghanistan]?
>   – What other provincial officials do you work with?
>   – What DSGs [district sub-governors] do you know best? How long have you known them?
>   – We heard that one can only become the DC [district commissioner] if he knows some governmental official. Is that true?
>   – We heard that one of Logar's DCs is the most powerful. Can you tell us who he is?[52]

Whereas the *Human Terrain Team Handbook* constantly reminds its readers that the information to be gathered will not be used for "targeting" and that the teams should avoid any sort of "direct involvement with tactical questioning," the *Counterinsurgency Field Manual* treats network analysis simply as a cultural technique of entrapment. There, according to Erhard Schüttpelz, "it remains a net for capturing prey."[53] In the appendix to the *Counterinsurgency Field Manual*, a section titled "Social Network Analysis and Other Analytical Tools" contains the following unequivocal comment: "Social network analysis (SNA) is a tool for understanding the organizational dynamics of an insurgency and how best to attack or exploit it." Here it is also mentioned that: "For an insurgency, a social network is not just a description of who is in the insurgent organization; it is a picture of the population, how it is put together and how members interact with one another."[54]

It is perhaps no surprise, then, that the authors immediately conclude that the "social network graph is the building block of social network analysis" and then go on to explain the essential concepts of graph theory, namely vertices, edges, weights, degree centrality, and betweenness.[55] Counterinsurgency operations, according the doctrine set forth in Petraeus's *Field Manual*, must first create an accurate representation of social networks in order to reduce the density of enemy networks and increase the density of friendly networks.[56] Network density is considered to be an indicator of a group's ability to undertake coordinated operations. The number of relations that a given individual has to others within a network provides information about his role and about the potential that, by removing this person from the network in question, it might begin to fragment. In counterinsurgency operations, the ability to change social graphs in accordance with one's own objectives is measured in terms of an operation's capacity for intervention:

---

[52]   Ibid., 114.

[53]   Schüttpelz, "Ein absoluter Begriff: Zur Genealogie und Karriere des Netzwerkkonzepts," 44.

[54]   *Counterinsurgency Field Manual*, § B-10.

[55]   See also Irina Kaldrack and Theo Röhle's contribution in this volume.

[56]   *Counterinsurgency Field Manual*, § B-10.

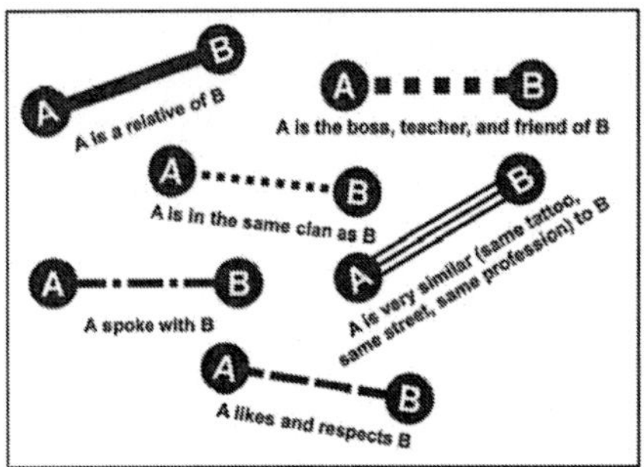

Figure B-5. Examples of dyads

Fig. 3: Source: Counterinsurgency Field Manual, § B-10

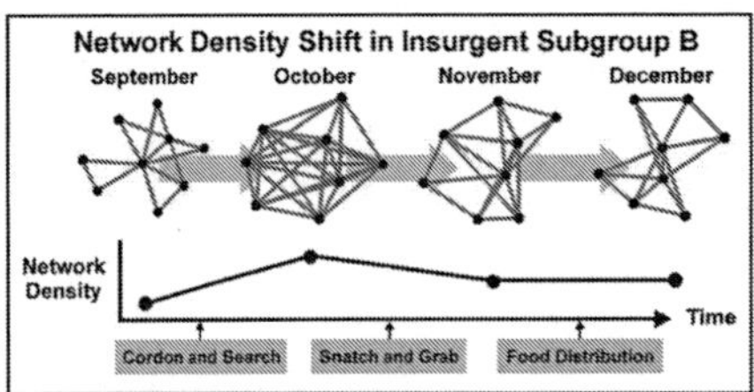

Figure B-7. Example of changes to tactics based on density shift

Fig. 4: Source: Counterinsurgency Field Manual, § B-12

Whereas the *Counterinsurgency Field Manual* makes only general statements about social graphs, the publications of West Point's Network Science Center have presented concrete data sets drawn from the formalized methods that have been used to fragment and weaken al-Qaeda's networks.[57] The authors, who are themselves veterans of counterinsurgency operations in Iraq and Afghanistan,[58] present algorithms with which the "leadership re-generation ability" of networks can be influenced in a targeted manner.[59] To do this, it is first necessary to determine, in mathematical terms, the extent of a given network's centrality, that is, the degree to which it is centralized or decentralized. Then it is possible to calculate which vertices of the network should be deactivated or manipulated in order to increase the fragility of the network in question. Fragility is thus formally defined as a problem of determining those vertices or nodes "whose removal would maximize the network-wide centrality."[60] The goal, in other words, is to use targeted attacks to make certain networks more hierarchical. In the nomenclature of graph analysis, higher levels of centrality entail higher levels of hierarchization. In turn, the more hierarchical a network is, the more vulnerable it is to external interferences. To explain this, the authors cite a graph that was made in the context of the 1998 attack against the American embassy in Tanzania:

---

[57]   See Devon Callahan et al., "Shaping Operations to Attack Robust Terror Networks" (November 6, 2012), http://arxiv.org/pdf/1211.0709.pdf (accessed on September 22, 2014).

[58]   See Philip Ball, "Unmasking Organised Crime Networks with Data," *BBC Future* (July 9, 2013), http://www.bbc.com/future/story/20130709-unmask-crime-networks-with-data; and "How Military Counterinsurgency Software Is Being Adapted to Tackle Gang Violence in Mainland USA," *MIT Technology Review* (July 4, 2013), http://www.technologyreview.com/view/516701/how-military-counterinsurgency-software-is-being-adapted-to-tackle-gang-violence-in/ (both websites were accessed on September 22, 2014).

[59]   Callahan et al., "Shaping Operations to Attack Robust Terror Networks," 1.

[60]   Ibid.

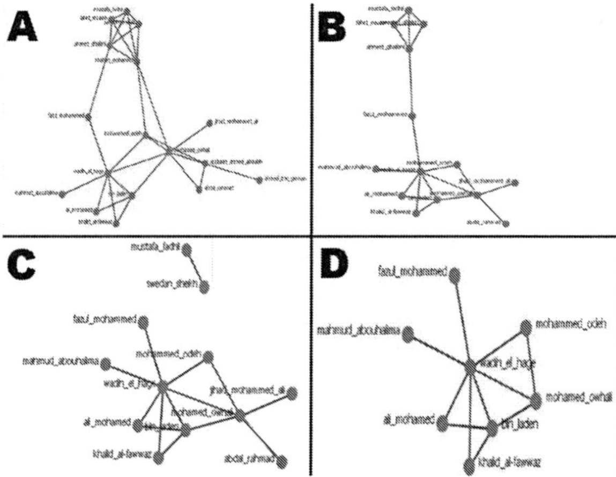

Fig. 5: A graph of the al-Qaeda network in Tanzania (1998). Graph A shows the original network; B is the network after the removal of three vertices; C is the network after five vertices, and D is network after the removal of nine. Over time, the graphs became more star-like in appearance, and Osama bin Laden moved closer to the center.[1]

---

[1]   Ibid.

VI. Producing Graphs in the Human Terrain System: Map-HT and the Analyst's Notebook

Social graphs are one of the main cultural techniques for topologizing socio-cultural relations and for converting a "social hieroglyph into a legible and administratively more convenient format."[61] They simultaneously produce both the legibility of social networks as well as a dynamic topology of spatial evidence and they represent human relations as navigable and manipulable quantities. In doing so, they are also able to scale up from small groups, like the al-Qaeda networks presented above, to entire national populations, and from there they can even scale up to represent transnational masses of people (think of the approximately one billion people represented by Facebook's graphs). Whereas, in the case of Facebook, the users actualize themselves graphically with their every interaction, the anthropologists engaged in counterinsurgency operations have to generate such knowledge by means of interviews and observations before they are able to create graphs pertaining to a given group of people. These graphs can then be implemented in so-called "shaping operations," which are targeted efforts to change a graph's features in accordance with the army's objectives.

Graphs are only able to fulfill their promise of being up-to-date and to preserve their dynamic quality, which is sensitive to events on the ground, if they are constantly being

---

[61]   Scott, *Seeing Like a State*, 3.

revised on the basis of thick descriptions. In the case of people who neglect to record and describe their own activity in writing – that is, in the case of people who avoid the internet and its social networks – constant and situationally flexible forms of data acquisition are needed to identify the main actors within a group and their relations and interactions with one another. Such information is of course a precondition for the creation and analysis of social graphs. In Iraq and Afghanistan classical media of authentication have been used to identify the roles of individuals; this has involved simple techniques such as creating databases of personal names and taking photographs to using more advanced technologies such as biometric instruments. This has also involved, whether secretly or not, marking pieces of clothing with radioactive dyes for purposes of tracking.[62] Once gathered and evaluated, data of this sort were entered into a software program called Map-HT, which is a database system that allows social graphs and events to be superimposed over geographic terrain.

The aim of the program was to ensure that interventions and their documentation took place simultaneously; it was based on the belief that, with a constantly updated data record, it would be possible to make the dynamics of human terrain legible and therefore manageable. The intention of the Human Terrain System and the Map-HT program, in other words, was to record and establish the legibility of a social environment that had hitherto remained illegible to those who wanted to read it. Of course, Map-HT is not accessible to the public, not even as a demo-program. I am only able to comment about it here on the basis of product descriptions and first-hand accounts that are circulating online. From such sources it can be said that Map-HT is a database system with a three-tiered hierarchy. The hierarchy consists of the software that is used for data acquisition on the ground, a middleware program for evaluating this data at regional sub-centers, and a centralized database located at the Human Terrain System Reachback Center in Fort Leavenworth. It is there that all of the data entered into Map-HT is stored and made available to analysts, who write background reports and respond to urgent requests from the regional teams. It was not long, however, before the Map-HT program proved to be too difficult and problematic to operate, and the laptops assigned for its use were put back on the shelf.[63] In the meantime, the Human Terrain Teams were networked to a different set of database systems, systems that had longer track records with the U.S. Army. Among these are the Tactical Ground Reporting System (TIGR), which is used by all active units for their daily reports,

---

[62]   Members of al-Qaeda's network are by now obviously aware of this practice, as is clear from documents that have been released by the Associated Press: "The Al-Qaida Papers – Drones" (2013), http://hosted.ap.org/specials/interactives/_international/_pdfs/al-qaida-papers-drones.pdf (accessed on September 23, 2014). For additional examples of tracking techniques, see David E. Sanger, *Confront and Conceal: Obama's Secret Wars and Surprising Use of American Power* (New York: Crown, 2012), 70–71.

[63]   See John Allison, "The Leavenworth Diary: Double Agent Anthropologist Inside the Human Terrain System," *Zero Anthropology* (December 5, 2010), http://zeroanthropology.net/2010/12/05/the-leavenworth-diary-double-agent-anthropologist-inside-the-human-terrain-system/ (accessed on September 23, 2014).

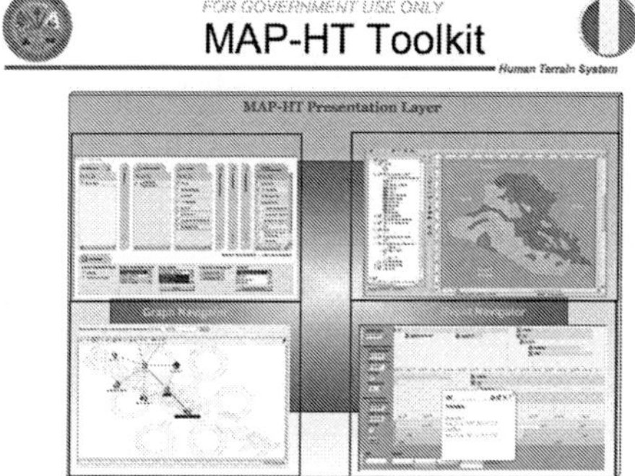

Fig. 6: The Map-HT Toolkit used by the Human Terrain System[1]

---

[1]   Steve Fondacaro and Montgomery McFate, "Human Terrain System Information Briefing for Army G3" (October 16, 2008), http://cryptocomb.org/Human%20Terrain%20System%20Info%20G3%20Briefing.pdf (accessed on September 23, 2014).

and the Software Analyst's Notebook. The latter is a commercial tool developed by IBM for analyzing social graphs and it has been used, for instance, for evaluating the success of advertising campaigns on social media. In addition to these systems, the American military and intelligence agencies have also used a variety of other network analysis programs, such as Palantir and ORA,[64] but there is no available information about how or whether they have been integrated into the Human Terrain System.

VII. Sovereignty and Opacity

The example of the Human Terrain System, which has been used to create and maintain the legibility of collectives, demonstrates that the ability to control legibility is an essential feature of sovereignty. During the Second World War, a perplexed British cryptographer is reported to have said the following to one of his colleagues at the Government Code and Cipher School in Bletchley Park: "You know, the Germans don't mean you to read their stuff, and I don't expect you ever will."[65] The Third Reich was sovereign because it could make itself illegible to its enemies, and the end of its sovereignty commenced as soon as the Turing machine at Bletchley Park began to rob it of its capacity to be opaque. It would be fitting to ask how and whether the participants in the "Facebook Revolutions" of the Arab Spring can be classified according to the distinction between legibility and illegibility, between regular and irregular soldiers. In this case, the relationship between legibility, friends, and enemies is certainly rather more complex, but several activists have nevertheless stressed that their global visibility on social media has served to protect them against repression. Of course, the actual role of social media in the Arab Spring remains a matter of dispute. German media theorists, for instance, have expressed their skepticism in this regard: "The assertion that Facebook played an essential role in the Arab Spring fails to pay due respect to the people who went out onto the streets and, for

---

[64]   See the paper issued by the Counter-IED Operations Intelligence Center (COIC): "Social Network Analysis (SNA) Tool Comparison: Working Paper" (November 28, 2011), https://info.publicintelligence.net/JIEDDO-SocialNetworkAnalysis.pdf (accessed on September 23, 2014).

[65]   Christopher Morris, "Navy Ultra's Poor Relations," in *Codebreakers: The Inside Story of Bletchley Park*, ed. Francis Harry Hinsley and Alan Stripp (Oxford: Oxford University Press, 2001), 231–46, at 242.

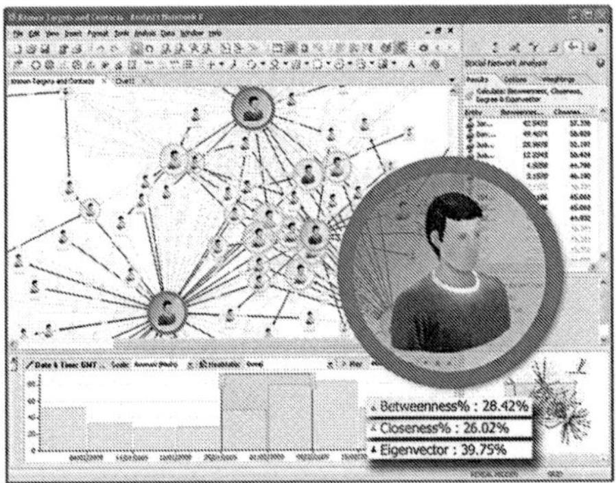

Fig. 7: The Analyst's Notebook (IBM)[1]

---

[1]   This image is borrowed from IBM's software site: http://www-03.ibm.com/software/products/en/analysts-notebook (accessed on September 23, 2014).

several weeks, risked their lives for democratic change. It suggests that the decisive capacity to act was made available by Western communication technologies."[66] The Egyptian author Essam Mansour, however, reached the opposite conclusion: "The Arab Revolutions, including the Egyptian Revolution, have largely been enabled by SNS."[67] This opinion was corroborated by the findings of the "Project on Information Technology and Political Islam," which has attempted to evaluate the effects of blogs, Facebook, Twitter, and YouTube: "Social media played a crucial role in the political uprising in Tunisia and Egypt. […] [B]y using digital technologies, democracy advocates created a freedom meme that took on a life of its own and spread ideas about liberty and revolution to a surprisingly large number of people."[68]

From the perspective of states that are struggling for their sovereignty, however, perhaps it is of little importance whether social networks are able to conceal any potential or actual threats of mobilization and subversion – or whether cryptography will enable certain segments of the population to hide their activity behind a veil of digital secrecy.[69] Perhaps they are more concerned with whether the legibility of social graphs should be one of their major objectives, that is, whether the improvement of such legibility will enhance their capacity to read and navigate through a given social terrain – whether social graphs, as this analysis of the Human Terrain System seems to indicate, number among the decisive media for establishing local order and thus represent a resource for preserving sovereignty, the control of which might ultimately serve to co-determine the survival of

---

[66]   Oliver Leistert and Theo Röhle, "Identifizieren, Verbinden, Verkaufen: Einleitendes zur Maschine Facebook, ihren Konsequenzen und den Beiträgen in diesem Band," in *Generation Facebook: Über das Leben im Social Net*, ed. Leistert and Röhle (Bielefeld: Transcript, 2011), 7–30, at 14.

[67]   Essam Mansour, "The Role of Social Networking Sites (SNS) in the January 25th Revolution in Egypt," *Library Review* 61 (2012), 128–59, at 148.

[68]   Philip N. Howard et al., "Opening Closed Regimes: What Was the Role of Social Media During the Arab Spring?" *Project on Information Technology and Political Islam* (January 2011), 3: http://pitpi.org/wp-content/uploads/2013/02/2011_Howard-Duffy-Freelon-Hussain-Mari-Mazaid_pITPI.pdf (accessed on September 23, 2014).

[69]   See Julian Assange, *Cyberpunks: Freedom and the Future of the Internet* (New York: OR Books, 2012).

one state or another.[70] Most recently in the case of the Arab Spring, social graphs and the control over their legibility or opacity have become concrete problems for agents of the state. Admittedly, Egyptian and Tunisian officials were able to shut down local internet servers and thereby hinder or prevent access to social networks, and yet in doing so they simultaneously made illegible the very segments of the population that they wanted to control, monitor, and inform the state's decision-making processes. In the case of the states in North Africa, the social graph of large and influential segments of their populations was unavailable to them.[71] The graph, after all, was being processed and stored on servers run by American internet companies and was ultimately accessible only to those with access to the servers in question. In addition to the obvious issue of militaries and security forces exploiting the social graphs that are created by Facebook, Twitter, and Google, the fact should not be ignored that, for more than six years, the American military has been using its Human Terrain System to graph the populations of countries in which Facebook and Twitter are hardly ever used. At least according to the army's own description of the program, another component of the Human Terrain System is to maintain a constantly updated "socio-cultural database," the contents of which are available both to the army and to other branches of the military.[72]

VIII. Anthropology and Social Media: Being Described and Describing Oneself

Historically, anthropology served as an ancillary science to the colonial powers by transferring the world, as experienced by illiterate and stateless collectives, into a legible form. Around the middle of the twentieth century, however, the field attempted to emancipate itself from its own state-sanctioned origins. At the same time, anthropology has nevertheless continued to study societies that other disciplines have deemed unworthy of description or whose activity has simply not yet been described in writing. In its attempts to fashion itself into a counterscience,[73] anthropology regards itself as being in

---

[70] On the history of generals being fascinated with graphs, see also Kittler, "The City is a Medium," 719.

[71] Regarding the North African groups who were using social media, see Howard et al., "Opening Closed Regimes," 2: "[S]ocial media was used heavily to conduct political conversations by a key demographic group in the revolution – young, urban, relatively well-educated individuals, many of whom were women. Both before and during the revolutions, these individuals used Facebook, Twitter, and YouTube to put pressure on their governments."

[72] See the website http://hts.army.mil/ (accessed on September 23, 2014); and Ferguson, "Plowing the Human Terrain," 117–22.

[73] On the notion of counterscience, see Michel Foucault, *The Order of Things: An Archaeology of the Human Sciences* (New York: Pantheon, 1970), 380. In this regard, structural anthropology found itself in a relatively comfortable position. It emerged as a discipline at the very moment of decolonization and thus evaded the suspicions of colonial complicity that were faced by other branches of anthropology. Of course, structural anthropology also relied extensively on the anthropological studies that had been conducted before its time.

opposition to the wishes of the state, especially when it comes to governing societies that lie beyond writing or description – societies, in other words, that either cannot or simply do not want to be read. These are groups of people whose manner of life underscores the extent to which governments need to be able to address and document their populations and who thus shed a critical light on the governance of mediality and on the mediality of governance. The military discourses under consideration here attest to just such a situation of "governmediality,"[74] a situation characterized by negotiations about the necessity and value of writing about or describing certain people. If nothing else, such negotiations about the proper use of media have created a field of tension between academic anthropologists, military institutions, the arms industry, and journalists. Media have perhaps become *the* main problem of government that needs to be included among the other objects of governmentality enumerated by Foucault.[75] Of course, security, territory, and population remain essential areas of activity for governments, but they have been redefined by the emergence of digital media in such a way as to seem medially preconditioned. In this regard it is not only sovereignty that allows such phenomena to exist; as the case of the Human Terrain System has demonstrated, security, territory, and population can also be defined by ensembles of oppositional and conflicting agents who may or may not affiliate themselves with a given state. Conflicts of this sort raise questions about which media are needed to govern, how and whether media can be governed, and how the government of media should itself be governed. At the same time, the internet can be understood as a machine for governmedialization that enables oppositional ensembles to come together on a large scale, and these ensembles further underscore the reciprocal relationship between governance and mediality. This is especially true regarding the practices that states have employed to document people and events, practices that, with the rise of the internet, are now confronted with a paradoxical problem. If the early-modern and modern history of governmediality can be characterized by the enormous amount of effort that was devoted to recording and describing people and things – tasks that required throngs of bureaucrats, secretaries, anthropologists and other state-employed pencil pushers – so it is now that the internet serves as a medium for generating such writing, that is, as medium in which people essentially describe or write about themselves (and thus about things as well).[76] It is no longer really necessary to record anything, and this is because the present transformation in media conditions has brought about a shift from modes of description to modes of self-description. In other words, that which is happening in the world no longer needs to be treated as something to write about because such happenings seemingly write about

---

74 See Christoph Engemann, "Write Me Down, Make Me Real: Zur Gouvernemedialität der digitalen Identität," in *Quoten, Kurven und Profile: Zur Vermessung der Gesellschaft*, ed. Jan-Hendrik Passoth and Josef Wehner (Wiesbaden: Springer, 2012), 205–27.

75 Michel Foucault, *Security, Territory, Population: Lectures at the Collège de France, 1977–1978*, trans. Graham Burchell (New York: Palgrave Macmillan, 2007).

76 See Christoph Engemann, "Verteiltes Überleben: Paul Barans Antwort auf die atomare Bedrohung," in *Überleben: Historische und aktuelle Konstellationen*, ed. Falko Schmieder (Munich: Wilhelm Fink, 2010), 381–93.

themselves. This situation is paradoxical because the paranoia about the chasm between the actual world and our administrative record of it, a sort of paranoia that had long accompanied the government of modern states,[77] has largely been eliminated, and yet the possibility has nevertheless remained out of reach – despite the assiduous efforts of pirate parties, corporate consultants, IT companies, hackers, ministerial e-government initiatives, etc. – to govern and document sovereignty or statehood with and within the internet.

It was in 2006 that Facebook, which remains the most successful format of its kind, was first made available to the general public. Innocuous questions – about such things as the last five people someone has spoken to or the five most important people someone knows – no longer need to be asked because they have always already been answered on Facebook. This is not the case, however, with the Human Terrain System, which (coincidentally or not) was initiated during the same year that Facebook became generally available, and which is concerned with those people (and things) that have not yet been described and are perhaps unwilling to be described. Unlike industrialized nations, Iraq and especially Afghanistan have not been pervaded by the internet. For the most part, the populations of these countries live on the other side of the digital gap; they are offline, not connected, or are simply unconvinced by the alleged benefits of every child having a laptop. Here, in place of digital media, anthropologists working for the Human Terrain System act as social media and describe people in terms of networks. Again, the people in question either live in societies that are not (or not yet) familiar with the self-descriptive practices of the internet or, for cautionary measures, intentionally refrain from such practices. In the latter case, at least, the Human Terrain System seeks to enforce the legibility of certain circumstances that have been created precisely to remain illegible. The social graphs generated by the Human Terrain System, moreover, remain inaccessible to those who are represented in them. They are in the control of the military and function as resources for establishing local order during ongoing or future interventions.

Does all of this represent – and I ask this question with Carl Schmitt in mind – a sort of spatial revolution, a media-technologically conditioned revolution of telluric ideas? If one can momentarily set aside the fascistically motivated and pseudo-mythological undercurrents of Schmitt's concept of the *nomos* and understand it instead as a media-historically indexable measure,[78] one that is limited to a given society's laws concerning the allocation of land and resources, then it ought to be asked whether graphs represent, as regards allocational laws of digital sovereignty, "the measure by which the land in a

---

[77] See Bernhard Siegert, *Passagiere und Papiere: Schreibakte auf der Schwelle zwischen Spanien und Amerika* (Munich: Wilhelm Fink, 2006); and idem, *Passage des Digitalen: Zeichenpraktiken der neuzeitlichen Wissenschaft, 1500–1900* (Berlin: Brinkmann & Bose, 2003).

[78] For historical discussions of authoritative media, see Bernhard Siegert's works on the genealogy of measuring instruments and Cornelia Vismann's contributions on the mediality of the law: Siegert, *Passage des Digitalen*; idem, "The Map Is the Territory," *Radical Philosophy* 169 (2011), 13–16; and Cornelia Vismann, *Files: Law and Media Technology*, trans. Geoffrey Winthrop-Young (Stanford: Stanford University Press, 2008).

particular order is divided and situated."[79] Without having to endorse Schmitt's fictional ideas about the genesis of the law, it is possible to maintain that, in the present situation, what is taking place is not the appropriation of territory or waterways but rather something that could be called the appropriation of graphs. For the moment, economics is the obvious driving force behind such appropriations and behind the acts of "division and distribution" that have been taking place in their wake.[80]

In Western societies, where the growth and consumption of the internet has already generated a governmediality of self-description and where people are busy recording their own activity quasi-synchronically and on a large scale, dynamic and constantly updated graphs of the relations between people and other people, between people and things, and between things and other things serve as the foundation of such businesses as Google, Facebook, Twitter, and LinkedIn. The media-materialistic infrastructures (server farms) that generate these graphs and keep them up-to-date are located predominantly in rural areas of the United States. Their steady migration to such locations began in 2006 with the success of Facebook and Twitter and with the smart-phone revolution brought about by Apple's iPhone and Google's Android. In 2005, only five percent of the world's mobile phones were equipped with an operating system by an American company. This number reached eighty-eight percent by 2012, at which time a full eighty percent of the world's most popular websites were also run by firms based in the United States.[81] From the recent disclosures by Edward Snowden and others of the expansive surveillance efforts that have been undertaken around the globe, it has become clear that governmental institutions such as the American National Security Agency and the German Federal Intelligence Service (*Bundesnachrichtendienst*) have had access to these data-processing centers and thus to the graphs themselves. The military analyst John Robb has referred to such centers as "system points" – the network-topological equivalent to Clausewitz's "centers of gravity" or "focal points"[82] – and they remain inaccessible to the self-describing individuals who provide them with information. Instead, they are controlled by the companies named above and made accessible to certain national-security officials and intelligence services. It can be presumed that the latter, with the awareness and support of military units, are the impetus behind the appropriations of graphs that are currently taking place and that their goal is to procure full access to up-to-date graphs of as many societies and social groups as possible.

A situation has thus arisen in which the generation and analysis of graphs is undergoing a process of generalization. At least from the perspective of American intelligence services, this process has two sides. Whereas graphs of the American population (and of

---

[79] Carl Schmitt, *The Nomos of the Earth in the International Law of the Jus Publicum Europaeum*, trans. G. L. Ulmen (New York: Telos, 2003), 70.

[80] Ibid., 81.

[81] Mary Meeker and Liang Wu, "Key Internet Trends" (May 2013), http://www.slideshare.net/klein-erperkins/kpcb-internet-trends-2013 (accessed on September 23, 2014).

[82] Robb, *Brave New War*, 95.

the populations in many other countries) can be extrapolated from data collected from the internet and other forms of telecommunication, the social graphs of war zones, as discussed above, are ultimately generated by the military anthropology practiced by Human Terrain Teams. "Like buttons" and "friend requests" may be innocent enough in allowing users to recognize, "within a crowd of eight hundred million, a new society of people to adore them in a different but no less genuine manner,"[83] but the media of social networks and the cultural technique of graph analysis have long since fallen, in Schmitt's words, "within the sphere of the political: the intense friend-enemy distinction"[84] – assuming, of course, that they were ever outside of this sphere. Although the division and distribution of social graphs have not yet been elevated into a pressing issue of international law, they have long been a part of governmedial negotiation processes. Struggles are well underway over access to social graphs and their legibility, over the control and representation of their "system points," and over the ability to harness their potential for creating local order and thus for establishing or maintaining sovereignty.

---

[83] Alexander Pschera, *800 Millionen: Apologie der sozialen Medien* (Berlin: Matthes & Seitz, 2011), 106.

[84] Schmitt, *The Nomos of the Earth*, 88.

III. Which Public Spheres?

The chapters in this section can be inscribed into the rich history of thinking about media upheavals, their political consequences, and their effects on the formation of public spheres. In the early twentieth century, this history was shaped by the likes of Bertolt Brecht and Walter Benjamin, who were then concerned with the new media of radio and film.[1] The first two sections of this book illustrated that, from a historical perspective, it is impossible to discuss the formation and effects of masses without also taking into account the question of their medial conditions. The current changes in the socio-technological configuration of mass phenomena therefore indicate (among other things) a reconfiguration of the political – perhaps even a technological shift in the way that the political is sensed and made sense of[2] – and this development should be regarded as one of the central issues in studies devoted to social media and new masses. In light of the distinction between connectivity and collectivity, which Claus Pias discussed above in his introduction to the second part of this book, the chapters in the present section share a common understanding of the interconnected nature of medial and social forms. On this basis, and in light of the new socio-technical constellation known as "digital cultures," their authors have endeavored to discern the implications of this interconnection as regards contemporary scenes of the political and the emergence of public spheres.

The texts in this section are thus united by their explicit concern with the contemporary situation. How, they ask, has the digitalization of nearly all aspects of life affected the creation of public spheres and the potential for political change? Both conceptually and empirically, they share an exploratory approach: What sort of mediated practices

---

[1] See Bertolt Brecht, "The Radio as an Apparatus of Communication," in *Communication for Social Change Anthology: Historical and Contemporary Readings*, ed. Alfonso Gumucio-Dagron and Thomas Tufte (South Orange, NJ: Communication for Social Change Consortium, 2006), 2–3; and Walter Benjamin, "The Work of Art in the Age of Mechanical Reproduction," in *Illuminations: Essays and Reflections*, trans. Harry Zohn (New York: Schocken Books, 1968), 217–251.

[2] Erich Hörl, "Die technologische Bedingung: Zur Einführung," in *Die technologische Bedingung: Beiträge zur Beschreibung der technischen Welt*, ed. Erich Hörl (Berlin: Suhrkamp, 2011), 7–53. See also Daniel Gethmann and Markus Stauff, eds., *Politiken der Medien* (Berlin: Diaphanes, 2005).

and organizational forms can be observed, and which concepts and descriptive forms are suitable for analyzing their political consequences?

One result of this is a pronounced engagement with the empirical phenomena of social media and the new masses, which are closely analyzed below, for instance, with regard to the processes and operations implemented by Anonymous, WikiLeaks, and Facebook. Another consequence is that the focus is not on the function of social media for politics in a conventional, institutional sense. The issue is not, for instance, that of the mass-media coverage of politics or the use of the media by political actors, and nor is it simply a matter of diagnosing the incorporation of the media apparatus and its mass effects in a certain regime of governmentality. Although the concepts used by the authors vary, on a more abstract level the contributions can be connected to the distinction between "politics" and "the political," a distinction that was fostered by Carl Schmitt and Hanna Arendt and has recently been revived by theorists such as Giorgio Agamben, Claude Lefort, and Jacques Rancière.[3] Here the political appears as the manifestation of the contingency of the social, as a rupture and an opening in the constellation of institutionalized apparatuses and practices. The public sphere is thus not something that is always already given; rather, the concern is with the creation of more or less temporary publics or public spheres.[4] In this regard, it is interesting that such a performative understanding of the public sphere seems to adhere to traditional ideas about the principle possibility of mass organization and its emancipatory potential.

However, insights into current forms of control and regulation, which have been discussed in terms of protocological control and in terms of the "micrological" distribution and modulation of affects and atmospheres,[5] have resulted in a fundamental sense of ambivalence that pervades the texts collected here. That we are now, as Wolfgang Hagen concluded in his chapter above, without crowds in the traditional sense, but are rather a crowd "at the zero point of the political," is a point that will warrant further discussion in light of the ideas presented in this section. Here it is shown with concrete examples how publics can be generated that at least hint at the potential of political struggle – even in the case of Facebook's user conditions, for instance, which are designed to serve commercial purposes. For sure, this is a far cry from the optimistic or utopian prospects that have been peddled by the so-called "Californian ideology," according to which unlimited access to new and powerful information technologies will inevitably lead to democratic transparency and large-scale participation in the political process. Whereas Alexander Galloway has likened the bipolarity of engaging with the political potential of networks to the structure of Aeschylus's tragedies, with the chain of triumph on one side and the

---

[3]   See Oliver Marchart, *Post-Foundational Political Thought: Political Difference in Nancy, Lefort, Badiou and Laclau* (Edinburgh: Edinburgh University Press, 2007).

[4]   See Michael Warner, *Publics and Counterpublics* (New York: Zone Books, 2002).

[5]   See Alexander R. Galloway, *Protocol: How Control Exists after Decentralization* (Cambridge, MA: MIT Press, 2004); and Tiziana Terranova, *Network Culture: Politics for the Information Age* (London: Pluto Press, 2004).

web of ruin on the other,[6] the studies collected here constitute a refusal or qualification of overarching arguments and "grand narratives". Rather, the struggle over the organization of digital cultures seems to be ongoing, and much can be gained from taking a closer look at current experimental attempts to reorganize what is visible and sayable.

In his chapter on the "Ornament of Mass Customization," therefore, Sascha Simons maintains that the public sphere of the Web 2.0 has been structured more and more according to the model of the shopping mall. However, with reference to Gabriel Tarde's sociology of imitation (and, as Simons rightly points out, of imitation's flaws and glitches), which here, too, is presented as highly applicable to current socio-medial processes, he nevertheless argues that present-day media can bring about the disappearance of older masses only to the extent that they help engender new ones. By analyzing a YouTube video montage by the artist Natalie Bookchin (titled *Mass Ornament*), Simons offers novel reflections about the social morphology and mobilizing effects of digital networks. In her artistic update of Kracauer's canonical study, Bookchin's dispersed YouTube dancers look less like emancipated "prosumers" than they appear to be exchangeable modules in a digital production process. In other words, the mass customization of individuality in our society of control has come to take the place of the industrial mass production that had been characteristic of the previous disciplinary society. The implicit morphological knowledge of Bookchin's dancers, however, is also indicative of the potential inherent in medially enabled processes of imitation and contagion, the variety of which reflects the permanent possibility of finding new audiences and of creating new forms of assembly and representation.

Perhaps the most influential recent experiment with such new forms has been the formation known as Anonymous, which is the focus of Carolin Wiedemann's chapter. Neither the anonymous communication processes used by this collective nor its amorphous, "formless form" can be understood with the help of classical theories of collectivity, group identity, and organization; such features rather require a new a way of thinking about the technologies or infrastructures of the common. Wiedemann's examination of Anonymous relies on the concepts of network, swarm, and multitude, on the basis of which she is able to describe and analyze this new form of collectivity without having to associate it exclusively with any one of them. Hardt and Negri's idea of the multitude, which is conceived as being free from mediation and thus different from mere crowds, seems especially unsuitable for explaining a collectivity like Anonymous, in which the "event of the common" cannot take place without the ambivalent enabling condition of mobile infrastructures, a condition that is as controlling as it is liberating and affecting (*affizierend*).

---

6   Alexander R. Galloway, "Networks," in *Critical Terms for Media Studies*, ed. W. J. T. Mitchell and Mark B. N. Hansen (Chicago: University of Chicago Press, 2010), 280–96, at 281.

As the example of WikiLeaks has made clear, the increasing prominence of the leak and the creation of a "networked fourth estate," in Yochai Benkler's terms,[7] are unthinkable without collaborative platforms and without the ability to organize masses of digital data. In "Toward an Ethics of the Leak," Christoph Bieber thus discusses WikiLeaks as a "programmed public sphere" and treats code as a new power structure at the intersection of media and politics. Such is the basis of the "formative public sphere," a new and dynamic type of public that is experimental in nature and offers alternatives to participating in institutionalized political processes. This development necessarily raises ethical questions about how to deal with certain sorts of knowledge and information, about the unanticipated and unintended consequences of its publication, and about the self-regulation and obligations of collaborative actors. The "ethical dissidence" of a "surveillance actor" such as WikiLeaks also creates a degree of ambivalence, given that the platform restricts access to its resources of power – that is, to its data and code.

To what extent can social media platforms such as Facebook, which aim to commercially exploit the activity of their customers as data providers, become public spaces? In his examination of Facebook's call for its (then 450 million) users to participate, seemingly, in the formulation of the website's "Statement of Rights and Responsibilities," Mirko Tobias Schäfer argues in his chapter that online platforms have become "hybrid forums for socio-political debates." How should we evaluate the political quality or political potential of such for-profit enterprises? With a number of examples and observations, Schäfer demonstrates how activities on commercial platforms connect to alternative sources of information and content. He identifies three factors, according to which the question of the emancipatory potential of new media platforms is to be analyzed and evaluated: The first is the ability to mass-mobilize in the name of political causes, the second is free access to information and data, and the third is the expansion of traditional political discourses into online public spheres. Each of these factors perpetuates classical ideas about the political potential of a critical and enlightened public and seeks to translate them into the digital age.

If profit-oriented social media platforms can be said to commodify mass communication and exchange in unprecedented ways, this is all the more true of the synthetic worlds of computer games and of the booming market that has developed around them. In his chapter "Between the Madness and Wisdom of Crowds: Computer Games and the Distraction Economy," Peter Krapp turns his attention to this understudied social, political, and economic field. A new sort of masses, in short, is "playfully" forming in synthetic worlds, which have come to be dominated by subscription services and secondary, grey-market transactions. Under the conditions of digital cultures, according to Krapp, media theorists not only need to concentrate on the quality of media products; they have to focus on numerical quantities as well. By examining the worlds of computer games, then, media studies can certainly gain certain insights into the emergence of new masses and recognize the extent to which the latter have been commodified. It seems questionable, however,

---

[7]   Yochai Benkler, "A Free Irresponsible Press: WikiLeaks and the Battle over the Soul of the Networked Fourth Estate," *Harvard Civil Rights-Civil Liberties Law Review* 46 (2011), 311–97.

whether the traditional model of self-enlightening public spheres can accommodate the economy of attention and distraction that such worlds entail.

Timon Beyes

Sascha Simons

The Ornament of Mass Customization
On the Collective Consciousness of Dispersed Examiners

"When one wakes up, the first feeling that he experiences is that of the position of his body and limbs and his orientation in space in relation to the furniture, the walls of the bedroom, the window, etc. Here is the primordial foundation of our mental life; on this all the rest is built and it needs nothing more in order to appear. The same thing holds true of a group: the awareness that it develops of its structure and movements is at the base of all social life."[1]

Whenever social protests have occurred in recent years, they have quickly been associated with catchwords and given labels such as "Twitter-Revolution," "Facebook-Revolution," or "YouTube-Revolution." The increasing use of such catchwords does not merely reflect the profound changes that have taken place in medial relations but rather glorifies this change as the originator of social dynamics and simplifies the complex connections between social and medial upheavals in a manner that is as striking as it is one-sided. All the talk of hyphenated revolutions has not only brought about a rhetorical metamorphosis, whereby private corporations are now explicitly treated as major servants of the common good; it has also identified medial and social upheavals in such a manner as to leave little leeway for making differentiated statements about the involved collectives.

Admittedly, social functions have come to characterize the aesthetic forms of the Web 2.0 to an extent that is novel in terms of media history.[2] However, even though the distance between active participation and mediatized enthusiasm has been significantly reduced, there is – contrary to the narrative of medially determined revolutions – no certainty that the oppositional groups in Tehran, Cairo, or New York can be merged with the so called intelligent swarms of the social web and thus be regarded as a homogeneous collective subject – regardless of whether all of their activity was coordinated via mobile applications and appeared in network-based forms of representation. Certain questions remain: Do the masses on the street have any correspondence in the social media? What happens

---

[1]   Maurice Halbwachs, *Population and Society: Introduction to Social Morphology*, trans. Otis Dudley Duncan and Harold W. Pfautz (Glencoe, IL: The Free Press, 1960), 200.

[2]   See Stefan Münker, *Emergenz digitaler Öffentlichkeiten: Die Sozialen Medien im Web 2.0* (Frankfurt am Main: Suhrkamp, 2009), 70–71.

to collective consciousness under the conditions of the social web? To what extent are smart mobs aware of their smartness, and what does it consist of?[3] In short: Who bears responsibility for the first element of these hyphenated revolutions, and according to what conventions do they behave?

The search for answers to these and similar questions must take into account the entanglement of medial and social forms: Today's protests are no longer merely characterized by a simultaneous "collective reception" (in Benjamin's sense),[4] but also by simultaneous and collective acts of production and distribution. More so than ever before, the Web 2.0 enables groups to come together around and by means of medial artefacts, the formation of which is largely left to their recipients. The social morphology of networks forms their sensually experienceable surfaces, and vice versa. On social network sites, blogs, and video portals, the implicit functional equivalence between mid-sized social habitus and medial form have become explicit, and it is now possible to sensually experience the modes of collective formation before every conceptual reflection.[5] Collective consciousness, as it is formulated by concepts of social networks, swarms, or multitudes, is sublated (*aufgehoben*) into media-aesthetic practices and the 'prosumer's' implicit knowledge of medial forms. The group figures that are formed by these examiners (in Walter Benjamin's sense), who are as distracted as they are dispersed, create latent socio-aesthetic structures that are actualized in an eventful manner and are capable of generating mobilization effects that are comparable to Elias Canetti's notion of "crowd crystals"[6] without similarly becoming identifiable or institutionalized. During the recent and ongoing instances of social unrest, it has been possible to observe how loosely connected collectives have become aware of their social situation. This awareness has had substantial consequences, and it is for this reason that the morphological dimensions of these protests should not be ignored. In order to analyze this process in an appropriate manner, it is thus necessary to take its collaborative composition seriously.

---

[3]   See Howard Rheingold, *Smart Mobs: The Next Social Revolution* (Cambridge, MA: Perseus, 2002), 157–82.

[4]   Walter Benjamin, "The Work of Art in the Age of Mechanical Reproduction," in *Illuminations: Essays and Reflections*, trans. Harry Zohn (New York: Schocken Books, 1968), 217–251, at 235.

[5]   Analogies between habitus and medial forms can be observed both at the level of descriptive language and at the level of object language. First, both function as a conceptual hinge between sociological or media-aesthetic micro-perspectives and macro-perspectives. Second, they equally designate phenomena of the cultural unconscious whose aesthetic conciseness depends on a non-conceptual *sensus communis*. See Pierre Bourdieu, "Structuralism and Theory of Sociological Knowledge," trans. Angela Zanotti-Karp, *Social Research* 35 (1968), 681–706, esp. 704–06; idem, "Postface to Erwin Panofsky, *Gothic Architecture and Scholasticism*," trans. Laurence Petit, in *The Premodern Condition: Medievalism and the Making of Theory*, by Bruce Holsinger (Chicago: University of Chicago Press, 2005), 221–42 (Appendix II); and Rainer Leschke, *Medien und Formen: Eine Morphologie der Medien* (Konstanz: UVK, 2010), 70–71.

[6]   Elias Canetti, *Crowds and Power*, trans. Carol Stewart (New York: Farrar, Straus and Giroux, 1984), 73–75.

I. The Redundancy and Recursivity of the Mass Ornament 2.0

This is precisely the approach taken by Natalie Bookchin in her video montage *Mass Ornament*.[7] Here the artist has compiled, in diachronic and synchronic rows, short YouTube videos of dancing adolescents in front of their webcams, and she has done so to reflect the ideas expressed by Siegfried Kracauer in his canonical essay of the same title. Kracauer's observations about the dance routines of the "Tiller Girls" provide a historical template that allows Bookchin to depict both the medial and aesthetic logic of web-based video platforms as well as the way that individual and collective identities are constructed on them. Like Kracauer's historical-material analysis, her aesthetic reconstruction is based entirely on the reflexivity of socio-economic relations as expressed in the forms of popular culture:

> The YouTube dancer alone in her room, performing a dance routine that is both extremely private and extraordinarily public is, in its own way, a perfect expression of our age. Just as rows of spectators in the 1920s and 1930s sat in movie theaters and stadiums watching rows of bodies moving in formation, with YouTube videos, single viewers sit alone in front of computer screens watching individual dancers voluntarily moving in formation, alone in their rooms.[8]

Although, in both cases, the chosen surface analysis is (not coincidentally) focused on dancing figures as viewing material, my concentration below will not by on this particular form of selection but rather on the forms of its construction or composition.[9] In this context, the fact that both Kracauer and Bookchin are concerned with dancing bodies seems less important than the formal construction of their choreographies.

Kracauer, too, was not terribly interested in the dancers themselves, whom he regarded as acting entirely in the service of the ornament.[10] It is precisely in their denial of organic forms that the common rationality of industrial capitalism and the mass ornament is re-

---

7   The montage can be viewed online at http://bookchin.net/projects/massornament.html (accessed on September 1, 2014).

8   Carolyn Kane, "Dancing Machine: An Interview with Natalie Bookchin," *Rhyzome.org* (May 27, 2009), http://rhizome.org/editorial/2009/may/27/dancing-machines/ (accessed on September 1, 2014).

9   On the relationship among forms of selection, construction, and composition, see Leschke, *Medien und Formen*, 161.

10 Admittedly Kracauer's occasional asides about bodies and the "disposition of the soul" can be read as biopolitical sketches *avant le lettre*. See Siegfried Kracauer, "The Mass Ornament," in *The Mass Ornament: Weimar Essays*, trans. Thomas Y. Levin (Cambridge, MA: Harvard University Press, 1995), 75–88, at 79, 85. In this sense, Kracauer's contemporary Fritz Giese similarly regarded American "girl culture" to be an expression of the "collective workers" that fundamentally differs from Russian ballet, German body culture, and French variety shows. See Fritz Giese, *Girlkultur: Vergleiche zwischen amerikanischem und europäischem Rhythmus und Lebensgefühl* (Munich: Delphin, 1925), 83, 9–11. As media of self control, bodies dancing in web videos thus warrant a study of their own, but this will have to be undertaken elsewhere. In this regard, reference should be made to Kathrin Peters and Andrea Seier, "Home Dance: Mediacy and Aesthetics of the Self on YouTube," in *The YouTube Reader*, ed. Pelle Snickars and Patrick Vonderau (Stockholm: National Library of Sweden, 2009), 187–203.

vealed. According to Kracauer, the individual dancers cannot be identified as individuals, nor is it possible to identify a single intention that is given expression within the dance. An end in itself, the mass ornament is pure surface, and one searches in vain for any indication of its content:

> The end result is the ornament, whose closure is brought about by emptying all the substantial constructs of their contents. Although the masses give rise to the ornament, they are not involved in thinking it through. As linear as it may be, there is no line that extends from the small sections of the mass to the entire figure.[11]

The mass ornament thus proves to be an emergent phenomenon, one in which there is no path that leads from its higher social grouping back to its individual elements. The unity of the ornament remains closed. It is only by imagining a bird's eye view of it that, according to Kracauer, the motions of the individuals come to form a homogeneous relation between the parts and the whole – just as it is only the surveillance flights of historical materialism that allows to reach the heights necessary for observing "the undistorted truth" lying behind "the *rational and empty form* of the cult" in the light of reason.[12] Kracauer goes on:

> The production process runs its secret course in public. Everyone does his or her task on the conveyer belt, performing a partial function without grasping the totality. Like the pattern in the stadium, the organization stands above the masses, a monstrous figure whose creator withdraws it from the eyes of its bearers, and barely even observes it himself.[13]

Kracauer thus has in mind a sort of hidden choreographer that, though being up to no good, nevertheless guarantees a degree of formal unity within the social ornament. Bookchin, who rather invokes a medial than a historical materialism, dissolves this authorial position in terms that are reminiscent of Michel Foucault:

> There is no need for a director or choreographer (or foreman) to keep production flowing or to keep the dancers moving in sync. It is a perfectly individualized self-generated, self-replicating system.[14]

Instead of suggesting a central controlling authority or a hierarchically organized type of discipline, the dance videos are rather indicative of the recursive operational mode of governmental control.[15] This can only be observed because Bookchin occupies the vacant

---

[11]   Kracauer, "The Mass Ornament," 77.

[12]   Ibid., 84

[13]   Ibid., 78.

[14]   Kane, "Dancing Machine: An Interview with Natalie Bookchin," n.p.

[15]   See Michel Foucault, "Governmentality," trans. Pascquale Pasquino, in *The Foucault Effect: Studies in Governmentality*, ed. Graham Burchell et al. (Chicago: University of Chicago Press, 1991), 87–104, esp. 100–04. For specific applications of Foucault's concept of governmentality to user generated

position of author or originator under the protective aegis of the art system. The sort of authorship practiced here, however, is based less on the originality of artistic genius than it is on Bookchin's ability to select, organize, and contextualize materials, an ability that would suit the job profile of a curator or editor. Bookchin uses her knowledge of the audio-visual products of our mediatized everyday life and their design patterns to give a surface to the process of collectivization that is coordinated by means of such footage. The unity of the social ornament, which Kracauer was still able to rely on, here has to be restored out of the presumed isolation of private bedrooms. Its shape is not due to a subsequent establishment of a center or to a fixation of social dynamics but rather to mere redundancy and recursivity – or to "the ornamental," in Niklas Luhmann's terminology.[16]

Only through repetition does it become clear that the apparently isolated dancers on YouTube form a figure whose identity systematically evades both the dancers and their observers. The constructive principle of this mass ornament 2.0 is that of self-similarity. What makes the "mash up" memorable is the redundant form of its *mise en scène, mise en cadre*, and montage. Each with the grainy footage of a webcam, the different videos depict surface images that are nearly identically structured. By arranging them into uniform rows, Bookchin is thus able to produce a morphological connection between the YouTube dancers and the "pure assemblage" of chorus lines.[17] Moreover, she compounds the movements on the surface of the videos with the corresponding dynamic of her arrangement. In this way, *Mass Ornament* radicalizes merely a fundamental analogous relationship that exists between the different videos, but it does so in a virtuoso manner. The result is a high degree of order and thus an aesthetic difference from the normal operations of YouTube.

The incorporation of video samples from YouTube's "suggestions," which are presented to the right of the main framework, creates image-to-image relations that underscore the constitutive significance of contoured formal borders, especially in light of the permeable interfaces of the internet: There is no image without a frame, and there is no web video without a video frame. Thanks to the redundancy of forms, moreover, Bookchin is also able to translate the informational space of user interfaces and the structure of databases into the simultaneity of split screens. Thus she stresses the spatial organization of online audience flow. Contrary to diachronic television programs, which are oriented toward continuity, YouTube and other video platforms continuously present similar videos and thus always direct the attention toward an imperative of alternatives, in order to lure their users into the infinitude of their archives:

---

content in general – and to dance videos on YouTube in particular – see Peters and Seier, "Home Dance: Mediacy and Aesthetics of the Self on YouTube," 201; and Ramón Reichert, *Amateure im Netz: Selbstmanagement und Wissenstechnik im Web 2.0* (Bielefeld: Transcript, 2008), 13–14.

[16] Niklas Luhmann, *Art as a Social System*, trans. Eva M. Knodt (Stanford: Stanford University Press, 2000), 220.

[17] Kracauer, "The Mass Ornament," 76.

> The arrangement of multiple clips in a single row across the screen mimics a chorus line but it also reflects the viewing conditions of YouTube, where videos are shown with an accompanying row of thumbnail images linking seemingly similar videos. The installation progresses from one video to many, reflecting the culture of video sharing, where one video can produce chain reactions – that can include hundreds of copies, responses, and variations.[18]

The social foundations and conditions of media use are thus taken into account not only by the display of "view counts" but above all by the repetition and self-referentiality of the videos, which reflect upon the analogous nature of the distributional and reduplicative excesses that exist on the social web.

The medial framework of the video frame thereby becomes the object of an aesthetic inversion. The forms of borders or edges are transformed into the formed center. By means of its recursivity, the video compilation makes visible and audible the phenomenological, media-technological, and social conditions of its visibility and audibility.[19] That this constructive principle is not only applicable to dancing teenagers – but is just as fitting for other forms of material – can be demonstrated with a comparison to similar "mash ups."[20] This is because the contrastive multiplication of videos relaxes their object of reference; they gain a degree of autonomy beyond their context and come to present themselves in the formal character alone. Instead of fading away behind a symbolic function, the screen is rather dominated by analogy, redundancy, and recursive closure. The web videos processed here are highly compatible because their content has been vacated. They are compatible, in other words, because they have been made into ornaments.

II. On the Social Reflexivity, Public, and Individuality of Mass Ornaments

How is it possible, however, to go beyond the matter of purely aesthetic immanence in order to examine the social reflexivity of the ornament, as both Kracauer and Bookchin claim to do? Can the historical place of our epoch truly be detected in them, just as Kracauer, with some confidence, saw his own era reflected in the mass ornaments of the time? In order to come close to answering such questions and to draw a connection between Kracauer and Bookchin, it is first necessary to free Kracauer's cultural-sociological diagnosis from the bounds of his teleological philosophy of history. Throughout her work, Bookchin indeed makes connections between comparable circumstances. However, whereas she allows perceptible forms to speak for the socio-cultural context of their development, Kracauer's reflections rely on written analysis. Accordingly, she is unable able to offer any radical

---

18   Kane, "Dancing Machine: An Interview with Natalie Bookchin," n.p.

19   For a similar argument, see Brian Willems, "Increasing the Visibility of Blindness: Natalie Bookchin's Mass Ornament," in *Video Vortex Reader II*, ed. Geert Lovink and Rachel Somers Miles (Amsterdam: Institute of Network Cultures, 2011), 293–305, esp. 304–05.

20   Bookchin's related projects – *Testament* (2009), *Now He's Out in Public and Everyone Can See* (2012), and *Long Story Short* (2013) – can be viewed online at http://bookchin.net/projects (accessed on September 2, 2014).

solutions to the problems that she has identified. Then again, it is precisely because her work depends on medial self-descriptions that she is able to offer significant insight concerning the interrelations of economic forms, social formations, and the dynamics of medial forms without having to make salvific claims in the name of reason (*à la* Kracauer) and without falling victim to the sort of media determinism that emanates from California.

In order to do justice to the socio-political dimension of Bookchin's work, both of the mass ornaments under discussion here have to be interrogated on the basis of the concepts of individuality and the public that are communicated by them. A historical comparison will allow conclusions to be reached about the changes that have taken place in social visibility and collective consciousness. It will also shed light on the disappointments of the emancipatory expectations of the past and point to new political potentialities. In this regard it will be instructive to refer to the work of Gabriel Tarde, who was deeply concerned with the mediation between crowds, the public, and individuality. His sociology of imitation provides an appropriate conceptual framework for examining both the social-theoretical issues and the media-aesthetic phenomena that are at stake here. The currency of Tarde's theories is evidenced by the fact that they are just as useful for explaining the present media-historical circumstances as they are for clarifying those of the Weimar Republic described by Kracauer.

Because, in Kracauer's opinion, the public staging of capitalist rationality results in significant gains with respect to aesthetic realism and social transparency, he obviously sees no need to forsake his bourgeois distance and infiltrate the private spheres of individual crowd members. For him it is rather the case that *all of reality is public.* The "formal principle" of capitalist production, on which masses are modelled, corresponds to "the same rationality that controls the bearers of the patterns in real life."[21] Work and leisure are subjected to the same rhythm of Tayloristic rationalization. Fritz Giese, who was Kracauer's contemporary, based his comparative analysis of German and American "girl culture" on a similar notion. For him, the developmental state of a nation's culture, technology, and economy had to be observed in the "marginal zones of being" and described in terms of phenomena that are "complementary to the official culture of technology and economics."[22]

---

[21] Kracauer, "The Mass Ornament," 79, 85. At best, the distinction between the visible and hidden realms of this public reality can be reconceived as an incorporation of the (invisible) private sphere into a broader understanding of the public sphere and thus as a sort of "re-entry" of the distinction between social visibility and invisibility.

[22] Giese, *Girlkultur*, 14–15. In this regard, both Giese and Kracauer refer to the strikingly anti-erotic nature of the Tiller Girls. As "dancing machines," the latter are not meant to be sexually stimulating; rather, they are representative of the "collective of all technology," which Giese considered to be the new basis of human culture (see ibid., 83, 119, 141–42). Despite their common premises Giese and Kracauer came to diametrically opposite conclusions: While Kracauer believed in the inevitability of the revolutionary progress, Giese was concerned about the total manageability of society and the stabilization of production conditions. See Helmut Lethen, *Neue Sachlichkeit, 1924–1932: Studien zur Literatur des "Weissen Sozialismus"*, 2nd ed. (Stuttgart: Metzler, 1975), 43.

Even though it would seem obvious to apply this notion of a public without boundaries tacitly to the present situation, it is first necessary to understand certain factors that have led to a significant shift in the relations between the public and the private. Initially, users imitate conventionalized poses and gestures from the repertoire of popular culture. These mimetic appropriations are then established, by their constant repetition, as virally distributed memes. The private appropriation of a public model is thus reinjected into the public realm of communication. The public sphere of social network sites, however, does not develop naturally or organically (if such a simplification will be allowed here for the sake of brevity); rather, it is founded or endowed (*gestiftet*). It is controlled by the private corporation Google, which, for providing the communicative infrastructure of the video platform, rewards itself by maintaining extensive control over its user data. In this context, Mark Andrejevic has turned to the Marxist concept of primitive accumulation, which manifests itself today as a sort of "digital enclosure":

> Contrary to conventional wisdom, social networking sites do not publicize community but rather privatize it. In that the digital production of online communities takes place within a private corporate structure, such sites are able to appropriate and use the power of communities for commercial purposes. Their ability to gain control over this information is at least partially based on their "free" access and on their user agreements, the conditions of which are set by the commercial enterprises that control the resources for forming communities. Commercial social networking sites are presumably communal productions, except when it comes down to establishing user conditions and sharing the profits that they generate.[23]

The public sphere of the Web 2.0 has been increasingly structured according the model of the shopping mall and not according to the model of the agora. Its conditions for participation are only as transparent as the terms that are established by the large network providers, which, as far as the rights of users are concerned, can hardly be interested in tipping the balance of power against their favor.[24] Kracauer's diagnosis, namely that the "production process runs its secret course in public,"[25] must therefore be expanded to include not only immaterial goods and services but also the private spheres of social individuals. The home, which has been integrated into the process of creating value, is consequently treated by Bookchin as a key actor in its own right. The distinction between the public and the private is embedded into a more comprehensive and entirely commercialized sphere of *privatized public intimacy*. Within this sphere, the users of certain services have become the providers of these services and, to the extent that they have accepted the terms of participating on a social web governed by large corporations, they

---

23   Mark Andrejevic, "Facebook als neue Produktionsweise," in *Generation Facebook: Über das Leben im Social Net*, ed. Oliver Leistert and Theo Röhle (Bielefeld: Transcript, 2011), 31–49, at 43.

24   See Oliver Leistert and Theo Röhle, "Identifizieren, Verbinden, Verkaufen: Einleitendes zur Maschine Facebook, ihren Konsequenzen und den Beiträgen in diesem Band," in ibid., 7–30, esp. 16; and Mirko Tobias Schäfer's contribution to the present volume.

25   Kracauer, "The Mass Ornament," 78.

(must) offer their activity for sale as a sort of good. Even though it is hardly transparent, the promise of inclusion, with which the growing data economy entices its customers, is in fact quite extensive. Whereas algorithmic routines process critical or subversive content with formalistic indifference, the companies are reluctant to reveal the composition of their data sets to the very people who produce them. That which is publically accessible is typically restricted to the interfaces on which users gather to attract one another's attention. In this case, the reduction of the user to clusters or portfolios of data is counterpoised by the users' pursuit of affiliation and individual differentiation through their communication of personal achievements, opinions, and daily activity. The generation of "big data" remains dependent on the interplay between public participation and social distinction. Its de-subjectifying effects are driven by the promise of participation, on the one hand, and, on the other hand, by the differentiating self-reassurance of the individual in relation to his or her group of fellow participants.

The economic motivation of this promise, however, approximates a degree of distrust toward the affective connection between users and networks: The evaluation or analysis of web-based interactions seems to impede, in advance, the fulfillment of the desired prospect of participation and, in doing so, to renew its demand in a perpetual manner. Quite literally, this practice would thus profit from a sort of desire whose supplementary *telos* would be an equitable community of intersubjective recognition, even though it contaminates the very conditions that would enable such a community to form. However, the idea that such practices function to hollow out this ideal of community must remain a mere matter of suspicion, at least while the relationship between the individual and the group remains unclear. Before it is possible to clarify the problem of social visibility within these processes with an eye toward understanding the political potential of web-based collectives, the historical forms of the mass ornament must first be interrogated in terms of the concepts of individuality that find expression in them.

Kracauer expressly forgoes a prominent *topos* of crowd psychology, namely that the bourgeois subject needs to be defended against the collective irrationality and manipulability of the crowd.[26] On the contrary, his argument against the social reflexivity and significance of art betrays a degree of skepticism as regards bourgeois culture and its definitive protagonist, the subject. "As a total personality – that is, as a harmonious union of nature and 'spirit',"[27] this subject is adequate neither for the age of capitalism nor for the age of reason that Kracauer is heralding. For though the mass ornament must renounce this utopian hope for a new humanity on account of its unilaterally instrumental implications, the abstract formalism of its aesthetic principle distinguishes it from a work of art in that it sufficiently "reduces the natural"[28] and ensures that "[t]he surface-level expressions, […] by virtue of their unconscious nature, provide unmediated access to the fundamental

---

[26]   See Hannelore Bublitz, *In der Zerstreuung organisiert: Phantasmen und Paradoxien der Massenkultur* (Bielefeld: Transcript, 2005), 48.

[27]   Kracauer, "The Mass Ornament," 83.

[28]   Ibid.

substance of the state of things."[29] In contrast to the self-conception of bourgeois cultural products, the surface of the mass ornament thus offers "conclusive testimony about [the] overall constitution"[30] of an era whose capitalist and social state of development shows no consideration for the organic or spiritual-intellectual (*geistige*) identity of mankind:

> Only as parts of a mass, not as individuals who believe themselves to be formed from within, do people become fractions of a figure. […] The Tiller Girls can no longer be reassembled into human beings after the fact. Their mass gymnastics are never performed by the fully preserved bodies, whose contortions defy rational understanding. Arms, thighs, and other segments are the smallest component parts of the composition.[31]

Here Kracauer makes a valuable reference concerning the reduction of the individual bearers of the mass ornament into even smaller parts, an idea that Gilles Deleuze would later revive in his description of the "dividuality" that is characteristic of crowds in so-called societies of control. Kracauer himself, however, does not follow this line of thinking but rather concentrates on the transcendence of the individual dimension in the unity of the ornament.

Whereas Kracauer dissolves the autonomous subject in the undifferentiated nature of the formed masses, Bookchin confronts viewers with a dynamic sort of interaction between parts and the whole. Contrary to Kracauer's historical prognosis, the mass ornament of today is more tolerant regarding the integrity or intactness of the body and the identity of its parts. In light of the transformed conditions of production and distribution, it is tempting to believe that the individual is now stronger than ever before.[32] Admittedly, recipients have in fact experienced some appreciation for their control over the media of production and distribution, and this appreciation has not simply been rhetorical. However, the idea that this alone has resulted in an impetus for political emancipation must be cast into doubt in light of the asymmetric balance of power, mentioned above, between the rights held by website operators and the rather meager rights reserved for their users. Also Bookchin's formal-aesthetic analyses dampen any euphoria over the emancipation of recipients.[33] With the public intimacy of their webcams, the users admittedly present themselves as individuals. In doing so, however, they simultaneously commit themselves to serving the purpose of the mass ornament. In Bookchin's perspective of morphological constellations, the ostensible individuality of emancipated prosumers is revealed to

---

[29] Ibid., 75.

[30] Ibid.

[31] Ibid., 76, 78.

[32] For an argument in favor of this position, see Henry Jenkins, *Convergence Culture: Where Old and New Media Collide* (New York: New York University Press, 2006), 24.

[33] They also put into perspective one-sided pessimistic diagnoses, such as Jürgen Habermas' dismissive remarks about the online public sphere. See Jürgen Habermas, "Political Communication in Media Society: Does Democracy Still Enjoy an Epistemic Dimension? The Impact of Normative Theory on Empirical Research," *Communication Theory* 16 (2006), 411–26, at 423–24 (note 3).

be a mere effect of the redundancy and conventionality of medial forms. If one follows Kracauer's critical model, their freedom seems to correspond precisely to the freedom of interchangeable modules in variable production processes. In the mass ornament 2.0, it is no longer the logic of industrial mass production that finds expression but rather the logic of mass customization. This logic diverges from the rigid linearity of assembly lines and at the same time extends them to the consumers. The allegedly emancipated users have become productive, in the truest sense of the word. Their individuality serves as ennobling seal of still mass-produced and uniformly finished products.

III. From the Crowd to the Public ... and Back?

The suggestive sounds of cultural criticism have emphatically drawn attention to the close connection between the mass ornament and forms of production. Although such sounds have muffled any doubts concerning the economic foundation of sociality on the Web 2.0, they are hardly receptive to the possible dissonances that might arise from the oppositional potential of these dynamics. A differentiated description of the social functions and effects of the ornament of mass customization thus requires a vocabulary that, in normative terms, is somewhat less captious. To this end it will be fruitful to revisit Tarde's comparative treatment of the crowd and the public.

In the context of mass phenomena, Tarde's is an interesting name because, along with Scipio Sighele and Gustave Le Bon, he is considered one of the pioneers of crowd psychology. Like Sighele's *La folla delinquente* ("The Criminal Crowd"), Tarde's early studies were motivated by criminology and concerned with the individual accountability of those who participated in mass crimes.[34] In clarifying the question of guilt he relied on a decidedly sociological approach that took into account the influence of social milieus and opposed Sighele's positivistic preference for criminal-anthropological axioms. Admittedly, Tarde's publications from the early 1890s stress the irrationality and danger of crowds in phrases and metaphors that are as drastic as they are pessimistic. At the same time, however, these works place the crowd within a framework of general social theory that goes beyond crowd psychology. Thus they pursue an objective that, all superficial similarities aside, could not differ more from Le Bon's efforts to interpret the crowd as an overarching explanation for any kind of social phenomenona.[35] If Tarde conceives of the crowd as an urban nucleus of social interrelations – the rural counterpart to which would

---

[34]   See Gabriel Tarde, *Penal Philosophy*, trans. Rapelje Howell (Boston: Little, Brown, and Company, 1912); idem, *Études pénales et sociales* (Lyon: A. Stork, 1892); and idem, "Les crimes des foules," *Archives de l'anthropologie criminelle* 7 (1892), 353–86. On Tarde's role in the development of this international discourse, see Christian Borch, *The Politics of Crowds: An Alternative History of Sociology* (Cambridge, UK: Cambridge University Press, 2012); Michael Gamper, *Masse lesen, Masse schreiben: Eine Diskurs- und Imaginationsgeschichte der Menschenmenge, 1765–1930* (Munich: W. Fink, 2007), 407–25; and Stefanie Middendorf, *Massenkultur: Zur Wahrnehmung gesellschaftlicher Modernität in Frankreich, 1880–1980* (Göttingen: Wallstein, 2009), 53–72.

[35]   See Gamper, *Masse lesen, Masse schreiben*, 434.

be the family – he does not do so to treat it as an ineluctable medium of the social (in Le Bon's sense). Rather, he does so because the crowd, by virtue of the physical proximity of its members and despite all of its destructive tendencies, enhances and multiplies the universal processes of imitation that he described in his *Laws of Imitation* as being a constitutive element of social processuality. According to Urs Stäheli, whose reading of Tarde has informed my considerations below, Tarde's assessment of the crowd is somewhat ambivalent: It is both a "venue of destructive forces" as well as an "epistemologically privileged setting."[36] Some degree of this ambiguity can already be found in Tarde's early writings, but its major consequences would not be felt until the publication of *L'opinion et la foule* ("Opinion and the Crowd").[37] The following considerations are thus less concerned with his positions within the discourse of crowd psychology than they are with his broader understanding of the public, which Tarde introduced as a complementary concept to the crowd in order to do justice to the medial innovations of the press. Tarde was interested in the reconfiguration of the technical mechanisms of book printing, telegraphy, and the railroad, which were materialized and institutionalized in the daily newspapers, primarily because of their social resonances, which had escaped the notice of his contemporary crowd theorists. For the collective addressed by the press transcends the conditions of copresence and exclusive participation that bind together the members of a crowd.

As Canetti observed, an assembled crowd is a phenomenon of increased density. It is only intensive physical contact that levels out individual distinctions and generates a sense of equality within an undifferentiated crowd. In contrast to this situation, the public sphere addressed by the press is spatio-temporally dispersed and thus allows its members to participate simultaneously in a variety of publics. Tarde, who recognized an essential aspect of modernity in this medially induced differentiation of public spheres, thus considered the findings of crowd psychology to be historically obsolete. Accordingly, his assessment of Le Bon's famous thesis concerning "the era of crowds" was unequivocal: "La foule est le groupe social du passé [...]."[38] For Tarde his time had been characterized

---

[36] Urs Stäheli, "Übersteigerte Nachahmung – Tardes Massentheorie," in *Soziologie der Nachahmung und des Begehrens: Materialien zu Gabriel Tarde*, ed. Christian Borch and Urs Stäheli (Frankfurt am Main: Suhrkamp, 2009), 397–416, at 410.

[37] This book also contains an explicit revision of his previous pessimism about crowds. This is true above all in the case of celebratory crowds, which Tarde here describes as a representation of naturally coalescing sociality in and of itself. In terms of their social productivity, Tarde values the harmonious and peaceful effects of these self-referential and affectionate crowds more highly than the destructive consequences of the crimes studied by crowd psychologists. See Gabriel Tarde, *L'opinion et la foule: Théoricien de l'opinion* (1901; Paris: Presses Universitaires de France, 1989), 26, 61. See also Gamper, *Masse lesen, Masse schreiben*, 480–82; Stäheli, "Übersteigerte Nachahmung," 408–10; and idem, "Emergenz und Kontrolle in der Massenpsychologie," in *Schwärme, Kollektive ohne Grenzen: Eine Wissensgeschichte zwischen Leben und Information*, ed. Eva Horn and Lucas Marco Gisi (Bielefeld: Transcript, 2009), 85–100, esp. 97–98.

[38] Tarde, *L'opinion et la foule*, 12. See Gustave Le Bon, *Psychology of Crowds* (Southampton: Sparkling, 2009), 7 (the original French version of this book was published in 1895; the translator of the English version is anonymous).

by a public that was pluralistic and functionally differentiated. As a specifically modern formation of the social, the nineteenth-century public inherited a majority of the functions that, during the eighteenth century, had been ascribed exclusively to the crowd, but it did not share the latter's excessively irrational and subversive characteristics. For, although the public was able to fuse together the convictions and desires of large masses of people, this "simple and powerful common opinion" did not come at the expense of individual differences. This civilizing "progress toward tolerance" allowed Tarde to view the crowd, in retrospect, as something other than a mere effect or indicator of social decay.[39] Instead, Tarde described the historical and social interplay that took place between the crowd and the public sphere, and his insights remain significant and applicable to the situation today.[40]

Within Tarde's sociological theory of evolution, the crowd necessarily precedes the genesis of the public. The crowd (especially the urban crowd) and the experiences of social quantity, density, and indifference that accompany it create developmental and logical conditions for the public. In light of the ideal conditions for imitation within the crowd itself, it can even be interpreted as a fundamental model for a type of sociality that is formed on the basis of social mimesis. Tarde thus rehabilitated the exceptional nature of crowds as the "keystone of a theory of modern society."[41] Although its ability to conduct "action à distance" distinguished the public sphere as a higher order of social organization, it nevertheless required a habitualized suggestion of proximity, as offered by the crowd. The public must therefore remain connected to its historical precursor. It is a media-technologically "dispersed crowd" (*foule dispersée*)[42] – that is simultaneously a "virtual crowd" (*foule virtuelle*)[43] able to act as an actual crowd even if it cannot be recognized as such. Within the public sphere, the social heritage of the crowd has not been overcome or abolished; it has rather been sublated (*aufgehoben*) and can be reactivated, depending on the external circumstances, from this latent condition. Thus transposed into a different social state of aggregation, the ephemeral phenomenon of the crowd can be also conserved after its physical dissolution without having to rely on being one of the limited and institutionalized communities that Canetti refers to as crowd crystals.[44]

---

[39] Tarde, *L'opinion et la foule*, 13, 19.

[40] On the crowd as a systems-theoretical figure of dedifferentiation (*Entdifferenzierungsfigur*) and as the outer side of the public, see Urs Stäheli, "Das Populäre in der Systemtheorie," in *Luhmann und die Kulturtheorie*, ed. Günter Burkart and Gunter Runkel (Frankfurt am Main: Suhrkamp, 2004), 169–88.

[41] Stäheli, "Übersteigerte Nachahmung," 405.

[42] Tarde, *L'opinion et la foule*, 30.

[43] Ibid., 13.

[44] Canetti, *Crowds and Power*, 73–75. In a side note, Canetti also recognizes "the newspaper reading public" to be a virtual crowd (see ibid., 52). His disdainful assessment of this "baiting crowd," which is admittedly stable but lacks any responsibility, could not be more different from Tarde's. In this regard, see also Susanne Lüdemann, "Unsichtbare Massen," in *Masse und Medium: Verschiebungen in der Ordnung des Wissens und der Ort der Literatur, 1800/2000*, ed. Inge Münz-Koenen and Wolfgang Schäffner (Berlin: Akademie Verlag, 2002), 81–91.

The condition for this is that Tarde not only recognizes the individuals gathered in the public sphere as a virtual crowd in their totality; he also regards each individual being a crowd itself, namely an intellectual or "cerebral crowd" (*foule cérébrale*) – meaning that each individual's brain is steeped in with a multitude of collective beliefs and desires that float the social world.[45] Due to this affective openness to others' suggestions individuals take part in various public spheres at the same time. In contrast to the pre-dominant understanding of physical crowds, these dispersed and intellectual crowds do not demand to gather physically and to give up individual capacities, but shape their participants' capacities inherently and independently from physical encounters.[46] The individual does not function as the original point of departure for social processes but rather as a temporarily stabilized culmination point of universal currents of belief and desire that are disseminated by means of social imitative practices and that are the driving forces behind society and history alike.[47] It is rather the case that Tarde's sociological adaptation of Leibniz's speculative natural philosophy does not allow for any irreducible minimal units whatsoever. According to Tarde, the basis of all sociality is formed by a network of interpenetrating monads that are in no way closed off or limited, as Leibniz had thought them to be: "At the basis of each thing are all real or possible things. [...] But this implies first of all that *everything is a society*, that every phenomenon is a social fact."[48]

Tarde's radical micro-sociology is not only applicable and valuable to Bruno Latour's actor-network theory;[49] it can also shed light on the mass ornaments of industrial society and on those of our present network society. For, according to Tarde's line of thinking, the individual and the crowd are phenomena that can be translated into one another and whose comparable nature is ensured by the medium of social mimesis:

> But when, instead of patterning one's self after one person or after a few, we borrow from a hundred, a thousand, or ten thousand persons, each of whom is considered under a particular aspect, the elements of thought or action which we subsequently combine, the very nature and choice of these elementary copies, as well as their combination, expresses and accentuates our original personality. And this is, perhaps, the chief benefit that results from the prolonged action of imitation.[50]

The basis for "all social resemblances" is formed by social imitation, i.e. a sequence of mimetic acts that always refer to previous imitations or counter-imitations – even if these

---

45   Tarde, *Études pénales et sociales*, 292. See also Stäheli, "Übersteigerte Nachahmung," 400–01. On the brain as an organ of repetition, see Gabriel Tarde, *The Laws of Imitation*, trans. Elsie Clews Parsons (New York: Holt and Company, 1903), 74–88.

46   See Gamper, *Masse lesen, Masse schreiben*, 483–84. See also ibid., 475–76.

47   See Tarde, *The Laws of Imitation*, 37, 144–45; and idem, *Monadology and Sociology*, trans. Theo Lorenc (Melbourne: Re.Press, 2012), 16–17.

48   Ibid., 27–28.

49   See Bruno Latour, "Gabriel Tarde and the End of the Social," in *The Social in Question: New Bearings in History and the Social Sciences*, ed. Patrick Joyce (New York: Routledge, 2002), 117–32.

50   Tarde, *The Laws of Imitation*, xxiv.

happen to be inventions that, though admittedly necessary for the dynamic of society, can nevertheless be explained as having derived from the innovative concurrence of mimetic activity.[51] For Tarde, imitation serves as the "the most general and abstract fundamental concept for the smallest social unit" and allows continuous scaling to take place between the individual and national societies, crowds, and publics.[52]

The latter are privileged spaces in Tarde's sociology. In various ways, both the crowd and the public provide especially favorable conditions for the dissemination of social imitation. The crowd demonstrates its modernity not only through its volatility and suddenness but above all because it renounces, more fervently than any other collective, the personality and social background of the individual. In doing so, it neutralizes the individual as an agent of self-referential and mutually self-contaminating processes of imitation. It is in a crowd that social mimesis achieves its maximum intensity. What is misses there is the "extensive dynamic" that characterizes, in the public sphere, the synchronization of dispersed individuals.[53] There, due to the support of media technology, imitation transcends the local limitation of immediate social contact in favor of a tendentially universal dissemination whose actual magnitude is coextensively bound to the dissemination media in question. It is this "suggestion at a distance"[54] that actualizes Tarde's definition of imitation as "the action at a distance of one mind upon another" without essentially forfeiting the excessive contagious potential of the crowd.[55] Because, in the public sphere, suggestion and imitation do not require physical contact, the process of infection or contagion is accordingly invisible. Quite literally, the public sphere provides a "suggestibilité purement idéale."[56]

In sum: Whereas the crowd, on account of its self-referential homogeneity, presents an ideal milieu for imitation, the public sphere is no less ideal on account of its lack of physical contact. Stäheli has drawn attention to yet another decisive distinction. Because of its spatial tolerance and plural constitution, the public sphere proves to be susceptible

---

[51] Ibid., 14, 37.

[52] Stäheli, "Übersteigerte Nachahmung," 411. Along with Georg Simmel Tarde can be considered as one of the pioneers of aesthetic sociology, since he borrowed the main concept of his sociology from aesthetic theory; and he assigned great significance to the morphology of art or beauty as a genuine object of imitation. See Tarde, *The Laws of Imitation*, 51–58; and Georg Simmel, "Sociological Aesthetics," in *The Conflict in Modern Culture and Other Essays*, trans. K. P. Etzkorn (New York: Teachers College Press, 1968), 68–80. It might be promising to revisit this neglected sociological project in order to readjust the theories of modernity and social practices in light of the aestheticized present. For an argument in favor of renewing sociological aesthetics, see Andreas Reckwitz's chapter "Elemente einer Soziologie des Ästhetischen" in his book *Unscharfe Grenzen: Perspektiven der Kultursoziologie* (Bielefeld: Transcript, 2008), 259–82.

[53] Stäheli, "Übersteigerte Nachahmung," 412. On the importance of dissemination media in Tarde's work, especially as regards the theory of inclusion, see Urs Stäheli, "Der Takt der Börse: Inklusions-Effekte von Verbreitungsmedien am Beispiel des Börsen-Tickers," *Zeitschrift für Soziologie* 33 (2004), 245–63, esp. 245.

[54] Tarde, *L'opinion et la foule*, 10.

[55] Tarde, *The Laws of Imitation*, xiv.

[56] Tarde, *L'opinion et la foule*, 10.

to interferences from various currents of belief and desire. These intersections and over-lappings result in inventions that aspire, in turn, to multiply and reproduce themselves by means of imitation. Within Tarde's conceptual architecture, invention serves as an indispensable complementary concept to imitation because it provides social associations with a measure of heterogeneity and asymmetry that enables social progress.[57] His sociology of imitation also happens to be a sociology of imitative errors. Because of its self-referential coherence, the "excessive and more intensive form of imitation,"[58] which is prevalent in crowds, does not represent a fitting milieu for such mistakes, which are integral to the social dynamic. It is only the irritation of large-scale suggestion that opens up a space of possibility for innovation and critique, which otherwise remain inaccessible to the crowd.[59] In comparison to the crowd, the public thus offers not only better conditions for the remote coordination of society but also the condition of possibility for oppositional action. Though this does not mean, of course, that such opposition cannot be realized in the form of a crowd.

IV. Dispersed and Distracted Examiners: The Public of the Social Web

The present state of argumentation cannot satisfactorily explain whether or how this potential for opposition will be actualized. First it is necessary to clarify how Tarde's sociological speculations are relevant to the two types of mass ornament that are being compared here. Kracauer's diagnosis can benefit, above all, from Tarde's concept of individuality. Both of them oppose the idea of an autonomous subject as something to be defended against the frenzy of the crowd. The opposition between the individual and the crowd, which formerly seemed indispensable, has been undermined by the increase in social mediatization. Hannelore Bublitz has described this process as the dispersion and distraction of the physical crowd, which has been replaced by a biopolitical instrument of regulation for the circular self-control of the individual and society. This dynamic "medium of social normalization"[60] presents individuals with the possibility of distinguishing themselves and thereby – in an only apparently paradoxical manner – provides them with the possibility of connecting to society. However, this connection does not take place in the form of a clearly defined and spatio-temporally situated body, as imagined by the psychology and phenomenology of crowds, but rather as a cluster of references for the obligatory normality of society. For Bublitz, the crowd functions both as a supplement to the individual and as an imaginary form of perceiving a generalized "other." It is a biopolitical feature that pervades every element of mass culture:

> Thus a new type of subjectivity is established: The individual does not then "disappear" in the
> maelstrom of the crowd; rather, the crowd is embedded into the individual. It constitutes the

---

57   See Tarde, *The Laws of Imitation*, 69–73.

58   Stäheli, "Übersteigerte Nachahmung," 403.

59   Ibid., 413.

60   Bublitz, *In der Zerstreuung organisiert*, 62

functional medium for the establishment of individual dispositions, which are due to a radical dynamization – to a practice of normalizing subjectivization. The crowd is characterized by the fact that individuals situate themselves within fields of normality, compare their own positions to the imagined positions of others, and adjust themselves accordingly.[61]

In this regard, Gamper has pointed out the discourse-historical affinity that exists between Tarde and Kracauer. Both of them, he notes, were seeking an explanation for the "establishment of a sort of social conformism [...] that occurs independently from a gathering of large numbers of people."[62] Tarde's model could be used to fill a gap in Kracauer's argumentation. Kracauer, according to Gamper, "admittedly acknowledges the historical advancement of the new, outward-oriented subjectivity of the 'dispersed masses,' but he is unwilling to attribute any autonomous meaning to it."[63] In turn, Kracauer's fascinating descriptions of the Weimar Republic can provide Tarde's sociological speculations with an extensive empirical basis. It is of no consequence that the Tayloristic rationalization of its subjects, as described by Kracauer, took place under the conditions of dispersion and distraction, and this is because the terms *foule dispersée* and *foule cérébrale* anticipate both the physical disposition of dispersion as well as its psychological counterpart, distraction. The presumably new form of mass individuality, which dominates the workplaces and entertainment venues in Kracauer's account, seems to be embedded in a socio-historical development whose continuity can be traced up to the present day and whose major moments have been closely associated with the introduction of new dissemination media – with the newspaper in the case of Tarde, with the cinema in the case of Kracauer, and with web videos in Bookchin's case.[64] Whereas the press first enabled the social synchronization of dispersed masses, and Kracauer's focus was on the distraction that characterizes urban locations, the present socio-medial constellation radicalizes

---

[61] Ibid., 58.

[62] Gamper, *Masse lesen, Masse schreiben*, 475.

[63] Ibid., 492.

[64] This three-step characterization of media history fails to account for the television, even though it mediates between the distributional features of the newspaper and the audiovisual experience of the cinema and, what is more, could be regarded as having been the epitome of mass media for decades. But precisely its role as a leading medium prevents me here from discussing the television in any detail. It lies beyond the scope of the present study. For the same reason, I will not be able to give consideration to David Riesman's concept of externally-governed individuality. Riesman's idea of the lonely crowd could not only be said to flank, in sociological terms, the vacancy of television; it could also be regarded as an extension of the discourse-historical series from Tarde to Kracauer. See David Riesman, Nathan Glazer, Reuel Denney: *The Lonely Crowd. A Study of the Changing American Character.* Abridged ed. with a 1969 preface. (New Haven CT, London: Yale University Press, 1950), 8. For further discussion of this topic, see Gamper, *Masse lesen, Masse schreiben*, 492–4; and Bublitz, *In der Zerstreuung organisiert*, 52–64. Regarding the relation between crowds and television, see Christine Bartz, *MassenMedium Fernsehen: Die Semantik der Masse in der Medienbeschreibung* (Bielefeld: Transcript, 2007).

both of these phenomena. Consequently, as Susanne Lüdemann has lamented, the crowd
no longer seems to exist in its familiar form:

> Bodies no longer have to *move* in order to participate in social and political affairs. [...] Images
> and sounds simply come to us in our homes. The 'new media' of today do not serve to liberate
> the masses but rather to bring about, with a sleight of hand, their ultimate disappearance.[65]

This diagnosis of loss, which has far-reaching political implications, warrants closer
inspection and should encourage us to follow the media-sociological line of development, as outlined above, even further. This should be done even if it means that, for the
moment, I will have to set aside the fruitful comparison between Kracauer's concept of
the public and Tarde's micro-sociological scaling from individual to the crowd and from
the crowd to the public sphere. On the media-historical threshold between Kracauer's
and Bookchin's mass ornaments can be found Walter Benjamin's figure of the examiner.
Distracted or absent-minded examiners, in whose hands Benjamin places the future of both
the media system and the political system,[66] exercise their discerning expertise no longer
as an immobile gathering in the anonymous darkness of the movie theater. In addition to
possessing intuitive knowledge for making sensitive evaluations of medial performances,
they now additionally possess productive and distributive capabilities.

To recall: In the case of the Tiller Girls, the crowd receives its ornament from the
outside. Accordingly, the form of the mass ornament is as clearly defined as the allocation
of roles in society. While the founding actor – just like the observing Kracauer – seems
to be removed from the situation, the social ornament is in fact formed by the groups of
dancers and spectators that are differentiated from one another by the spatial mechanism
of the stage. In Bookchin's case, this functional divide has become just as fragile as the
contours of the ornament. The gap between the stage and the spectator space has disappeared. Production, distribution, and reception have become non-exclusive and equally
viable options of activity. The form of the ornament, moreover, is no longer determined by
musical scores and stage directions; it is rather continuously created by the self-addressing
acts of the user. The collectives of these dispersed and distracted examiners are connected
less by a binding idea or representation than they are by mediatized acts of imitation.
Such acts are hardly restricted to the performed movements of dancers; rather, they are
characteristic of entire stages of web-based communication.[67] The mimetic repetitions

---

[65]   Lüdemann, "Unsichtbare Massen," 89. Although Lüdemann is chiefly concerned here with tele-media
       such as the television, her argument is no less valid in the case of social networking media. In the
       end, the internet has further enhanced the mixture of the private and public spheres that Lüdemann
       is criticizing.

[66]   See Benjamin, "The Work of Art in the Age of Mechanical Reproduction," 238–41.

[67]   Hans Bernhard Schmid has pointed out that Tarde's ideas of social somnambulism and the *évolu-
       tion par association* strike a practical balance between subject-based and memetic perspectives. In
       light of the renaissance of the meme concept as a self-descriptive category of web communication,
       this "middle way" warrants further investigation. Tarde seems to offer a particularly apt and timely

in front of the camera and on the screen, which are highlighted in Bookchin's montage, furnish the ornaments of mass customization with the recognition value of a likewise social and medial figure.

Tarde's evolutionary sociology of imitation and (not to be forgotten) faulty imitation thus offers a fitting conceptual instrument for understanding these processes of socio-medial self-control, the recursivity and iterability of which Bookchin has made so apparent. It cannot (and need not) be addressed here whether Tarde was right to believe that society is generated by imitation. The line of argumentation is rather the other way around: A social association by imitation serves as circumstantial evidence in a trial concerning the generalizability of the observed socio-medial processes, and Tarde has been called as a witness. In light of the precarious shape (*Gestalt)* of the social web ornament, his concept of the crowd seems less adequate in this regard than his concept of the public or public sphere. Not only can the latter concept compensate for the loss of externally founded social ornamentality; it can also shed light on its consequences for social and political participation.

V. The Ornament of Mass Customization and its Political Potential

By way of conclusion, I can now revisit the question concerning oppositional potential and the relationship between virtual mass ornaments and physically present crowds of protesters. Of concern here is thus the potential for mobilization that is inherent to the ornament of mass customization.[68] Whereas Kracauer stated that the "masses organized" in large dance troupes "come from offices and factories,"[69] today's media technology and the use of outsourcing make it unnecessary to extract people from such places. Or, to put it in more extreme terms, today's masses can simply stay at home.

For Gilles Deleuze, it is precisely this dissolution of internment that distinguishes societies of discipline from societies of control:

> The factory constituted individuals as a single body to the double advantage of the boss who surveyed each element within the mass and the unions who mobilized a mass resistance; but the corporation constantly presents the brashest rivalry as a healthy form of emulation, an excellent motivational force that opposes individuals against one another and runs through each, dividing

---

vocabulary for describing the so-called viral communication that takes place on the Web 2.0. See Hans Bernhard Schmid, "Evolution durch Imitation: Gabriel Tarde und das Ende der Memetik," in *Soziologie der Nachahmung und des Begehrens: Materialien zu Gabriel Tarde*, ed. Christian Borch and Urs Stäheli (Frankfurt am Main: Suhrkamp, 2009), 280–310.

[68] Kracauer himself referred quite openly to the mobilizing effects of classical (mostly cinematic) mass ornaments in the service of National-Socialist propaganda. Here I will have neglect this issue in order to remain focused on the present situation. See Siegfried Kracauer, *From Caligari to Hitler: A Psychological History of the German Film* (Princeton: Princeton University Press, 1947).

[69] Kracauer, "The Mass Ornament," 79.

each within. [...] Individuals have become *"dividuals,"* and the masses, samples, data, markets, or *"banks."*[70]

Whereas one of such post-Fordistic forms of controls has already been imagined in terms of the digital enclosure,[71] the "question of resistance in times of dividual desire" remains open.[72] Open, too, is Deleuze's question concerning the potential for mobilization through which the potential for resistance can be realized. Gerald Raunig has associated the potential for resistance with the development of "ethical and aesthetic ways of existing," believing that these "will allow our mechanized forms of operating to function no longer (simply) by means of social and economic apparatuses. Rather, they will allow us use new technologies and forms of organization in a virtuoso manner."[73] Paolo Virno has also stressed the importance of virtuosity to the constitution of such alternative forms of organization, though he has been quick to point out its ambivalent character.[74] As a variation of the Marxist idea of "general intellect," virtuosity admittedly represents a generally accessible and *a priori* public element that precedes any form of socialization. However, as long as it is "evoked over and over again in its role as productive force," it merely reproduces and internalized techniques of suppression. It is only when it has been retransferred into the public sphere of a political community that virtuosity can serve as a "possible root of political action, as a different constitutional principle,"[75] one that does not simply or inevitably strengthen the power relations that are already in place.

Teeming as it is with social monads, Tarde's public sphere offers a fitting model for imagining the political public of the social web. Neither in philosophical nor sociological terms did Tarde consider social monads to be subject to binary distinctions. He rather regarded them – with a sort of quantitative logic – "as each individual's reciprocal possession, in many varied forms, of every other."[76] They are not faced with the choice between being (*Sein*) and not being respective being present (*Dabei-Sein*) and not being present; they rather aspire to participate as fully as possible and to affiliate themselves with other monads. This reciprocal permeation may encourage competition and hegemonic pretenses,

---

[70]   Gilles Deleuze, "Postscript on the Societies of Control," in *Cultural Theory: An Anthology*, ed. Imre Szeman and Timothy Kaposy (Chichester: Wiley-Blackwell, 2011), 139–42, at 140.

[71]   A detailed analysis would have to take this metaphor seriously and describe the primitive accumulation of data as form of disciplinary enclosure. Accordingly, Deleuze's historical separation of societies of discipline and societies of control would have to be interrogated in terms of its transitions and intersections.

[72]   Gerald Raunig, "Dividuen des Facebook: Das neue Begehren nach Selbstzerteilung," in *Generation Facebook: Über das Leben im Social Net*, ed. Oliver Leistert and Theo Röhle (Bielefeld: Transcript, 2011), 148–60, at 158. See also Carolin Wiedemann's chapter in the present book.

[73]   Ibid., 159.

[74]   Paolo Virno, *A Grammar of the Multitude: For an Analysis of Contemporary Forms of Life*, trans. Isabella Bertoletti and James Cascaito (Cambridge, MA: Semiotexte, 2003), 61–70.

[75]   Paolo Virno, *A Grammar of the Multitude: For an Analysis of Contemporary Forms of Life*, trans. Isabella Bertoletti and James Cascaito (Cambridge, MA: Semiotexte, 2003), 67.

[76]   Tarde, *Monadology and Sociology*, 51.

but it also promotes social transformation and can ultimately be regarded as giving rise to "the marvels of civilization."[77] Tarde's plea for a philosophy of possession highlights "the underexposed side of social networking," which, according to Raunig, is occupied by the desire "to communicate in public, share (or communicate) one's information, and share (or divide) oneself."[78] Tarde's critical impulse is not to discover the identity of social individuals and groups but rather to comprehend the quantifiable intensity of common desire and common beliefs. As regards the situation of the Web 2.0, this means that its dividuals can be statistically measured or registered more easily than ever before. This also means that such dividuals are admittedly more susceptible than their predecessors to the normalizing forces of biopolitical controls. However, the permanent possibility that the public will change or shift in one way or another hinders its addressability and thus also hinders the possibility of manipulating the public in the service a given idea or representation.

The dividuals of the social web may not form an obviously social body, as did the public masses in Kracauer's time, but even the dispersed masses, as Virno has noted with respect to the post-Fordistic multitude, "need a form of unity, of being a One."[79] Whereas Virno recognizes the unified milieu of these decentralized collectives in the Aristotelian *topoi koinoi*, Bookchin's mass ornament suggests that this basic idea needs to be expanded. It is not only linguistic or logical commonalities, but also aesthetic and morphologic commonalities, that form the foundation for the centrifugal movement of collectivization from the one to the many and that, contrary to technological infrastructure, resist total privatization. The schemes of medial forms enable a transition from the (technological) connectivity of the network to the (social) collectivity of the swarm and consequently enable the tactical development of a "combination of collectivity and connectivity" for purposes of political mobilization.[80]

In no way have crowds been shattered or done away with; they are simply no longer formed exclusively in public venues such as the streets, movie theaters, or stadiums. However, they can nevertheless be mobilized as quickly and as unpredictably as before. This potentiality is actualized in an event-based manner when the threshold between online and offline crowds has been crossed, a phenomenon that can currently be observed in several places.[81] The moment of escalation may be attributed to the formation of a

---

[77] Ibid., 56.

[78] Raunig, "Dividuen des Facebook," 156.

[79] Virno, *A Grammar of the Multitude*, 25.

[80] Eugene Thacker, "Networks, Swarms, Multitudes (Part One)," *CTheory.net* (May 18, 2004), http://www.ctheory.net/articles.aspx?id=422 (accessed on September 8, 2014). For Thacker, networks produce connectivity that is formed in clusters, whereas swarms produce a sort of collectivity that has a specific purpose. He argues against rashly identifying one or the other according to technological or biological models for social organization and he locates the political impulse of the multitude in the oscillation between these two poles.

[81] The potential for mobilization exhibited by these medial groups depends above all on whether they are able to synchronize the social moments of isomorphically constituted fields. If the situational in-

collective consciousness (or swarm consciousness). This is preceded, however, by an implicit and internalized morphological knowledge that is possessed by dispersed and distracted examiners, as Bookchin's montages have demonstrated. In her mass ornaments, these heterogeneous crowds are made visible at a stage of functional latency, that is, before the exponential escalation of their social dynamic.[82] Lüdemann's complaint about the disappearance of crowds can now be relativized with reference to the invisible and large-scale processes of suggestion that take place in the public sphere of the social web. The media of the present day cause the older crowds to disappear only to the extent that they liberate new ones. It is precisely against the presumed invisibility of crowds, moreover, that Bookchin's audiovisual strategy is directed. Her *Mass Ornament* captures historical, social, and aesthetic constellations in a snapshot of interrelations that translates both its socio-cultural and aesthetic frameworks into the formal aesthetic arrangement of its surface. Out of forms of construction, forms of composition emerge that transform abstract structural homologies (between medial and social situations) into an aesthetic experience. Bookchin's split screen montages suggest that there must be close morphological ties among any number of similarly produced "mash ups." Although my discussion here has been limited to a single telling example, I hope to have provided at least partial insight into a broader panorama of morphological interrelations.[83] With any luck, further investigations will bring even more of this panorama to light.

---

terferences between medial forms and social forces are consolidated into temporarily stable relations, the latency of the socio-aesthetic constellation will manifest itself as a historical event. Regarding the idea that historical events are caused by overlapping and synchronized crises, of several social fields see Pierre Bourdieu, *Homo Academicus*, trans. Peter Collier (Stanford: Stanford University Press, 1988), 173–79. On the significance of medially generated synchronicity to the self-consciousness of Tarde's public sphere, see Stäheli, "Der Takt der Börse," 258.

[82]　Thus they correspond to the self-reinforcing chain reactions of web communication. On the latency and escalation of social swarms, see Eva Horn, "Schwärme – Kollektive ohne Zentrum: Einleitung," in *Schwärme, Kollektive ohne Grenzen: Eine Wissensgeschichte zwischen Leben und Information*, ed. Eva Horn and Lucas Marco Gisi (Bielefeld: Transcript, 2009), 7–26.

[83]　For a discussion of the potential and limitations of sociological panoramas, see Bruno Latour, *Reassembling the Social: An Introduction to Social-Network-Theory* (New York: Oxford University Press, 2005), 174–90.

Carolin Wiedemann

Collectivity without Identity
Anonymous, Flexible Infrastructures, and the Event of the Common

Introduction

Anonymous has become famous as a label under which a variety of individuals and groups organize in common. It represents a cluster of ideas and ideals held by various hackers, geeks, and human rights activists whose common principle is that of anonymous communication[1] – online, such communication takes place under the pseudonym "Anonymous," whereas offline it is characterized by the Guy Fawkes mask, which allows everyone to have the same face.[2] With actions such as the anti-Scientology movement and its pro-WikiLeaks campaign at the end of 2010, not to mention its support for protestors in Egypt and Tunisia in early 2011, Anonymous made its way into the headlines. The media referred variously to the group as "hackers," "a hacktivist organization," and "cyberterrorists," but none of these terms seemed appropriate. As it gradually became clear that Anonymous is not an organization that can be defined by its members, that its existence is not based on a set of statutes and objectives, and that it is also not a group of hackers, other voices began to chime in. Some celebrated Anonymous as a sort of online flash mob that stands for new democracy, the freedom of expression, and open participation. Moreover, scholars such as Gabriella Coleman and Felix Stalder have discussed Anonymous as a new form of collectivity that functions differently from traditional collectives such as nations, political parties, and unions, each of which relies on narratives of shared identity.[3] As with the Occupy Wall Street movement and the earlier May Day protests, it

---

[1]   See Gabriella Coleman, "Our Weirdness Is Free: The Logic of Anonymous – Online Army, Agent of Chaos, and Seeker of Justice," *Triple Canopy* 15 (2012), http://www.canopycanopycanopy.com/contents/our_weirdness_ is_free (accessed on April 15, 2015).

[2]   The offline activity of Anonymous and the use of the Guy Fawkes mask are beyond the scope of this chapter, which will focus on Anonymous's online activity.

[3]   See Coleman, "Our Weirdness if Free"; and Felix Stalder, "Enter the Swarm: Anonymous and the Global Protest Movements" (February 9, 2012), http://felix.openflows.com/node/203 (accessed on April 15, 2015). Both of these writers, however, remain faithful to a classical concept of the subject instead of investigating the intertwined nature of material and affective elements in the constitutional processes of collectivity.

was thus assumed that Anonymous can no longer be understood with traditional notions of group identity and that its coherence is not primarily based on representations of the common. These assumptions are part of the fundamental expansion of social-scientific perspectives to include logics of collectivity formation that go beyond traditional attributions of identity. In recent years, above all, researchers have described the emergence of collectivities that hardly have any basis in representational logics; rather, discussions of swarm intelligence and the network society have focused increasingly on the material, operative, and media-technical conditions of collectivities.[4]

Here I would like to discuss Anonymous as an example of a presumably new sort of collectivity. In doing so, I will investigate the extent to which the communication techniques of the Internet – as infrastructures of the common – can be constitutive of certain forms of collectivity and how it might be possible to conceptualize dynamic constellations of such heterogeneous elements as technical programs and social practices.[5] To this end, my first aim will be to outline the rise of Anonymous on 4chan. Turning to the theoretical distinction between three concepts of "new" collectivity – swarms, networks, and multitudes – I will then examine the extent to which Anonymous conforms to any of these models. For definitions of the first two concepts, I have mainly relied on Eugene Thacker's typology of collectives without a center.[6] Within the "network society," such collectives reformulate

---

[4]   In their treatment of collectivity, media theorists have admittedly (and from the very beginning) focused on *pre-semantic* (i.e., media-technical) structures, though in doing so they have somewhat neglected the relation of these structures to *semantic* media contents. See Friedrich Kittler, *Discourse Networks 1800/1900*, trans. Michael Metteer and Chris Cullens (Stanford: Stanford University Press, 1990); Georg Keer et al., eds., *Bruno Latours Kollektive: Kontroversen zur Entgrenzung des Sozialen* (Frankfurt am Main: Suhrkamp, 2008); and Claus Pias, *Computer Spiel Welten*, 2nd ed. (Zurich: Diaphanes, 2010). In the field of sociology, on the contrary, scholars have concentrated primarily on the (discursive, normative, and symbolic) construction processes of (collective) identity instead of on material, operative, and media-technical conditions. See, for instance, Benedict Anderson, *Imagined Communities: Reflections on the Origin and Spread of Nationalism* (London: Verso, 1991). At this point I would like to extend my thanks to Urs Stäheli and his Hamburg-based research group "New Collectivities," which takes both of these levels (and their interrelations) into account and has inspired much of my argumentation in this chapter.

[5]   This perspective is informed by the ideas of the "material turn" in cultural studies and the social sciences. Above all, Manuel De Landa, Jane Bennett, and Bruno Latour have stressed the operations of connecting or assembling in the creation of collectivity. See Manuel De Landa, *A New Philosophy of Society: Assemblage Theory and Social Complexity* (London: Continuum, 2006); Jane Bennett, *Vibrant Matter: A Political Ecology of Things* (Durham: Duke University Press, 2010); and Bruno Latour, *Politics of Nature: How to Bring the Sciences into Democracy*, trans. Catherine Porter (Cambridge, MA: Harvard University Press, 2004). Other works that have inspired discussion about this material turn, particularly as it relates to communication and information technology, include Donna Haraway, *Modest_Witness@Second_Millenium.FemaleMan©_Meets_OncoMouseTM: Feminism and Technoscience* (New York: Routledge, 1997); and Jussi Parikka, *Digital Contagions: A Media Archaeology of Computer Viruses* (New York: Peter Lang, 2007).

[6]   Eugene Thacker, "Networks, Swarms, Multitudes: Part One," *Ctheory* 18 (2004), http://www.ctheory. net/articles.aspx?id=422; idem, "Networks, Swarms, Multitudes: Part Two," *Ctheory* 18 (2004),

the body politic without falling back on the paradigm of modern sovereignty. In addition to networks and swarms, Thacker also regards multitudes as mutations of the present-day body politic. Thacker's description of the multitude derives largely from its treatment in the works of Michael Hardt and Antonio Negri, on which I will also rely below.[7] In general, the multitude is understood as a form of opposition against recently decentralized manifestations of sovereignty in today's Empire, and this conception shares criteria with the other two types of collectivity: decentrality and horizontality. To the multitude belongs the concept of the common (*des Gemeinsamen*), which, more than the models of the swarm and network, provides insight into the question of what can be constitutive of present forms of collectivity beyond the creation of collective identity and beyond the classical logics of representation and their procedures of inclusion and exclusion. Yet the theory of the multitude, as reflected for instance in its conceptual opposition to the "old masses" and in the stress that it places on the freedom from mediation, reverts in part to the notion of classical sovereignty, which is incompatible with the interconnectedness and multifariousness of collaborative constitutional processes.

In an effort to theorize about a collectivity such as Anonymous, however, it might be beneficial to foreground the infrastructures that first enabled this sort of collective activity, for to do so would be to challenge the opposition between mediation and emergence, between institution and revolution. In light of protocols and codes, which lie behind the infrastructures in question, an argument can be made with respect to Anonymous that social media are not social because they enhance the formation of social movements – despite all of the Web 2.0 hype that has proclaimed as much   but rather because they affect the very constitution of the social.[8] Regarding the role of mobile infrastructures in current processes of constitution, the question of new forms of collectivity on and by means of the Internet ultimately demands that we focus our attention not on the matter of representation but rather on the experience and the event of the common.

The Rise of Anonymous

Anonymous originated in an anonymous exchange on the Internet. 4chan, a site at which, in 2003, multiple users simultaneously appeared under the name "Anonymous," is an imageboard forum whose central content (as is the case of such forums in general) is created by the users of the platform, who in turn can comment on each other's posts.[9] On the technical level, 4chan distinguishes itself from other platforms in two respects: First,

---

http://www.ctheory.net/articles.aspx?id=423 (both accessed on April 18, 2015)

[7]   Michael Hardt and Antonio Negri, *Multitude: War and Democracy in the Age of Empire* (New York: Penguin, 2004).

[8]   See Soenke Zehle and Ned Rossiter, "Organizing Networks: Notes on Collaborative Constitution, Translation and the Work of Organization," *Cultural Politics* 5 (2009), 237–64.

[9]   Perhaps the term "ProdUser," which was coined by Axel Bruns, might be more appropriate here. See Axel Bruns, *Blogs, Wikipedia, Second Life, and Beyond: From Production to Produsage* (New York: Peter Lang, 2008). Although not every concept lends itself to a poststructuralist approach,

it is impossible for users to register on the site; second, posted content is not archived but rather deleted as soon as it ceases to receive clicks and has thus reached the bottom of the page. Users are not given any fixed identity; each time they contribute to the site, they can do so with a new name, be it a pseudonym, their real name, or any other designation. These designations are therefore not protected but can rather be used simultaneously by others. If a user chooses to leave the space blank (that is, to enter no name at all), his or her post will appear under the name "Anonymous." The effect of this, as Jana Herwig has summarized in her recent analysis of the imageboard, is as follows:

> When "Anonymous" posts a contribution to the site, and this post receives responses from "Anonymous" and "Anonymous," it is no longer possible for an observer to figure out who is "speaking." […] The model of user-determined representations of identity is relinquished in favor of subject positions that manifest themselves individually with every new post. The latter can themselves no longer be assigned any sort overarching identity: Instead of reacting to users or identities, one is forced to react to opinions and positions.[10]

Any exchange of opinions and positions on 4chan that was not associated with individual authors or speakers can be regarded as the beginning of Anonymous,[11] and thus the communication technology can be regarded as a constitutive element of the phenomenon: As a collectivity and as an idea of collectivity, Anonymous first emerged and continues to appear in online communication.[12] This fact also distinguishes Anonymous from collectives that, on the basis of a common ideology, have been using hacking and "virtual sit-ins" as a form of politics since the early 1990s. In the case of Anonymous, it is impossible to identify any originating idea or initiator. Chris Poole, who created 4chan at the age of fifteen, has told me that he never anticipated that users would elect not to use a pseudonym and suddenly start contributing more and more posts as "Anonymous."[13]

Diverse forms of technical mediation and affective connection have modulated that which first enabled Anonymous's collective online activity. In the case of Anonymous, communication and information technology can thus be ascribed a more fundamental role than can, for instance, an understanding of collective identity. Cultural studies and

---

such a discussion might be fruitful in this case. In the present context, however, I have chosen for pragmatic reasons to stick with the term "user."

[10] Jana Herwig, "'Post Your Desktop!' 4chan als Sonderfall der Verhandlung von Nähe und Identität im Web," in *Medialität der Nähe: Situationen, Praktiken, Diskurse*, ed. Pablo Abend et al. (Bielefeld: Transcript, 2012), 65–83, at 71.

[11] For a comprehensive analysis of the 4chan platform and its role in the constitution of collectivity, see Carolin Wiedemann, "Digital Swarming and Affective Infrastructures: A New Materialist Approach to 4chan," in *Neighborhood Technologies: Media and Mathematics of Dynamic Networks*, ed. Sebastian Vehlken and Tobias Harks (Berlin: Diaphanes, 2015), 197–214.

[12] Other forms of protest, such as anonymous DDoS and hacking, were likewise first enabled by the Internet, but these will not be addressed in this essay.

[13] I first had the opportunity to interview Chris Poole after his presentation at the third annual re:publica conference, which was held in Berlin in early 2009.

poststructuralist approaches have admittedly focused their efforts on deconstructing precisely these identities, though in doing so they have failed to undermine the classical notion of "community," expressed for instance in the work of Ferdinand Tönnies, as a given number of people who affiliate with one another on the basis of shared values, feelings, and interests.[14] Poststructuralists and constructivists have thus analyzed collectivity mainly in the context of the discursive generation of identity.

A phenomenon such as Anonymous, however, requires us to focus on the operative level in the creation of collectivity, on the ability to forge a temporary community out of a coincidental gathering of various bodies or elements. This focus is shared by theories of "collective behavior," which derive from theories of the masses and do not underscore the process of collective construction but rather seek to elucidate unintentional, decentralized, and unorganized concepts of collectivity.[15] Such theories can thus serve as a guide to dealing with new collectivities, at least to the extent that affection (*Affizierung*) and contagion play a central role in them. That said, their concern is exclusively with direct forms of congregation and with the relationships between people in public venues (for instance). The phenomenon that is under investigation here, however, possesses an altogether different quality of collectivity. For Anonymous, communication technology is a constitutive element of convening in the "digital sphere"; it participates in the processes of affection that create collectivity out of connectivity.

In what follows, Anonymous will be treated as a constellation of heterogeneous elements that, in their relation to one another, come to achieve their effectiveness as a whole. It remains to explore whether models of collectivity such as the swarm, network, or multitude are appropriate for describing this phenomenon.

Methodological Considerations

The concept of affect seems to be of central significance to the form of collectivity at issue here; it offers a theoretical framework for understanding processes that create relations between various elements, and it does so without recourse to the idea of representation. Current theories of affect can roughly be divided into two camps. One side approaches affect primarily through its discursive elements, whereas the other focuses on processes of affection that interrupt and undermine the discursive level.[16] Affect theories of the latter

---

[14] See Ferdinand Tönnies, *Community and Civil Society*, trans. Margaret Hollis and José Harris (Cambridge: Cambridge University Press, 2001). The original German publication – *Gemeinschaft und Gesellschaft* – was first published in 1887.

[15] See, for instance, Herbert Blumer, "Collective Behavior," in *New Outlines of the Principles of Sociology*, ed. Alfred M. Lee (New York: Barnes & Noble, 1969), 167–221. For further discussion of Anonymous in light of Blumer's concept of circular reaction and Gabriel Tarde's theory of imitation, see Carolin Wiedemann, "Between Swarm, Network, and Multitude: Anonymous and the Infrastructures of the Common," *Distinktion: Scandinavian Journal of Social Theory* 15 (2014), 309–26.

[16] See Carsten Stage, "The Online Crowd: A Contradiction in Terms? On the Potentials of Gustave Le Bon's Crowd Psychology in an Analysis of Affective Blogging," *Distinktion: Scandinavian Journal*

type are more or less "new materialist." While Sara Ahmed, for instance, treats affect as being channeled or even motivated by discourses,[17] new-materialist thinkers such as Brian Massumi have borrowed ideas from Deleuze and Guattari (who in turn were indebted to Spinoza) and defined affect as a pre-personal phenomenon, though one that is neither asocial nor ahistorical.[18] Though I tend to side with the new-materialist camp and will adopt its approach here, it is not without certain difficulties. The attempt to "protocol" affection *in actu* and *in situ* hardly seems possible in light of the fact that processes of affection, according to the new-materialist understanding, are precisely defined as being unascertainable and unmeasurable.[19] In the tradition of Spinoza, affection is rather understood in terms of the increase or decrease of a body's ability to act. In this case the body is not conceived as a counterpart to the mind (*Geist*) and is also not necessarily associated with a "human" body; it is rather understood as something that can be related to the interplay among various infrastructural elements and other bodies. Affection is thus that which cannot be ascertained in the moment but only after the fact. Traces of affection, however, are left behind in linguistic material, for instance when, in interviews, narratives are suddenly interrupted or abandoned altogether.[20] Self-ascriptions of emotional experiences can accordingly lead to situations in which a state or condition is registered (or re-registered) in language after it has been experienced otherwise; the skin, after all, is faster than the word.[21] Inspired by the work of Carsten Stage, who likewise refers to Massumi in his discussion of affective blogging,[22] the present analysis of Anonymous will trace both the processes of affection as well as the development of an agenda in discursive material. The agenda in question is evident in the contents of the posts and commentary on 4chan, in discussions on Internet Relay Chats (IRCs), in press releases, and in interviews with people who have been involved with Anonymous's operations. I will further examine the rhythms and speeds of the postings and their feedback loops, particularly as they relate to digital architectures, programs, interfaces, and codes.

---

of Social Theory 14 (2013), 211–26.

[17] Sara Ahmed, *The Cultural Politics of Emotion* (New York: Routledge, 2004).

[18] Affects or processes of affection can be located within the *agencements* between human and non-human bodies or entities and thus they are not subject, despite many claims to the contrary, to a sort of "asocial" and "ahistorical" immediacy. See Marianne Pieper and Carolin Wiedemann, "In the Ruins of Representation: Affekt, Agencement und das Okkurente," *Zeitschrift für Geschlechterforschung und visuelle Kultur* 55 (2014), 66–78.

[19] See Marianne Pieper et al., "'Making Connections': Skizze einer Net(h)nographischen Grenzregime-analyse," in *Generation Facebook: Über das Leben im Social Net*, ed. Oliver Leistert and Theo Röhle (Bielefeld: Transcript, 2011), 221–48.

[20] See Brian Massumi, *Parables for the Virtual: Movement, Affect, Sensation* (Durham, NC: Duke University Press, 2002), 26.

[21] Ibid., 25.

[22] Stage, "The Online Crowd: A Contradiction in Terms?"

Swarms and Networks

I would like to explore the dynamic interaction of human bodies and media technology in light of Thacker's theoretical distinction between networks and swarms, both of which being collectives without a center,[23] and I would like to do so to address the question of new forms of politics in the age of computerization. As Thacker has pointed out, it is not necessary to draw immediate comparisons in order to suggest that "politics is self-organized life, or that life is political self-organization."[24] The goal is rather to deduce "a better idea of two concepts that inhere in both of these examples: collectivity and connectivity."[25] Like Thacker, I find it important to maintain this distinction because, on the one hand, many analyses of network phenomena seem to believe that connectivity immediately implies collectivity, thus equating the two terms, and, on the other hand, they tend to describe every collectivity in terms of the emergence of a political form – "often, a more direct or unmediated form of democracy."[26] The extent to which this applies to the case of Anonymous will be discussed below in light of Thacker's definition of networks and swarms, each of which, depending on the circumstances, can be more representative of either connectivity or collectivity.

Whereas in the case of networks, whose genealogy he derives from graph theory, decentralization represents a static topology of nodes and edges, swarms are based on a dynamic of permanent becoming. According to Thacker, networks thus differ from swarms by means of their temporal horizons: Networks are based on permanent connectivity; the elements of a network are permanently connected.[27] Connectivity is characterized by a pattern, while collectivity is characterized by a cause or purpose.[28] Thus a network can only be regarded as a collectivity if it has a cause; this is what allows collectivity to emerge from mere connectivity. In contrast to this, swarms are formed on the basis of spontaneous purposes or causes; they can thus be understood as collectives, though only briefly connected: "[N]etworks can form a collectivity, through connectivity, while swarms can initiate a connectivity, but only through collectivity."[29] This, however, requires a minimum threshold of connectivity, for collectivity is constituted by connectivity.[30]

---

[23] Thacker, "Networks, Swarms, Multitudes: Part One," n.p.

[24] Ibid.

[25] Ibid.

[26] Ibid.

[27] See Thacker, "Networks, Swarms, Multitudes: Part Two," n.p.

[28] Ibid.

[29] Ibid.

[30] Ibid.

Like Felix Stalder or Rick Falkvinge,[31] Thacker defines online swarms as decentralized, self-organizing, and spontaneous.[32] Anonymous originated in a similar manner on 4chan. The platform is not a network with fixed nodes and ridges – users are not registered there; it is rather a point at which an ever-changing group of users consistently forges short-term connections, and therefore it reaches the minimum threshold of connectivity. Anonymous emerged as a swarm at the moment in which it suddenly gathered on 4chan to exchange pictures of cats or to send large-scale emails to governmental websites, causing them to crash.[33] In her discussion of swarms as a type of collectivity, Eva Horn has – like Thacker – stressed the constitutive force of affect. In her opinion, the concept of affect is of great significance precisely because it makes no assumptions about the intentions, the "consciousness" (in the Marxist sense), or reasons of individual actors; it reacts only to the fact that, here, "a person is influenced, affected, and mobilized by another, and this affection proceeds on a mass scale."[34] Anonymous is constituted as a collectivity at the moment in which affects are circulated.[35] The example of "Lolcats" and "Caturday" illustrates both the extent to which Anonymous fits the definition of an online swarm and the effectiveness of mutual affect in the development of collectivity and creativity on 4chan,[36] that is, in the constitution of Anonymous itself: Users have told me that, in 2006, someone posted a picture of a cat, someone else gave the picture a caption, other anonymous users imitated this activity, and others posted comments and designated the phenomenon "Lolcats."[37] Within a few hours there were hundreds of Lolcats on 4chan,

---

[31] See Felix Stalder, "Schwärme, Anonymous und die Rebellion im Netz," *Le monde diplomatique* (February 10, 2012), http://www.monde-diplomatique.de/pm/2012/02/10.mondeText.artikel,a0009. idx,0 (accessed April 19, 2015); and Rick Falkvinge, "Swarmwise: What is a Swarm?" *Falkvinge & Co. on Infopolicy* (January 8, 2001), http://falkvinge.net/2011/08/01/swarmwise-what-is-a-swarm/ (accessed April 19, 2015).

[32] Thacker, "Networks, Swarms, Multitudes: Part One"; idem, "Networks, Swarms, Multitudes: Part Two."

[33] This was achieved in January of 2011, for instance, with repeated DDoS attacks against institutions in Egypt, including various government ministries.

[34] Eva Horn, "Schwärme – Kollektive ohne Zentrum: Einleitung," in *Schwärme – Kollektive ohne Zentrum: Eine Wissensgeschichte zwischen Leben und Information*, ed. Lucas Marco Gisi and Eva Horn (Bielefeld: Transcript, 2009), 7–26, at 17.

[35] On the constitutive role of affects, see also Massumi, *Parables for the Virtual*; and Urs Stäheli, "Von der Herde zur Horde? Zum Verhältnis von Hegemonie- und Affektpolitik," in *Diskurs, radikale Demokratie, Hegemonie: Zum politischen Denken von Ernesto Laclau und Chantal Mouffe*, ed. Martin Nonhoff (Bielefeld: Transcript, 2007), 123–38. Regarding Anonymous in particular, see Carolin Wiedemann, "'Greetings from the Dark Side of the Internet': Anonymous und die Frage nach Widerstand in Zeiten der Informatisierung," in *Subjektivierung 2.0: Machtverhältnisse digitaler Öffentlichkeiten*, ed. Tanja Carstensen and Tanja Paulitz (Wiesbaden: Springer, 2014), 143–62.

[36] For further discussion, see Wiedemann, "'Greetings from the Dark Side of the Internet'."

[37] While in New York in April of 2012, I had the opportunity to interview several people who had participated in a variety of Anonymous's activities. I was able to locate them because they had already been identified by the FBI, which indicates the shortcomings of the software that Anonymous activists

and a few weeks later the event known as "Caturday" was initiated. So began a trend that has already involved tens of thousands of users.[38]

Like swarms, Anonymous is "more than the sum of its parts."[39] The chains of association result in emergences that cannot be traced back to individual elements; the ideas and actions of Anonymous are not brought about by the engagement of individual users but rather through their interaction. According to Thacker, the central criterion of a swarm is that it must exhibit directional force without centralized control.[40] Self-organization is thus defined as the emergence of a global pattern out of local interactions. As in the case of swarms, Anonymous, at least at this first phase, can be described as an act without an actor and as a heterogeneous whole that always remains in motion.[41]

It is important to note, however, that although Anonymous appeared from the beginning as a swarm-like entity, it has come to develop increasingly stable nodal points on the Internet; these include, for instance, AnonNews.org, a moderated forum on which reports by other news providers are recirculated, on which Anonymous publishes its own press releases, and on which every visitor can post comments anonymously. For speakers of German, there is also du-bist-anonymous.de, a website meant to justify and clarify Anonymous's activities and to provide links to a diverse variety of blogs and forums.[42] By developing stable nodal points on the Internet, that is, by establishing individual blogs and forums in the name of Anonymous (so to speak), Anonymous has thus fulfilled the central criteria of the network, which Thacker has defined, in terms of Eulerian graph theory, as "a map of fixed nodes (or things) and stable edges (or relations)."[43]

If this network were merely a purposeless concatenation of individual elements, it would not, according to Thacker, constitute a collectivity. Yet the network that in fact developed – that furnished Anonymous with a pattern and sustainable connectivity – emerged from the swarms that, in the moment of swarming, each had their own purpose. At first, Anonymous was operated and collectively produced on and by 4chan; with the subsequent creation of AnonNews or IRC cannels, however, additional infrastructures appeared in which it was possible to communicate and cooperate anonymously.

On December 16, 2010, immediately after Operation Payback, the founders of Anon-News stated in an anonymously conducted interview with the magazine *Computer und Technik* that Anonymous possesses a "creative power" that "generates" operations such as

---

    had been using in the past. This aspect, like forms of hacking and DDoS, deserves a discussion of its own and will not be treated here.

[38] From 4chan, the trend spread throughout the Internet and became an email phenomenon; see the Wikipedia entry on Lolcats: http://en.wikipedia.org/wiki/Lolcat (accessed on April 20, 2015).

[39] Thacker, "Networks, Swarms, Multitudes: Part Two," n.p.

[40] Ibid.

[41] Ibid.

[42] I conducted research for this article in 2012 and 2013; since that time, this website has changed considerably.

[43] Thacker, "Networks, Swarms, Multitudes: Part One," n.p.

Leakspin, Operation Paperstorm, or websites like www.AnonNews.org and IRC channels.[44]
They thus denied their role as the creators of the site, one of the central nodal points of
the network, by asserting that a creative power within Anonymous was also responsible
for AnonNews. In a similar manner, one of my interview subjects, who had participated
in a variety of Anonymous's operations, explained why it was that, within the network,
no single Anon could be credited as the author of any given document, video, action, or
new nodal point in the network:

> If you put something out there, it no longer *truly* belongs to you. You can feel proud that you
> wrote something that became so popular. But you did not truly *make* it popular; the people around
> you did. You did not circulate it thousands of times. You did not pull parts of it and put it into
> something else. You may have written the original thing, but you have no claim to how famous
> it became. The thing belongs to Anonymous now because, had you written it for anything else,
> it would have gone nowhere and because *you* decided to give it to the group when you posted
> it to the network, saying it was for the operation.

This is essentially a description of the principle of collective, swarm-like authorship.[45] The texts that circulate online have a multiplicity of origins; they bring attention
to Anonymous by means of the anonymous cooperation that is conjured by it. Before
they are posted, documents are thus spontaneously authored by users who have been
engaged in anonymous exchanges on an IRC (for instance), and it is this sort of process
that yields ideas for action.[46] An extra chat room can be created whose address is posted
in the previous chat room and, theoretically, everyone interested in the topic can click on
it. Depending on how much reception the idea receives from users chatting on the channels, and depending on how many of them modify the idea itself and further distribute it,
it can then "function" as Anonymous.

This suggests that infrastructures in which anonymous communication and cooperation can take place lend themselves particularly well to the behavior of swarms. All
of the nodal points of the network, especially IRC channels, are meant to be spaces in
which people can communicate anonymously (as on 4chan), in which the "creative
power" of Anonymous can "generate" something (as mentioned in the interview), and in
which – to use Thacker's swarm vocabulary – intentionality can operate without inten-

---

[44]   See Jan-Keno Jannsen, "Anonymous verändert sich gerade dramatisch: Interview mit MacherInnen
       von AnonNews.org," *c't magazin* (December 16, 2010), http://www.heise.de/ct/artikel/Anonymous-
       veraendert-sich-gerade-dramatisch-1154156.html (accessed on April 20, 2015).

[45]   For an overview of the historical precursors to collective authorship, see Marco Deseriis, *Improper
       Names: The Minor Politics of Collective Pseudonyms and Multiple-Use Names* (Doctoral diss.: New
       York University, 2011).

[46]   As noted above, IRC is an abbreviation for Internet Relay Chat, which is a purely text-based chat
       system: On various "channels," a given number of users can chat with each other; new channels
       can be opened by anyone at any time, and it is possible to participate simultaneously on multiple
       channels. See http://en.wikipedia.org/wiki/Internet_Relay_Chat (accessed on April 21, 2015).

tion and a directional force can operate without centralized control.[47] At this point it can thus be claimed that the swarms of Anonymous have created infrastructures that in turn encourage the formation of additional swarms. This in fact could be thought of as its "purpose," something which Thacker regards as constitutive of swarm collectivity.[48] The infrastructures that have been created are networks in which users can permanently communicate and cooperate anonymously, and this provides Anonymous with a pattern and signifies enduring connectivity. Anonymous moves in between the two points of tension in Thacker's classification of "group phenomena"[49] – collectivity/connectivity and purpose/pattern – and thus as a collectivity it is a hybrid of a network and a swarm. The network that has developed under the name Anonymous is not a purposeless chain of individual nodes but rather seems to fulfill a lasting purpose, namely the creation of infrastructures in which people can communicate anonymously.

But is this a matter of swarming for the sake of swarming, as previous discussions of Anonymous have implied? Or can such swarming be attributed any significance? Has a long-term cause been developed that the (co)operations and productions of Anonymous have in common? As I intend to show, the purposes of Anonymous's individual swarms can all be traced back to just such a common cause. This cause, however, can only be identified at a level that is not shared by traditional protest groups, for which causes constitute the common nature of the group and only then lead to communication and cooperation. In the case of Anonymous, things are precisely the other way around; anonymous exchanges on the network lead to the development of common narratives. To what extent, however, do such narratives function differently from traditional logics of representation?

The Multitude and the Common

The question of the meaning or narrative that develops in swarm networks is ultimately that of the role that the two axes *connectivity-collectivity* and *pattern-purpose* play on the level of political ontology. A swarm that swarms simply for the sake of swarming, like a network without a cause, is not yet something that can be regarded as political. It seems obvious at this point to devote some attention to a model of decentralized collectivity that political theorists refer to as the multitude, something that Thacker also addresses in his discussion of networks and swarms.[50] At first glance, the model of the multitude corresponds well with Anonymous precisely because, in theory, the multitude is not constituted by logics of identity but rather by their denial. Here I would like to summarize a few aspects of Hardt and Negri's idea of the multitude in order to test the extent to which it might be applicable to Anonymous.

---

[47]   Thacker, "Networks, Swarms, Multitudes: Part Two," n.p.

[48]   Ibid.

[49]   Ibid.

[50]   Ibid.

The multitude is theorized as an oppositional collectivity against the current form of capitalist exploitation and hierarchy within Empire.[51] For Hardt and Negri, Empire designates a situation in which national and governmental regulation is dissolved, resulting in a new framework for global capitalism. In the case of Empire, sovereignty has transformed into a sort of governmentality that no longer needs a central authority.[52] It operates by means of harnessing "biopower," the technology of power that subsumes all of life under capitalism. In doing so, however, surpluses of sociability and creativity are generated in various branches of post-Fordist society; unable to be exploited, it is these surpluses that give rise to the common – the basis of the multitude.[53] Through communication and cooperation, an intersection of affects, themes, and experiences is formed that stands in opposition to Empire's individualizing logic of profit.[54] The common is not constituted by representational logics and the attribution of particular commonalities: "Insofar as the multitude is neither an identity (like the people) nor uniform (like the masses), the internal differences of the multitude must discover *the common* that allows them to communicate and act together. The common we share, in fact, is not so much discovered as it is produced."[55] It is a type of common that does not create a common identity but rather, as Marianne Pieper has summarized, is based on the "association of a multiplicity of heterogeneous and non-hierarchical actors that rely neither on a higher authority nor on the self-assurance of the identity-based positions of collective subjectivities."[56]

This is reminiscent of Anonymous's own self-descriptions, which have been circulating online since Operation Payback or at the latest since its intervention during the Arab Spring. As far as my line of questioning is concerned, it is noteworthy that Anonymous has come to develop an increasingly concerted narrative, one that manages to convey the common experience of anonymous online exchanges. It is a sort of self-reflection of the way in which Anonymous functions with users who in turn become the very cause of Anonymous; it this act of "producing the common" that seems to correspond so well to the model of the multitude. In "An Open Letter to the World," one of Anonymous's most widely circulated documents, the idea is expressed as follows: "We have begun telling each other our own stories. Sharing our lives, our hopes, our dreams, our demons. [...] As

---

[51]   See Hardt and Negri, *Multitude*, 29.

[52]   Michael Hardt and Antonio Negri, *Empire* (Cambridge, MA: Harvard University Press, 2000), 339.

[53]   See Vassilis Tsianos et al., *Escape Routes: Control and Subversion in the Twenty-First Century* (London: Pluto Press, 2008), 251–53. The authors of this book refer to the post-industrial value system as "embodied capitalism" and argue that the surplus of sociability destabilizes social regulation or is not entirely governable because it is incompatible with the current system of measuring the productivity of labor.

[54]   See Paolo Virno, *A Grammar of the Multitude: For an Analysis of Contemporary Forms of Life*, trans. Isabella Bertoletti and James Cascaito (Cambridge, MA: Semiotexte, 2003), 41–42.

[55]   Hardt and Negri, *Multitude: War and Democracy in the Age of Empire*, xv (the emphasis is original).

[56]   Marianne Pieper, "Biopolitik: Die Umwendung eines Machtparadigmas," in *Empire und die biopolitische Wende: Die internationale Diskussion im Anschluss an Hardt und Negri*, ed. Thomas Atzert et al. (Frankfurt am Main: Campus, 2007), 215–44, at 236.

we learn more about our global community a fundamental truth has been rediscovered: We are not so different as we may seem."[57] The letter goes on to add that Anonymous stands for the welfare of all mankind, which is achievable by means of the freedom of information and communication. In the case of anonymous communication on the Internet, that is, all voices are equal, such that people can experience their commonality without prejudice. Anonymous's cause is to promote the experience of a non-unified unity that does not require any identity-based conditions for membership. This has thus amounted to a figure of inclusion that functions differently from traditional inclusive identities such as "Germans," "women," or "citizens." One of the people whom I interviewed described to me how, while chatting with others on anonymous IRC channels, she would share spontaneous stories and talk about what she was up to; in doing so, she said, she felt connected with all of humanity because her chat partners could have been anyone in the world. Just as with the multitude, a common has been produced here that unifies without making anyone the same. Although the similarities between Anonymous's self-descriptions and the theoretical description of the multitude may be obvious, further analysis reveals certain characteristics that disagree with the multitude and even cast doubt on it as an analytical category.

Emergence and Mediation

In its present form, as has been shown, Anonymous fulfills both the defining criteria of swarms (it is dynamic, spontaneous, and a directional force without centralized control) as well those of networks (it is a pattern composed of distributed nodes and edges). Now it also seems as though Anonymous, given that it has a cause and can thus be regarded as political, likewise conforms to the model of the multitude. Assuming that the multitude unites the regimes of the other two types of collectivity, as Thacker notes,[58] one might quickly reach the conclusion that Anonymous is a realization of the multitude. According to Thacker, the criteria of the swarm, which "is not one, homogenous thing, but rather a dynamic and highly differentiated collectivity of interacting agents,"[59] reemerge in the idea of the multitude.

At least according to its Eulerian-Kantian definition, however, the criteria of the network in part contradict the notion of the multitude. The multitude, as has already been demonstrated, cannot be conceived as a sort of network that can be used to describe the form of Anonymous. It is this observation that reveals the extent to which Anonymous does not correspond to the model of the multitude. Hardt and Negri fail to provide a precise definition of the form that the multitude is supposed to adopt as a new organizational model for mobilizing the common. They rather depict it as something that is entirely free

---

[57] The letter can be read at http://www.moggies.co.uk/articles/letter.html (accessed on April 24, 2015).

[58] See Thacker, "Networks, Swarms, Multitudes: Part Two," n.p.: "Networks and swarms are what *inform* and *transform* multitudes" (emphasis original).

[59] Ibid.

from mediation, as something that is autonomous, pure, and decoupled from any sort of infrastructure.

Although they often use the term "network" to describe the form of the multitude,[60] they do not specify which network model they have in mind. Instead, they simply assume that the networked multitude is anti-hierarchical and equally shared, and that every node (or singularity) is furnished with the same access to the common – with a common link that, as Linda C. Brigham has remarked, is not suppressed by the uniqueness of the nodes that it connects.[61] Hardt and Negri assume, that is, that the multitude will result in pure and direct democracy without organization or representation. The conceptual purity attributed to the multitude, as William Mazzarella has mentioned, is stressed all the more by the fact that Hardt and Negri's multitudes are thought of as being opposed to the masses or crowds of people that always require a form of mediation.[62] Referring exclusively to LeBon's concept of the masses, Hardt and Negri remark: "Crowds are fundamentally irrational and susceptible to external influence; they naturally and necessarily follow a leader whose control maintains their unity through contagion and repetition."[63] According to Hardt and Negri, the energy of the multitude is thus productive only when it is not mediated or represented. This is their central argument for distinguishing the multitude from crowds or the masses, the productive energy of which has to be mediated, in their estimation, by a leader or by institutions.

In the case of Anonymous, an opposition between infrastructure intertwined in power relations and the emancipatory swarm has never been recognized. Whereas the characteristics of the multitude allow it to be conceived as a pure swarm, Anonymous only exists as a swarm at the moments in which a given number of users achieve something that no single individual has planned. Yet, in Anonymous's case, this emergence is always based on a shared infrastructure; even the very first Anonymous swarm was connected by means of a decentralized network (the Internet) and a specific address (4chan) before it could commence its swarming. And such infrastructure is crucial to the creation of the swarm because the latter is produced through the mediation of technical and social codes, much like the circulation of affects (which are themselves not unmediated). In the case of Anonymous, digital media are actors in the processes of constitution and production; they are that which permanently reconstitutes Anonymous. The fact that the self-organization

---

[60]   See Hardt and Negri, *Multitude*, xii, 57, 91–92.

[61]   Linda C. Brigham, "Networking the Multitude," *Electronic Book Review* (December 18, 2005), http://www.electronicbookreview.com/thread/endconstruction/networked (accessed on April 24, 2015).

[62]   William Mazzarella, "The Myth of the Multitude, or, Who's Afraid of the Crowd?" *Critical Inquiry* 36 (2010), 697–727. See also Christian Borch, *The Politics of Crowds: An Alternative History of Sociology* (Cambridge, UK: Cambridge University Press, 2012), 291.

[63]   Hardt and Negri, *Multitude*, 260. Had they relied on another concept of the masses, they would have had a more difficult time differentiating the multitude as rigidly as they did (see Borch, *The Politics of Crowds*, 291). See also the chapters by Christian Borch and Christiane Heibach in this volume.

of the multitude, on the contrary, theoretically needs no self-control exposes a deficiency in the concept that can be attributed to its political teleology.[64]

By stressing the opposition between emergence and mediation, Hardt and Negri have perpetuated the contrast between group energy and social order, which serves as the basis of older theories of the masses.[65] As Christian Borch has summarized: "Hardt and Negri in effect turned Le Bon upside-down."[66] With this close theoretical affinity, the concept of the multitude comes to contradict Hardt and Negri's own poststructuralist perspective.[67] Although they align themselves with Foucault, for whom there is nothing *outside of* power relations, they nevertheless attempt with the multitude to demonstrate the transition to an alternative that breaks away from existing power relations to seek its own autonomy.[68] At such places in their work they thus revert to the traditional notion of sovereignty, which liberates the multitude from any form of mediation. It is this idea that, they believe, will allow for the formation of an oppositional power and enable a truly democratic global society.[69] How this is supposed to take place and how the common of the multitude is supposed to be constituted while fostering difference, in Thacker's terms,[70] are questions that Hardt and Negri are unable to answer on account of the contradiction in their work. The revolutionary climax that they envision treats the multitude as a political ideal instead of as a model of a certain type of collectivity.

It is questionable whether Anonymous or any other new collectivity will become a force of opposition and enable a truly democratic society, and this is not the place to speculate about such matters. Of greater interest is rather the diversity and interconnectedness of collective processes of constitution within societies of control. And the latter cannot be understood if the forms of mediation within these processes are not taken into account. When theorizing about a collectivity such as Anonymous, on the contrary, the opposition between mediation and emergence – between infrastructure and event – can best be challenged by foregrounding the very infrastructures that enable collective production.

---

[64] See Thacker, "Networks, Swarms, Multitudes: Part Two," n.p.

[65] See Mazzarella, "The Myth of the Multitude," 720.

[66] Borch, *The Politics of Crowds*, 294.

[67] Reference to the historical appearance (post-Fordism, etc.) of biopolitical productivity, upon which the multitude is based, situates its potential and at the same time represents it not as something external to Empire but rather as something immanent to it. The opposition to the crowd confirms Thomas Lemke's critique of "Hardt and Negri's ontologization of biopolitics," which also ontologizes the multitude as an antithesis to Empire. See Thomas Lemke, "Imperiale Herrschaft, immaterielle Arbeit und die Militanz der Multitude: Anmerkungen zum Konzept der Biopolitik bei Michael Hardt und Antonio Negri," in *Biopolitik – in der Debatte*, ed. Marianne Pieper et al. (Wiesbaden: VS Verlag, 2008), 109–28, at 123.

[68] See Michael Hardt and Antonio Negri, *Commonwealth* (Cambridge, MA: Harvard University Press, 2008), 102.

[69] Hardt and Negri, *Multitude*, 264.

[70] See Thacker, "Networks, Swarms, Multitudes: Part Two," n.p.

Mobile Infrastructures and the Experience of the Common

Whereas the multitude has been described as an act of emancipation from the post-Fordist networks of Empire, the exploitative structures of which are inseparably intertwined with their infrastructures,[71] Anonymous does not emerge within exploitative networks but rather on 4chan. Little by little, Anonymous has formed a network of its own in order to organize itself as Anonymous; as mentioned above, more and more stable nodal points, such as AnonOps and AnonNews, have come to be established. The space in which Anonymous emerges is structured by an architecture of codes and protocols, out of *dispositifs* that organize the field of visibility and effability.

The interaction of cultural practices and technical infrastructure,[72] which constitutes Anonymous, is always controlled and mediated; that is, it is coded on two different but related levels. On the one hand, code is the fundamental technical process – the set of rules and instructions – that lies behind interfaces, algorithms, and protocols. On the other hand, code is also a cultural framework that is socially and performatively controlled and interpreted. The form and expression of Anonymous are coded; they are bound to the framework provided by codes. And thus the idea has to be ruled out that the other Anons (with whom the interviewee quoted above was communicating) could in fact be anyone in the world. Aside from people who lack a computer or (unrestricted) Internet access,[73] it must be said that, even among those who come together as Anonymous, hierarchies are developed by the situation and hegemonies inherent to communication, by efforts to understand, and by the fact that Anonymous comes into being on a publicly coded field. Particularly because I wish to describe the processes of affection as being effective when they interact with those infrastructures that are a constitutive element of the *dispositifs* of control societies, it must also be taken into account how such infrastructures can be used to govern both affects and swarm behavior.

According to Sebastian Vehlken's account of swarming as a cultural technique, swarms have become relevant as structures of organization and coordination, as effective optimization strategies and zoo-technological solutions for "the governmental constitution of the present itself, in which operationalized and optimized multitudes have emerged from the uncontrollable data drift of dynamic collectives."[74] The logic of contagion, which is linked to the mathematics of epidemics and theories of organization, becomes a key tactic in commercial, security, and technological contexts within current forms of capitalism. As

---

[71]   See Hardt and Negri, *Empire*, 339–43.

[72]   See Alexander R. Galloway, *Protocol: How Control Exists after Decentralization* (Cambridge, MA: MIT Press, 2004).

[73]   As Deleuze also stressed, societies of control perpetuate in themselves certain elements of disciplinary societies, so that it is never possible for "everyone" to be included and connected. See Gilles Deleuze, "Postscript on the Societies of Control," in *Cultural Theory: An Anthology*, ed. Imre Szeman and Timothy Kaposy (Chichester: Wiley-Blackwell, 2011), 139–42.

[74]   Sebastian Vehlken, "Zootechnologies: Swarming as a Cultural Technique," *Theory, Culture & Society* 30 (2013), 110–31, at 127.

Tony Sampson has noted,[75] the notion that spontaneous collective moods can be guided toward specific goals seems to be the latent exertion of an affective biopower over an increasingly connected population. This governmental constitution, which is exhibited for example in viral marketing, attempts to capitalize on affectability, that is, on the capacity of users to affect (and be affected). The infrastructures in which Anonymous swarms emerge create a dynamic informational space that is "suitable for the spread of contagion and [the] transversal propagation of movement (from computer viruses to ideas and affects)."[76] And thus they also create a space in which new types of collectivity are able to emerge and suggest new forms of politics.

With respect to "old" media infrastructures, Urs Stäheli has described the collectivization that occurs by means of infrastructures with the example of the ferry.[77] Ferries orchestrate the experience of a crowd in such a way that it experiences a journey *simultaneously*, thereby creating an experiential collective (*Erlebniskollektiv*). Anonymous can likewise be referred to as an experiential collective on the basis of its simultaneously used infrastructure, though in this case there is a central difference that could further intensify the simultaneous experience: The gathering of multiple anonymous chatters serves no other purpose beyond becoming a collective by sharing a common experience. Whereas a journey on a ferry serves to bring people closer their destination, and their common experience – that is, their collectivization – is merely an unplanned effect, the users who believe in Anonymous create, each according to his or her capabilities, ferries of their own simply for the sake of experiencing the common.[78] They create infrastructures that encourage unplanned and emergent behavior – infrastructures that enable "creative power" to be harnessed. IRCs are admittedly opened by individuals who can in turn close them, and AnonNews.org admittedly has moderators who are able to modify or delete content posted by others, but if these moderators intervene in such a way that restricts anonymous communication, AnonNews would then no longer be part of Anonymous. Thus the nodes and edges of the network known as Anonymous are constantly changing. Tutorials, for instance, have therefore been designed on how to use IRCs, and these are meant to facilitate access for new users; they are essentially instruction manuals for modulating Anonymous that can in turn, at least in theory, be modified by all users.

Certain practices and their infrastructures are legitimized within Anonymous while others are disqualified, and this depends on the extent to which they correspond to the cause that is underway. It is the cause, after all, that assigns meaning to the infrastructure

---

[75] Tony Sampson, *Virality: Contagion Theory in the Age of Networks* (Minneapolis: University of Minnesota Press, 2012), 126.

[76] Tiziana Terranova, *Network Culture: Politics for the Information Age* (London: Pluto Press, 2004), 67.

[77] Urs Stäheli, "Infrastrukturen des Kollektiven: alte Medien – neue Kollektive?" *Zeitschrift für Medien- und Kulturforschung* 2 (2012), 99–116, esp. 108–12.

[78] Stäheli cites yet another central difference of new media, namely that the simultaneous experience of new collectivities on the Internet can potentially be enhanced by the fact that there is no fixed travel schedule – that is, by the fact that they create their own schedules (see ibid., 111).

in which it is able to emerge. Anonymous communication and cooperation on the network function as conditions for non-hierarchical community and creativity, for swarms of solidarity in which the common is able to take place. It is for this reason that the comments by users who post with their real names or with pseudonyms – users who make themselves distinguishable – are ignored by those chatting anonymously. For this reason, too, a platform such as AnonOps was hardly used for a certain period of time; certain users had begun to recognize one another's writing styles, schedule meetings, and thus develop hierarchies. The principle of Anonymous thus ceased to function there.

Any definition of collectivization as an event of the common by means of media infrastructures can also be related to Gerald Raunig's ideas about orgiastic media.[79] According to Raunig, orgiastic media are not means of acquiring information or mediating an event; rather, they are the enabling conditions of events themselves.[80] It is thus no longer possible to separate mediation and emergence. This is not to say that media should be understood as solutions to problems – as is often the case in emancipatory discourses about the Internet and Web 2.0 – but rather that they should be regarded, in Raunig's terms, "as an opening up of the possible."[81] As mentioned in my introduction, social media are not "social" because they enhance the formation of social movements but rather because they affect the constitution of the social itself.[82] In terms of new forms of collectivity created on and by means of the Internet, Anonymous reveals, more than any other before it, the intertwined nature of the symbolic and operative levels in the creation of collectivity. Both of these levels, that is, possess characteristics that are controlling as well as liberating, coding as well as affecting. In the case of Anonymous, infrastructure and cause – pattern and purpose – require one another.

Conclusion and Outlook

Anonymous thus poses a challenge to the two types of tension in Thacker's classification of "group phenomena,"[83] namely the tension between collectivity/connectivity and that

---

[79] Gerald Raunig, "Eventum et Medium: Event and Orgiastic Representation in Media Activism," *European Institute for Progressive Cultural Policies* (June 2006), http://eipcp.net/transversal/0707/raunig/en (accessed on April 26, 2015).

[80] Raunig thus aligns himself with the thinking of Walter Benjamin and Bertolt Brecht: "If we do not want to conceive of this middle as a vacant market for the trading of information goods, two preconditions must be clarified: one is that the transmitting of the medium itself is never to be understood as neutral, and more important, the specific form of the transmission can change the medium as a production apparatus." With reference to Deleuze, Raunig also differentiates between organic and orgiastic representation: "Unlike the paradigm of organic representation, an *orgiastic* medium appears not only as a pure means of information, of mediating an event, but instead concatenates with the event, ultimately becoming an event itself" (ibid., n.p.; emphasis original).

[81] Ibid.

[82] See Zehle and Rossiter, "Organizing Networks," 250.

[83] Thacker, "Networks, Swarms, Multitudes: Part Two," n.p.

between purpose/pattern: If Anonymous *exists*, then purpose and pattern merge into one and connectivity and collectivity are mutually dependent on one another. In Anonymous's case, self-organization is always a mixture of self-control – that is, an internal control mechanism that seeks to establish infrastructures of anonymous exchange, thus stabilizing networks and restraining their *affects* – and the circulation of these very affects, which is essential to producing and experiencing the creative power of the common.

It might be most accurate, then, to regard Anonymous as a *living network*, something which Thacker holds in contrast to networks of the Eulerian-Kantian sort.[84] Older definitions of the network were concerned only with the *network effect*; they neglected the level of *network affects*.[85] Such affects circulate in those moments about which, after the fact, we can speak of swarms. The latter consist of individuals who only in retrospect can identify themselves as having been part of a swarm, which does not *exist* but rather occurs *in actu* as an unmediated emergence.[86] Neither a swarm nor a network in the traditional sense, Anonymous is rather a *living network*. It is thus neither a multitude nor a mass in the traditional sense but rather a *new mass* that calls into question the conditions of the masses before it by unifying emergence and institutionalization – by causing nodes to shift around in a state of swarming oscillation.

---

[84] Ibid.
[85] Ibid.
[86] See Horn, "Schwärme – Kollektive ohne Zentrum," 16.

Mirko Tobias Schäfer

Unstable (Counter)Publics
Online Platforms as Hybrid Forums
for Socio-Political Debates

I. A Civic Awakening in the Virtual Shopping Mall?

In April of 2009, Mark Zuckerberg reached out to the (then) 450 million users of Facebook with a video message. Striking a rather statesmanlike pose, the young CEO urged his audience to participate in a vote to determine the code of conduct that should govern the website. Facebook had previously translated its "Statement of Rights and Responsibilities" into numerous languages and posted it on its governance page for the sake of discussion.[1] As Zuckerman was openly proud to note, the world's largest social organization now had the opportunity to comment on the rules crafted by the company. Presumably, the company took these comments into account when redrafting its regulations, and now it was asking its users to decide which changes should be adopted in the binding version. Later, the adopted changes to the terms of use were announced on Facebook's governance page and users were asked yet again to provide commentary and recommendations.[2] To the attentive user it is not entirely clear how the voting process actually worked and how the integrity of the results could be assured. It was also unclear to what extent the company would be obliged to carry out the users' decisions. More interesting, however, is Facebook's effort to establish a sort of legitimate sovereignty. In this situation, the CEO of the company is presented as a quasi-president, but the laws of the land are ultimately to be determined by the extensive involvement of users in the decision-making process. It has not always been the case that Facebook seemed so eager to convince its customers about the legitimacy of its terms of use. Novel, too, is its trend of using the participation of its users to establish a platform-wide form of legitimate sovereignty. This was possibly a response to criticism – voiced by users, politicians, and data-protection agencies – concerning its rather loose handling of private information. Or was it perhaps the realization that the popular online

---

[1]   Facebook's page devoted to "site governance" can be found at http://www.facebook.com/fbsitegov-ernance (accessed on July 31, 2014).

[2]   The updates posted on Facebook's governance page are of the following sort: "We've proposed updates to our Privacy Policy and Statement of Rights and Responsibilities. We encourage you to read through the proposed documents and offer your comments on the 'Discussions' tab of this page by 12:00am PDT on April 3, 2010" (http://www.facebook.com/fbsitegovernance).

Fig. 1: Mark Zuckerberg implores Facebook users to vote. (A screenshot of Facebook's Governance Page)

platform was in fact not a shopping mall whose visitors have to check their civil rights at the door before abandoning themselves to the pleasures of casual shopping?

As so-called "social media" have gained more and significance, the providers of such platforms have developed something that, in Foucault's terms, could be called an "art of government."[3] This has not only involved the imitation of certain symbols and activities that are generally associated with the legitimate exercise of power; it has also involved the development and implementation of techniques with which mass numbers of users can control and manage themselves. The graphical interfaces of popular web applications, moreover, implicitly serve to control the activity of users while, behind the scenes, such activity is automatically collected, assessed, and (when necessary) removed in response to the feedback of other users.[4] So it was that Zuckerberg appeared, as statesmanlike as possible in a video resembling a televised address by an elected official, to call his users to vote on the Facebook "Statement of Rights and Responsibilities." This appearance was merely a symbolic gesture to emphasize a notion of participation, not to invoke real democratic decision processes.

---

[3]   Michel Foucault, *Security, Territory, Population: Lectures at the Collège de France, 1977–1978*, trans. Graham Burchell (New York: Picador, 2007), esp. 87–114.

[4]   Regarding the structure and implications of Facebook's open graph protocol, see the chapter by Irina Kaldrack and Theo Röhle in this book.

In light of this background, my goal here is to focus on the political quality of social media. In particular I would like to explore how "platform policies" are used to construct legitimacy and how "platform designs" are used to govern the behavior of their users. This form of management is associated with the politicization of users, who demand civil rights and cultural freedom from such platforms and also rely on them to hold societal debates and to run political campaigns. As Stefan Münker has observed, "social media" have thus developed into "public spaces."[5] My concentration below will be on the potential exhibited by these efforts toward politicization.

II. Platforms for Commerce and Criticism

It must be kept in mind that the original intent of these platforms was to find, in one way or another, commercial applications for their users' activity. Whereas the media industry of the twentieth century still created content and made it available alongside advertisements, the aspiring media industry of the twenty-first century offers platforms on which users can create their own content independently. The contributions of individuals have come to take the place of professionally developed media content. Efforts to make profits are now focused on individualized advertising, licensing content to third parties, and evaluating user data.

The technical design of platforms is oriented toward these ends and is thus chiefly concerned with user interfaces and software applications. This is clear to see, for instance, in Facebook's "like button," which quite intentionally has no counterpart in the form of a "dislike button." In this case, the Facebook design presents users with fewer options than did the Roman circus, where the plebs could at least respond negatively with their thumbs down.[6] For their part, comment sections seem to be designed explicitly to prevent long debates; rather, they lend themselves to ephemeral expressions of mutual recognition or to offering positive feedback to posted content with a quick click of the "like button." Other elements of Facebook's design prevent users from posting hyperlinks to BitTorrent files. For some time it was even impossible to post "Bit.ly links," which are automatically shortened hyperlinks, because Facebook feared that these could link to sources that might violate copyright provisions or might be regarded as SPAM.[7] YouTube has likewise implemented several design elements that are meant to protect the company from potential

---

[5] See Stefan Münker, *Emergenz digitaler Öffentlichkeiten: Die sozialen Medien im Web 2.0* (Frankfurt am Main: Suhrkamp, 2009).

[6] Facebook has entertained the idea of introducing a "want button." Similar to the "like button," this would allow users to make knee-jerk positive assessments (in this case to express their desire to own something) and thus it would fit seamlessly into Facebook's commercial logic. See Laura Stampler, "Here's What Facebook's New 'Want' Button Will Look Like," *Business Insider* (October 9, 2012), http://www.businessinsider.com/what-facebooks-want-button-will-look-like-2012-10 (accessed on August 5, 2014).

[7] Ben Parr, "Facebook Breaks All Bit.ly Links, Marks Them as Abusive," *Mashable.com* (July 16, 2010), http://mashable.com/2010/07/16/facebook-bitly-broken/ (accessed on August 5, 2014).

lawsuits concerned with copyright infringement. Videos posted by users are automatically run through a database in order to see whether they contain any unauthorized music. A similar process is used to prevent people from reposting videos that YouTube has already removed. Yet another filter serves to prevent swear words and discriminatory language from appearing in the comment sections.[8] Any user, moreover, is able to mark a given video as being "offensive" simply by clicking on the so-called "flag button." Videos flagged in such a way are then evaluated by an editor and, when necessary, removed from the site. YouTube's "flag button" corresponds to a button on Facebook labeled "report." If someone uses this button to file a report about offensive content, the material in question is then reviewed by a content moderator to see whether it might violate Facebook's "community standards." If so, it is removed.[9] Most discussions of "social media" have overlooked the extent to which user-generated content is controlled, evaluated, and moderated.[10] Recently, however, the popular blog *Gawker* devoted some attention to the dubious guidelines behind Facebook's content moderation.[11] In only a few cases has the daily censorship that takes place on these platforms been brought to the public's attention. Some attention, for instance, has been given to a cover of *Zeit Magazin* that Facebook censored, to the company's removal of a campaign advertisement posted by the Dutch GreenLeft party, and to the general censorship of art.[12] Perhaps in retaliation, *Die Zeit* has published a story about acts of censorship committed by Apple, Amazon, Facebook, and Google.[13]

The terms of use implemented by such platforms as well as their technical designs serve to regulate user activity in rather heavy-handed manner. So-called "user-generated content" is therefore always the result of a hybrid evaluation process and is thus subjected quite extensively to the controls and regulations instituted by the companies in questions. On

---

[8] Matthew Moore, "YouTube's Worst Comments Blocked by Filter," *The Telegraph* (September 2, 2008), http://www.telegraph.co.uk/news/newstopics/howaboutthat/2668997/YouTubes-worst-comments-blocked-by-filter.html (accessed on August 5, 2014).

[9] For Facebook's own description of this process, see its page titled "What Happens After You Click 'Report'": https://www.facebook.com/notes/432670926753695/ (accessed on August 5, 2014).

[10] In a highly informative article in *The New York Times*, Brad Stone reported about the work of companies such as Caleris, which are contracted by large web platforms to control user-generated media content. See Brad Stone, "Policing the Web's Lurid Precincts," *The New York Times* (July 18, 2010), http://www.nytimes.com/2010/07/19/ technology/19screen.html?_r=0 (accessed on August 5, 2014).

[11] Adrian Chen, "Inside Facebook's Outsourced Anti-Porn and Gore Brigade, Where Camel Toes Are More Offensive than Crushed Heads," *Gawker.com* (February 16, 2012), http://gawker.com/5885714/inside-facebooks-outsourced-anti-porn-and-gore-brigade-where-camel-toes-are-more-offensive-than-crushed-heads (accessed on August 5, 2014).

[12] See the blog post "Facebook löscht Penis Cover," *Futurzone.at* (July 28, 2012), http://futurezone.at/digital-life/facebook-loescht-penis-cover/24.583.678; and Bas Paternotte, "Facebook verwijdert iconische PSP poster," *HP/De Tijd* (August 23, 2012), http://www.hpdetijd.nl/2012-08-23/facebook-verwijdert-iconische-psp-poster/ (both websites were accessed on August 5, 2014).

[13] Götz Hamann and Marcus Rohwetter, "Vier Sheriffs zensieren die Welt: Wie Apple, Facebook, Amazon und Google dem Internet ihre Gesetze aufzwingen," *Zeit Online* (August 6, 2012), http://www.zeit.de/2012/32/Zensur-Apple-Facebook-Amazon-Google (accessed on August 5, 2014).

one hand, it is in the interest of the providers to offer advertiser-friendly platforms whose orientation toward consensus fosters a form of consumer-friendliness. On the other hand, platform providers are ever in fear of being held responsible for any copyright violations that might be committed by their users.

Above all, companies have implemented strict terms of use to protect or distance themselves from potential lawsuits. The network Xbox Live, for instance, has the following language in its "End User License Agreement":

> We may change the Service or delete or discontinue features, games, or other content at any and for any reason (or no reason). We may cancel or suspend your Service at any time. Our cancellation or suspension may be without cause and without notice. Upon Service cancellation, your right to use the Service stops right away.[14]

The company reserves all rights for itself and offers no protection whatsoever to its users. The language is similar in Facebook's "Statement of Rights and Responsibilities." Essentially, the document lists the obligations and limitations with which its users must comply, whereas the obligations of the company itself are restricted to a rhetorical claim: "We respect other people's rights, and expect you to do the same." The statement goes on to enumerate all the rights that have to be respected.[15] Simply by using Facebook, people are legally committed to following these rules. Moreover, any developer who hopes to design applications for the platform is subject to Facebook's "Platform Policies." This general attitude is reflected in the company's treatment of its users' personal information, as Kurt Opsahl has summarized:

> Viewed together, the successive policies tell a clear story. Facebook originally earned its core base of users by offering them simple and powerful controls over their personal information. As Facebook grew larger and became more important, it could have chosen to maintain or improve those controls. Instead, it slowly but surely helped itself – and its advertising and business partners – to more and more of its users' information, while limiting the users' options to control their own information.[16]

As the number of users has grown, however, so too has the number of critical users. Such users value the importance of data protection and cultural freedom and are also able to generate awareness about these themes. On all of the present platforms, debates and campaigns have emerged that are directly concerned with the freedom of users and with the terms of use dictated by the companies. When Flickr only made its web application available to German users with its so-called "SafeSearch" filter, this prompted a protest

---

[14]   Quoted from http://www.xbox.com/en-NZ/Live/LIVETermsOfUse (accessed on August 5, 2014).

[15]   Facebook's "Statement of Rights and Responsibilities" can be read at https://www.facebook.com/note.php?note_id=183538190300 (accessed on August 5, 2014).

[16]   Kurt Opsahl, "Facebook's Eroding Privacy Policy: A Timeline," *Business Insider* (April 30, 2010), http://www.businessinsider.com/facebooks-eroding-privacy-policy-a-timeline-2010-4 (accessed on August 5, 2014).

Figure 2: An image posted in protest by a user of Flickr (CC: caro-li)

that took place on the platform itself.[17] The company decided to take such controversial measures on account of Germany's strict attitude toward protecting minors from pornographic images. Users, however, posted numerous photographs that accused the site of censorship.

On Facebook, too, people have used the infrastructure and interface to raise criticism about the company's guidelines and practices. With status updates, users warned one another about the newly adopted changes to privacy settings and gave each other tips on how to ensure that as little of their content as possible would be shared with potential advertisers. These efforts soon went "viral" on the site itself. In numerous petitions for a "dislike button" (with which users could object to certain data-protection provisions and other issues), attempts were made to confront the company with direct criticism. These protests were not restricted to the platform's own infrastructure but rather took place on various websites; in fact, a site called "Facebook Protest" was even set up for this very purpose.[18] William Uricchio was right to point out that the debates about cultural freedom and terms of use – debates that suddenly transformed users or consumers into citizens – have raised important questions about the very role that companies ought to play.[19] As citizens, users can urge legislators to ensure that such companies will abide by data-protection laws. In the case of popular sites like Facebook, a critical dynamic has quickly developed and spread to the point of entering the political discourse; politicians, in other words, are now feeling pressure to enact the agenda of a new focus group.[20] Companies have attempted to counteract these developments by sending lobbyists of their own to sway the discourse in their favor.[21]

In addition to the possibility of using platforms to voice criticism about the companies that run them, it is also possible for designs to be appropriated. A plug-in for Firefox called "Unfuck Facebook" allows people to use the site in a form that is stripped down

---

[17]   See Konrad Lischka, "Zwangsfilter: Flickr verbietet Deutschen Nacktfotos," *Spiegel Online* (June 14, 2007), http://www.spiegel.de/netzwelt/web/zwangsfilter-flickr-verbietet-deutschen-nacktfotos-a-488542.html (accessed on August 5, 20014).

[18]   See http://facebookprotest.com/.

[19]   William Uricchio, "Cultural Citizenship in the Age of P2P Networks," in *European Culture and the Media*, ed. Ib Bondebjerg and Peter Golding (Bristol: Intellect, 2004), 139–64.

[20]   On a similar note, the Pirate Party in Germany has been using its internet competence to fill a gap in the German political landscape.

[21]   See Javier Cáceres, "Internetkonzerne schreiben bei Datenschutzregeln mit," *Süddeusche.de* (February 11, 2013), http://www.sueddeutsche.de/digital/lobby-einfluss-auf-neue-eu-verordnung-internet-konzerne-schreiben-bei-datenschutzregeln-mit-1.1596560 (accessed on August 5, 2014).

to its basic functions. A site called Open Book demonstrates the extent to which personal status updates on Facebook are made accessible to the broader public if users do not take it upon themselves to adjust their privacy settings. An application known as "Give Me My Data" allows users to download and export all of the information they have posted on Facebook.[22] Like the somewhat older but lesser-known service "Seppukoo," the service referred to as the "Web 2.0 Suicide Machine" enables irritated users of Facebook, Twitter, or Linked-In to deactivate their profiles.[23] An annual "Quit Facebook Day" has been established to encourage discontent users to abandon the network, and nearly forty thousand of such users promised to leave the site on May 31, 2010.[24] Whereas these examples are creative forms of expressing dissent by means of web applications (not by means of petitions), there is also the possibility of simply using alternative platforms. One alternative to Facebook, as Geert Lovink noted in 2010, is a platform called Diaspora, which was then still under development.[25] Diaspora is a social network site much like Facebook or Google Plus, which it resembles quite closely in appearance, but unlike the commercial providers it aims to grant users the maximum amount of control both over the technology itself and its terms of use. Participation in the site is not supposed to be like the merely ostensible participation in Facebook's votes, mentioned above, but will rather involve a systemically inherent integration into the decision-making process, an open discussion of design elements and terms of use, and the implementation of shared values into the software design. Diaspora would thus correspond more closely to the model of Wikipedia, where the difficult processes of user participation and communal decision-making have more or less been resolved.[26] However, Diaspora was never able to live up to these expectations. Shortly after it was launched, its development team fell apart, and the platform never created enough momentum to lure a significant number of people away from Facebook. In 2014, the "Facebook killer" was supposed to be a platform called Ello, which was enthusiastically welcomed by commentators critical of Facebook. As of now, however, it has yet to prove whether it can be viable alternative. If Lovink offers any criticism regarding alternative platforms and the rebellious activity of their users, it is that they will inevitably confront problems when trying to evade the economic logic of the internet.[27] A large-scale exodus of users from the popular social networks, however

---

[22] See http://givememydata.com/ (accessed on August 6, 2014).

[23] See http://seppukoo.com and http://suicidemachine.org (both accessed on August 6, 2014).

[24] See http://quitfacebookday.com/ (accessed on August 6, 2012).

[25] Morgan Curie, "Geert Lovink: 'Critique of the Free and Open' Keynote," *Masters of Media* (November 10, 2010), http://mastersofmedia.hum.uva.nl/2010/11/10/geert-lovink-critique-of-the-free-and-open-keynote/ (accessed on August 6, 2014). This is a summary of Lovink's keynote address delivered in Berlin at the Open Culture Research Conference, which was held on October 8–10, 2010.

[26] See Joseph Reagle, *Good Faith Collaboration: The Culture of Wikipedia* (Cambridge, MA: MIT Press, 2010).

[27] Whereas Wikipedia has managed to remain financially independent and has been able to rely on voluntary contributions from the Wikipedia community (in addition to the administrative work of

maligned they might be, is highly unlikely on account of social reasons. Jonathan Zittrain
has discussed this sort of "social lock-in" in the following terms:

> [These are] winner-take-all network effects that say that, after a particular appliance or platform
> is dominating the [user's] environment, there are reasons why it would be awfully hard to leave.
> I can't necessarily leave Facebook with all the stuff I've contributed, all the mouse droppings
> that comprise my newsfeed, [and] all the other people can't simultaneously leave with me.[28]

It hardly would have been necessary for Facebook to take any legal action against the
creators of the "Web 2.0 Suicide Machine." Its users are not overwhelmingly ready to
leave the site on account of the protests, and most people are unwilling to give up all the
contacts that they have formed there, not to mention all the communication that has been
saved and the social status that they have cultivated. In fact, Facebook has responded to
criticism in a rather flexible manner. Privacy settings have been set up that at least leave
users with the impression that they are better able to control their personal information.
It is now even possible for users to download all the data that have posted on the site,
including all the communication that they have contributed to the social network. Within
the limits of its business model, the company has gone some way to meet its customers'
demands, and these gestures have only been possible because of its vast number of users.
The example of MySpace has shown how quickly even a large and successful platform
can lose its participants; in April of 2011 alone, approximately ten million people left
what was once the model project of the "social web."

In this light, Mark Zuckerberg's statesmanlike appearance in the video message to
Facebook's users seems to have been based on his awareness that the merely rhetorical
notion of participation had to be followed by a more genuine, though limited, form of the
same. It is for this reason that critical users are now treated as constructive collaborators
and offered the opportunity to critique the company's guidelines in comment sections.
The rather effective result of this is that the "sovereignty" of the company and of its
regulations has been established and legitimized collectively. Zuckerberg's appearance
also fits neatly into the political discourse that he wishes to foster; he and other internet
entrepreneurs have been invited to conferences and summit meetings convened by leading political figures.[29]

While both politicians and the commercial providers of platforms have been paying
lip service to the idea of civic participation, empowered user groups have demanded a
genuine reevaluation of these new public spheres. The cuddly notion of community togetherness, which Clay Shirky and Charles Leadbeater have considered to be the basic
quality of popular web platforms, is in fact the depoliticized and commodified form of

---

its permanent staff), Diaspora has yet to establish such an infrastructure.

[28] Jonathan Zittrain, "Jonathan Zittrain on Big Think," *BigThink.com* (2009), http://bigthink.com/
jonathanzittrain (this site is no longer active).

[29] Zuckerberg was invited to the G8 summit in Paris, and Barack Obama has held a so-called "town
hall meeting" at Facebook's headquarters. The event streamed live on Facebook.

"social media."[30] Here the political is reduced a "like button," with which it is possible to show one's sympathy for the democratic activists in the Near and Middle East. Academics have criticized the popular web platforms chiefly on account of their dubious power structures,[31] and this criticism has focused especially on the companies' violations of the private sphere (the misuse of personal information) and on their generation of profit from work that has been performed by others.[32] As I discussed above, the users of such platforms also criticized their regulations, but they did so within the limits set by the technical designs of the platforms themselves. Even if the economic logic of web-based industries poses a considerable challenge to alternative models, it is also true that the mere "social" connection that people have with the popular platforms will discourage large numbers of users from moving to an alternative provider.

While popular platforms such as Facebook, Twitter, YouTube, or Flickr have evoked criticism from their users, they have simultaneously served as important infrastructures for socio-political debates. Independent of the criticism directed at the platforms themselves, these discussions have generated awareness for political themes, organized activism, and helped to spread information. Commercial providers, in other words, have not only provoked critical responses from a limited number of their own users; they have also provided a service to civic activists by offering an infrastructure for political organization. In doing so, the platforms reveal their potential for generating public spheres. They contribute a network of numerous applications and activities that have considerably expanded the sphere of public discourse. Noteworthy, too, is the heterogeneity of public spheres in digital space, where commercial platforms are directly connected to the content provided by alternative, independent, or non-commercial sources.

III. Technology-Driven Political Change

Ever since "social media" such as Facebook and Twitter were attributed a central role in the uprisings of the so-called Arab Spring, they have been described as a new form of civic activism. This has ranged from the innocent enthusiasm of their users to serious efforts to assign the platforms a prominent role in American foreign policy. In his programmatic essay "The Political Power of Social Media," Clay Shirky has pointed out the emancipa-

---

[30] See Clay Shirky, *Cognitive Surplus: Creativity and Generosity in a Connected Age* (New York: Penguin, 2010); and Charles Leadbeater, *We-Think: Mass Innovation, Not Mass Production* (London: Profile, 2008).

[31] See Geert Lovink and Miriam Rasch, eds., *Unlike Us: Social Media Monopolies and Their Alternatives* (Amsterdam: Institute of Network Cultures, 2013).

[32] See, for example, Trebor Scholz, "Market Ideology and the Myths of Web 2.0," *First Monday* 13 (2008), http://firstmonday.org/article/view/2138/1945; Michael Zimmer, "The Externalities of Search 2.0: the Emerging Privacy Threats When the Drive for the Perfect Search Engine Meets Web 2.0," *First Monday* 13 (2008), http://www.firstmonday.org/ojs/index.php/fm/article/view/2136/1944 (both sites were accessed on August 6, 2014); and Trebor Scholz, ed., *Digital Labor: the Internet as Playground and Factory* (New York: Routledge, 2013).

tory effects of social media in the process of transforming repressive regimes.[33] With his great trust in media technology as an agent of political change, Shirky thus situates himself within the long history of media being used for political ends.[34] As early as the 1950s, Marshall McLuhan made the following remark: "We can win China and India for the West only by giving them the new media. Russia will not give these to them."[35] As Secretary of State, Hillary Clinton of course did have complete trust in the use of technology for political change; in her initiative for "internet freedom," however, she did stress that free access to information can be a catalyst for social and economic progress:

> We are convinced that an open internet fosters long-term peace, progress, and prosperity. The reverse is also true. An internet that is closed and fractured, where different governments can block activity or change the rules on a whim – where speech is censored or punished, and privacy does not exist – that [...] is an internet that can cut off opportunities for peace and progress and discourage innovation and entrepreneurship.[36]

While these warnings about a closed and fractured internet were implicitly directed toward the Chinese government, the political establishment in the United States – in an ironic twist – was simultaneously pressuring corporations and institutions to cut off all resources to WikiLeaks, a platform for whistleblowers.[37] This is an especially vivid example of the balancing act of politics. After welcoming the emancipatory potential of internet-based forms of civic self-organization, the political sphere then turned around to treat the phenomenon with skepticism. For years, politicians had ignored the socio-formative potential of dispersed and internet-based public spheres while also underestimating the extent to which society was being transformed.[38] For some time, the internet was perceived simply as a new money-making zone for e-commerce and the information economy, and political participation was largely restricted to the liberalization of telecommunications

---

[33] See Clay Shirky, "The Political Power of Social Media," *Foreign Affairs* 90 (February 2011), http://www.foreignaffairs.com/articles/67038/clay-shirky/the-political-power-of-social-media (accessed on August 6, 2014).

[34] For an excellent description of media innovations that were politically motivated, see Dieter Daniels, *Kunst als Sendung: Von der Telegraphie zum Internet* (Munich: Beck, 2000).

[35] Marshall McLuhan, *Counterblast*, 2nd ed. (Berkeley: Transmediale, 2011), n.p.

[36] Quoted from Dan Sabbagh, "Hillary Clinton's Speech: Shades of Hypocrisy on Internet Freedom," *The Guardian* (February 15, 2011), http://www.theguardian.com/world/2011/feb/15/hillary-clinton-internet-freedom (accessed on August 6, 2014).

[37] On the case of WikiLeaks, see the contribution by Christoph Bieber in this volume.

[38] Citing the example of the German Green Party, a recent article in the *Frankfurter Allgemeine Zeitung* discussed the failure of established political parties to recognize the socio-political aspects of the internet. Incompetence regarding the internet, however, can be attributed to all the major parties; in fact, it was such incompetence that fueled the recent formation of thematic parties such as the Pirate Party. See Jan Ludwig, "Grüne und Piraten: Die Freibeuter der Leere," *Frankfurter Allgemeine Zeitung* (November 24, 2011), http://www.faz.net/aktuell/ feuilleton/debatten/digitales-denken/gruene-und-piraten-die-freibeuter-der-leere-11538418.html (accessed on August 6, 2014).

markets. During all of this, civil society was supposed to play the role of consumer. This attitude is exemplified, for instance, in the Clinton Administration's conception of the "information superhighway," which Al Gore described as follows in 1997:

> We are on the verge of a revolution that is just as profound as the change in the economy that came with the industrial revolution. Soon electronic networks will allow people to transcend the barriers of time and distance and take advantage of global markets and business opportunities not even imaginable today, opening up a new world of economic possibility and progress.[39]

In the case of social media and their easy-to-use interfaces, this new world of economic possibility and progress has expanded to include broader aspects of society, including civic participation and collective production. According to the so-called "Eurobaromator," which was used by the authors of the comprehensive *Study on the Social Impact of ICT*, almost all young Europeans and almost all Europeans with an advanced degree use the internet. Twenty-five percent of the poorly educated population is online, and thirty-eight percent of the older generation uses online services in one way or another. The differences between urban and rural areas are considered to be insignificant.[40] The online activity of these users differs little from the online activity in the United States, which the Pew Research Center has investigated in numerous studies.[41] The most common activities include using social network sites, downloading music and videos, shopping and banking online, and the rather vague "searching for information."[42] That said, the *Study on the Social Impact of ICT* also shows that, at least in the European Union, the new information infrastructures and new media practices have not been seamlessly integrated into broader society or civic life. The authors note that the political sphere has not succeeded in using new media to increase civic participation. On the contrary, Jan A. G. M. van Dijk refers explicitly to the gradual decline of European citizens' engagement in public life that has been taking place over the last twenty-five years.[43] Although Van Dijk acknowledges the emancipatory potential of new media, he finds that their use, far from constituting a sort of collective and socio-formative undertaking, can best be described as individualized activity:

---

[39] William J. Clinton and Albert Gore, "A Framework for Global Economic Commerce" (December 1, 1997), http://www.w3.org/TR/NOTE-framework-970706 (accessed on August 6, 2014).

[40] Of course, the study also claims that there is "digital divide" in Europe between the West and East (and the North and South). The Scandinavian countries are the most connected of all and have the most diversified online media practices, whereas the Eastern European countries have room to grow in this regard. See Gyorgy Lengyel et al., "Report on Findings from Flash Eurobarometer," in *Study on the Social Impact of ICT*, Topic Report 3 (April 30, 2010), 474–587, at 492 (http://ec.europa.eu/information_society/newsroom/cf/itemdetail.cfm?item_id=5789; accessed on August 6, 2014).

[41] For Pew's findings regarding online trends, see http://www.pewinternet.org/three-technology-revolutions/ (accessed on August 7, 2014).

[42] Ellen Helsper et al., "Consumption (Incl. Media and Entertainment)," in *Study on the Social Impact of ICT*, 181–225, at 182–83.

[43] Jan A. G. M. van Dijk, "Conceptual Framework," in *Study on the Social Impact of ICT*, 1–31, at 20.

> Online activities contribute to the individualized kind of participation and individual citizen emancipation described. The contemporary citizen acts from his/her own environment and experiences and s(h)e inserts these experiences in public opinion, among others the online public sphere. There is less deductive reasoning from collective political, social or cultural interests.[44]

Sobering, too, are the results of the study regarding the efforts of political administrations to encourage citizens, by means of new media, to participate actively in society, culture, and politics. The authors maintain that there is no indication at all that administrations have had any success in their efforts to reach out to citizens via eParticipation initiatives. Such government-imposed initiatives promise to be less successful than the so-called grass-roots activities initiated by the citizens themselves. In fact, it can be said that governments and political administrations have experimented with electronic participation *not* to include citizens in the political decision-making process but rather simply to bolster their own legitimacy: "The main motive for governments and public administration to start experimenting with eParticipation is to close the gap that is perceived to be growing between governments and citizens and to boost the legitimacy of government policy and administrative decisions."[45] It is therefore hardly surprising that the big players in the internet industry (Zuckerberg among them) are regularly invited to participate in political summit meetings. With their pseudo-democracy and extensively controlled user activities, commercial platforms are presumably regarded as prototypes for the online democracy that governments wish to establish. Zuckerberg's jovial and patriarchal dominion is opposed by ad-hoc collectives, by temporary zones of autonomy, and by the multiplicity of "alternative" media tools and practices.[46] The critics of Web 2.0 and social media often overlook the fact that, at least temporarily, its free applications can be used in ways that are far different from their intended purpose. Platforms are exchangeable and their economy is subject to their volatile user numbers. For distributing messages, for instance, established social media are better suited than obscure alternatives, where there are fewer users to disseminate information. As Ethan Zuckerman has pointed out, the popular platforms are, for a variety of reasons, quite useful for inciting political dissent. For example, if authorities take down a service like YouTube, this action will not go unnoticed. The technical infrastructures of these large platforms are better equipped to handle large numbers of requests, and they are even able to withstand DDOS attacks.[47]

---

44   Ibid., 21.

45   Jan A. G. M. van Dijk, "Participation in Policy-Making," in *Study on the Social Impact of ICT*, 31–79, at 67.

46   Such alternatives have been the topic of the three "Unlike Us" conferences that have been sponsored by Institute of Network Cultures at the University of Amsterdam.

47   See Ethan Zuckerman, "The Cute Cat Theory Talk at ETech," *My Heart's in Accra* (March 8, 2008), http://www.ethanzuckerman.com/blog/2008/03/08/the-cute-cat-theory-talk-at-etech/ (accessed on November 11, 2014).

In discussions about the emancipatory potential of new media, three elements can be identified that need to be examined in closer detail. First is the possibility of mobilizing masses and raising awareness about certain issues; second is free access to information or data; and third is the expansion of traditional political discourses into online public spheres. These three elements are directly connected to one another. In the popular discourse, they are often reduced to particular platforms, whose brand names then become synonymous with the media practice itself. The mobilization of the masses in the Near East is now inseparably associated with Twitter; free access to information is usually discussed with the term "open data"; and the promise of transparency and free access to sensitive information is identified with WikiLeaks. The third aspect, namely the expansion (or multiplication) of the public sphere, was associated with the "blogosphere" until social media usurped the dominant position of the blog.

The old fantasy of a critical and enlightened public is inherent to each of these elements and is treated in various ways in the popular discourse. However, the ambivalent nature of technology and the heterogeneity of media practices prevent us from unequivocally ascribing an emancipatory character to the media themselves. That said, the media are central actors in the transformation of the public sphere. Stefan Münker has shown that the "social" aspect of "social media" manifests itself in the constitution of spaces and practices that have traditionally been understood as "public spheres" in the Habermasian sense.[48] However, the public sphere should not be reduced to Habermas's normatively formulated concept of a homogeneous citizenry. With reference to a more recent definition of the public sphere, suggested by Habermas himself, it is perhaps best to understand it as a network for communicating information and opinions.[49] In light of this pragmatic reduction, and in light of Nancy Fraser's concept of "strong publics" and "weak publics,"[50] the partial public spheres that exist online can certainly be described as "weak." Although it has admittedly been questioned whether online platforms can be regarded as forming public spheres,[51] such media practices and technologies ultimately do nothing else than constitute a network for disseminating information and opinions. In general, this network cannot be said to fulfill the normative demands for rational debate, for egalitarian participation, and for the strict separation of governments and citizens. On the contrary, the following examples will show that the new media encourage heterogeneous and dispersed public spheres, within which specific media practices are used in attempts to reach a broader public audience.

---

[48] Münker, *Emergenz digitaler Öffentlichkeiten* (cited in note 5 above).

[49] See Jürgen Habermas, *Between Facts and Norms: Contributions to a Discourse Theory of Law and Democracy*, trans. William Rehg (Cambridge, MA: MIT Press, 1996).

[50] Nancy Fraser, "Rethinking the Public Sphere: A Contribution to the Critique of Actually Existing Democracy," *Social Text* 25/26 (1990), 56–80, esp. 74–77.

[51] See Jodi Dean, "Why the Net is Not a Public Sphere," *Constellations* 10 (2013), 95–112; and Zizi Papacharissi, *A Private Sphere: Democracy in a Digital Age* (Cambridge, UK: Polity, 2010).

IV. Mobilizing the Masses

The network qualities of new media make it possible to mobilize large numbers of participants. Howard Rheingold has referred to these groups, which are supported by communications technologies, as "smart mobs."[52] Mobile phones and text messages can temporarily function as "tactical media" that are able to spread information far more effectively than the established media services.[53] In an information vacuum or in a strongly regulated media environment, these alternative means of spreading information can reach quite a large audience. As an example of this, Rheingold cited the organization of demonstrations against the Philippine president Joseph Estrada in 2001. Shirky has added the example of the demonstrations in Spain in 2004; in this case, citizens used text messages to organize protests against the conservative government and its response to the terrorist bombings in Madrid.[54] Activists at the Institute for Applied Autonomy have attempted to formalize such practices and to develop applications for the promotion of civic autonomy. Among such applications is "TXTMob," a program that allows text messages to be sent to a large number of mobile phones.[55] Its purpose is to enable demonstrators to organize more effectively and to send quick messages regarding police activity. The commercial counterpart to TXTMob, namely Twitter, has been credited for the successful mobilization of demonstrators after the elections in Iran.[56] In 2009, the U.S. State Department allegedly intervened with Twitter's maintenance schedule to ensure that the service would be available to Iranians on their election day.[57] Whereas Twitter, YouTube, and Flicker were used to disseminate news from Tehran and other Iranian cities, proxy servers were set up for activists to circumvent Iran's tightly controlled internet infrastructure.[58] Both Google and Facebook posted Persian translations of their services.[59] On the so-called Insurgency Wiki, the loose collective known as "Anonymous" urged users to wage a "denial of distributed services attack" to shut down a website run by the Iranian security forces.[60] While the dispersed online public spheres were busy expressing sympathy for

---

[52] Howard Rheingold, *Smart Mobs: The Next Social Revolution* (Cambridge, MA: Perseus, 2003).

[53] See Geert Lovink, *Dark Fiber: Tracking Critical Internet Culture* (Cambridge, MA: MIT Press, 2002), 254.

[54] Shirky, "The Political Power of Social Media," n.p.

[55] For more information about TXTMob visit the website of Institute for Applied Autonomy: http://www.appliedautonomy.com/txtmob.html.

[56] Lev Grossman, "Iran Protests: Twitter, the Medium of the Movement," *Time* (June 17, 2009), http://content.time.com/time/world/article/0,8599,1905125,00.html (accessed on August 6, 2014).

[57] Ibid.

[58] Here it should be noted that Internet Relay Chat (IRC), though typically overlooked in the popular discourse, has been a frequently used channel of communication.

[59] Cyrus Farivar, *The Internet of Elsewhere: The Emergent Effects of a Wired World* (New Brunswick: Rutgers University Press, 2011), 156.

[60] The website in question was Gerdab.ir, which published photographs of demonstrators with the hope that visitors would identify them. Anonymous responded by asking users to install a program called *Epic Fail Cannon*, which can be used to bombard a targeted address with a vast number of

democratic activists in repressive regimes, the criticized authorities attempted to win over public opinion in the blogosphere and to block the communication channels of activists with (mostly Western) technologies.[61]

V. The Expansion of Political Discourses

The media practices mentioned above require varying levels of technological competence. In general, it is crucial for participation in online public spheres to be possible with minimal or even no technical knowledge. Such is the case, for instance, with blogging services such as Google's Blogger.com. For their part, Twitter and Facebook allow internet users to publish online without any technical know-how. This simplification of the publication process has led to an exponential increase in the number of blogs.[62] The blogosphere consists in large part of casual bloggers who write about their favorite topics. There is also a large number of authors whose blogs are associated with their professional interests or are directly related to their professional activity. Only a small group of people earn their living by blogging. The blogosphere provides a space for commentary and serves as an alternative outlet for ideas that are not always expressed or covered by the established media.[63]

In addition to "traditional" blogs, there are now micro-blogging services such as Twitter.[64] In a study of the Dutch political "Twittersphere," my colleagues and I have shown that this short-messaging service is by now an integral component of both the blogosphere and the traditional media landscape. In fact, an analysis of actively tweeting members of parliament and a select group of Twitter accounts (each of which is followed by at least four politicians) suggests that Twitter should be regarded as an expansion of the

---

requests. In an updated version of the program, called *Low Orbit Ion Cannon*, the application can be controlled by a third party to exhaust the computing and network capacities of targeted websites. For a good description of this process, see Aiko Pras et al., "Attacks by 'Anonymous' WikiLeaks Proponents not Anonymous," *CTIT Technical Report 10.41* (December 10, 2010), http://doc.utwente.nl/75331/1/2010-12-CTIT-TR.pdf (accessed on August 6, 2014).

[61] Farivar, *The Internet of Elsewhere*, 6. In his book *The Net Delusion: How Not to Liberate the World* (New York: Public Affairs, 2011), Evgeny Morozov offered a counter-argument against the success stories of internet activism and demonstrated how repressive regimes have used new media with great success to oppress dissent and activism.

[62] See *Technorati*'s annual reports on the "State of the Blogosphere," a feature that was renamed in 2013 as the "Digital Influence Report": http://technorati.com/report/2013-dir/ (accessed on August 8, 2014).

[63] Such outlets also include politically radical platforms such as the German anti-Muslim blog *Politically Incorrect*: http://www.pi-news.net/ (accessed on August 8, 2014).

[64] Twitter allows messages to be sent that do not exceed 140 characters. Twitter users can subscribe to receive the messages of other users by "following" them, and many users are followed by thousands of people. For instance, Geert Wilders, the leader of the Dutch Party for Freedom, has more than 330,000 followers.

public sphere.[65] On a qualitative level, we were able to show that the participants in this sample were largely engaged in discussing political issues, running campaigns, and calling attention to their respective positions. Communication took place between members of civil society, politicians, numerous journalists, and various PR representatives. Here there is thus a mixture of the strong and weak publics, those that are actively engaged in the legislative process and those that are engaged in formulating political opinions. Such debates are closely associated with the daily political commentary in the traditional media. Almost every other tweet in our sample contained a hyperlink to a website, many of which belonged to established media outlets. These outlets themselves are actively tweeting, either from accounts representing the media companies in question or from accounts used by journalists to promote their own publications. The tweets by politicians are often direct responses to reports in the press.[66]

With Twitter, users are able both to send and receive messages. Politicians like Geert Wilders use their accounts exclusively as senders and never respond to messages that have been sent to them with the request to "@reply." The analysis became rather interesting at the micro-level, however. Here it was revealed that small networks of relations were created within the national Twittersphere by the mutual exchange of tweets (@reply and @mention). Figure 3 shows a "retweet" network from the Dutch political sphere; in particular, it displays the accounts retweeted by member of the Dutch parliament. The more popular an account became, the more frequently it would be retweeted, and the more an account has been retweeted by the overall political spectrum, the more it is emphasized in the visualization. At the core of this process are journalists, political commentators, PR experts, young politicians (who are especially willing to make use of new means of communication), bloggers, and engaged citizens of the online public sphere in the Netherlands. The result is an intricate and informal information network that represents a new channel beyond the networks that are already in place. Of course, not everyone participates in this medium, but the network is nevertheless surprisingly heterogeneous and shows that the distance between journalists, bloggers, active citizens, and professional politicians has become smaller. There is some indication, moreover, that active Twitter users are capable of generating a good deal of public attention and debate about political issues.

The mobilization of participants, the generation of attention, access to information, and the establishment of networks of political discourse are each integral elements of the transforming public sphere. However, the often-presumed emancipatory potential of such activity on Twitter is only one side of the story. Applications such as Facebook can also

---

[65] See Mirko Tobias Schäfer et al., "Politiek in 140 tekens," in *Voorgeprogrammeerd: Hoe Internet ons leven leidt*, ed. Christian van 't Hof et al. (The Hague: Rathenau Instituut, 2012), 193–214. Over the course of five weeks in October and November of 2011, we saved all the tweets produced by our sample, which consisted of ninety-seven politicians in the Dutch parliament and 383 Twitter users that were "followed" by at least four politicians. The number of saved messages reached 124,000.

[66] Over the course of our study, the most "tweeted-about" media production was the television program *Pauw & Wittemann*, a political talk-show.

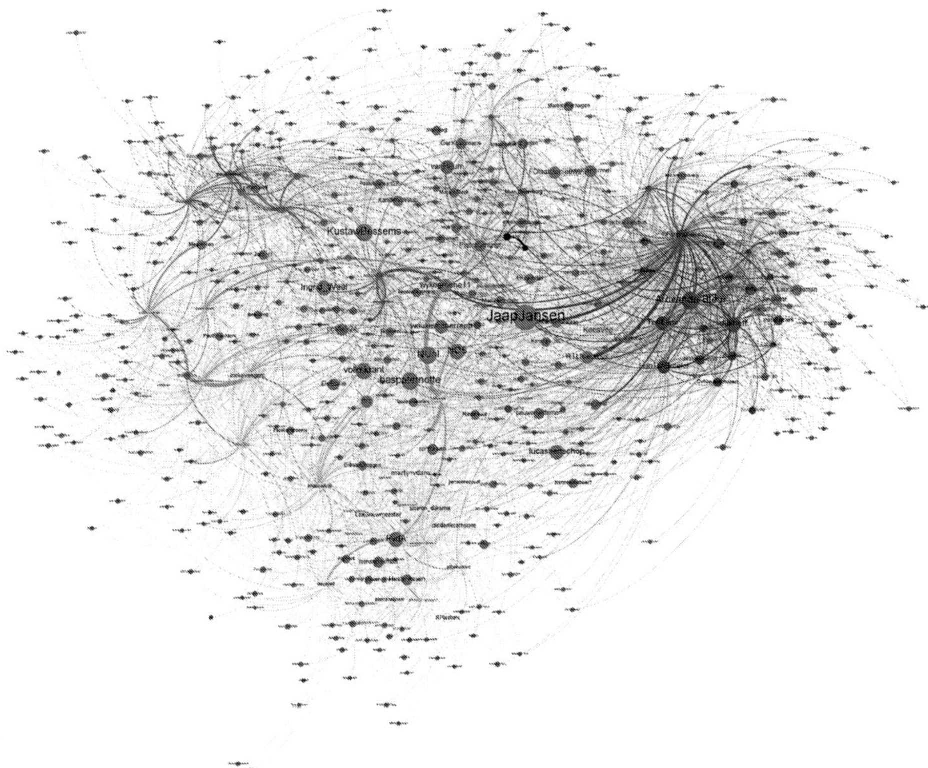

Figure 3: A graph of the "retweets" exchanged by members of the political Twittersphere in the Netherlands (created by Thomas Boeschoten with Gephi visualization software and the algorithm Force Atlas 2)

serve as platforms for political criticism, just as Twitter can be used as a pure broadcasting medium or as an effective PR instrument to make a politician seem "internet savvy."

VI. The Public Sphere in Transition

The extensive integration of new media into all aspects of society has brought about a new set of challenges. For one, the multiplication of public spheres now means that every opinion can find a publication niche on the internet. At the same time, many of these internal discourses are associated with those of the mainstream media and can occasionally capture the attention of the broader public. A homogeneous public sphere exists neither online nor offline. Yet the dynamic of fragmentation and clustering appears to be even more volatile online than offline. The audiences for political discussions are volatile, and attention can only be held temporarily. Debates concerning geopolitical issues resemble those concerning the technical designs of web applications, at least to the extent that they focus on cultural freedom or the personal integrity of users. Often enough, online attention is dictated by instant reactions, gut feelings, shock, and amusement. The sensational, the appalling, the shocking receives a great deal of attention and creates an incredible noise of redundancy, inadequacy, ignorance and immaturity. This noise distorts informed debate and fuels populism.

The commercial platforms of the "social web" are often treated like public space, even though they are administered by entities that lack democratic legitimacy. Facebook's various programs encouraging user participation are attempts to give off the appearance of collectively legitimized sovereignty. With their attempts to initiate technology-based civic participation, governments, too, seem to be doing nothing more than waging PR campaigns to corroborate their own legitimacy.

For engaged citizens, the new media certainly offer certain possibilities to participate in socio-political debates. It has become commonplace in the new media landscape for the discourse to be opened up to those who are not members of the professional media. The question remains about how governments and political administrations intend to use the new media, that is, whether they are genuinely interested in integrating civic engagement or are rather inclined to follow Facebook's model of controlled participation. These questions, among others, will have to be negotiated in light of the new role assigned to citizens and users on social media, that is, on the "commodified" version of the internet. Here lawmakers will have the opportunity to limit the ability of companies to control user data and to profit from such information.

In the end, a new and dynamic type of interaction has emerged between the emulation of traditional forms of political organization and the constitution of new (counter)publics with online media. It has also become clear, moreover, that questions of proprietorship and the legal integration of platforms are not the only issues of socio-political importance. Significant, too, is the role of software design, which ultimately contributes to the formation of something like a "programmed public sphere."[67] In light of governmental efforts to use new media to encourage electronic civic participation and to model these efforts according to the regulatory structures imposed by the leading companies in the internet industry, it is necessary to hold an informed and critical discussion about these new technologies and their socio-political implications. The challenge facing the field of media studies is to develop methods for analyzing the technological foundation that underlies both current representations of power and the oppositional establishment of counterpublics.

---

[67]   For more on the notion of the programmed public sphere, see Christoph Bieber's chapter in this book.

Christoph Bieber

Toward an Ethics of the Leak?
WikiLeaks as a Programmed Public Sphere

As the example of WikiLeaks has made clear, the new technological means of creating, reproducing, and disseminating documents have contributed to the rise of what might be called an "economy of the leak." Digitalization, above all, has made it possible to share not only "simple" written documents and audio recordings but also film sequences, abstract collections of data, and shorter texts in the form of emails and text messages. The process of sharing information has changed as well. Whereas the so-called "fourth estate" had once functioned as the somewhat autarkical caretakers of information, by now there are NGOs such as WikiLeaks and specialized watchdog organizations that are likewise engaged in spreading news. The latter organizations, which are decentralized networks, are also able to protect whistleblowers in ways that are more secure than the protections offered by the conventional media. Jay Rosen has underscored the innovative potential of these new configurations by referring to WikiLeaks as "the world's first stateless news organization."[1] For Yochai Benkler, the case of WikiLeaks is an important indicator of the emergence of a "networked fourth estate," one that already has considerable influence over the political media content that is available.[2] In light of the technological implications involved with the new digital practices of divulging information, as exemplified by WikiLeaks, it is possible to speak of a "programmed public sphere." Throughout this development, the effects of "massification" have played an essential role, both by creating collaborative digital platforms with highly flexible divisions of labor and by treating digital information as a universally accessible raw material that can be received, organized, and disseminated in an automated manner.

My discussion below will be divided into six parts. In the first I will examine, from the perspective of political science, the different ways of characterizing the documents released by WikiLeaks. Here a specific distinction will be drawn between *policy*-oriented

---

[1] Jay Rosen, "The Afghanistan War Logs Released by WikiLeaks, the World's First Stateless News Organization," *PressThink* (July 26, 2010), http://pressthink.org/2010/07/the-afghanistan-war-logs-released-by-wikileaks-the-worlds-first-stateless-news-organization/ (accessed on July 17, 2014).

[2] Yochai Benkler, "A Free Irresponsible Press: WikiLeaks and the Battle over the Soul of the Networked Fourth Estate," *Harvard Civil Rights-Civil Liberties Law Review* 46 (2011), 311–97.

leaks and leaks that are oriented toward *politics*. My second aim will be to describe WikiLeaks as a "transparency activist," the role of which is dependent on the creation of a particular sort of public sphere. In this regard it will be shown, third, how WikiLeaks has experimented with various strategies in order to reach a public audience, strategies that have oscillated from acting as a closed and self-sufficient online platform to functioning as a part of a "networked fourth estate." My fourth concern will be to demonstrate the significance of code in the generation of "programmed public spheres." This will be followed, fifth, by a brief theoretical sketch of the concept of "formative public spheres" (*"Gestaltungsöffentlichkeiten"*) and this sketch will enable me to describe the nature of various leaking processes. Finally, some considerations will be offered concerning the new phenomenon of transparency activism and the "ethics of the leak" associated with it.

I. Policy and Politics: Two Types of Leak

What is immediately striking about the "WikiLeaks revelations," at least from the perspective of political science, is that it was not until the release of the *fourth* leak, in 2010, that a truly intensive public discussion ensued. Before that time, the transparency activists working around Julian Assange had only managed to attract relatively minor attention. Serious attention was attracted above all by the distribution, on April 5, 2010, of a video titled "Collateral Murder," which depicts a U.S. helicopter attack on a group of civilians in Bagdad and which had been made available on an anonymous website.[3]

This visual intervention into the debates about the Iraq War was soon followed, in July and October of the same year, by the respective publications of the so-called "Afghan War Logs" and "Iraq War Logs," which were released in association with prominent media outlets such as *The New York Times*, *The Guardian*, and *Der Spiegel*.[4] These releases contained military protocols with detailed descriptions of combat activity in both countries,

---

[3]   See ibid., 321–26; Raffi Khatchadourian, "No Secrets: Julian Assange's Mission for Total Transparency," *New Yorker* (June 7, 2010), http://www.newyorker.com/magazine/2010/06/07/no-secrets?currentPage=all (accessed on July 21, 2014); Micah L. Sifry, *WikiLeaks and the Age of Transparency* (Berkeley: Counterpoint, 2011); Christoph Bieber, "Lessons of the Leak," in *A Companion to New Media Dynamics*, ed. John Hartley et al. (Chichester: Wiley-Blackwell, 2013), 322–35; and the website www.collateralmurder.com (accessed on July 17, 2014).

[4]   All three of these media outlets provided "exclusive" background information about the editorial practices that were used during the process of publishing the leaks. Regarding *The New York Times*, see Alexander Star and Bill Keller, *Open Secrets: WikiLeaks, War, and American Diplomacy* (New York: Grove Press, 2011); as regards *The Guardian*, see David Leigh et al., *WikiLeaks: Inside Julian Assange's War on Secrecy* (New York: Public Affairs, 2011); and regarding *Der Spiegel*, see Marcel Rosenbach and Holger Stark, *Staatsfeind Wikileaks: Wie eine Gruppe von Netzaktivisten die mächtigsten Nationen der Welt herausfordert* (Munich: DVA, 2011). Later in the year 2010, WikiLeaks expanded its publishing network to include *Le Monde* in France and *El Pais* in Spain. In June of 2011, moreover, the organization began to cooperate with *Pública*, a non-profit media outlet in Brazil that initiated a feature called "Semana WikiLeaks" ("WikiLeaks Week"); see http://apublica.org/2011/08/semana-wikileaks/ (accessed on July 21, 2014).

including the documentation and interpretation of incidents that undoubtedly constituted war crimes. The materials in question were provided by a "leak," an unauthorized (and still unidentified) source from within the U.S. military who decided to share classified information. They were quite obviously copied from insecure computer networks and passed along. WikiLeaks received the information, made it legible (when necessary) and published it either independently or in conjunction with its partners in the media. Already at this point it is clear that the practice of sharing sensitive data has changed considerably and that this shift was brought about by a change in media technologies. Although the leak of the so-called "Pentagon Papers" in 1969 represented a similar effort to disclose classified information, the analogue nature of these documents (nearly 7,000 pages) severely hindered their distribution and publication.[5]

Each of the three examples mentioned above can be said to constitute a sort of "policy leak." They are leaks of information concerned with specific areas of U.S. foreign policy and their aim was to discredit the political agendas of those operating within these spheres. In other words, the "Collateral Murder" video and the millions of documents concerned with Iraq and Afghanistan were released in order to influence public opinion, bring the wars to an end, and thus to initiate a major change in American foreign policy. The material was released in particular to discredit political figures whose "official" positions were shown to contradict the contents of the leaked documents.

It was hoped that political change could be realized by using communication channels and resources that lay outside of the formal structures and processes employed by government bureaucracies. Along with the disclosure of general malfeasance and individual wrongdoing, the goal of ushering forth an age of transparency is reminiscent of a structural principle of modern government according to which political agents, by means of the mass media, will use the public as a sounding board before implementing their own political agendas. Such attempts to sway public opinion are made in order to predefine the course of political or parliamentary decision processes in such a way as to weaken the position of political opponents. WikiLeaks has appropriated this very concept in order to install a mechanism for political critique "from the outside," and its efforts have come to be used as a representative blueprint by other "transparency activists."[6] The leaks served to provide a connection between the secure and "secretive" *modus operandi* of political networks (of which the U.S. State Department, U.S. military, and their international allies were all a part) and the general public. They also, however, made sensitive information available to the wartime enemies of the United States.

This policy-oriented exertion of influence by an organization outside of conventional (and democratically legitimized) processes must be distinguished from the leaking of diplomatic dispatches during November of 2011, for these published documents were of

---

[5]   See Benkler, "A Free Irresponsible Press," 351–54.

[6]   As Micah L. Sifry has discussed in his book *WikiLeaks and the Age of Transparency*, such activism is concerned with holding political figures accountable and with using digital platforms (among others) to disclose errors, wrongdoing, contradictions, and illegal behavior in the political process.

an entirely different nature. The object of the latter leak was the contents of communication within a single agency. The fact that the leaked materials concerned the U.S. State Department, which operates around the globe, increased their effects considerably. The so-called "diplomatic cables" contained profiles of prominent international politicians as well as dossiers about the internal affairs of certain countries and the notes taken by American foreign-service officers during diplomatic meetings. The contents of the individual dispatches covered an entire range of topics; that is, the leaked material did not focus on one particular political issue or another. For this reason, the "Cablegate" episode (as it came to be called) can be said to represent a *politics*-oriented leak, one that involved the publication of documents concerned with general political processes. Specifically, the leaked material consisted of an agency's "throughput" documents that were certainly not meant to be published, or at least not immediately.

At first, the disclosures made by WikiLeaks served to expose the secretive communications processes that took place within an important agency. The released "cables" thus provided insight into the agency's "informal operations," and such operations were not necessarily associated with political activity or any specific "output" or goal. Rather, the leaked information often consisted of subjective statements and positions, confidential deals and judgments, or simply incomplete collections of raw data. The British historian Timothy Garton Ash summed up this distinction with the following appropriate remark: "A diplomat's nightmare is a historian's dream."[7]

II. WikiLeaks and Transparency Activism

The text released alongside the "Collateral Murder" video is unequivocal about WikiLeaks's activism on behalf of transparency:

> WikiLeaks obtained this video as well as supporting documents from a number of military whistleblowers. WikiLeaks goes to great lengths to verify the authenticity of the information it receives. We have analyzed the information about this incident from a variety of source material. We have spoken to witnesses and journalists directly involved in the incident. WikiLeaks wants to ensure that all the leaked information it receives gets the attention it deserves. In this particular case, some of the people killed were journalists that were simply doing their jobs: putting their lives at risk in order to report on war. Iraq is a very dangerous place for journalists: from 2003–2009, 139 journalists were killed while doing their work.[8]

To this day, little is known about the specific form of the organization "behind" the various leaks. At first, the public statements by Julian Assange and Daniel Domscheit-Berg (then under the pseudonym Daniel Schmitt) were contested and attributed to Assange

---

7   Timothy Garton Ash, "U.S. Embassy Cables: A Banquet of Secrets," *The Guardian* (November 28, 2010), http://www.theguardian.com/commentisfree/2010/nov/28/wikileaks-diplomacy-us-media-war (accessed on July 21, 2014).

8   Quoted from http://www.collateralmurder.com/ (accessed on July 17, 2014).

alone. In the meantime, this gesture of personalization led to the unfortunate conflation of an organization (WikiLeaks) with a person (Assange). Even during the early discussions between Assange and Schmitt, the argument had been raised that, as an organization, WikiLeaks could operate only "anonymously" or "in secrecy," for there would be no other way to protect the activists engaged in its "operations." Beyond a few journalistic reports and Domscheit-Berg's own "insider" account,[9] there is hardly any information about WikiLeaks's organizational structure, operations, or internal policies. The organization's self-description on its website concentrates on its mission but makes no mention of formal or structural issues:

> WikiLeaks is a non-profit media organization dedicated to bringing important news and information to the public. We provide an innovative, secure and anonymous way for independent sources around the world to leak information to our journalists. We publish material of ethical, political and historical significance while keeping the identity of our sources anonymous, thus providing a universal way for the revealing of suppressed and censored injustices.[10]

In his numerous statements concerning the idea, self-conception, and political positions of WikiLeaks, Assange has regularly described it in terms of providing a new form of investigative journalism that can operate in conjunction with the established media in various ways:

> [I]t was my view early on that the whole of the existing Fourth Estate was not big enough for the task of making sense of information that hadn't previously been public. To take our most recent case as an example, all the journalists in the world would not be enough to make complete sense of the 400,000 documents we released about Iraq, and, of course, they have other things to write about as well.[11]

On account of its close collaboration with established media outlets, Assange's self-assured comments on its website, and the portrayal of Assange as a leading media activist and face of the operation, WikiLeaks quickly established the reputation of being a new – though rather vague – media organization. According to Benkler, WikiLeaks gained this position over the course of a "battle" with the established media and with the political apparatus.[12] As an unwanted intruder, it was thus incessantly criticized or even demonized, and Julian Assange was painted to be a massive threat to American society:

---

9   See, for example, Khatchadourian, "No Secrets: Julian Assange's Mission for Total Transparency"; and Daniel Domscheit-Berg, *Inside Wikileaks: My Time with Julian Assange at the World's Most Dangerous Website* (London: Crown, 2010).

10   Quoted from http://www.wikileaks.org/About.html (accessed on July 17, 2014).

11   These remarks by Julian Assange are quoted from Hans Ulrich Obrist, "In Conversation with Julian Assange, Part I," *e-flux* (May 2011), http://www.e-flux.com/journal/in-conversation-with-julian-assange-part-i/ (accessed on July 17, 2014).

12   Benkler, "A Free Irresponsible Press," *passim.*

Throughout the events, Assange and WikiLeaks emphasized their role as journalists. Inverting the practices of those who sought to analogize WikiLeaks to terrorists, some commentators and reporters emphasized the basic argument that WikiLeaks is a reporting organization, fulfilling a reporting function.[13]

In one of the early posts on his blog *Press Think*, Jay Rosen referred to WikiLeaks as the "world's first stateless news organization" in order to distinguish it from other political and media organizations. In particular, it is different because of its

> release of information without regard for national interest. In media history up to now, the press is free to report on what the powerful wish to keep secret because the laws of a given nation protect it. But WikiLeaks is able to report on what the powerful wish to keep secret because the logic of the Internet permits it. This is new.[14]

What Rosen regards as crucial is thus not the legally established freedom of the press, which guarantees the right to publish opinions that are potentially critical of the state, but rather WikiLeaks's media-technological and logical independence from any single state apparatus, that is, its dispersed infrastructure and decentralized organization of information. Charlie Beckett and James Ball have formulated one of the few positive responses to the question of WikiLeaks's status as an organization. Looking back with hindsight at the leaking process during the year 2010, they also suggest that WikiLeaks's model might be sustainable:

> It is a hybrid entity that exploits the global digital information network both to source its material and to distribute it. While theoretically subject to legal and extra-legal actions, it has avoided sanctions and remains at one distinct remove from being a conventional media or political enterprise. [...] WikiLeaks looks set to continue with its model of an independent organization that enters into collaboration with other media to process and publish classified information – transnational, if not transitory.[15]

Although WikiLeaks differs in several fundamental respects from established media outlets (in terms of its formal organization and legal status, its size, financial security, and degree of professionalization), Benkler argues that it must be treated in a similar manner and – what is more – that it must likewise be offered constitutional protection:

> The difference between the constituents of the networked fourth estate and the mass media cannot, then, be organizational size or complexity. Functionally, it is more important to provide robust

---

13   Ibid., 348.

14   Jay Rosen, "The Afghanistan War Logs Released by Wikileaks, the World's First Stateless News Organization," *PressThink* (July 26, 2010), http://pressthink.org/2010/07/the-afghanistan-war-logs-released-by-wikileaks-the-worlds-first-stateless-news-organization/ (accessed on July 17, 2014).

15   Charlie Beckett and James Ball, *WikiLeaks: News in the Networked Era* (Cambridge, UK: Polity Press, 2012), 147.

constitutional protection to the weaker members of the fourth estate, who have less public visibility and wherewithal to withstand pressure from government officials, than it is to emphasize the rights of the organizationally and economically stronger members of the press.[16]

Much of WikiLeaks's distinctness is that it is far more undefined than most of the members of the "fourth estate." Under the conditions of digital and interactive communication environments, the classical features of mass-media communication – such as high circulation and broad coverage, organization, and institutionalization – now exist alongside other strategies for taking over the media's functions in society, including the creation of transparency in the public sphere and the role of criticizing and controlling political activity. The question of whether the practice of leaking represents a new manifestation of investigative journalism is, at least in the United States, the dominant issue in the public debates about WikiLeaks. Even if Benkler's argument is accepted and it is assumed that WikiLeaks warrants protection as a new member of the fourth estate, the result is still a certain degree of ambivalence. For the fact of the matter is that WikiLeaks itself, a self-proclaimed organization for transparency activism, operates in a manner that is inconspicuous and secretive – that is, as intransparently as possible:

It is telling, however, that even WikiLeaks does not stand for a world of total transparency. Instead, it engenders new secrets of its own, given that the people behind the organization act according a double standard. [...] Whereas the organization treats the personal consequences faced by diplomats and their sources as mere "collateral damage" in the struggle for transparency, it operates with hardly any transparency itself, it is not controlled by anybody, and it ensures the total protection and anonymity of its own sources. In such a way, WikiLeaks has simply created a new set of secrets. Regarding foreign policy, it is no longer the state that decides which information should be kept secret; it is rather a group of people that is entirely unaccountable.[17]

However fruitful it might be here to conduct a thorough sociological analysis of WikiLeaks as an agent of change, the paucity of sources about the organization and its leader happens to preclude the possibility of such an investigation. According to Felix Stalder, this dilemma can be avoided by assuming that Assange is in fact a so-called "super-empowered individual" who is able to exert a vast amount of influence with the support of only a small group of people. In this regard, the great importance of WikiLeaks's informality comes to light, and Stalder goes so far as to describe the website with terminology that is usually reserved for cells or networks of terrorists, the existence of which

---

[16] Benkler, "A Free Irresponsible Press," 357.

[17] Wolfgang Ischinger, "Das WikiLeaks-Paradox: Weniger Transparenz, Mehr Geheimdiplomatie," in *WikiLeaks und die Folgen: Die Hintergründe. Die Konsequenten*, ed. Heinrich Geiselberger (Berlin: Suhrkamp, 2011), 155–63, at 160. See also Lucia Görke and Kathrin Morgenstern, "Ambivalente Transparenz: Vorgehensweise und Funktion von Wikileaks," *Politische Studien* 439 (2011), 16–29.

depends on opaque and furtive activity.[18] In any case, he discusses the concept of the super-empowered individual in the following terms:

> It [...] highlights how individuals, or more likely, small groups, can affect these systems dispro-
> portionately if they manage to interfere with these critical nodes. Thus, individuals, supported
> by small, networked organizations, can now intervene in social dynamics at a systemic level,
> for better or worse. This picture fits WikiLeaks, organized around one charismatic individual,
> very well.[19]

This underscores the importance of lacking a specific, comprehensible, and visible structure. Informality and intransparency are the keystones of WikiLeaks's organizational principle, and thus it is able to deal with its partners and participants in a highly flexible manner. The ambivalent nature of WikiLeaks's self-conception and self-organization is especially significant for the development of an "ethics of the leak," which I will return to at the end of this essay.

III. WikiLeaks and the Media

Digitalization has resulted in multiple new ways of creating, reproducing, and disseminating documents in a variety of different formats. People can now deal with texts, images, and videos in such a way that it can be difficult to ascertain any differences between the personal and professional generation of media. It is highly likely that this explosion of digital data will soon lead to an "economy of the leak," and it is just as likely that WikiLeaks will come to be regarded as a prefiguration of this development. At least as far as technology is concerned, it has become easier and easier to distribute sensitive information. A typical example of this is the leaked CD containing the names of German tax evaders (the so-called *Steuersünder-CD*). Over the past few years, more and more account information of this sort (typically from banks in Switzerland and Liechtenstein) has been brought to the attention of German authorities. This process would have been far more difficult under analogue conditions, given that the data would have had to have been laboriously copied before being handed over.

In addition to these technological aspects, the process of digital leaking also has consequences for the recipients of the information. Whereas sensitive information had typically been passed along in a clandestine manner to representatives of the traditional mass

---

[18] Despite the use of the term "cell" and the emphasis placed here on (extremely) small organizational structures, activism is not necessarily trending toward "miniaturization." The possibility of networked communication also enables the mobilization of larger groups such as the activist collective known as "Anonymous."

[19] Felix Stalder, "Contain This! Leaks, Whistle-Blowers and the Networked News Ecology," *Mute* 3 (November 4, 2010), http://www.metamute.org/editorial/articles/contain-leaks-whistle-blowers-and-networked-news-ecology (accessed on July 22, 2014).

media,[20] today it is the case that NGOs, associations, and even individual bloggers can serve as relay stations for such leaks. In several respects, however, professional journalists have proven to be highly useful in this process, above all by sifting through and editing large collections of unstructured data. Even WikiLeaks could not have accomplished its self-proclaimed goal of global visibility without the assistance of professional media companies such as *The New York Times*, *The Guardian*, or *Der Spiegel*. WikiLeaks's main contributions were to receive the data, archive it, and "cleanse" it of any digital traces that might incriminate whoever had been involved with the leak.

WikiLeaks has also made substantial changes to the "division of labor" that is typical of conventional investigative journalism. It can offer far better protection to people wishing to disclose "dangerous information" than can be offered by any of traditional representatives of the fourth estate. One reason for this, in addition to its ability to eliminate any digital traces that might connect a leaked document with a given informant, is the fact that WikiLeaks is a decentralized shadow organization that is positioned somewhere in the gaps between various national legal systems.[21] In contrast, the strength of professional journalism lies in its adeptness at validating and authenticating raw data as well as in its development of narratives and its editorial activity, which is necessary in order to make large amounts of data available and intelligible to a large audience.

Although WikiLeaks was not the only platform that distributed the military documents and diplomatic cables, it is quite clear that the organization, and Julian Assange in particular, were the driving forces behind the leaking process. WikiLeaks's pursuit of the largest possible audience, which took various turns during the publications released throughout 2010, made it likewise clear that the use, image, and place of the news media were all undergoing radical changes and that these changes were of immediate relevance to the societal construction of medial and political public spheres. Although the political public sphere continues in large part to be created by means of the traditional mass media, the many publications "powered by WikiLeaks" strongly suggest that a new sort of public sphere has emerged.

That WikiLeaks is not a singular example is evidenced by the efforts of several organizations to "copy" its model, especially in the wake of the lawsuit filed against Assange and the house arrest that resulted from it. These "heirs to WikiLeaks," as they were known early on, are similarly engaged in receiving leaked digital information, a process for which

---

[20] Some of the most prominent representatives of this former stage of leaking were also mentioned on several occasions in the debates about WikiLeaks: Daniel Ellsberg, who had copied the so-called "Pentagon Papers" and passed them along to *The New York Times*, as well as Bob Woodward and Carl Bernstein, who as reporters for *The Washington Post* had received information concerning the Watergate scandal from an anonymous source ("Deep Throat"). It is thus hardly a coincidence that the Pentagon Papers have been cited as a precedent in the legal discussions about WikiLeaks's activity. See Benkler, "A Free Irresponsible Press," 351–52; and Mercedes Bunz, "Das offene Geheimnis: Zur Politik der Wahrheit im Datenjournalismus," in *WikiLeaks und die Folgen: Die Hintergründe. Die Konsequenten*, ed. Heinrich Geiselberger (Berlin: Suhrkamp, 2011), 134–51.

[21] Benkler, "A Free Irresponsible Press," 356.

they have developed various strategies and approaches. One of such "heirs," for instance, is OpenLeaks.org, which was initiated by Domscheit-Berg and Herbert Snorrason, both of whom were formerly associated with WikiLeaks.[22] A website was set up for this organization in January of 2011, but it is no longer active. There is no evidence, moreover, that OpenLeaks.org ever received or published any sensitive information. Nevertheless, the short-lived or dormant platform has made some substantial contributions to our understanding of leaking as a communicative process. Domscheit-Berg and his fellow activists developed a model according to which the process of leaking is divided into four distinct stages. In this regard, OpenLeaks.org hoped to concentrate on the reception and "cleansing" of leaked digital documents, whereas the acts of editing and publishing them would be left to others. By such means, it was thought that certain problems that are specific to one stage or another could be dealt with more effectively:

> There are two major parts to the process of leaking: submission of material and publication of it. By concentrating on the submission part we attain two desirable goals: 1) increasing the security for all parties involved, 2) improving scalability by minimizing bottlenecks and reducing complexity in our organization.[23]

The developers of OpenLeaks thus focused their attention primarily on ensuring security and anonymity during the processing of digital documents. The importance of such issues came to light especially in the rash efforts of professional media outlets to set up leaking portals of their own. The most prominent example of this is *The Wall Street Journal*'s short-lived establishment of something called "SafeHouse,"[24] which failed to live up to its own security standards. The project was abandoned after it had received criticism for not adequately protecting the anonymity of its contributors.[25]

---

[22] The platform's website (www.openleaks.org) is now defunct. For a description of this new organization, see the last chapter of Domscheit-Berg's book *Inside Wikileaks*, the title of which is "The Promise of OpenLeaks."

[23] Quoted from OpenLeaks's page devoted to frequently asked questions, which is archived at the following site: http://archive.today/xfrHX (accessed on July 17, 2014).

[24] See http://online.wsj.com/public/page/news-tips.html (accessed on July 24, 2014).

[25] See Adam Martin, "Privacy Advocate Doesn't Trust the Wall Street Journal's Safehouse," *The Atlantic* (May 5, 2011), which is now available online at http://www.thewire.com/business/2011/05/privacy-advocate-doesnt-trust-wall-street-journal-safehouse/37410/ (accessed on July 24, 2014); and Dan Gillmor, "Wall Street Journal's Fail(Safe)House: Keep Trying," *Mediactive* (May 6, 2011), http://mediactive.com/category/privacy/ (accessed on July 17, 2014). A similar project was begun in Germany by the *Westdeutsche Allgemeine Zeitung*. The newspaper's research team has set up a website that offers potential informants a secure platform for exchanging information (see http://www.derwesten.de/recherche). As of now there have been no reports that the site has been infiltrated. In the paper's semi-annual report, the service was described as being a great success, even though its users have been more inclined to provide tips about potentially noteworthy material than to provide the documents themselves. See http://www.derwesten-recherche.org/2011/07/in-eigener-sache-nachrichten-aus-anonymen-quellen/ (accessed on July 24, 2014).

Whereas *The New York Times*, *The Guardian*, and *Der Spiegel* have been reluctant to institute their own leaking portals, the news broadcaster Al-Jazeera has created a so-called "Transparency Unit." The occasion for this was the publication of several documents pertaining to the Israeli-Palestinian conflict (the so-called "Palestine Papers"). The initiative has been described as a new sort of "participative journalism":

> The Al Jazeera Transparency Unit (AJTU) aims to mobilize its audience – both in the Arab world and further afield – to submit all forms of content (documents, photos, audio & video clips, as well as "story tips") for editorial review and, if merited, online broadcast and transmission on our English and Arabic-language broadcasts.[26]

With the success of WikiLeaks's activities in mind, professional news outlets have been patently eager to make use of and process leaked information, even if such information concerns the media system itself. There are still reservations, however, about whether these platforms are able to offer enough security and protection to informants. Moreover, the legal status of these services is frequently unclear because their terms of use have been formulated rather imprecisely. Professional observers are therefore undecided about the security measures that the classical media companies can offer to those who are willing to hand over controversial, classified, or even dangerous documents.

The journalist and author Dan Gillmor, for instance, has expressed mixed feelings about the efforts of traditional journalism to adopt the methods of WikiLeaks:

> While I tend to believe that every news organization should have a drop-off point for documents from whistleblowers, there's always going to be a question of how much a leaker should trust any private company on which a government can exert pressure, apart from the issue of whether the company itself can always be trusted.[27]

At this point it is clear that there is a close connection between the leaking process and the political system. For even if documents are released that have no immediate relevance to any particular political figure, the possibility nevertheless remains that political influence will be exerted over the people and platforms engaged in the leak. Even though the growing number websites devoted to disclosing information provides evidence for a booming "economy of the leak," the example of WikiLeaks also demonstrates that there are ways and means to quell or impede the unwanted dissemination of official documents.[28]

---

[26] Quoted from Al Jazeera's page titled "About the Transparency Unit": http://transparency.aljazeera.net/en/ aboutus/ (accessed on July 17, 2014).

[27] Dan Gillmor, "Wall Street Journal's Fail(Safe)House: Keep Trying," *Mediactive* (May 6, 2011), http://mediactive.com/category/privacy/ (accessed on July 17, 2014).

[28] An example of this is the so-called "financial blockade" that was set up against WikiLeaks's activity. Credit card companies and certain providers of online financial services froze the organization's accounts, thereby suspending its ability to spend money. Even though this blockade was instituted without any official request from the U.S. government, several politicians insinuated that the companies in question would have faced certain consequences had they continued to facilitate WikiLeaks's

IV. WikiLeaks, Code, and the Programming of Public Spheres

As a platform for digital transparency, WikiLeaks is devoted to receiving and distributing a special form of information. The fundamental idea of publishing raw data, which had been passed along to the organization, had as its final goal yet another form of specialization. This was to release a vast amount of information that could not be processed by a single individual (by an investigative journalist, for instance) but rather first had to be sifted through and analyzed in a collaborative manner.

However, the "digital imperative" entailed by the WikiLeaks publications led to a paradoxical situation in which the opaque and informal organization could only reveal information or make it transparent if it happened to be available in the form of digital data records. The entire leaking process, which is characteristic of WikiLeaks's operations and those of similar platforms, is thus based on technical formalizations of programmed code: "Code at its most simplistic definition is a set of unambiguous instructions for the processing of elements of capta in computer memory. Computer code [...] is essential for the operation of any object or system that utilizes microprocessors."[29] Data processing and data description – by means of programming software – are undertaken with the goal of making such data available both for automated search routines and human perception (reading, viewing):

> Regardless of the nature of programming, the code created is the manifestation of a system of thought – an expression of how the world can be captured, represented, processed, and modeled computationally with the outcome subsequently doing work in the world. Programming then fundamentally seeks to capture and enact knowledge about the world – practices, ideas, measurements, locations, equations, and images – in order to augment, mediate, and regulate people's lives.[30]

In this light, even the act of systematically searching through materials, something which is undertaken by the "masses" that have been activated by the leaking platforms themselves, corresponds to a "formalization process" that gives order to vast and otherwise

---

transactions. See Rick Cohen, "The Financial Blockade of WikiLeaks and Its Meaning for the Non-profit Sector," *Nonprofit Quarterly* (October 28, 2011), https://nonprofitquarterly.org/policysocial-context/17171-the-financial-blockade-of-wikileaks-and-its-meaning-for-the-nonprofit-sector.html; and Ryan Singel, "Key Lawmakers Up Pressure on WikiLeaks and Defend Visa and MasterCard," *Wired.com* (December 9, 2011), http://www.wired.com/2010/12/wikileaks-congress-pressure/ (both websites were accessed on July 24, 2014).

[29] Rob Kitchin and Martin Dodge, *Code/Space: Software and Everyday Life* (Cambridge, MA: MIT Press, 2011), 24. According to Kitchen and Dodge, "capta" are units of information that are selected from the totality of available data about a person, a topic, and so on: "In other words, with respect to a person, data is everything that is possible to know about [him or her]; capta is what is selectively captured through measurement" (ibid., 5).

[30] Ibid., 26.

unmanageable amounts of raw data.[31] This involves two aspects of "new mass quantities" that are closely associated with one another. On the one hand, digitalization has led to an exponential increase in available digital data ("big data," as it is called); on the other hand, new technological infrastructures now allow for flexible collaboration to take place among the networked users of online platforms.

To this extent, the result of internet-based leaking processes has been a new type of public sphere that is based on the code used during the development of online platforms.[32] Here, in contrast to previous forms of the public spheres, which were based on various sorts of mass media, it is neither the journalistic activity of editing nor the structures of production and distribution that make information available to users. Instead, "programmed public spheres" are formed by receiving, decrypting (when necessary), processing, and structuring digital data. This requires an extensive understanding of the form of the received material and of the possible ways that, by means of code, it can be formalized and made legible for a general audience. This new logic of production when dealing with publishable material furnishes WikiLeaks and other digital transparency activists with certain advantages over the "classical" media outlets, whose core competence consists primarily in editing content and distributing this content to global media markets.[33]

The fact that programmers are using digital data more and more frequently to generate spontaneous and situation-specific public spheres is also evidenced by the numerous examples of digital political activism and protests. Numerous data-based public spheres were created, for instance, in the context of the #occupy protests. Among other things, these involved the technique of "crisis mapping," which enables location-specific reports of protest events to be visualized on maps without the assistance of professional journalists. The conceptualization of the #occupy movement as an "application programming interface" also points in this direction. In this case, the ideas, instruments, and strategies

---

[31] This also applies, incidentally, to WikiLeaks's collaboration with established media outlets such as *The New York Times*, *The Guardian*, and *Der Spiegel*. In this case, too, a degree of order was given to the undefined mounds of data concerned with the wars in Iraq and Afghanistan, and it was this order that allowed the material to be investigated by third parties. However, this formalization was not achieved by technical means alone but also with the help of traditional editorial activity involving research and the verification of facts.

[32] For detailed discussions of the significance of algorithms in the creation of public spheres, see Mercedes Bunz, *Die stille Revolution: Wie Algorithmen Wissen, Arbeit, Öffentlichkeit und Politik verändern, ohne dabei viel Lärm zu machen* (Berlin: Suhrkamp, 2012); and Tarleton Gillespie, "The Relevance of Algorithms," in *Media Technologies: Essays on Communication, Materiality, and Society*, ed. Pablo J. Baczkowski et al. (Cambridge, MA: MIT Press, 2014), 167–94.

[33] The current developments toward "data-driven journalism" indicate that a gradual orientation toward dealing with digital material is taking place. This process, moreover, has enabled new types of journalists to penetrate the structures of the media system. Assange has referred directly to the need for established media activity to be modernized, and he has described WikiLeaks as a sort of auxiliary structure that can help to balance out such deficits (see Obrist, "In Conversation with Julian Assange, Part I").

of protest activity are treated as elements of an openly accessible reservoir of data that can be reconfigured by "reprogramming" the specific protest codes in question.[34]

The growing importance of digital data and the growing number of ways in which it has become possible to intervene, actively and formatively by means of programming knowledge, into the process of creating public spheres provide an appropriate conceptual bridge to the concept to be discussed next, namely that of "formative public spheres" (again, *"Gestaltungsöffentlichkeiten"*). Whereas the theoretical development of this concept has been dominated by the notion of its dynamic elements and potential for giving rise to innovation and reform, here I hope to lend it an additional contour. The digital programming of the public sphere, which admittedly uses the structures of electronic mass media but simultaneously updates them and makes them more open, underscores the formative potential of the new agents generating public information.[35]

In the sense of the classical theories concerned with the public sphere,[36] WikiLeaks exemplifies a new group of "speakers and communicators." This new group, however, not only has access to the arenas addressed by the mass media; it also possesses the means to produce, develop, and network together novel subsets of the public.[37] With respect to transparency activism, the key resources happen to be the possession or access to previously secret or classified information and, above all, an understanding of how to formalize and further process digital data. In this particular process of digitalization, code has become a new power structure at the intersection of media and politics.

V. WikiLeaks and the Model of the Formative Public Sphere

From a theoretical perspective, the model of the "formative public sphere" offers new approaches for describing and systematizing the various developmental phases of WikiLeaks's activity. In the broader theoretical debates about the nature of the public

---

[34] See Alexis C. Madrigal, "A Guide to the Occupy Wall Street API, or Why the Nerdiest Way to Think About OSW Is So Useful," *The Atlantic* (November 16, 2011), http://www.theatlantic.com/technology/archive/2011/11/a-guide-to-the-occupy-wall-street-api-or-why-the-nerdiest-way-to-think-about-ows-is-so-useful/248562/ (accessed on July 25, 2014); and Peter Mörtenböck and Helge Mooshammer, *Occupy: Räume des Protests* (Bielefeld: Transcript, 2012).

[35] In their analysis of the occupy movement, Mörtenböck and Mooshammer often point to the significance of "collective logics," which, in today's protest movements, function by means of digital communication: "Together with smart phones, the social media used during the latest protest movements have decisively altered the relationship between individuals and collectives. They have also managed to shift the public sphere away from the institutional realm toward a new sort of communicative space" (ibid., 91).

[36] See Jürgen Habermas, *Between Facts and Norms: Contributions to a Discourse Theory of Law and Democracy*, trans. William Rehg (Cambridge, MA: MIT Press, 1996); Friedhelm Neidhardt, "Öffentlichkeit, öffentliche Meinung, soziale Bewegungen," *Kölner Zeitschrift für Soziologie und Sozialpsychologie: Sonderheft* 34 (1994), 7–41; and Bernhard Peters, *Die Integration moderner Gesellschaften* (Frankfurt am Main: Suhrkamp, 1993).

[37] In this regard, see also the chapters by Carolin Wiedemann and Mirko Tobias Schäfer in this volume.

sphere itself, this concept is seldom mentioned; it is typically used to discuss the various types of communication that political and societal processes can generate between and among the realms of politics, the media, and civil society. Such discussions have been instigated by a variety of experiences of uncertainty and formlessness in society's negotiation processes, experiences that, alongside consultations with traditional experts, have opened access to additional stocks of knowledge and information. In this regard, formative public spheres can be understood as a flexible but unstable dimension between volatile event-based public spheres (*Veranstaltungsöffentlichkeiten*) and the established processes and arenas of deliberative democracy.[38]

In order to apply the concept of the formative public sphere to the case of WikiLeaks, the latter must not be understood as an advisory agent. The approach offered by formative public spheres expands the traditional reservoir of agents, which consists of the combination and intersection of various communicative processes, to include the decision-making processes employed by a given political system. This enables, according to Stefan Böschen and his colleagues, "various perspectives on the structuring of problems to be made transparent and it highlights certain types of knowledge that had previously been outside of or irrelevant to the advisory process."[39] In this regard, WikiLeaks is not "invited" to participate as an external stimulus; rather, it brings itself into play by presenting information to a broad public audience, information that had previously been accessible only to select members within the political system. To this extent, WikiLeaks admittedly does not generate a "new" stock of knowledge but rather contributes to the disclosure of knowledge that had previously been kept secret. By divulging information about various topics, the possibility emerges (at least for the short term) of reorienting and restructuring societal debates in such a way that political figures are compelled to reconsider, if not change, their own decisions and actions.

Formative public spheres are characterized primarily by their dynamic and open-ended form, by their flexible constellation of participants (each with different connections to the political system), and by their fundamental and thematic openness. To these features, WikiLeaks has added the possibility of changing the functional basis of public space. By means of its innovative ability to make digital information available to an expansive public audience, WikiLeaks as an organization has not only contributed to the disclosure of new bodies of knowledge. It has also created a new manifestation of the "formative public sphere."[40] Such innovative activity suits the concept quite well, given that, in the words of Böschen and his co-authors, "formative public spheres [...] can be understood as

---

[38] Regarding the public spheres generated by political events, see Jürgen Gerhards, "Politische Veranstaltungen in der Bundesrepublik: Nachfrager und wahrgenommenes Angebot einer 'kleinen' Form von Öffentlichkeit," *Kölner Zeitschrift für Soziologie und Sozialpsychologie* 44 (1992), 766–79.

[39] Stefan Böschen et al., "'Gesellschaftliche Selbstberatung': Visualisierung von Risikokonflikten als Chance für Gestaltungsöffentlichkeiten," in *Von der Politik- zur Gesellschaftsberatung: Neue Wege öffentlicher Konsultation*, ed. Claus Leggewie (Frankfurt am Main: Campus, 2007), 223–46, at 224.

[40] A similar claim can be made about the Pirate Party of Germany, whose "entrance" into the established party landscape (by being elected to the state parliament of Berlin) led to disruptive but also formative

thematically centered arrangements of discourses, institutions, and agents that reflect the 'real-world experimental' conditions for embedding specific innovations within society."[41] WikiLeaks's publication of documents can be described as a series of such "real-world experiments." Over the course of these experiments, the organization's commitment to openness (as suggested by the concept of the "wiki") weakened and ultimately led to internal conflicts. In this matter, too, WikiLeaks accords quite well with the dynamic concept of the formative public sphere:

> Although formative public spheres evince the fundamentally open-ended nature of public spheres, they are simultaneously structured. They inscribe specific orders of knowledge to a particular object and predetermine institutional patterns of behavior. They are the result of power plays and societal conflicts (about knowledge) and they operate according to a dynamic of openings and closings.[42]

Such "openings and closings" are clear to see in WikiLeaks's publication history. Between 2006 and 2009 it functioned as an open and collaborative platform for distributing predominantly raw data. This stage was followed in early 2010 by the independent online release of the decrypted and edited video "Collateral Murder." The leaks released during the second half of that year (the "Afghan War Logs," "Iraq War Logs," and "Diplomatic Cables") were quite different, however, in that they were published in collaboration with established media companies and thus signaled a renunciation of the open model of collaboration. In the case of the "Guantanamo Files," which were made available in April of 2011, it was unclear through which channels the fully edited interrogation protocols were distributed. In contrast, the publication of approximately 55,000 unedited diplomatic cables, which took place in August of the same year, was clearly meant to involve the evaluative efforts of the "interested masses."

After a period of internal disputes, which led several people to leave the organization, WikiLeaks returned in the fall of 2011 to its original idea of being a "wiki" for disclosing information. Although the diplomatic cables had at first been released incrementally in association with various media partners, WikiLeaks ultimately decided to make the entire set of data available to the public.[43]

---

effects in the political public sphere. See the articles collected in Christoph Bieber and Claus Leggewie, eds., *Unter Piraten: Erkundungen in einer neuen politischen Arena* (Bielefeld: Transcript, 2012).

[41] Böschen et al., "'Gesellschaftliche Selbstberatung'," 224.

[42] Ibid.

[43] See Steffen Kraft, "Leck bei WikiLeaks," *Der Freitag* (August 25, 2011), https://www.freitag.de/autoren/steffen-kraft/leck-bei-wikileaks (accessed on July 28, 2014). The precise circumstances of the complete publication, which consisted of more than 250,000 individual documents from the U.S. State Department, are not entirely clear. Whereas members of the professional media claimed that there had been a data breach or a "leak at WikiLeaks," the organization itself claimed that it had "officially" made the material available through its website in order to enable interested users to sift through and evaluate the material collaboratively.

By briefly turning its back on the wiki principle of open collaboration, WikiLeaks systematically hindered the ability of common citizens to engage with the digital material at its disposal. By concentrating on its business partnerships with the professional media, in other words, WikiLeaks had more or less become a conventional participant in political-medial system. This resulted in a formal shift. At the height of its success, WikiLeaks was in fact not and open public platform based on decentralized cooperation but rather an exclusive organization devoted to dealing with sensitive information and thus an integral element of the "networked fourth estate" (in Benkler's terms).[44] Beckett and Ball have noted that WikiLeaks is in a permanent state of change and thus inherently unstable: "WikiLeaks has changed in its short history, and as it moves forward it might change again. This is not a stable project."[45]

Paradoxically, this situation also accounts for WikiLeaks's stabilizing effect in the process of social communication. Without continuously publishing classified information – be it as an independent agent or in association with established media companies – WikiLeaks never would have provoked any serious debates about the fundamental importance of transparency and secrecy in the political process.[46] Even the internal conflicts that have plagued the organization do nothing to change this assessment. It is ultimately the case that WikiLeaks's activity inspired the development of additional leaking platforms (OpenLeaks.org, GreenLeaks.com, IrishLeaks.ie, etc.) and prompted media companies to incorporate "leaking portals" into their services (at Al Jazeera, *The Washington Post*, *Der Westen*, for instance).[47] All of this has long-lasting implications for the development of political public spheres.

It thus seems appropriate to classify WikiLeaks as an organizer and stabilizer within a thematically centered network of agents. With its policy-related leaks about Afghanistan, Iraq, and Guantanamo, it suggested an interpretation of events that differed considerably from the depictions offered by the political figures who were immediately responsible for them. Even the leaks related to politics ("Cablegate," for example) are interesting from the perspective of formative public spheres. In this case, WikiLeaks operated in the opposite direction, namely as a "destabilizer" that laid bare the communicative practices of political operatives and thus provided society with fresh insight into their activity. Yet even here it is possible to speak of a learning process or a process of knowledge forma-

---

[44] Benkler, "A Free Irresponsible Press," 311.

[45] Beckett and Ball, *WikiLeaks: News in the Networked Era*, 141–42.

[46] See Ischinger, "Das WikiLeaks-Paradox," 155–63; and John C. Kornblum, "WikiLeaks und die Ära des radikalen Wandels," in *WikiLeaks und die Folgen: Die Hintergründe. Die Konsequenten*, ed. Heinrich Geiselberger (Berlin: Suhrkamp, 2011), 175–89.

[47] See Stefan Mey, "Jenseits von WikiLeaks: Tyler, OpenLeaks & Co.," *Hyperland* (January 6, 2013), http://blog.zdf.de/hyperland/2013/01/jenseits-von-wikileaks-tyler-openleaks-co/ (accessed on July 28, 2014).

tion, though less in the sense of a productive appropriation of new knowledge than in the sense of a critical confrontation with the techniques of power.[48]

In addition to its creation of a specific public sphere by means of programming, WikiLeaks can also be described as a contributor to public discourse from the perspective of content. Its special place outside of the classical structures of political systems goes beyond the particular nature of formative public spheres, which enable the integration or networking of new actors who, in phases of discursive indeterminacy, provide impulses for societal debates about relevant topics. In conventional formative public spheres, a connection to political processes is realized by means of various forms of consulting (conferences, committees, councils, and so on). As an agent of a new digital media arena, however, WikiLeaks offers new possibilities for participating in the political process. Characteristic in this regard is its position outside of the jurisdiction of political and legal systems and its ability to open up new resources (digital data, code) for the specific development of political public spheres.

VI. The Ethics of the Leak?

By treating the leaking processes as a manifestation of a new sort of "formative public sphere," a connection can also be made to the debate concerning the ethical aspects of dealing with sensitive information. Thus far, such issues have not played a significant role in the discussions of WikiLeaks's activity; in fact, the question of media ethics has hardly been raised at all, or at least not in a serious manner.[49]

The new configurations and structures of medial and political public spheres have distracted attention away from the fact that leaks can be a source of ethical conflicts when dealing with information. In this regard, the motivation for "exposing wrongdoing" could very well be used as a point of contact for evaluating the ethical components of leaking processes. Are leaks to be judged according the amount of (societal) injustice or unlawfulness that they have exposed? Or does the dissemination of information "only" serve to damage the reputations of certain individuals or institutions to the advantage of others'? Are unintended consequences taken into consideration, and who bears the responsibility in such cases? Such questions have gained considerable significance as leaking processes have become the topic of an unfolding public debate. The release of new stores of knowledge by means of novel sorts of "formative public spheres" requires

---

[48] Here there is a clear connection to Assange's writings about "conspiracy as governance," in which he regards the targeted disruption of communication between the members of a conspiracy as a subversive act. In this matter, the communication process instigated by the "formative public sphere" aims to paralyze the network of conspirators outright (that is, it does not intend for there to be a constructive learning process). From a functional perspective, it can be said that these leaks take on the role of "anti-formative public spheres."

[49] For introductory discussions of the matter, see Beckett and Ball, *WikiLeaks: News in the Networked Era*, 67–83, 92–114; and Caja Thimm, "WikiLeaks und die digitale Bürgerschaft," in *Medien und Zivilgesellschaft*, ed. Alexander Filipović et al. (Weinheim: Juventa, 2012), 132–42.

us to come to terms with the intended and unintended consequences of such revelations. An ethical dimension is thus inherent to the act of leaking information.[50]

Along the lines of such questions, rather few attempts have been made to distinguish between "good" and "bad" leaks.[51] In such discussions, the argumentation hinges almost exclusively on the individual motivations for disseminating or holding back information, which is quite similar to the fundamental dilemma faced by "whistleblowers."[52] The leap from here to the ethical dimension of WikiLeaks can be achieved by translating the concept of a corporate or organizational perspective into a point of intervention that is societal or systems-oriented: "Whistleblowers are thus 'ethical dissidents,' that is, people with civil courage who are selflessly motivated to 'sound alarms' without any concern for the consequences of such behavior. They do this to reveal and remedy suspect activity or processes at their workplace or within their sphere of influence."[53] The position of the "ethical dissident" is of course quite familiar to Julian Assange. In his essays "State and Terrorist Conspiracies" and "Conspiracy as Governance," he outlines a concept that can be regarded as the theoretical foundation for the subsequent operations of the WikiLeaks platform. It is in these works that he made a claim for "radical transparency," a concept that has been used as a model or point of orientation for several other leaking portals. Crucial to this concept, too, is the role of technological innovation, which can provide a new basis for monitoring and controlling political activity: "To radically shift regime behavior we must think clearly and boldly for if we have learned anything, it is that regimes do not want to be changed. We must think beyond those who have gone before us and discover

---

50   A fundamental discussion of such "grappling with moral issues" could take place within the framework of a formalized process of "ethical decision-making." According to the "Zurich Model," this multi-step process would involve determining boundary conditions, identifying stakeholders, stating a moral question, developing and evaluating arguments, and finally recommending a course of action. See Barbara Bleisch and Markus Huppenbauer, *Ethische Entscheidungsfindung: Ein Handbuch für die Praxis* (Zurich: Versus, 2011). In the present context, the moral question when dealing with information would be to ask whether the benefits of releasing it (exposing criminal behavior, etc.) will outweigh whatever possible damages the release might cause. In general, a comprehensive discussion of the "ethical practices of dealing with digital information" remains a desideratum.

51   See Kirk O. Hanson and Jerry Ceppos, "The Ethics of Leaking," *Los Angeles Times* (October 6, 2006), http://articles.latimes.com/2006/oct/06/opinion/oe-ceppos6); and Mike Labossiere, "The Ethics of WikiLeaking, Revisited," *Talking Philosophy* (December 2, 2010), http://blog.talkingphilosophy. com/?p=2384 (both websites were accessed on July 29, 2014).

52   Dieter Deiseroth has defined whistleblowing according to the criteria of "revealing wrongdoing," "going outside," "serving the public interest," and "risking retaliation." See his article "Was ist Whistleblowing?" in *Zivilcourage lernen: Analysen – Modelle – Arbeitshilfen*, ed. Gerd Meyer et al. (Bonn: BPB, 2004), 124–35. Central to the action of whistleblowers is their level of authority within a given organization, for the (legal) consequences of "sounding the alarm" will vary depending on a whistleblower's position. In this regard, see Guido Strack, "Whistleblowing in Germany," *Whistleblower-Netzwerk.de* (2008), http://www.whistleblower-net.de/pdf/WB_in_Germany.pdf (accessed on July 29, 2014).

53   Deiseroth, "Was ist Whistleblowing?" 125.

technological changes that embolden us with ways to act in which our forebears could not."[54] In his extensive analysis of Assange's writings, Alan Bady came to the conclusion that, if WikiLeaks can be regarded as a sort of society-driven portal for whistleblowing, then it should not be left out of any discussions concerning an "ethics of the leak": "The question for an ethical human being – and Assange always emphasizes his ethics – has to be the question of what exposing secrets will actually accomplish, what good it will do, what better state of affairs it will bring about."[55] In the case of leaking platforms, as I hope to have shown above, it is not enough to devote critical attention to their associations with professional media outlets; it is also necessary to evaluate the profile of activity within these new "investigative divisions of labor." In this light, WikiLeaks's ambivalent character as an "intransparent transparency activist" certainly beckons criticism. Then again, as a stimulus for formative public spheres that is defined by its outsider position and "political indeterminacy," WikiLeaks can also bring about positive effects.

Furthermore, it is necessary to question the level of self-regulation, self-responsibility, and self-restraint of those who voluntarily choose to collaborate with WikiLeaks and other such organizations.[56] That platforms such as WikiLeaks have played a significant role in creating (or limiting) "formative public spheres" is evident in the history of publications that have already been released. Here, too, a key aspect is the manner in which the organization has dealt with the new resource of code. This happens to provide yet another example of ambivalence: Despite WikiLeaks's promises of transparency, its source code remains proprietary (this is true in the case of other leaking platforms as well). Contrary to the principles of the "open-source" movement, the architecture of its platform was developed in secrecy and is only accessible to the "initiated." Although such secrecy has often been justified in the name of security, it has the effect of placing a considerable amount of responsibility and pressure on the operators of transparency platforms. The ability to access and control the key resources of data and code puts those in charge in a fundamental position of power, one that can easily be abused by dishonest or unethical behavior. A basic consensus thus needs to be reached among those engaged in developing

---

54   Julian Assange, "State and Terrorist Conspiracies," *me@iq.org* (November 10, 2006), http://cryptome.org/0002/ja-conspiracies.pdf (accessed on July 17, 2014).

55   Aaron Bady, "Julian Assange and the Computer Conspiracy 'To Destroy this Invisible Government'," *Zunguzungu* (November 29, 2010), http://zunguzungu.wordpress.com/2010/11/29/julian-assange-and-the-computer-conspiracy-%E2%80%9Cto-destroy-this-invisible-government%E2%80%9D/ (accessed on July 17, 2014).

56   There has yet to be a study of the "second degree" of participation, of those who do not participate directly in WikiLeaks's leaking process but make use of the platform for collaborative research and systemization processes. As with investigations of the demographics of WikiLeaks's users, it would be hoped in this case that information could be provided about the actual extent to which users participate in the platform and about the specific nature of this participation during their collaborative efforts.

such platforms. As for now, however, the closed nature of their operational structures has made it difficult to conduct any investigations.[57]

An "ethics of the leak" (or an "ethics of leaking") also has implications at the macro-level. Digital transparency activists, who are devoted to monitoring and controlling the behavior of political figures and thus represent a functional extension of the "fourth estate," can also be described as activists for "sousveillance." This concept was introduced by the media artist Steve Mann as a subversive counter-strategy against forms of media surveillance:

> The word "surveillance" is French for "to watch from above." It typically describes situations where person(s) of higher authority (e.g. security guards, department store owners, or the like) watch over citizens, suspects, or shoppers. [...] The author has suggested "sousveillance" as French for "to watch from below." The term "sousveillance" refers both to hierarchical sousveillance, e.g. citizens photographing police, shoppers photographing shopkeepers, and taxi-cab passengers photographing cab drivers, as well as personal sousveillance (bringing cameras from the lamp posts and ceilings, down to eye-level, for human-centered recording of personal experience).[58]

Whereas Mann is chiefly concerned with photographs and video recordings, transparency activists such as WikiLeaks offer the possibility of different forms of "communal sousveillance." Collaborative engagement with leaked documents certainly shares much in common with "watching from below," a practice that, after information has been leaked, can lead to confrontations with the political system and subsequent changes in society.[59]

There is finally the question of how ethical standards should be established in the future. Whereas it has long been the case that centralized institutions, committees, and commissions have been charged with developing principles of "good practice," "ethical behavior," or "good governance," it is clear by now that the dispersed and non-hierarchical structures of decentralized communication networks are also capable of formulating norms and regulations. Even if WikiLeaks has reached a dead end as an organization and

---

[57] During WikiLeaks's recent rounds of publications, the risky nature of this situation was made evident by the controversial positions held by those involved. This led to public disputes and ultimately to a falling out between Assange and former leaders of the group such as Domscheit-Berg.

[58] Steve Mann, "Sousveillance: Inverse Surveillance in Multimedia Imaging," in *Proceedings of the 12th Annual ACM International Conference on Multimedia* (New York: Association for Computer Machinery, 2004), 620–27, at 620 (quoted from the abstract).

[59] An example of "sousveillance" is offered by the online platforms that recently unveiled acts of plagiarism committed by various German politicians. In this case, a number of users made contributions "from below" by taking it upon themselves to double-check the research that had been published by those in public office. The most notable perpetrator was certainly Karl-Theodor zu Guttenberg, the former Federal Minister of Economics and Defense. See Julius Reimer and Max Ruppert, "Der Ex-Minister und sein Schwarm," *Journalist* 4 (2011), 76–80; and the articles collected in Oliver Lepsius and Reinhart Meyer-Kalkus, eds., *Inszenierung als Beruf: Der Fall Gutenberg* (Berlin: Suhrkamp, 2011).

is perhaps too closely tied to the personal fate of Julian Assange, the principles behind the platform – and the overall debate about global transparency that it helped to spearhead[60] – should provide ample material for further developments.

---

[60] See especially Sifry, *WikiLeaks and the Age of Transparency*.

Peter Krapp

Between the Madness and the Wisdom of Crowds
Computer Games and the Distraction Economy

Digital culture promises a business model that oscillates between blockbusters and niche products. This model leads to upheavals in the market that directly affect, for instance, the quality and availability of computer games. Just as we rely on cognitive models in our interactions with individuals, our understanding of complex social situations depends, accordingly, on models of a larger scale, based on longitudinal studies of our basic assumptions. In the field of finance, for instance, there are those who, trusting the rational expectation that markets will "naturally" correct themselves, seek "beta" in the wisdom of crowds, and there are reflexive behaviorists who, assuming that the world is in a constant state of flux or disequilibrium, look for "alpha" opportunities in the madness of the marketplace. Media studies is similarly divided between those who regard crowdsourcing as an impetus for transformation and progress (from the printing press to the mass media of the twentieth century and on to the highly differentiated media of networked cultures) and those who believe that the dispersion of the masses into ever more channels has produced a droning noise that threatens to smother whatever informational value or entertainment value might exist.[1]

In an effort to mediate between these seemingly irreconcilable positions, I have examined the planning cycles of the entertainment-software industry, although of course the disclaimer must be kept in mind that past performance is no guarantee of future results, whether we are dealing with finance or media studies. The question is what media studies may gain when speaking of the "new masses," regardless of whether such insight can be expressed as formulaically as an alpha or beta deviation, in looking into to the business cycles of American computer-game developers.[2] In this context, an interesting

---

[1]   On the Lombard effect generated by such noise, see Peter Krapp, *Noise Channels: Glitch and Error in Digital Culture* (Minneapolis: University of Minnesota Press, 2011).

[2]   This project was supported by the California Institute for Telecommunications and Information Technology and by the 2008 Undergraduate Research Opportunity Project at UC Irvine. My research is based on industry data from 1996 to 2010, particularly on market research conducted by NPD Group (http://www.npdgroup.com), publications by the industry advocacy group ESA (http://www.theesa.com), and investment analyses by Deutsche Bank and UBS. I owe special thanks to Jeetil

role is played by Metacritic and Gamerankings, two websites that aggregate criticism on the Internet.[3] These sites have become so influential in the gaming industry that they are often used to determine the salaries and bonus packages of its managers and executives. Finally, the discussion will turn to synthetic worlds, for it is time for observers of new media to familiarize ourselves with trends in the entertainment software industry that have come to govern both the quality and the variety of the products being offered. While media studies typically approached the phenomenon of computer games in terms of media archaeology or of ideological critique, my intention here is to underscore the influence of management and of journalistic criticism over the hardware and software that are developed for this new mass medium.

I. The New Masses

Just as cars, radios, televisions, and record players enriched the experience of our daily lives, the same now goes for computer culture, and especially for computer games. It is an axiom of media economics that one observes a dual market: an exchange of wares on the one hand and the package and sale of attention on the other.[4] Technical infrastructures enable and facilitate the development of creative content, which is then advertised and made available to consumers, but media consumption is not only the consumption of films or computer games; it is also the consumption of the time that someone is willing to devote to such things. In this regard, the supply and demand of production flows in the opposite direction of the supply and demand of attention. Information can be packaged and sold without being scarce or used up by that process; digital media bring a highly segmented and fragmented audience in contact with suppliers of content and distraction. While it is true that attention is limited, for media economics it is just as relevant that the consumption of a film, a CD, or a game does not use them up – they remain available for further circulation. At the same time, it is no less relevant to note that, both in terms of quantity and quality, consumer goods in the entertainment sector exhibit a growth rate that far exceeds the growth rate of attention itself. Whereas more movies, music, and software

---

Patel (Deutsche Bank, San Francisco) and Benjamin Schachter (UBS, New York). Some preliminary findings related to this study have been published online; see Peter Krapp, "Ranks and Files: On Metacritic and Gamerankings," *Flow* (December 2012), http://flowtv.org/2012/12/ranks-and-files/; and idem, "MMO Models: Crowd-Sourcing Economedia," *Flow* (March 2013), http://flowtv.org/2013/03/mmo-models/.

[3] See http://www.metacritic.com and http://gamerankings.com.

[4] See Alan B. Albarran, *The Media Economy* (New York: Routledge, 2010); Alison Alexander, ed., *Media Economics: Theory and Practice* (Mahwah, NJ: Lawrence Erlbaum, 2004); Gillian Doyle, *Understanding Media Economics* (London: Sage, 2002); Thomas H. Davenport and John C. Beck, *The Attention Economy: Understanding the New Currency of Business* (Boston: Harvard Business School Press, 2001); Aleida Assmann, ed., *Aufmerksamkeiten* (Munich: Fink, 2001); Bernhard Waldenfels, *Phänomenologie der Aufmerksamkeit* (Frankfurt am Main: Suhrkamp, 2004); and Georg Franck, *Ökonomie der Aufmerksamkeit: Ein Entwurf* (Munich: Hanser, 1998).

become available every year, the collective attention of the new masses does not increase proportionally. In the past, moreover, when it was difficult to start a new television station, radio station, or newspaper, the supply of such products was limited to a far greater extent by the barriers to market entry. A classic example of this is the vertical integration of Hollywood studios during the 1950s and 1960s.[5] In the case of traditional media, their business has mostly been limited by the costs of infrastructure, operation costs, and production costs, whereas the price they have paid for attention has been relatively low. Today, attention is no longer so cheap. In 1982, television advertising in the United States occupied only six minutes of every hour of broadcasting, yet this number had doubled by 2001 and has continued to climb. The same trend applies to newspapers, magazines, and radio stations. For these investments in attention, it is relatively insignificant to distinguish between advertising time and advertising expenditures; as long the participants in these industries find it more advantageous to invest in advertising instead of in production quality or infrastructure, the budgets allocated for advertising will continue to grow. The implication of this for entertainment software is that attention is not a factor in the creation of quality, at least so long as it is cheaper to purchase attention than it is to develop a computer game. Although it would be nice if the market were such that quality and popularity went hand in hand, within the sphere of the mass media there is an inefficient relation between production quality and public success, and this inefficiency is modulated only by a sharp rise in advertising costs. A film can be marketed in the movie theater, on a DVD, on television, in foreign countries, as well as in the form of toys, books, posters, T-shirts, and so on. This explains why film producers depend on blockbusters and why the music industry relies so heavily on hit songs. During the past two decades, the computer-game industry has come closer and closer to adopting this model. As advertising costs continue to rise, however, less money is left for the production of quality; thus either the investment in production must rise overall, or quality will suffer.

The Internet age promised to provide greater flexibility for producing, distributing, and marketing media content in novel ways, but this hope raises questions about the reality and nature of the vaunted new masses. The assumption was that the new media landscape will no longer be dominated by production costs but rather by the costs of attention, because new technologies would lower the cost of production and distribution. Nonetheless it is doubtful that these new media conditions will lead to direct correlation between the popularity of a product and its quality. A detailed analysis of the computer-game market in the United States will reveal why this is the case.

The American computer-game industry has been boasting since 2007 that its earnings surpassed those of the film and music industries. The total market size of nearly nineteen billion dollars for 2007 was three times larger more than a decade earlier; half of that money was spent on entertainment software and the other half on hardware, with consoles and mobile devices accounting for larger share than computers and displays. Whereas the American music industry shrank by nearly ten percent between 2002 and 2007, and the

---

[5]   See Tim Wu, *The Master Switch: the Rise and Fall of Information Empires* (New York: Knopf, 2010).

film industry remained stagnant, game manufacturers grew by more than twenty-eight percent. Of course the price of a game is usually higher than that of a movie ticket or a CD. Of the sixty or so dollars charged for a new console game, a quarter represents the markup by the retailer, an additional fifteen to twenty percent pays for royalties or licenses (to comic-book authors, athletes, film studios, or other copyright holders), ten percent is set aside for refunds and theft, ten percent pays for amortized investments in software (in the Unreal Engine, Massive, or any other code that serves as the basis for multiple games), and another ten percent is often paid to hardware manufacturers such as Nintendo, Sony, or Microsoft for providing their interface. After packaging and distribution are taken into account, this means that approximately twenty percent of a game's retail price goes to its development.

Over the past ten years, however, development costs have soared while retail prices have remained stable. Because of the demand for more complex graphics, larger game worlds, and more sophisticated interactions, the average investment in a new title has increased from approximately fifty thousand dollars for a sixteen-bit game to three million dollars for a sixty-four-bit game. In other words, it typically cost around two million dollars to develop a game for the original PlayStation, games for the Xbox could cost between three and seven million dollars and games for the Wii cost as much as twelve million; but for the PS3 and Xbox360, the cost of developing a game easily exceeded twenty million dollars, and several ambitious projects in fact made even that number seem rather low. At the same time, the development cycle for games has become longer and longer, and this puts further pressure on profit expectations. Thus it is no surprise that the fastest-growing sector on the internet has been so-called "massively multiplayer online role-playing games" (MMORPGs). For in addition to being able to reach a broader demographic, online games of this sort also generate additional revenue streams beyond the one-time sale of packaged software, through subscriptions, advertisements, and secondary markets.

Before we turn to online games, however, a few observations about the market for console games should be made. There is a basic distinction between game developers that produce their own hardware (such as Microsoft, Sony, or Nintendo) and those that are not bound to any single platform and thus enjoy the benefit of having multiple options at their disposal (such as Ubisoft, Activision Blizzard, Electronic Arts, Take Two, or THQ). Within the game industry, the software market share of hardware developers is relatively small. Nintendo's sits around eleven percent, Sony's around four percent, and that of Microsoft is little more than three percent. The remainder of the market is divided among the large hardware-independent developers, with Electronic Arts leading at twenty-four percent, followed by Activision Blizzard with twenty percent, Ubisoft hovering above six percent, and a long list of smaller companies behind them. Formerly influential brand names such as Disney or Sega hardly play a role any more, while up-and-comers such as Valve and Zynga have entered the fray. Although it can be advantageous for hardware-independent developers to offer a given game on multiple consoles (examples include Take Two's *Grand Theft Auto* or Ubisoft's *Assassin's Creed*), over the past few years it has also been quite profitable to combine one's own hardware and software. In this regard it should not be forgotten that both Sony and Microsoft have strategically lowered the price of their consoles in order to stimulate software sales, so much so that both the Xbox360 and PlayStation 3 have at times been selling below cost. During the last development cycle, a great many below-average games were sold for the PlayStation, but now Nintendo's Wii and DS are the most obvious niches in the market without any direct correlation between game sales and game quality. In the past, Electronic Arts, Activision, and THQ were able to remain profitable not only by selling big hits like *Call of Duty* but also by selling a number of other products that were predominately targeted at children or casual players. In 2009, however, when Electronic Arts laid off a tenth of its employees in order to save 120 million dollars, the CEO explained that advance reviews in trade publications and on industry websites had begun to influence sales. Two websites, in particular, were identified as responsible for aggregating a game's ratings and providing its overall score, a score that is in turn influencing sales, market shares, and stock prices: Metacritic (which also rates films and music) and Gamerankings.[6]

Unlike film and music criticism, which is at least informed by the total impression made by one work or another, game journalists usually have to file their reports about new products long before they can become completely familiar with the entertainment software under review (even if they have a full week to play a given new game). It is characteristic of the new media landscape for these two websites to aggregate and summarize game critiques from European, Japanese, Canadian, Australian, and American magazines in a single collective score, even if these magazines themselves do not use a grading scale. Metacritic and Gamerankings typically publish formulaic summaries of journalists' first impressions about a game even before any sales data has been made available, and this is the source of their influence over the industry, over Wall Street, and over the general public itself.

When Activision's game *Spiderman 3* reached the stores on a Friday in May of 2007, for example, the tepid early reviews by industry journalists (50/100) reverberated in the form a five-percent loss in the company's share price, followed by additional stock price drops in subsequent weeks. In August of the same year, by contrast, the game *Bioshock* received a nearly perfect score (96/100) in its advance reviews, and Take Two's stock rose by twenty percent within a few days. According to Activision's CEO Robert Kotick, a systematic study of 789 games for Sony's PlayStation 2, conducted during the year 2005, had demonstrated a clear correlation between game ratings and sales numbers. Sales of an Activision game doubled for every five points it received over 80, and for this reason developers became convinced that ratings not only reflected the quality of games but their sales potential as well. "Everyone wants 85 or better," as Jim Ward, the president of

---

[6] Both Gamerankings and Metacritic belong to CNET, which has been owned by CBS Interactive since 2008. The website Rottentomatoes.com offers a similar service for film criticism; it will not be taken into account here, however, because it does not cover computer games.

LucasArts, in 2007 told the *Wall Street Journal*.[7] Since 2005, in fact, numerous developers including Activision and Take Two have incorporated these collective game ratings into their employment contracts. Even industry partners take such aggregate scores into account during their contract negotiations. Since 2004, for instance, Warner Brothers has directly relied on such ratings when calculating the licensing fees for games based on its movies: The better the game, the lower the fees, whereas more is charged for lower-quality games that risk tarnishing a film's reputation.

It was not until early 2011 that the industry influence of Metacritic and Gamerankings began to wane. The turning point was when the game *Homefront* (a THQ product in which the North Korean army invades the United States in the year 2027) enjoyed respectable sales despite its low ratings. Early reviews of the game were negative enough to cause the company's stock price to drop by more than twenty percent in a single day, and yet the sales numbers stubbornly went on to defy expectations.[8] Metacritic had given *Homefront* an overall rating of 72. Although twelve of the twenty-eight reviews were positive (80/100 or better), most reviewers thought the game was a flop (the ratings ranged from 40 to 93). Nevertheless, *Homefront* spent nearly an entire month as a bestseller on Amazon and elsewhere and quickly turned a profit for THQ, which ultimately sold some two million copies of the game.[9] Such occurrences are interesting for media studies because they complicate the conventional distinction between quantity and quality. Under the conditions of digital culture, media theorists have to concern themselves not only with matters of quality but with quantitative data as well.

It can be revealing to correlate aggregate ratings of games with sales data collected by the NPD Group, a market research company, and it casts a grim light on the role of criticism – in the entertainment software scene it no longer plays, it seems, the role arbiter of cultural merit. Whereas film criticism rarely reflects the taste of the general public,

---

[7] Nick Wingfield, "High Scores Matter to Game Makers Too," *Wall Street Journal* (September 2007), http://online.wsj.com/article/SB119024844874433247.html (accessed on June 24, 2014). See also Joe Dodson, "Mind Over Meta," *GameRevolution* (July 2006), http://www.gamerevolution.com/features/mind_over_meta (accessed on June 24, 2014).

[8] See Matt Peckham, "Homefront Reviews Torpedo THQ Stock Price, Metacritic Broken," *PC World* (March 2011), http://www.techhive.com/article/222293/homefront_reviews_torpedo_thq_stock_price.html; Alex Pham and Ben Fritz, "Bad Reviews of Homefront Send THQ Shares Tumbling," *Los Angeles Times* (March 2011), http://articles.latimes.com/2011/mar/16/business/la-fi-ct-thq-homefront-20110316; and Alex Pham, "THQ May Profit from Homefront Video Game Despite Poor Reviews," *Los Angeles Times* (March 2011), http://articles.latimes.com/2011/mar/26/business/la-fi-ct-thq-homefront-20110326. Each of these sites was accessed on June 24, 2014.

[9] It is important not to overestimate the significance of online sales numbers. In the United States, ninety-four percent of all purchases are still made offline, though the number of online purchases has been growing steadily. According to Forrester Research, the percentage of online sales jumped from 1.7 in 2001 to 4.9 in 2007, with an expected market share of 6.8 percent in 2013. E-commerce continues to grow in Germany as well, although the growth rates there have fallen over the past few years. Between 2003 and 2004, online sales in Germany increased by thirty percent, whereas the increase between 2010 and 2011 was only eleven percent.

and music criticism usually has little patience for pop hits, in the world of computer games there is a direct and quantifiable correlation between a game's reviews and its popularity. Games with the highest ratings (again, these scores are simply an average of the first impressions reported by a few dozen industry journalists) sell three times as well as games with collective ratings between 80 and 90. The latter, in turn, sell twice as well as games rated between 70 and 80, which themselves have twice the sales of games with ratings between 60 and 70. It is therefore no surprise that a mere four percent of all the games sold between 2000 and 2006 were responsible for a third of all revenues, and that this situation has become even more pronounced in recent years. By now, a fourth of the titles sold are responsible for eighty-six percent of the industry's total earnings. Both UBS and Deutsche Bank conducted longitudinal studies (released in 2007 and 2010, respectively) that together analyzed more than 1,600 games. According to UBS's findings, the fifty games with ratings over ninety, which constituted no more than three percent of all available games, outsold all the other games combined, while twenty-three percent of the games on the market had received an aggregate score of 60 or lower. UBS also compared the multi-year average ratings of products by Activision, Electronic Arts, Take Two, and THQ with those of the products made by Microsoft, Sony, and Nintendo. Between 1997 and 2006, the market share held by the hardware producers dropped from forty-four to seventeen percent, while that of the four large American third-party developers increased from sixteen to forty-seven percent. Whereas Activision did quite well with *Call of Duty*, *Marvel Ultimate Alliance*, *Tony Hawk*, and *Guitar Hero*, a number of its film adaptations – notably *Spiderman 3*, *Shrek 3*, and *Transformers* – performed rather poorly. During the same time period, Electronic Arts was able to rely primarily on *Madden Football* and *Need for Speed*, which respectively accounted for twenty percent and five percent of the company's five-year revenues, while its own film adaptations, namely *Harry Potter* and *Lord of the Rings*, likewise proved to be less profitable (each accounted for a mere five percent of revenues). CEO John Riccitiello blamed Electronic Arts' lost market share directly on aggregate game ratings: "We did not have any internally developed breakaway titles and none of EA's internally developed titles reached a Metacritic rating of 90 or greater."[10] Take Two relied even more heavily on a single franchise, *Grand Theft Auto*, which earned more than a billion dollars between 2000 and 2005 (more than half its total earnings), while other offerings such as *Midnight Club* and *Max Payne* were worth only a tenth of that. For its part, THQ was mainly reliant on licensed games from Disney, Pixar, Nickelodeon, and World Wide Wrestling Entertainment. In the case of these games (think of *SpongeBob SquarePants*, *Scooby Doo*, *Rugrats*, *Finding Nemo*, and *Power Rangers*), the correlation between sales and reviews was less explicit. The

---

[10] Quoted from Matt Martin, "Riccitiello: 'Short-Term Pain Necessary for Further Growth'," *Games-Industry International* (February 2008), http://www.gamesindustry.biz/articles/riccitiello-short-term-pain-necessary-for-further-growth. See also Andy Chalk, "Riccitiello Won't Dodge 'Short-Term Pain' at EA," *The Escapist* (February 2008), http://www.escapistmagazine.com/forums/read/7.53966-Riccitiello-Wont-Dodge-Short-Term-Pain-At-EA. Both websites were accessed on June 24, 2014.

overarching trend, however, has led the industry to change its ways and tilt increasingly to the winner-take-all model: A decade ago, the twenty-five best-selling games accounted for a quarter of the market, whereas now the same number of bestsellers makes up more than forty percent of the games sold.

In this precarious situation, it is no wonder that the industry went looking for a hedge – and they went online. Regardless of whether they belong to the latest 256-bit generation or to the old 128-bit platform, game consoles are increasingly faced with the challenge of having to compete with networked home computers, which can simultaneously be used as digital television sets, chat interfaces, and telephones (not to mention the convenience of shopping, banking, etc). Nintendo, Sony, and Microsoft have thus devoted more and more of their resources to networking technology, and console games are being touted more and more frequently for their networked gaming modes over WiiWare, the PlayStation Network, or Xbox Live. In its first six months, Activision's *Call of Duty: Modern Warfare 2* was responsible for 1.75 billion minutes of play on Xbox Live, and prompted twenty million transactions for additional game content.[11] Xbox Live (available since November of 2002) connects more consoles than WiiWare (available since March of 2008) or the PlayStation Network (available since May of 2006), but the greatest variety of networked games is available on the Wii (the PlayStation Network has the fewest users). Whereas both the PlayStation Network and Xbox Live offer access to Facebook, Twitter, and Netflix, this is not true of the Wii (which only started offering Netflix recently). Game consoles, however, have been losing market share as well, and this is because entertainment software has been changing under the growing influence of web and mobile culture. Many game developers are looking for new markets; their interest is not only on producing casual games for Facebook or smart phones, which are inexpensive to create yet not that highly profitable, but also in developing large-scale online games with thousands or even millions of participants. The first titles of this sort were produced by newcomers like PopCap, Zynga, and Playdom, which tested new strategies for releasing their products, including making them available as iPhone or Android apps and on portals such as Pogo, Yahoo Games, Bebo, or WildTangent. Now, however, American developers are trying to learn from Asian MMORPGs and to lure, from among the players of popular adolescent titles such as *Habbo Hotel*, more and more subscribers to new online offerings. This, above all, is the great promise of the game market that the new masses are expected to fulfill.

II. Virtual World Economies

Four fifths of the Internet users in the United States work or play in synthetic worlds. The American market for computer games amounted to some nineteen billion dollars in 2007, as mentioned above, and this number is projected to reach thirty billion or more.

---

[11]   Here I will have to set aside the important matter of whether there is any difference between playing *Guitar Hero* on a plastic guitar, which is included with the Xbox360 console, and simply playing it on a Blackberry. Do media-specific differences alter such games in a significant manner?

One of the most noteworthy trends has been the strong growth of MMORPGs and synthetic worlds, which have millions of users in Asia and North America. At peak times, the game *World of Warcraft* alone has had between ten and twenty million players and earned the Vivendi company more than a billion dollars of annual revenue. Nintendo offers *MapleStory* on its DS platform; Square Enix's games include *Final Fantasy* and *Dragon Quest*, while Electronic Arts is responsible for *Ultima Online* and *Dark Age of Camelot*. These worlds are distinguished by their great variety of simulated economic activities, from simple trades and auctions to opportunities for earning or losing "gold" or other items in the game. Because the division of labor is such a prevalent aspect of role-playing games, it comes as no surprise that this economic structure has led to a number of secondary markets. Everything from virtual swords and magic elixirs to entire characters and player accounts are available for sale on eBay, IGE, PlayerAuctions, ItemMania, and other websites. My first personal encounter with these markets occurred fifteen years ago when one of my neighbors was promoted from programmer to usability manager. One of his first tasks was to figure out how, precisely, his company's software was being used. One product line was an inexpensive alternative to Photoshop, and as he found out it was being used by numerous hobbyists to design virtual armor, buildings, flags, and animals that could be incorporated into various game worlds. Many game developers count on the creativity of their subscribers and allow or encourage the use of skins, maps, loot, and other "user-generated content" in their online games. As Samuel Weber has commented, a distinction needs to be drawn between those who turn virtual goods into real currency (which itself is somewhat virtual) and those who dream of creating a different life through their consumption.[12]

Regardless of whether online game worlds are interpreted in anthropological terms as meeting a basic need or in historical terms as a critique of technologized modernity, they are popular because role-playing allows for different styles and motivations to coexist and interact. Players can meet others, explore virtual territory, solve puzzles, conquer, dominate, spy, cast spells, heal, and so on. Avatars enable embodied forms of communication to take place in a common space; they are less expensive than teleconferences or business trips; and they are equipped with faces and bodies chosen by their users, which suggests that, as far as communication is concerned, virtual worlds offer at least as much as the telephone. Interactivity with a steadily growing number of other participants entails that the quantity of entertainment will be translated into quality, and so long as the experience remains enjoyable, it can be assumed that synthetic worlds will continue to expand. There is no guarantee, however, that this will happen. For instance, there has been some controversy about the practice of selling virtual currency for actual money instead of earning such currency by laboring through a given game. When virtual goods (skins, coins, elixirs, property, etc.) can be bought and sold directly instead being acquired within a game, purists regard this not only as a degradation of the playing experience but

---

[12] Samuel Weber, "A Virtual Indication," in *Digital and Other Virtualities: Renegotiating the Image*, ed. Antony Bryant and Griselda Pollock (London: I. B. Tauris, 2010), 63–78.

also as an imbalance that reflects negatively on the game's design. More than anything else, MMORPGs promise to provide escapist fantasy worlds of dungeons and dragons in which the pressure to buy and sell things, so persistent in everyday life, can temporarily be avoided. Yet this boundary is rapidly beginning to crumble as auctions and other secondary markets continue to skew the balance between the time that a player invests in a game and the abilities that can be acquired by other means.

Most of the efforts to secure the border between virtual worlds and "reality" have proved to be overly expensive and complicated. Moreover, many players go far beyond mere escapism and construct virtual existences for themselves in which virtual income and virtual life go hand in hand. This, in turn, raises the question of whether such income should be taxed and perhaps even the question of whether an "exodus" into virtual worlds is under way.[13] As soon as such worlds develop a sophisticated division of labor and become socially differentiated, players will expect certain opportunities to acquire things in exchange for the time that they have invested elsewhere in the game, and fictitious game currencies will come to be exchanged, at a more or less regular rate, with national currencies. Experts have estimated that the value of such currency trading lies somewhere between one and two billion dollars per year. Just how games become economically productive is evident in the sweatshops, in places like China and Mexico, that employ cheap labor to level up virtual characters on behalf of interested customers. Their customer base includes not only casual gamers who lack the patience to cultivate their avatars for months on end, but also for instance documentary film makers who need a particular character for machinima, or marketing companies that seek to make profits in virtual worlds.[14] Other customers might include game journalists who want to write about a virtual world without having to spend months of precious time in it; game developers who need to explore the worlds designed by their competitors; or players who occasionally want to acquire additional magic objects, weapons, gold, or avatars for their guilds.

All of this commerce has made synthetic worlds into a social, political, and economic reality that has yet to be fully understood or appreciated. In an interview with the University of Chicago Press, Edward Castronova made the following insightful comparisons:

> In virtual worlds – or synthetic worlds, "virtual" having lost much of its meaning – only the icons around which human interactions flow are nonreal. The interactions themselves are as real as any we have outside synthetic worlds. When six soldiers take out a machine-gun nest at Fort Bragg, the machine gun is real and the teamwork is real. When the same six soldiers take out a dragon in a synthetic world, the dragon is not real but the teamwork is. In synthetic worlds, the things we trade may be fantastic, but the process and value of the trade is real.[15]

---

[13] See Edward Castronova, *Exodus to the Virtual World: How Online Fun Is Changing Reality* (New York: Palgrave Macmillan, 2007).

[14] On machinima, see Peter Krapp, "Über Spiele und Gesten: Machinima und das Anhalten der Bewegung," *Paragrana: Internationale Zeitschrift für historische Anthropologie* 17 (2008), 296–315.

[15] University of Chicago Press, "An Interview with Edward Castronova" (2005), http://www.press. uchicago.edu/ Misc/Chicago/096262in.html (accessed on June 24, 2014).

Along with other developers and researchers, Richard Bartle has traced such practices back to 1987, when they began to feature in multi-user dungeons and other online forums. As early as 1997, players of *Ultima Online* were able to purchase virtual goods on eBay, which was a fairly new site at the time. In 2001, Brock Pierce founded the Internet Gaming Exchange, which provided a means for customers to purchase virtual currencies and goods. The serious academic study of virtual economies began with Castronova's analysis of the macroeconomic activity in *EverQuest II*, a game that had become available on Sony Online in 1999. According to his calculations, the average hourly wage on the fictional planet of Norrath ($3.42) was competitive with that in Bulgaria; moreover, Norrath's per capita GNP of $2,226 exceeded that of China and India during the year under investigation.[16] In 2003, Linden Lab inaugurated *Second Life*, a synthetic world that requires all of its players to purchase so-called Linden Dollars with real currency (by credit card or through PayPal). Since then there has hardly been a single MMORPG whose currency and avatars have been treated any differently. Avatars can be auctioned on eBay, while swords, horses, gold, and other virtual objects can likewise be sold for real money to the highest bidder.

If it is indeed true that almost half of all the players in synthetic worlds exchange money and engage in commerce, then it might be beneficial to give this market a closer look and to evaluate its consequences for our understanding of "games" – and for the bottom lines of the companies that operate them. The best observations thus far have come from commentators, such as Castronova and Julian Dibbell, who are participants themselves.[17] For 750 Linden Dollars (about $2.25 at the time), Dibbell offered his work as an eBook that could be read by an avatar in *Second Life*, and he also offered it as a hardcopy for 6,250 Linden Dollars (approximately $18.75). Autographed editions of both versions were also available for auction, and all of this was done under the following motto: "On behalf of Julian Dibbell, 'Julian Dibbell' is selling *Play Money* for play money." Castronova, for his part, found nearly twenty million dollars of commerce on eBay that was related to *EverQuest II*, and from this he concluded that there must be even more of such economic activity within the game itself. A good deal of discussion has surrounded the idea that "real-money trading" has degraded or distorted the concept of "games," pointing in part to the influence of limited restrictions on trade, and partly to the very real existence of transaction costs. But players and developers do not have many options at their disposal: because every game has participants who insist on their right to conduct such business, companies have been forced to react in one way or another. There have been three general approaches to the issue of introducing trade and barter into the gaming worlds: prohibition, segmentation, and integration. A comparison of these approaches will allow us to speculate about how things might look if any of the competing companies had chosen to implement

---

16   Edward Castronova, *Synthetic Worlds: The Business and Culture of Online Games* (Chicago: University of Chicago Press, 2005).

17   In addition to Castronova's book cited in the previous note, see Julian Dibbell, *Play Money, or How I Quit My Day Job and Made Millions Trading Virtual Loot* (New York: Basic Books, 2006).

an alternative model. In each scenario, social, cultural, and economic values are transferred back and forth between synthetic worlds and the real market in a self-perpetuating loop.

Blizzard has expressed its appreciation for the continuous feedback provided by the large numbers of players of its games, though it has done so with some reluctance. Jeff Kaplan, one of the lead designers of *World of Warcraft*, pointedly cited the value of internet forums such as Wowhead,[18] though he is quick to qualify his assessment: "The community agrees on nothing, but is never wrong; it pretends to agree with one another, but it is not good at problem solving; and it is not good at game design, but is a good tool to identify issues."[19] That said, the company has left the players of *World of Warcraft* with little doubt about its corporate position; both its End-User License Agreement and its Terms of Use are unambiguously draconian. Real-money trading is taboo, any players engaged in it will be banned from the game, and their WoW accounts will be closed. Linden Labs, however, provides stable and reliable tools not only for designing avatars and their environments but also for all sorts of commerce on *Second Life*, from selling virtual real estate to exchanging certain services for Linden Dollars. Sony in turn decided to set up two different types of servers for *EverQuest*, one that prohibits real-money trading entirely (because it undermines certain approaches to the game) and one in which Sony permits the trading style of play, and itself functions as the broker. In the latter case, real-money trading is not only permitted; it is also linked to something called Station Exchange, which allows Sony to take part in the secondary market. Several questions come to mind in light of these three models: Do transaction costs hinder the free flow of social, cultural, and economic capital? What methods are available for players and developers to reduce these costs, and to what extent can the effects of such methods be observed? Answers to these questions are suggested by the qualitative, quantitative, and anecdotal evidence furnished by the existing scholarship devoted to "ludocapitalism," by interviews with players, and by my own experiences in *EverQuest II*, *World of Warcraft*, and *Second Life* between 2006 and 2011. While pursuing such answers, however, I was quickly confronted by another phenomenon associated with these games, namely with the use of secondary software in synthetic worlds. This phenomenon radicalizes the issues surrounding games and markets even further.

III. End Users

On October 25, 2006, three representatives from Blizzard arrived unannounced at Michael Donnelly's home office in Phoenix, Arizona: a lawyer, a vice president from corporate parent Vivendi, and a private detective. Donnelly, the owner and founder of MDY Industries, is the creator of WoWGlider, a popular and controversial piece of automation software for *World of Warcraft*. Although he has maintained that his business in no way violates Blizzard's rights, the company accused him of infringing upon their contracts, copyrights,

---

[18]   The forum can be found at http://www.wowhead.com/premium.

[19]   This quotation is from a personal conversation that I had with Kaplan on January 25, 2012.

trademarks, and of breaching the Digital Millennium Copyright Act as well. According to Blizzard, MDY Industries has detracted from the value of their game, from the nature of MMORPGs, and from the legitimacy of intellectual property itself.[20] Donnelly's appeal, which was (curiously enough) delivered to Vivendi's offices on the same day, maintained that Blizzard's representatives had threatened him. Interesting, too, is the fact that Blizzard's counter-appeal was not filed until February 20, 2007; it demanded that MDY shut down WoWGlider's website, surrender the source code to Blizzard, and indemnify Blizzard for accrued losses. The speed with which Donnelly filed his suit suggests that he and his lawyers had already been in contact with Blizzard and were ready to go to court. Though somewhat unusual, Blizzard's four-month delay indicates that the two parties were then undergoing some negotiations. At any rate, there was no doubt that the case would have enormous implications for End-User License Agreements and Terms of Use. According to Blizzard, MDY's violation of contract law, copyright law, trademarks, and the Digital Millennium Copyright Act led to unfair competition and unjustly earned profits. Equating contracts with intellectual property, the company argued that the experience of *World of Warcraft*'s legitimate players was under constant attack from impostors attempting to appropriate the game for their own unlawful purposes.

Blizzard's draconian licensing is yet another indication of how, on the Internet, contracts matter much more than laws.[21] The problem in this case is not one of copy protection (WoWGlider functions independently from *World of Warcraft*'s code), nor is it plausible that Blizzard loses any profits when people let "bots" play the game in their absence (their subscriptions continue to be paid regardless). It might seem as though the main issue of the dispute is whether Blizzard loses any money when players are "banned" from the game, but this is also unlikely. Committed fans of *World of Warcraft* simply return to the game with a new subscription, and in many cases they even use the same credit card to pay for it. If there are any losses at all, these seem to be suffered by the players themselves, who have to start over with the game; this is another reason, in fact, why it is enticing to use WoWGlider. I found one user of the service who proudly posted a list of all his banned accounts:

---

[20]   See Dan Burk, "Authorization and Governance in Virtual Worlds," *First Monday* 15 (May 2010), http://firstmonday.org/htbin/cgiwrap/bin/ojs/index/php/fm/article/view/2967/2527: "Blizzard had placed software safeguards, dubbed Warden, on its system to detect and prevent botting or similar impermissible game modifications. The Warden software restricted access to the Blizzard servers by scanning a user's computer at logon to look for unauthorized programs, and by requesting periodic updates on memory use from the client software during play. Users whose equipment failed either of these automated inspections were disconnected and refused access. In order to function, Glider bypassed the Warden detection features; Blizzard characterized this as circumvention of a technical protection."

[21]   See Joshua Fairfield, "Anti-Social Contracts: The Contractual Governance of Virtual Worlds," *McGill Law Journal* 53 (2008), 427–76; and Dan Burk, "Copyright and Paratext in Computer Gaming," in *Emerging Ethical Issues of Life in Virtual Worlds*, ed. Charles Wankel and Shaun Malleck (Charlotte, NC: Information Age Pub., 2010), 33–53.

~~Glided~~
1-60 Undead (Holy) Priest *BANNED*
1-60 Undead (Frost) Mage *BANNED*
1-60 Undead (Shadow) Priest *BANNED*
1-60 Troll (Fire) Mage *BANNED*
1-60 Troll Shaman *BANNED*
1-42 Undead Rogue (Melee classes aren't for me so I gave up on this one) *BANNED*
~~Gliding~~
1-46 Troll Hunter *BANNED*
1-49 Tauren Druid *BANNED*

A conservative estimate of how long it typically takes for five avatars to reach level sixty, and another three to reach level forty, suggests that this single player paid something like the following amount of money to Blizzard: $20 × 8 new accounts + a subscription of $15 × 12 months = $340 or $28.33 per month. That is twice the amount of what the average player pays. One study has estimated that it takes fifteen days of playing time to reach level sixty by normal means.[22] Even if it is assumed that the use of WoWGlider does not considerably slow down this process, it would take at least four months to accomplish what this player did. Taking into account the interruptions brought about by being banned, one could realistically estimate that the process might require an entire year to complete. It must be supposed, then, that diehard fans represent a considerable source of income for Blizzard, not a loss. I myself know that among my students there were at least twenty-seven players who have used WoWGlider, and each one of them had three accounts (on average). In other words, each of them paid Blizzard an average of $250 per year, which, despite any interruptions, is a third more than the company could have expected from a typical player.

More generally, it is worth asking to what extent the use of WoWGlider even affects the gaming experience of others. Is Blizzard able to demonstrate how many of its customers stopped playing the game because of their distaste for real-money trading or automation software? How many players have actually cancelled their subscriptions for this reason? And do these players object to auctioning off their avatars to players who, in large part, have no problems at all with such transactions or with WoWGlider? The main reasons why people stop playing *World of Warcraft* probably involve time management, a loss of interest in the contents of the game, and problems with the guilds. So why did Blizzard really want to sue MDY? In short, it came down to Blizzard's unwillingness to yield any influence over the nature of their game. The new style of play, supported by secondary markets and software, would lie outside of Blizzard's authority. This was problematic for the company because as always the main concern of game design is with maintaining a balance between rules that govern play and the leeway a player has while playing. Designing games is a matter of both limiting risks and allowing players to discover whatever

---

[22] Nicolas Ducheneaut et al., "Building an MMO with Mass Appeal: A Look at Gameplay in *World of Warcraft*," *Games and Culture* 1 (2006), 281–317.

risks remain. The involvement of secondary markets and software causes a game to shift fundamentally; Blizzard's concern was less about the content of *World of Warcraft* than it was about the playing conditions of the game. What the company's stance has entailed for *World of Warcraft*, however, is an unstable economy, doubts about the value of the game's concept, high regulatory costs, reduced liquidity, and an authoritarian approach to the game's management. Interestingly, Blizzard has been more tolerant in Europe, where the price for gold on the *World of Warcraft* servers is only an eighth of what it is in the United States.[23]

Sony's introduction of server-specific auctions through Station Exchange has provided players of *EverQuest II* with a means of buying and selling items as they please on particular servers, whereas the company's other game servers do not permit such activity. This solution has both reduced Sony's customer-service costs and brought in new fees. What this has meant for *EverQuest II* is a stable economy that ensures lower costs for players and steady profits for Sony Online. In 2007, the first year that this model was implemented, in-game trading of $1.87 million produced $274,083 in fees and commissions for Sony. At the same time, the segmentation of the game community reduced Sony's administrative costs by about thirty percent.[24] If we assume that this demand for real-money trading is proportional to that in *World of Warcraft*, then it is clear that, in 2007, the approximately 8.5 million players of that game could have been responsible for roughly eight million dollars in WoW trade volume. For Blizzard, this could have amounted to around $1.3 million in commissions. Moreover, the legendarily high operating costs of the game could have been lowered as well. Blizzard employs approximately 1,300 "game masters" to monitor the internal activity of the game (this is one my students' favorite part-time jobs). By applying Sony's model, Blizzard could have cut nearly four hundred of these employees (at a wage of ten dollars per hour), a move that might have saved the company around eight million dollars that year.

For *Second Life*, from the very beginning Linden Labs established a stable economy with clear property rights. Everything created in the game belongs to the player who created it, while Linden Labs control only the tools and manages the game. Given that Linden Dollars are necessary for playing the game, the model is specifically designed for exchanging currency (the exchange rate fluctuates, but only minimally). The result for Linden Labs is low operating costs, productive play, and a profitable market. When I asked Maty Roberts, general counsel for Linden Lab, about Blizzard's experiences, he sidestepped the question, stating only that game developers usually do not share such information with one another.[25]

---

[23]   See the study "WoW Gold Price Research: A World of Warcraft Economic Study" *GamerPrice.com*, http://www.gamerprice.com/wow-gold-study.html (accessed June 27, 2014).

[24]   See Noah Robischon, "Station Exchange: Year One (White Paper)" (2007), http://www.gamasutra.com/features/ 20070207/SOE%20Station%20Exchange%20White%20Paper%201.19.doc. This link is no longer active. A copy of the article can now be found at http://www.fredshouse.net/images/ SOE%20Station%20Exchange% 20White%20Paper%201.19.pdf (accessed June 30, 2014).

[25]   Our conversation was held on March 4, 2010.

The spectrum of reactions to the productive or unproductive frictions between the planned economies of online games and the actual market economy of the software industry indicates that, even in the case of computer games, the masses have become a commodity. If the growth of the American computer-game market has by now come to be dominated less by packaged goods than by subscriptions and secondary transactions, this means that the focus of the industry has shifted from goods, services, and demographic niches to the much-anticipated "new masses." In this regard it should be noted that the scene in Asia is already far ahead of that in the United States. There, a much larger portion of players is engaged with online games, and at least a fifth of all gamers deal with online goods, services, and currencies.[26] On the one hand, then, there is the rational expectation that the economies of computer games will find a natural equilibrium between rigorous central planning and playful self-regulation, and on the other hand there is the assumption of reflexive behaviorists that inherently unstable game worlds will lose cohesion as more and more people participate in them. It is only in the tension between these two positions that the new mass media have been able to commodify the masses.

---

[26]   See Kim Zetter, "Bullion and Bandits: The Improbable Rise and Fall of E-Gold," *Wired* (June 2009), http://www.wired.com/2009/06/e-gold/ (accessed on June 30, 2014).

Images:

Figure 21: Xbox Live Members (Dec 2005 – Jun 2010) – (in millions)
>10x in less than 5 years
30
25
20
15
10
5
0
2
3
4
5
6
7
10
12
14
17
20
23
25
Dec 05
Jun 06
Sep 06
Dec 06
Mar 07
Jun 07
Dec 07
Jun 08
Sep 08
Dec 08
Jun 09
Dec 09
Jun 10
Source: Microsoft

Figure 11: US Publisher Market Share 2000A-2009A
25.0%
20.0%
15.0%
10.0%
5.0%
0.0%
2000 2001 2002 2003 2004 2005 2006 2007 2008 2009
Activision
Electronic Arts
Take Two
THQ
Ubisoft
Source: NPD, Deutsche Bank Estimates.

Figure 26: US Online PC Gaming Market Segment Breakout ($ in millions)
MMO & Casual Subscription
Premium Full Game & Add-On Download
Advertising & Microtransactions
$10,000
$9,000
$8,000
$7,000
$6,000
$5,000
$4,000
$3,000
$2,000
$1,000
$0
2009 2010E 2011E 2012E 2013E 2014E
$1,042
$910
$1,479
$1,136
$1,348
$1,963
$1,500
$1,935
$2,585
$1,873
$2,474
$3,218
$2,275
$2,474
$3,733
$2,698
$2,583
$4,211
Source: IDC, Deutsche Bank Estimates

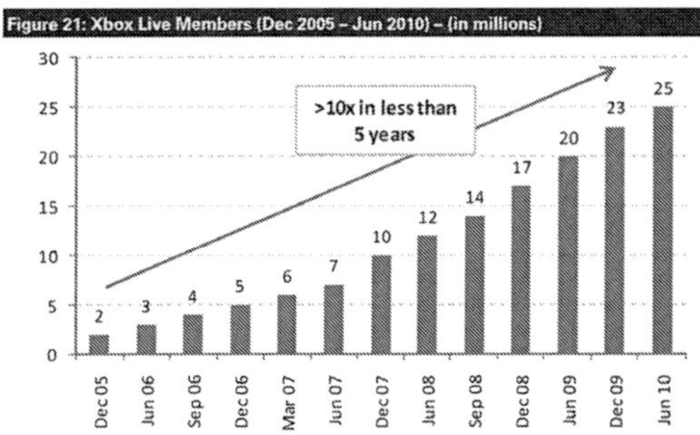

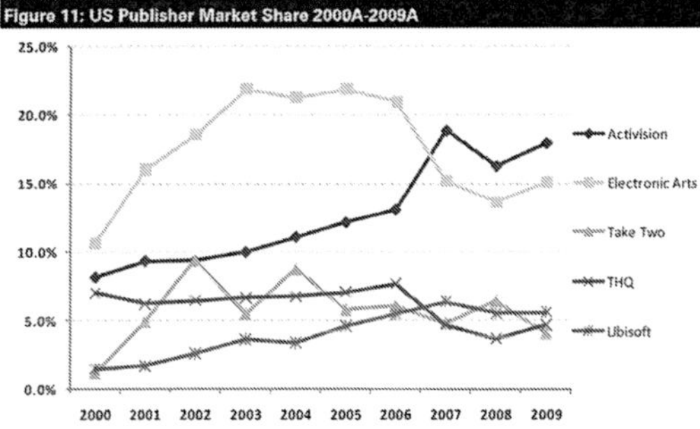

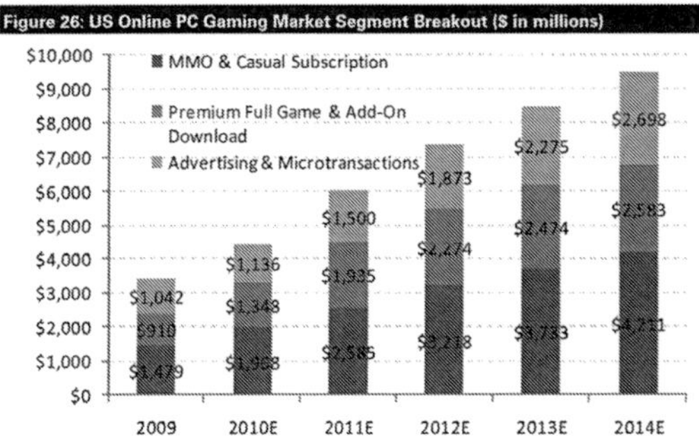

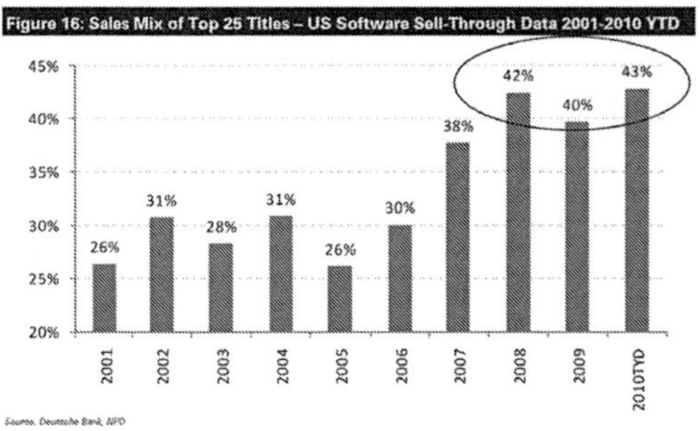

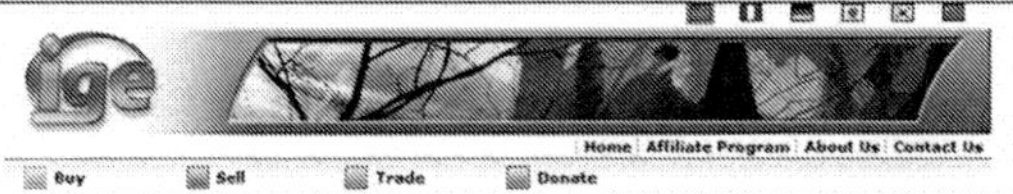

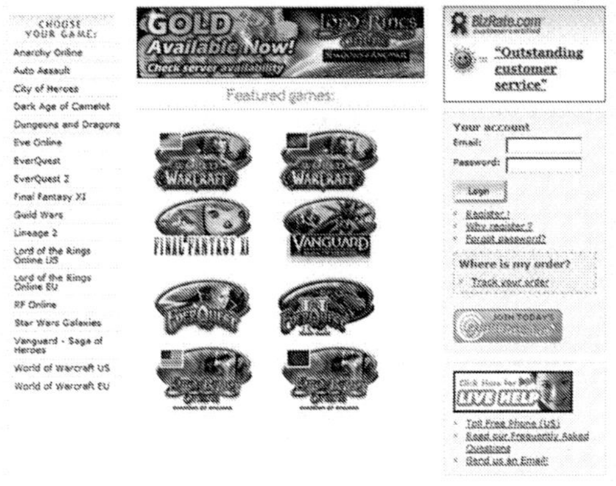

Figure 27: Comparison of Subscription-Based MMOs and Free-to-Play / Credits

SUBSCRIPTION-BASED

Title	Release	Subscribers (1)	Monthly Fee (2)	Description
World of Warcraft	2004	12,000,000	$14.38	Blizzard franchise with strong engaged user base
Aion	2009	3,500,000	$15.00	NC Soft title, developed in Korea, fantasy genre game, recently Westernized
RuneScape	2001	1,200,000	$5.95	Jagex developed game, popular free MMORPG with 15m accounts
Lineage II	2003	1,000,000	$7.50	NC Soft title, developed in Korea
Final Fantasy XI	2002	500,000	$12.95	Square enix game, popular in Japan
Dofus	2005	500,000	$7.00	Ankama Games, pay-to-play game, new version in beta test Wakfu
Warhammer Online	2008	300,000	$14.99	Electronic Arts game, developed by Mythic, 800k users in Sept 2008
EVE Online	2003	245,000	$14.95	Science fiction game developed by CCP games, Iceland

FREE MMORPG

Title	Release	Subscribers (1)	Monthly Fee (2)	Description
Habbo	2000	116,500,000	Free/Credits	Social networking website targeting teens, interacts in virtual hotel
MapleStory	2005	5,000,000	Free/Credits	Developed by WizNet, uses micro-transactions for virtual currency
Guild Wars	2005	5,000,000	Free/Credits	NC Soft title, created by senior Blizzard developers
Knight Online	2004	4,250,000	Free/Credits	Mgame developed game (Korea), requires SSN to register, some pay features
Second Life	2003	1,701,827	Free/Credits	Developed by LindenLab, the virtual world has own economy using virtual dollars
Hattrick	1997	604,000	Free/Credits	Online browser based soccer game (Sweden), pay-to-play features

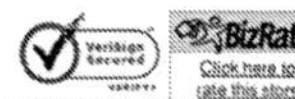

An evening with Julian Dibbell
New Globe: 94/168
Thursday, July 27
Noon PST:
Book signing and informal chat
with Julian.
6PM PST:
Interview with Hamlet Au followed
by audience Q&A and book signing.
Event sponsored and produced by:
Millions of Us
PLAY MONEY
JULIAN DIBBELL

LindeX official L$ Exchange
Buy or Sell L$ here!

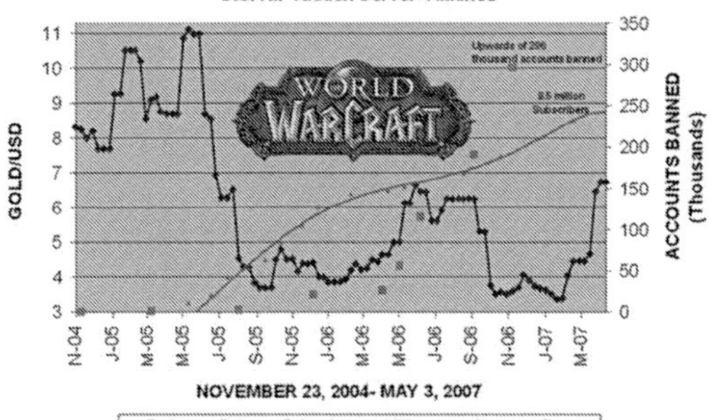

WORLD OF WARCRAFT DOLLAR EXCHANGE RATES
U.S. Kil' Jaeden Server- Alliance
GOLD/USD
ACCOUNTS BANNED (Thousands)
Upwards of 296 thousand accounts banned
8.5 million subscribers
WORLD WARCRAFT
NOVEMBER 23, 2004- MAY 3, 2007
Exchange Rate Subscriptions (Millions) Accounts Banned

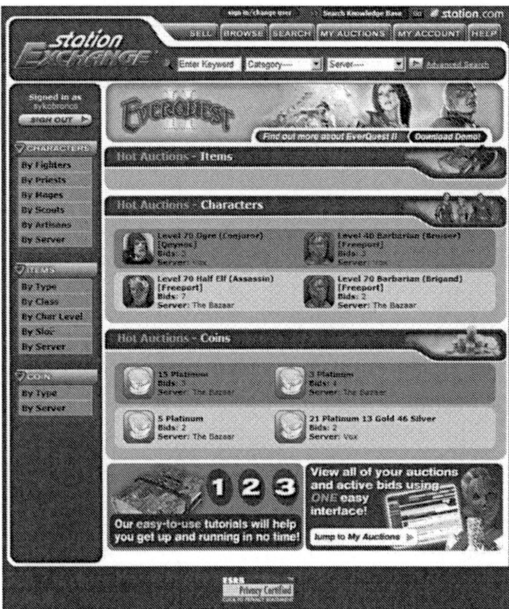

station.com
station EXCHANGE
SELL BROWSE SEARCH MY AUCTIONS MY ACCOUNT HELP
Search Knowledge Base
Enter Keyword Category---- Server---- Advanced Search
Signed in as
sykobronco
SIGN OUT
CHARACTERS
By Fighters
By Priests
By Mages
By Scouts
By Artisans
By Server
ITEMS
By Type
By Class
By Char Level
By Slot
By Server
COINS
By Type
By Server
EVERQUEST
Find out more about EverQuest II Download Demo!
Hot Auctions - Items
Hot Auctions - Characters
Level 70 Ogre (Conjuror) [Qeynos] Bids: 5 Server: Vox
Level 40 Barbarian (Bruiser) [Freeport] Bids: 3 Server:
Level 70 Half Elf (Assassin) [Freeport] Bids: 7 Server: The Bazaar
Level 70 Barbarian (Brigand) [Freeport] Bids: 2 Server: The Bazaar
Hot Auctions - Coins
15 Platinum Bids: 3 Server: The Bazaar
3 Platinum Bids: 4 Server: The Bazaar
5 Platinum Bids: 2 Server: The Bazaar
21 Platinum 13 Gold 46 Silver Bids: 2 Server: Vox
1 2 3
Our easy-to-use tutorials will help you get up and running in no time!
View all of your auctions and active bids using ONE easy interface!
Jump to My Auctions
ESRB Privacy Certified

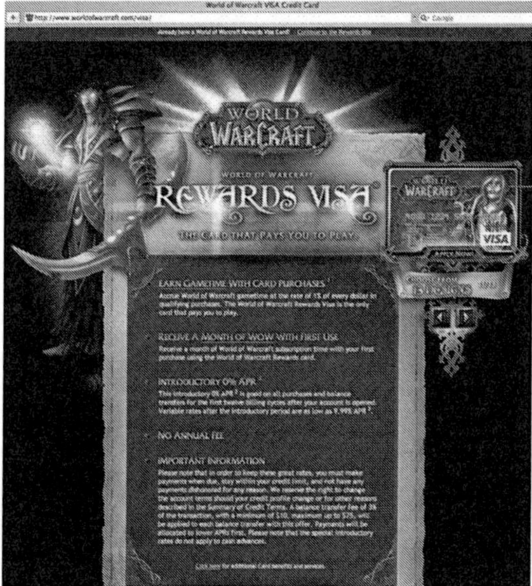

IV. Commentaries

Marie-Luise Angerer

Short-Circuiting the Masses

Toward the end of Stieg Larsson's *The Girl with the Dragon Tattoo*, the character Mikael Blomkvist expresses his suspicion that Lisbeth Salander, the very girl with the dragon tattoo with whom he has collaborated so successfully, must suffer from something along the lines of Asperger's Syndrome: While seemingly autistic in her dealings with people and her environment, she exhibits a great talent for recognizing patterns and structures, an equally great talent for hacking into networks and computers, and an even greater talent for tracking things down.[1] In her appearance and behavior, however, Lisbeth Salander happens to share much in common with the way in which young women have been portrayed (and have portrayed themselves) in recent films, television shows, advertisements, fashion shoots, and other media. Spot on with the trend, she is androgynous to the point of being asexual, fixated with her work, experienced with sexual abuse and drugs, a computer specialist, a hacker, and a motorcycle rider. This is not even to mention her tautly sculpted body, which can mercilessly prevail over any physical challenge that it confronts.[2]

The discourse concerned with new social media (and their "masses") contains two noteworthy peculiarities. The first is its strong tendency to associate the agents of these networked worlds with mental, physical, and social qualities that are stereotypically feminine.[3] The second is its conspicuous strategy to redefine otherness in terms of "neuro-

---

[1] Stieg Larsson, *The Girl with the Dragon Tattoo*, trans. Steven T. Murray (London: Quercus, 2011), 399: "*Asperger's Syndrome*, he thought, *Or something like that. A talent for seeing patterns and understanding abstract reasoning where other people perceive only white noise*" (the italics are original).

[2] Similar examples include the CIA agent played by Jessica Chastain in Kathryn Bigelow's film *Zero Dark Thirty* (2012), who supposedly resembled one of the "real" CIA agents quite closely, and Claire Danes's character Carrie Mathison in the television program *Homeland* (2011-), who is a CIA officer suffering from bipolar disorder.

[3] In a recent article titled "War ich heute schon gut genug?" ("Was I Good Enough Today"), for instance, the *Süddeutsche Zeitung* summarized a debate about politics and senior management in which both sides agreed that the social competencies associated with women – such as listening skills, empathy, and communication – have come to be considered absolutely necessary qualities in the digitally connected world. Yet these same characteristics belong to an entire canon of others; think of multitasking, fitness, health consciousness, child care, nurturing friendships, and so on. Like the

diversity." As a result of this strategy, medical diagnoses such as Asperger's Syndrome are no longer classified as illnesses but rather as potentially alternative forms of perception and behavior. Moreover, they have also been reclassified as a potentially alternative form of social interaction that is not based on empathy as much as it is on object references and technological connections.[4]

Ten years after the publication of Donna J. Haraway's essay "A Cyborg Manifesto" (1984),[5] Sadie Plant declared women to be the first real cyborgs, and this is because women and cyberspace together constitute a peculiar symbiosis.[6] According to Plant, this symbiosis is conspicuous in the fact that our society continues to function through the exchange of women. Women have existed exclusively as a medium, as a transition, as an object of transaction among men; they have been the intermediaries, the "in-betweens," the figures sent by embassies of men to tally his sums, bear his children, and thus pass on his genetic code. Up to this point, Plant's analysis concurs with Friedrich Kittler's definition of women working at typewriters and telephone switchboards.[7] Yet by now, in her estimation, the digital revolution has annulled the opposition between a material (feminine) base and an ideal (masculine) superstructure. Here Plant was playing both with the Marxist idea of base and superstructure as well as with the traditional Western way of thinking that places the feminine on the "inferior" side of things and equates it with nature, the body, and emotions. Yet today, according to her argument, doubt has been cast on this humanistic subject. New sorts of connections have led to digital, mental, and material hybridities, and these have brought an end to "project mankind," just as Michel Foucault had predicted they would in *The Order of Things*.[8] According to Plant, moreover, this is an end of an era to which women, having never been integrated into man's project to begin with, have suffered no pain in saying farewell. It is men who, as the former shapers of history, are now struggling to define their future with any clarity.

---

corresponding societal expectations faced by young men, these expectations are known to lead to mental illnesses, such as anorexia and bulimia, that have characterized the image of girls and young women for decades.

[4] According to a report in the magazine *Der Spiegel*, the company SAP has begun to hire autistic software testers because of their ability to recognize structures and patterns, their high level of concentration, etc. See Martin Motzkau, "Autisten bei SAP: Super-Talente mit Überraschungseffekt," *Spiegel Online* (May 2013), http://www.spiegel.de/wirtschaft/unternehmen/sap-stellt-autisten-ein-a-901090.html (accessed on July 1, 2014).

[5] Donna J. Haraway, "A Cyborg Manifesto: Science, Technology, and Socialist-Feminism in the Late Twentieth Century," in *Simians, Cyborgs, and Women: The Reinvention of Nature*, by Haraway (London: Free Association Books, 1991), 149–83.

[6] Sadie Plant, "The Future Looms: Weaving Women and Cybernetics," *Body & Society* 1 (1995), 45–64.

[7] Friedrich Kittler, *Gramophone, Film, Typewriter*, trans. Geoffrey Winthrop-Young and Michael Wutz (Stanford: Stanford University Press, 1999).

[8] See Michel Foucault, *The Order of Things: An Archaeology of the Human Sciences* (New York: Pantheon, 1970), 386–87: "One thing in any case is certain: man is neither the oldest nor the most constant problem that has been posed for human knowledge. [...] As the archaeology of our thought easily shows, man is an invention of recent date. And one perhaps nearing its end."

This description of the situation dovetails quite well with the development and evaluation of so-called "feminine qualities," as described briefly in my third footnote above. The societal shift diagnosed by Plant, however, also entailed a general reevaluation of the "masses" (especially by the media).

Since their first sociological and psychological definitions by Gustave Le Bon, Sigmund Freud, and others, masses or crowds of people have been described (often implicitly) as feminine, irrational, fear-driven, panic-fueled, and hysterical. According to Freud's psychoanalysis, crowds become enchanted by a super-ego or leader (who could only have been imagined as masculine), whereby the boundaries of individual egos begin to fade. This notion of the masses persisted throughout most of the twentieth century in theories about the mass media and their audience. It was not until the 1970s that British cultural theorists such as Stuart Hall, John Fiske, and Ien Ang rejected the presumed obtuseness of "couch potatoes" and began to analyze male and female television viewers as competent agents. Until then, television consumers in particular had been regarded as passive victims who were helpless and defenseless against the ideological manipulations of the consciousness industry (and thus placed in an implicitly feminine position).

In the meantime, Sadie Plant's analysis of women as the first cyborgs has taken hold. The fitness and beauty industries have long welcomed the cyborgization of the body, and the work conducted by synthetic biologists, especially on the artificial and technological production of human beings, has for some time promoted the idea of a "different" sort of humanity. Alongside these developments, the traditional mass medium of the television has begun to lose its "readers" (in Stuart Hall's terms), as more and more people (especially the young) have begun to organize themselves as swarms or clouds by means of smart phones and other signal networks.

Throughout this process, however, the time or interval of time in which people act and react – unconsciously, reflexively, uncontrollably, and unintentionally – has come to play a prominent role. (I will return to this role over the course of my argument, which will ultimately return to *The Girl with the Dragon Tattoo*. In the meantime, I will propose a new understanding of the masses, which have certainly not become more intelligent but rather – following a logic that is implicitly masculine – have possibly come to be controlled "more intelligently.") First, however, a few words are in order regarding this small but decisive interval of time.

In the middle of the nineteenth century, Hermann von Helmholtz became the first person to measure the amount of time that was lost between stimuli and reactions. He did this in laboratory experiments first conducted with frogs and later on with humans.[9] In her investigations of childhood television viewing, which were conducted more than a century later, Hertha Sturm measured a "missing half-second" that led children to react

---

[9]	See Henning Schmidgen, *The Helmholtz Curves: Tracing Lost Time*, trans. Nils F. Schott (New York: Fordham University Press, 2014).

to the screen in a manner that was "somehow out of place."[10] Since then, Benjamin Libet's "short delay" between signals and reactions has become "common sense" in media studies and in other disciplines that have been influenced by the findings of neurology.[11] In his studies devoted to "technics and time," Bernard Stiegler has also called attention to the impending "grammaticalization of consciousness" by means of the new programming industries, which have stimulated a tertiary memory (in Husserl's terms) whereby the pace or rhythm of humanity has reached a new dimension.[12] In 1993, Stiegler and Jacques Derrida held a conversation about the advanced media-technological developments of the time. Their conversation was prompted, in particular, by CNN's live coverage of the American bombing of Bagdad: "Broadcast in real time, television achieves a sort of *plusquampraesens* that, during the production of images, causes any potential for selection and manipulation to disappear behind a supposedly objective actuality or up-to-dateness."[13] During their conversation, Derrida, the philosopher of *différance* – of originary postponement as an absent precondition for every positivity – wrestled with the question of how it might be possible "to think one's time." "The time of this very speaking," he concluded, "is artificially produced. It is an *artifact*."[14]

The new media (and the new masses) have been decisive factors in the discussion about this "artifact of time." At the end of the nineteenth century, this interval – a half-second or a "tenth of a second" (in Jimena Canales's terms)[15] – was described by Henri Bergson as a "zone of sensation," as a moment that encroaches between one movement and the next. It is the moment that Gilles Deleuze, in his books on the cinema, refers to as a zone in which affect can be overcome and transcended as a technical occurrence.[16] It is

---

[10] See Hertha Sturm and J. Ray Brown, eds., *Wie Kinder mit dem Fernsehen umgehen: Nutzen und Wirkung eines Mediums* (Stuttgart: Klett-Cotta, 1979); and Hertha Sturm, *Fernsehdiktate: Die Veränderung von Gedanken und Gefühlen. Ergebnisse und Folgerungen für eine rezipientenorientierte Mediendramaturgie* (Gütersloh: Bertelsmann Stiftung, 1991).

[11] See Peter Hankins, "Libet's Short Delay," *Conscious Entities* (June 2005), http://www.consciousentities. com/libet.htm; and Marie-Luise Angerer, "Vom Lauf der 'halben Sekunde'," *Kunsttexte.de: E-Journal für Kunst und Bildgeschichte* 1 (2011), http://edoc.hu-berlin.de/kunsttexte/2011-1/angerer-marie-luise-6/ PDF/angerer.pdf (both sites were accessed on July 1, 2014).

[12] Bernard Stiegler, *Technics and Time*, 3 vols., trans. Richard Beardsworth et al. (Stanford: Stanford University Press, 1998–2009).

[13] Jacques Derrida and Bernard Stiegler, *Echographien: Fernsehgespräche*, trans. Horst Brühmann (Vienna: Passagen, 2006), 2: "In Echtzeit zielt das Fernsehen auf ein *Plusquampräsens*, das alle Selections- und Manipulationsmöglichkeiten bei der Produktion der Bilder hinter einer vermeintlich objektiven Aktualität verschwinden läßt." This sentence is absent from the English version of the book, which will be cited in the following note.

[14] Jacques Derrida and Bernard Stiegler *Echographies of Television: Filmed Interviews*, trans. Jennifer Bajorek (Malden, MA: Blackwell, 2002), 3 (the emphasis is original).

[15] Jimena Canales, *A Tenth of a Second: A History* (Chicago: University of Chicago Press, 2009).

[16] Gilles Deleuze, *Cinema 1: The Movement Image*, trans. Hugh Tomlinson and Robert Galeta (London: Continuum, 2005); idem, *Cinema 2: The Time Image*, trans. Hugh Tomlinson and Robert Galeta (London: Continuum, 2005).

the moment that Brian Massumi would ultimately equate with Hertha Sturm's "missing half-second" in order to argue (*contra* Sturm) that in fact so much happens during this time frame that our consciousness is unable to register any of it.[17]

With reference to recent developments in media technology, however, efforts are being made today to challenge the idea that this "time gap" is an interval at all. The notion of time, it is thought, should rather be reconsidered yet again. In his essay "The Temporal Gap," Wolfgang Ernst has argued that auditory and visual channels operate at different speeds and are not equally well suited for perception. Whereas auditory perception captures the real, he maintains that visual perception is always dependent on the imaginary; it is always creating abstractions because the eye is unable to apprehend exceedingly fast activity.[18] Mark B. N. Hansen, for his part, has taken a step further and contended that the missing half-second does not even exist; it is rather the case, he proposes, that the interval was simply "made up" by various recording techniques. In his book *Feed-Forward*, Hansen refines Husserl's model of time-consciousness and self-affection to argue that time can only be experienced in a technical manner.[19]

One of Bergson's contemporaries, Gabriel Tarde, had long been overshadowed by his rival Emile Durkheim before his theory of monads and imitation became attractive to today's media theorists. Tarde revived Leibniz's monadology in order to confront the scientific impulses of his time with a corresponding quantity, namely the smallest unit of intelligent existence. Science, according to Tarde, "tends to pulverize the universe and to multiply beings indefinitely."[20] It also wishes to overcome the Cartesian duality of mind and matter and thus it leads to "psychomorphism," according to which each and everything is accorded something like a soul. He thought that the existence and activity of these souls could be recognized in the two universal forces of "movement" and "sensation," forces which he discussed in terms of universal "belief" and universal "desire":

> By the universality of their presence in all psychological phenomena, both human and animal, by the homogeneity of their nature from one end of their immense gamut to the other, from the slightest inclination to believe or to want up to certainty and passion, […] belief and desire play exactly the same role in the ego, with respect to sensations, as do space and time in the external world with respect to material elements.[21]

My question now is whether Gabriel Tarde's monadology, with its psychomorphism, can be regarded as having reemerged today in the form of "mediamorphism" – a media-

---

[17] Brian Massumi, "The Autonomy of Affect," *Cultural Critique* 31 (1995), 83–109.

[18] Wolfgang Ernst, "The Temporal Gap: On Asymmetries within the So-Called 'Audiovisual' Regime (in Sensory Perception and in Technical Media)," in *Synaesthesia and Kinaesthetics*, ed. Jörg Fingerhut et al. (Berlin: Peter Lang, 2011), 225–40.

[19] Mark B. N. Hansen, *Feed-Forward: On the Future of Twenty-First-Century Media* (Chicago: University of Chicago Press, 2014).

[20] Gabriel Tarde, *Monadology and Sociology*, trans. Theo Lorenc (Melbourne: Re.Press, 2012), 15.

[21] Ibid., 16–17.

morphism that returns like a boomerang to the end of the nineteenth century in order to encounter there the *"need for society"* that is as manifest in atoms, trees, and stars as it is in human beings.[22]

Since the 1970s, psychoanalytically oriented film and media theorists had largely dispensed with the concept of imitation, which in their eyes had been too rigidly formulated as a psychological and social process by scholars in the humanities and social sciences. Instead of the sociologically charged concept of imitation, they rather preferred the psychoanalytic concept of identification, which focused more heavily on the dimension of the unconscious. By now, however, interest in psychoanalysis has waned considerably and the issue of imitation has found itself at the forefront of public debates. In Deleuze and Guattari's reading, moreover, Tarde's notion of imitation has been correlated with a structure of desire that happens to be highly relevant to today's intellectual trends. As Christian Borch and Urs Stäheli have stressed, Tarde's "sociology of desire" or "sociology of affect" is so important to today's theoretical discussions because it does not reduce desire to a "psychoanalytic passion play about identification."[23] Rather, it takes the idea of "mimetic repetition" seriously and demonstrates how imitation can be encouraged or discouraged by the forces of desire and belief.

Gabriel Tarde wrote the following words in 1893: "Difference is the alpha and omega of the universe; everything begins with difference [...]; everything ends with difference. [...] It seems to me that all similarities and all phenomenal repetitions are only intermediaries, which will inevitably be found to be interposed between some elementary diversities which are more or less obliterated."[24] More than a century later, this idea of "mediation-as-difference" – between matter and desire, between micro-levels and macro-levels, between nanotechnology and the body – is experiencing renewed interest from animistic and neocybernetic thinkers alike. During the middle of the 1990s, Sadie Plant argued that the digital conquest of the world would cause the opposition between mind and matter to dissolve. In the figure of the cyborg, an imminent future was imaginable in which the waves, the climate, bacteria, the currents, the wind, and the clouds would come to dictate "culture" – a future in which all traces of an active human subject will already have disappeared.[25] Today the concern is no longer about the difference between culture and nature, or about one overcoming the other; of interest now is rather what, against the backdrop of fundamental digitalization, can (still) be called life. "And so," Derrida asks

---

22   Ibid., 14 (the emphasis is original).

23   Christian Borch and Urs Stäheli, "Einleitung – Tarde's Soziologie der Nachahmung und des Begehrens," in *Soziologie der Nachahmung und des Begehrens: Materialien zu Gabriel Tarde*, ed. Christian Borch and Urs Stäheli (Frankfurt am Main: Suhrkamp, 2008), 7–38, at 11.

24   Tarde, *Monadology and Sociology*, 40–41.

25   See Sadie Plant, "The Virtual Complexity of Culture," in *FutureNatural: Nature, Science, Culture*, ed. George Robertson et al. (New York: Routledge, 1996), 203–17, esp. 214: "Culture emerges from the complex interactions of media, organisms, weather patterns, ecosystems, thought patterns, cities, discourses, fashions, populations, brains, markets, dance nights and bacterial exchanges. There are ecosystems under your fingernails. You live in cultures, and cultures live in you."

in his conversation with Stiegler, "how to proceed without denying ourselves these new resources of live television (the video camera, etc.) while continuing to be critical of their mystification? And above all, while continuing to remind people and to *demonstrate* that the 'live' and 'real time' are never pure, that they do not give us intuition or transparency, a perception stripped of interpretation or technical intervention."[26]

The classical age of mass media – the age of film, radio, and television – is nearing its end. This end is comparable to that of national politics and of societies formed on the basis of "ideological state apparatuses" (in Louis Althusser's terms). The social dimension of such societies was built around "master narratives," the demise of which Jean-François Lyotard had predicted as early as the 1980s.[27] Gilles Deleuze equated this ending with the downfall of disciplinary societies and with the transition, which has long since been undertaken, into the age of control societies. Controls, in Deleuze's estimation, are "a *modulation*, like a self-deforming cast that will continuously change from one moment to another, or like a sieve whose mesh will transmute from point to point."[28] In other words, controls represent a departure from so-called "spaces of enclosure" such as families, schools, or churches, which had all been rather porous for some time, and an analysis of their logic reveals that it is one of "limitless postponements."[29] Such postponement is characterized by constant motion (in the form of ongoing education, services, etc.), by the fact that nothing is ever fully achieved and no one is ever fully satisfied, and by perpetual work for its own sake and for everything else. Whereas the man of disciplinary societies, according to Deleuze, "was a discontinuous producer of energy," the man of control is "undulatory" (for which reason he thought that surfing had superseded all other sports).[30]

A shift that began gradually in the 1990s has since quickened its pace. The technical figure of the cyborg, which was first introduced by researchers to illustrate how someone might be able to survive in outer space as an (irreversibly) technological symbiosis, has by now become doubly attractive as something both realistic and media-"metaphorical." The cyborg, as understood by Haraway, is a girl in order to be radically non-feminine. It is a monad in its need for society. It is a monad that perpetually modulates itself (and must do so), one that can be assigned to neither one side nor the other; it is thus neither active nor passive, neither intelligent nor irrational, but rather brutally demands a type of existence like that of the girl with the dragon tattoo. Compelled by a desire to affect and be affected, it must rely on its body, on its motorcycle, on its drugs, cables, plugs, gadgets, and other elements of connection in order to enter momentary alliances – even if such moments last no longer than half a second.

---

[26] Derrida and Stiegler, *Echographies of Television*, 5 (the emphasis is original).

[27] Jean-François Lyotard, *The Postmodern Condition: A Report on Knowledge*, trans. Geoff Bennington and Brian Massumi (Minneapolis: University of Minnesota Press, 1984).

[28] Gilles Deleuze, "Postscript on the Societies of Control," in *Cultural Theory: An Anthology*, ed. Imre Szeman and Timothy Kaposy (Chichester: Wiley-Blackwell, 2011), 139–42, at 140 (the emphasis is original).

[29] Ibid.

[30] Ibid., 141.

CHARLES ESS

Falling Between Two Chairs – or Three, or …
Comments on the Second Symposium of Media Studies (Medienwissenschaftliches Symposium) of the German Research Society (Deutsche Forschungsgemeinschaft, DFG), "Social Media–New Masses?"

I must begin with my profound thanks to Prof. Dr. Claus Pias and Prof. Dr. Wolfgang Coy for their kind invitation to attend the Symposium as a discussant, and most certainly to the symposium's sponsor, the German Research Society (Deutsche Forschungsgemeinschaft), represented here by Dr. Claudia Althaus. With the same breath – many thanks to the participants whose papers and conversations have proven to be so insightful and inspiring. It was both a very great honor and an enormous pleasure to rejoin the world of German-language scholarship and research over these two days.

I was especially heartened by the interdisciplinary character of the symposium, first of all because the participants and organizers exemplified what I take to be a primary virtue necessary for such interdisciplinary collaborations to succeed – namely, what I think of as an *epistemological humility*: in this posture – one not, shall we say, commonly found or practiced in most academic settings – we do not simply tolerate but openly welcome the views and perspectives of those outside our own primary disciplines. The following comments are offered in turn in such a posture, precisely because I am an Outsider in so many ways. I hope that my observations and suggestions will succeed in their intention – namely, to provide some useful insights from an external perspective.

Very broadly, this was been an exceptionally rich two days, ones that opened up for me a huge bundle of new ideas, new *theoretische Ansätze*, and new insights. The *Reader* collecting your first papers in preparation for the Symposium is especially valuable – and I could not be more pleased but that much of the Reader, revised and enhanced through subsequent revision, is now available to a larger audience through this volume. I have every confidence that the book will quickly establish itself as a watershed publication in Media Studies.

Still broadly speaking: I found here in good measure what I anticipated from the outset – namely, *deutsche Akribie, Gründlichkeit, und vor allem Kritik*. To begin with: I found several of the readings and presentations especially valuable for the sharp critique they offered of what for me are otherwise prevailing frameworks and assumptions in English-language new media and digital media research and scholarship. *Contra* the tendency, still apparent in some circles of English-language work, towards an uncritical, indeed frankly celebratory enthusiasm for new technologies, I found here a refreshing and beneficent series of critical comments and insights, beginning with carefully developed conceptions of civil society, civil rights, and democracy, often taken up as some version of parliamentary democracy.

Moreover, I found the focus on new masses as the defining thematic of the symposium – on how to rethink and reconceptualize what we might understand by these in light of historical changes and media influences – to be simply ingenious (*genial*). While numerous contributions shed significant new light in these directions, I found Carolin Wiedemann's analysis of Anonymous to be especially helpful, as it begins by clearly showing how the group, from its "organization" (or lack thereof, in at least previous ways of thinking) through its effects on the larger world, simply springs apart our received categories and frameworks for thinking about social groups and their potential democratic roles. Taken together, these are thematic foci, critical insights, and fruitful suggestions that I have not encountered elsewhere for how to move beyond frameworks and assumptions that clearly no longer work well in the age of new media and social media. Manifestly, these are clearly central and urgent – both to our work as scholars and researchers and, even more importantly, to our larger societies as this work unfolds new insights that may well have profound implications for the practices, policies, and fundamental self-conceptions of especially democratic societies. Hence the contributions gathered here have every likelihood of dramatically contributing to and radically transforming the theoretical and research landscapes of media as pursued in other national traditions and languages.

At something of a meta-level: it was tremendously encouraging to see interdisciplinary work being furthered through the Symposium – and so fruitfully, as these initial comments suggest. I have pursued interdisciplinary work in one form or another since the 1980s. In my experience, institutional enthusiasm for interdisciplinarity peaked sometime in the 1990s (depending in part, of course, on specific national and cultural contexts). As but one example: the Center for Interdisciplinary Studies at Drury University, established in the 1990s and which I briefly directed, was dissolved this spring (2012). This closure of such a center is, sadly, but one of many that have taken place in recent years – in particular, in the United Kingdom as draconian budget cuts brought on in part by the financial crises of 2009 and onward have forced drastic reductions in staff and research centers. So it is profoundly heartening to see interdisciplinarity – as threatened to the point of extinction in other quarters – surviving and thriving in German-language scholarship and research.

At the same time, of course, the eternal tensions of such interdisciplinary efforts were apparent here as well. Inge Baxman, for example, helpfully pointed out the difficulties of doing interdisciplinary work that "doesn't flatten the differences" between the disciplines so brought together. Hartmut Winkler gave a particular memorable expression to another difficulty of undertaking interdisciplinary work – namely, our risking "being grilled like shrimp" when we dare to venture into the fields and disciplines that are not our own.

Suggestions for future collaborations

Finally, as a newly arrived visitor to the Symposium and the many traditions and backgrounds it represents, I was struck by the incredible richness of these backgrounds and traditions. Indeed, I felt as if I had stepped into nothing less than a new universe of a hundred thousand insights. It was also profoundly interesting to see how much of the work presented here represented already very strong international orientations and collaborations – first of all, in my view, because there is so much here that will be of compelling interest and foundational importance to media studies as pursued in other national traditions and languages.

At the same time, however, my perspective as an Outsider – one whose experience and work in media studies has been primarily in the English-speaking worlds and, more recently, in Scandinavia – made me aware of at least four ways in which such international collaborations could be expanded.

Let me suggest these possibilities for such new connections and expansions by way of four *questions* that occurred to me over the course of the Symposium.

1. Where is the subject?

As has been kindly explained to me, the "subject" disappears in the so-called "material turn" in *Medienwissenschaft* inaugurated by F. Kittler and his appropriation of M. McLuhan. As this Symposium amply demonstrated, this material turn has led to a raft of important new insights and helpful perspectives, ones that promise to both enrich and dramatically reshape media studies more broadly.

But this loss of the subject is problematic in at least two ways. Broadly, the "subject" is making a come-back in a range of disciplines, including philosophy of technology, phenomenology, neuroscience, philosophy of mind – and thereby in media studies as requiring, in my view, some form of a philosophical anthropology that provides us with a robust account of the *persons* who design, implement, take up, and respond to new media. *Contra* earlier, predominantly Cartesian and dualistic accounts of subjectivity as radically divorced from the body and thereby a larger material world, these new conceptions focus on the many ways in which our identity, agency, multiple forms of knowing and multiple forms of navigating the world – including by way of new media – are inextricably interwoven with and interdependent upon the body, our tools, and the larger world around us. Especially as grounded in the growing insights of neuroscience, conceptions of selfhood collected under notions of enactivism and the embedded or embodied mind are reshaping earlier understandings of human beings in philosophy and media studies[1]. Against this larger background, further exploration and discussion regarding conceptions of the subject and selfhood would seem vital for the field of media studies.

---

[1]   Charles Ess, "At the Intersections Between Internet Studies and Philosophy: "Who Am I Online?" (Introduction to special issue), *Philosophy & Technology*, 25/3 (September 2012): 275–284. DOI 10.1007/s13347-012-0085-4.

Second, especially if we wish to take up *ethical* or *normative* issues in robust ways, it seems we have no choice but to re-introduce some notion of the subject in its function as a moral agent. To be sure, our understandings of moral agency and responsibility have been dramatically transformed most especially by the rise of various forms of communication and media facilitated by networks and the Internet. As but one example, it is becoming increasingly common to attempt to understand ethical responsibility as a *distributed* responsibility – i.e., one shared precisely across the network of relationships and communications made possible by new communication technologies[2]. However all of this might work out over the next decades – it is difficult to see how such reflection and related research can move forward without a cogent and robust conception of the subject.

Attention to the ethical dimensions of new media technologies, finally, seems both inevitable and a very useful direction for media studies. Simply put: the rise of new media, most especially as interwoven with the Internet and the multiple communicative engagements it facilitates, evokes in every society a raft of new ethical concerns, both for the various professionals whose work directly contributes to the technologies involved and for "the rest of us," i.e., everyday users, including parents and children whose lives are increasingly interwoven with and interdependent upon the Internet and related media. Nation-states and more international bodies, beginning with the European Union and extending through the United Nations, are forced to grapple with these various ethical dimensions in ever-growing ways, following the rapid development and diffusion of the technologies themselves. It seems obvious to me that the scholarship and research in media studies must play a primary role in these debates, deliberations, and, ultimately, the decisions shaping design, implementation, and use of new media – first of all, because only media studies can deliver the empirically-grounded accounts of media use and possible impacts required for such debate and decision. Hence I would urge more engagement in the discussions of ethics wherever possible – but again, this would seem to require revisiting and revitalizing conceptions of the subject as an ethical agent.

2. *Where is religion?*

Of course, in strongly secular societies such as those of Northern Europe and Scandinavia, it may well seem that "religion" is not a necessary or useful analytical concept or category. Indeed, if the proponents of the so-called secularization thesis had been correct – i.e., that post-Enlightenment secularization would necessarily lead to the end of religion as an institution with meaningful interactions with and significance for the larger society – there would be no reason for scholars and researchers to pay "religion" any further attention. In that light, the absence of attention to religion in this Symposium is not unusual at all.

---

[2] Luciano Floridi, "Foundations of Information Ethics", in Kenneth Einar Himma and Herman T. Tavani, eds., *The Handbook of Information and Computer Ethics* (Oxford: Wiley-Blackwell, 2008), 3–23.

But it appears that the secularization thesis is more problematic than its proponents believe: rather, for better and for worse, religion – like the subject – is making a comeback, first of all "on the ground" as many religious institutions and movements continue to gain new adherents and influence around the world. But this further means, secondly, that attention to religion in media studies is also growing steadily – perhaps most notably in the domain of so-called "digital religion"[3].

It would seem to me that media studies of religion in Germany would be enormously interesting. Obviously, the religious landscapes of Germany are complex, as they include both very old traditions of Christendom and more recently introduced Islamic and non-Western traditions. In some ways, these religious landscapes are thus a microcosm of a larger world of religious development and transformation as facilitated by globalization, immigration – and new media. Careful research and reflection on the multiple interactions between religious communities and new media is thus both urgently needed and of great potential for enriching the field of media studies in these increasingly important directions.

3. Where is methodology discussion – and with it, research ethics discussion?

Perhaps it's an accident of the make-up of this particular conference, but I did not see much discussion of the methodologies we might use in diverse approaches to media studies – a discussion that in other languages and traditions is compelling and important precisely because of the strongly *interdisciplinary* approaches required by media studies. That is, our efforts to blend diverse methodologies and other starting points defining specific disciplines demands precisely critical reflection on the hybrid methodologies that arise as we do so.

Directly related to these methodology discussions, at least in my experience, are equally intense attention to and discussion of questions of *research ethics*. To be sure, the focus on media research ethics, and especially Internet research ethics (IRE) began in the United States – whose tradition of requiring university Institutional Review Boards (IRBs) responsible for approving research involving human subjects long preceded the advent of the Internet – and then extended first of all to other English-language countries such as Canada, the U.K., and Australia which have also developed strong traditions of institutional oversight of research. But my experience is that many of the reasons compelling attention to research ethics – beginning with changing privacy laws and institutional developments that parallel the rise of IRBs in the U.S. – are forcing researchers in other countries and traditions, including Scandinavia, for example, to come to grips with research ethics. Minimally, if there is no need for such attention in German-language scholarship, it would be enormously interesting to explain to the rest of us why this this so. Maximally, if there is indeed a growing recognition of the importance of attention to research ethics by scholars in media studies – this would then be a good time to inaugurate such attention in a systematic way.

---

[3] Pauline Hope Cheong, Peter Fischer-Nielsen, Stefan Gelfgren, and Charles Ess, eds., *Digital Religion, Social Media and Culture: Perspectives, Practices and Futures* (Oxford: Peter Lang, 2012).

4. Where are the "other" theoretical traditions?

On the one hand, I've certainly been impressed with the depth and scope of theoretical traditions represented and expanded upon here. At the same time, however, there are several important traditions that I expected to see in play here, but were apparently absent.

As a reference point, in his Spring, 2012, PhD course in media theory, my Aarhus (Denmark) colleague Jesper Tække highlighted four theoretical traditions that students would work through:

> The Canadian Medium Theory tradition (Innis, McLuhan, Meyrowitz,…)
> The systematic media theory tradition (Parsons, Luhmann, and others)
> Actor-network theory traditions (Latour, Callon, Woolgar, Debray…)
>
> and
>
> Critical Theory traditions (Adorno, Habermas, and others).
> (To this last I would further add the work of Andrew Feenburg, Maria Bakardjieva, Christian Fuchs, and others.)

Most certainly, the theoretical and methodological traditions of German-language media studies have much to offer to your colleagues abroad who are, to begin with, not necessarily familiar with Kittler and the material turn, for example. More broadly, it would seem to me that many seminars and symposia could be most fruitfully devoted to work seeking to explore the commonalities, differences, and potentially useful new conjunctions of this expanded list of theoretical traditions

Concluding remarks: invitation to (more) dialogue

Let me close by reiterating that the above comments are intended <u>not</u> as criticisms but as invitations to new dialogues and collaborations that seem to me can only benefit and enrich the already exceptionally rich and insightful research traditions and approaches represented here. In addition to pursuing new connections along the four directions I've outlined above, I would further call your attention to the Association of Internet Researchers (AoIR – <aoir.org>) as a primary scholarly resource for pursuing such connections. The AoIR mailing list is free to join, and immediately puts you in touch with over 2000 scholars and researchers from a great diversity of disciplines around the globe who are pursuing a great number of research directions that would be of immediate interest and value to their German counterparts. AoIR prizes precisely the sort of interdisciplinarity that you have demonstrated here in exemplary ways. Queries and their replies on the mailing list are consistently among the most interesting and generous in my experience as a scholar.

Again, a thousand thanks for these two profoundly inspiring and enjoyable days in Lüneburg. I hope the above comments may contribute in some small way to further iterations of the Symposium.

List of Contributors

Michael Andreas is a researcher at the Ruhr University in Bochum, where he is affiliated with the Institute for Media Studies. His current research interests include the history and mediality of migration in Germany, postcolonial studies, visual culture, and identity politics. He is the co-editor (with Natascha Frankenberg) of *Im Netz der Eindeutigkeiten: Unbestimmte Figuren und die Irritation von Identität* (Bielefeld: Transcript, 2013); and the co-author (with Bastian Blachut) of "Bildverhältnisse: Politische Bilder und ihre Verhandlung im Dokumentar- und Protestfilm," in *Protest, Empörung, Widerstand: Zur Analyse der Dimensionen, Formen und Implikationen von Auflehnungsbewegungen*, ed. Iuditha Balint et al. (Konstanz: UVK, 2014), 131–56.

Marie-Luise Angerer is a professor of media and cultural studies at the Academy of Media Arts in Cologne, where she served as rector from 2007 to 2009. In late 2013 and early 2014 she participated as a senior research fellow in the research group Media Cultures of Computer Simulation at the Leuphana University in Lüneburg. Much of her research is concerned with affect, technology, and social fantasies, though she is also engaged with the ideas of nature-culture and nature-media. Her book *Vom Begehren nach dem Affekt* (Zurich: Diaphanes, 2007) has been translated into English as *Desire after Affect* (New York: Rowman & Littlefield Intl., 2014), and she is the co-editor of two recent volumes: *Timing of Affect: Epistemologies, Aesthetics, Politics* (Zurich: Diaphanes, 2014); and *Choreographie, Medien, Gender* (Zurich: Diaphanes, 2013).

Dirk Baecker is a professor of cultural management at Witten/Herdecke University in Witten, Germany. He is also the co-founder of the consulting firm Management Zentrum Witten and a co-editor of the journals *Soziale Systeme* and *Revue für postheroisches Management*. His areas of expertise are sociological systems theory and cultural theory, and his recent publications include *Neurosoziologie: Ein Versuch* (Frankfurt am Main: Suhrkamp, 2014); *Ökonomie der Werte: Festschrift zum 65. Geburtstag von Michael Hutter* (Marburg: Metropolis, 2013), co-edited with Birger P. Priddat; and *Beobachter unter sich: Eine Kulturtheorie* (Berlin: Suhrkamp, 2013).

Inge Baxmann is a professor of theatre studies at the University of Leipzig. She is a member of the editorial board for the journal *Zeitschrift für Medienwissenschaft*. She has been an associate director at the Fondation de la Maison des Sciences de l'Homme in Paris and a fellow of the Alexander von Humboldt-Stiftung. The primary concerns of her research are modern concepts and staging of national and transnational communities in Europe and Latin America and a historiography of bodily knowledge and media technologies from modernity to the present. Some of her publications: *Mayas, Pochos and Chicanos: Die transnationale Nation* (Munich: Wilhelm Fink 2008), *Arbeit und Rhythmus: Lebensformen im Wandel* (Munich: Wilhelm Fink, 2009), co-edited with Melanie Gruß, Sebastian Göschel and Vera Lauf; and *Les Archives Internationales de la Danse 1931–1951 (Paris: Editions du CND 2007),* co-edited with Claire Rousier and Patrizia Veroli.

Timon Beyes is Professor at the Department of Management, Politics and Philosophy, Copenhagen Business School (Denmark), and a Visiting Professor at Leuphana University, Lüneburg (Germany), where he is a director of the Centre for Digital Cultures. His research focuses on the processes, spaces and aesthetics of organization in the fields of media culture, art, cities as well as education. His research has been published in a range of monographs and edited collections as well as in leading German-speaking and international journals. Forthcoming publications in English include *The Routledge Companion to Reinventing Management Education* (ed., with Martin Parker and Chris Steyaert; Routledge, 2016); *Performing the Digital: Performance studies and performances in digital cultures* (ed., with Martina Leeker and Immanuel Schipper; Transcript, 2016); "Colour and Organization Studies" (*Organization Studies*, 2016).

Christoph Bieber, a professor of political science at the University of Duisburg-Essen, has written extensively on ethics and responsibility in politics, ethics in the field of political management, transparency and public communication, and the role of media in democracy. Among other recent studies, he is the author of "Von der Computer-Demokratie zur Liquid Democracy: Zur Modernisierung politischer Beteiligung im Kontext technologischer Entwicklung," in *Handbuch Innovationen: Interdisziplinäre Grundlagen und Anwendungsfelder*, ed. Manfred Mai (Wiesbaden: Springer, 2014), 189–208; "Die Veränderung politischer Kommunikation im Internetzeitalter: Medien und Demokratie und die These von der Postdemokratie," *Jahrbuch für Christliche Sozialwissenschaften* 54 (2014), 155–180; and the co-editor (with Claus Leggewie) of *Unter Piraten: Erkundungen einer neuen politischen Arena* (Bielefeld: Transcript, 2012).

Christian Borch is professor of political sociology at the Department of Management, Politics, and Philosophy, Copenhagen Business School, Denmark. His current research focuses on crowd theory and financial markets. He is the author of several books, including *Foucault, Crime and Power: Problematisations of Crime in the Twentieth Century* (Routledge, 2015); *The Politics of Crowds: An Alternative History of Sociology* (Cambridge University Press, 2012); and *Niklas Luhmann (Key Sociologists)* (Routledge,

2011); and editor of volumes such as *Urban Commons: Rethinking the City* (Routledge, 2015; co-edited with Martin Kornberger); *Architectural Atmospheres: On the Experience and Politics of Architecture* (Birkhäuser, 2014); and *Soziologie der Nachahmung und des Begehrens: Materialien zu Gabriel Tarde* (Suhrkamp, 2009; co-edited with Urs Stäheli).

Christoph Engemann is a media theorist whose interests as a teacher and researcher include digital identity (and its history), e-government and e-health, the genealogy of transaction, rurality, and barns. After holding positions at the University of Bremen, Stanford, the University of Texas at Austin, and the International Research Institute for Cultural Technologies and Media Philosophy in Weimar, he was made an assistant director of the research group Media Cultures of Computer Simulation at the Leuphana University in Lüneburg. Among other works, he is the author of "Deutschland, die USA und digitale Identitätssysteme," *Zeitschrift für Medienwissenschaft* 11 (2014), forthcoming; "Elektronische Gesundheitsakte oder Fallakten: Medizinische Archivmacht und die elektronische Gesundheitskarte," in *Qualität in der Medizin dynamisch denken: Versorgung – Forschung – Markt*, ed. Ralph Kray et al. (Wiesbaden: Springer Gabler, 2013), 149–75; and "Im Namen des Staates: Der elektronische Personalausweis und die Medien der Reigerungskunst," *Zeitschrift für Medien- und Kulturforschung* 2 (2011), 211–28.

Charles Ess is a professor at the Institute for Media and Communication at the University of Oslo and is currently the president of the International Society for Ethics and Information Technology (INSEIT). With interests in the ethics of digital media, the democratizing potential of new media, online religion, and internet studies, he is the author of *Digital Media Ethics*, 2nd ed. (Cambridge, UK: Polity, 2014); the co-editor (with Pauline Cheong, Peter Fischer-Nielsen, and Stefan Gelfgren) of *Digital Religion, Social Media and Culture* (New York: Peter Lang, 2012); and the co-editor (with William Dutton) of "Internet Studies: Perspectives on a Rapidly Developing Field," which is a special issue of the journal *New Media & Society* (2013).

Wolfgang Hagen is a professor of media studies at the Leuphana University in Lüneburg, Germany. He has been a visiting scholar and lecturer at several institutions, including the University of California – Santa Barbara, the University of St. Gallen and the Humboldt University in Berlin. In 2012 he finished his professional career in radio as head of the cultural departments of Deutschlandradio Kultur, Berlin. He is the author of numerous works on the history and epistemology of media, with emphasis on radio and the computer. His most recent publication is *Ethos, Pathos, Powerpoint – On the Epistemology and (Silicon-Valley-) Rhetorics of Digital Presentations* (Frankfurt, 2015).

Christiane Heibach is a professor for Media Aesthetics at the Institute of Information and Media, Language and Culture at the University of Regensburg. Her research focuses on the epistemology of media, the history and theory of multi- and intermedial art forms, the aesthetics of new media, and the literary and media theories of the twentieth century.

She is the author of *Multimediale Aufführungskunst: Medienästhetische Studien zur Entstehung einer neuen Kunstform* (Munich: Wilhelm Fink, 2010), the editor of *Atmosphären: Dimensionen eines diffusen Phänomens* (Munich: Wilhelm Fink, 2012), and the co-editor, with Friedrich W. Block and Karen Wenz, of *Poesis: Ästhetik digitaler Poesie/ The Aesthetics of Digital Poetry* (Ostfildern-Ruit: Hatje Cantz, 2004).

Irina Kaldrack is a postdoctoral researcher at the Digital Cultures Research Lab (Leuphana University in Lüneburg), where her work concerns new methods in the digital age, the mediality of technical media, the history of media, the scientific history of motion, and the cultural history of mathematics. She is the co-editor (with Hannelore Bublitz, Theo Röhle, and Mirna Zeman) of *Automatismen: Selbst-Technologien* (Munich: Wilhelm Fink, 2013); the co-editor (with Hannelore Bublitz, Theo Röhle, and Hartmut Winkler) of *Unsichtbare Hände: Automatismen in Medien-, Technik-, und Diskursgeschichte* (Munich: Wilhelm Fink, 2011); and the author of *Imaginierte Wirksamkeit: Zwischen Performance und Bewegungserkennung* (Berlin: Kadmos, 2011).

Peter Krapp is Chair of Film and Media studies, and Professor of English, at the University of California in Irvine, where he is also affiliated with the Donald Bren School of Information and Computer Sciences. His research interests include digital cultures, media theory, cultural memory, the history of simulation, and computer game culture. The author of two monographs – *Déjà Vu: Aberrations of Cultural Memory* (2004) and *Noise Channels: Glitch and Error in Digital Culture*, both of which were published by the University of Minnesota Press – he has also co-edited a forthcoming volume entitled *Sprache – Kultur – Kommunikation: Ein internationales Handbuch zu Linguistik als Kulturwissenschaft* (Berlin: De Gruyter, 2016), together with Ludwig Jaeger, Werner Holly, and Samuel M Weber.

Roland Meyer is a doctoral student at the Karlsruhe University of Arts and Design, where he is currently finishing his Ph.D. project, titled "Operative Portraits". His research focusses on the question of identifiability in the history of visual media as well as on the mediality of architecture. He has recently co-edited a special issue of *ZfM – Zeitschrift für Medienwissenschaft* 12 (2015): "Medien / Architekturen", with Christa Kamleithner and Julia Weber; and the reader *Architekturwissen: Grundlagentexte aus den Kulturwissenschaften*, 2 vols. (Bielefeld: Transcript, 2011–2013), with Susanne Hauser and Christa Kamleithner.

Claus Pias is Professor for History and Epistemology of Media at the Institute for Culture and Aesthetics of Digital Media (ICAM), Director of the Institute for Advanced Study in Media Cultures of Computer Simulation (mecs), the Centre for Digital Cultures (CDC) and the Digital Cultures Research Lab (DCRL) at Leuphana University in Lueneburg. In the 2015 summer term Claus Pias was a Senior Fellow at the Institute for Advanced Study „Kulturelle Grundlagen von Integration" Konstanz. Main areas of interest are the

media history and epistemology of computer simulations, the history of media studies, and the history and epistemology of cybernetics. Some recent publications: *Computer Game Worlds*, (Amsterdam: Amsterdam University Press 2016); ed.: *Was waren Medien?*, (Zürich: diaphanes 2012); Ed. with T. Brandstetter und S. Vehlken: *Think Tanks. Die Beratung der Gesellschaft*, (Zürich: diaphanes 2010).

Theo Röhle is a researcher for the project "Business Games as a Cultural Technique," which is funded by the German Research Foundation and associated with the Institute for Media Research at the Braunschweig University of Art. From 2009 to 2013 he was a postdoctoral fellow at the University of Paderborn, where he worked with a team of researchers on the topic of automatisms. His interests include science and technology studies, surveillance and power, and digital orders of knowledge. Along with Oliver Leistert, he edited the volume *Generation Facebook: Über das Leben im Social Net* (Bielefeld: Transcript, 2011), and he is the author of *Der Google-Komplex: Über Macht im Zeitalter des Internets* (Bielefeld: Transcript, 2010).

Mirko Tobias Schäfer is an assistant professor in the Department for Media and Culture Studies at Utrecht University and principal investigator at the Utrecht Data School. His teaching and research concern the cultural and socio-political aspects of computer technology and software. In 2012 he was appointed as a research fellow at the Vienna University of Applied Arts and in 2014 he became a research fellow at the Centre for Humanities at Utrecht University. He is one of nine authors responsible for "Participations: Dialogues on the Participatory Promise of Contemporary Culture and Politics. Part III: Politics," *International Journal of Communication* 8 (2014), 1129–51; he is the author of the book *Bastard Culture! How User Participation Transforms Cultural Production (*Amsterdam: Amsterdam University Press, 2012; and he co-edited the anthology *Digital Media: Tracing New Media in Everyday Life and Technology* (Amsterdam: Amsterdam University Press, 2009). www.mtschaefer.net

Sascha Simons is a research associate at Leuphana University's Digital Cultures Research Lab in Lüneburg and a member of the editorial collective of the web journal *spheres* (www.spheres-journal.org). He is currently completing his doctoral thesis on the aesthetics of authenticity and the social testimony of web videos. He is interested in the aesthetics, theory, and history of social media, the interplay of medial and social morphology, and theories of the event. He has recently published "Mobilizing Memes – The Contagious Socio-Aesthetics of Participation" (in *Reclaiming Participation: Technology – Mediation – Collectivity*, edited by Mathias Denecke et al., Bielefeld: Transcript, 2015), which can be considered as a complement to his essay in this book.

Florian Sprenger is a postdoctoral researcher at the Digital Cultures Research Lab (Leuphana University in Lüneburg), where he is completing projects on the media history of electricity and the conceptual history of the environment. From 2010 to 2012 he was a

fellow at the International Research Center for Cultural Studies in Vienna. Among other topics, his research concentrates on the history of media studies, the media of architecture, and the epistemology of the environment. In the past few years he has published *Die Enden des Kabels: Kleine Mediengeschichte der Übertragung* (Berlin: Kadmos, 2014), a book co-authored with Daniel Gethmann; *Medien des Immediaten: Elektrizität, Telegraphie, McLuhan* (Berlin: Kadmos, 2012); and *Blitzlicht* (Zurich: Diaphanes, 2010), co-edited with Katja Müller-Helle.

Sebastian Vehlken is an assistant director of the Institute for Advanced Study on Media Cultures of Computer Simulation, which is funded by the German Research Foundation. From 2005 to 2007 he was a member of the graduate school "Media of History – History of Media" at the Bauhaus University in Weimar; from 2007 to 2010 he worked as a research associate (PreDoc) in Epistemology and Philosophy of Digital Media at the University of Vienna's Institute for Philosophy; and from 2010 to 2013 he was as a research associate (PostDoc) at the Institute for Culture and Aesthetics of Digital Media (Leuphana University in Lüneburg). His interests include the theory and history of digital media (especially computer simulation), the media history of supercomputing, and oceans as areas of knowledge. His recent publications include *Zootechnologien: Eine Mediengeschichte der Schwarmforschung* (Zurich: Diaphanes, 2012); and *Think Tanks: Die Beratung der Gesellschaft* (Zurich: Diaphanes, 2010), which he co-edited with Claus Pias and Thomas Brandstetter.

Carolin Wiedemann is a freelance journalist and a doctoral student in the Department of Sociology at the University of Hamburg, where her research has focused on new forms of collectivity, subjectivity and subversion, and theories of digital networks. Among her recent publications are the articles "Between Swarm, Network and Multitude. Anonymous and the Infrastructures of the Common," *Distinktion: Scandinavian Journal of Social Theory,* 15 (2014), 309–326; and "In den Ruinen der Repräsentation? Affekt, Agencement und das Okkurente," *Zeitschrift für Geschlechterforschung und visuelle Kultur* 55 (2014), 66–78 which she co-authored with Marianne Pieper. Along with Soenke Zehle she edited the book *Depletion Design: A Glossary of Network Ecologies* (Amsterdam: Institute of Network Cultures, 2012).